2013年度浙江省社科联省级社会科学学术著作
出版资金全额资助出版

浙江省哲学社会科学规划课题研究成果

当代浙江学术文库

DANGDAI ZHEJIANG XUESHU WENKU

滕 超 著

权力博弈中的晚清法律翻译

中国社会科学出版社

图书在版编目（CIP）数据

权力博弈中的晚清法律翻译 = Legal Translation in Late Qing Dynasty's Power Game ／滕超著 . —北京：中国社会科学出版社，2014. 12

ISBN 978 - 7 - 5161 - 5363 - 5

Ⅰ. ①权… Ⅱ. ①滕… Ⅲ. ①法律—翻译—语言学史—研究— 中国—清后期 Ⅳ. ①D90 - 055②H159 - 092

中国版本图书馆 CIP 数据核字（2014）第 303372 号

出 版 人	赵剑英
选题策划	田 文
责任编辑	夏 侠
特约编辑	赵博艺
责任校对	郝阳洋
责任印制	王 超

出 版	中国社会科学出版社
社 址	北京鼓楼西大街甲 158 号（邮编 100720）
网 址	http://www.csspw.cn
	中文域名:中国社科网 010 - 64070619
发 行 部	010 - 84083685
门 市 部	010 - 84029450
经 销	新华书店及其他书店

印 刷	北京君升印刷有限公司
装 订	廊坊市广阳区广增装订厂
版 次	2014 年 12 月第 1 版
印 次	2014 年 12 月第 1 次印刷

开 本	710 × 1000 1/16
印 张	26. 75
插 页	2
字 数	452 千字
定 价	78. 00 元

总　序

浙江省社会科学界联合会党组书记　郑新浦

　　源远流长的浙江学术，蕴华含英，是今天浙江经济社会发展的"文化基因"；三十五年的浙江改革发展，鲜活典型，是浙江人民创业创新的生动实践。无论是对优秀传统文化的传承弘扬，还是就波澜壮阔实践的概括提升，都是理论研究和理论创新的"富矿"，我省社科工作者可以而且应该在这里努力开凿挖掘，精心洗矿提炼，创造学术精品。

　　繁荣发展浙江学术，当代浙江学人使命光荣、责无旁贷。我们既要深入研究、深度开掘浙江学术思想的优良传统，肩负起继承、弘扬、发展的伟大使命；更要面向今天浙江经济社会的发展之要和人文社会科学建设的迫切需要，担当起促进学术繁荣的重大责任，创造具有时代特征和地方特色的当代浙江学术，打造当代浙江学术品牌，全力服务"两富"现代化浙江建设。

　　繁荣发展浙江学术，良好工作机制更具长远、殊为重要。我们要着力创新机制，树立品牌意识，构建良好载体，鼓励浙江学人，扶持优秀成果。"浙江省社科联省级社会科学学术著作出版资金资助项目"，就是一个坚持多年、富有成效、受学人欢迎的优质品牌和载体。2006 年开始，我们对年度全额资助书稿以"当代浙江学术论丛"（《光明文库》）系列丛书资助出版；2011 年，我们将当年获得全额重点资助和全额资助的书稿改为《当代浙江学术文库》系列加以出版。多年来，我们已资助出版共 553 部著作，对于扶持学术精品，推进学术创新，阐释浙江改革开放轨迹，提炼浙江经验，弘扬浙江精神，创新浙江模式，探索浙江发展路径，产生了良好的社会影响和积极的促进作用。

2013 年入选资助出版的 27 部书稿，内容丰富，选题新颖，学术功底较深，创新视野广阔。有的集中关注现实社会问题，追踪热点，详论对策破解之道；有的深究传统历史文化，精心梳理，力呈推陈出新之意；有的收集整理民俗习尚，寻觅探究，深追民间社会记忆之迹；有的倾注研究人类共同面对的难题，潜心思考，苦求解决和谐发展之法。尤为可喜的是，资助成果的作者大部分是我省的中青年学者，我们的资助扶持，不唯解决了他们优秀成果的出版之困，更具有促进社科新才成长的奖掖之功。

我相信，"浙江省社科联省级社会科学学术著作出版资金资助项目"的继续实施，特别是《当代浙江学术文库》品牌的持续、系列化出版，必将推出更多的优秀浙江学人，涌现更丰富的精品佳作，从而繁荣发展我省哲学社会科学，充分发挥"思想库"和"智囊团"的作用，有效助推物质富裕、精神富有现代化浙江的加快发展。

2013 年 12 月

序

年轻学者滕超寄来新作《权力博弈中的晚清法律翻译》书稿，嘱我作序，不敢推脱，遂于暑期拨冗仔细研读，及至主线渐趋明晰，再细细揣摩，不禁油然慨叹，便欣然命笔，记录点滴所思所想，以为序。

译事难，法律翻译更难。作者的选题还不止于此，而是基于法律翻译进行研究，涉及法律的权力博弈，聚焦清朝晚期若干重要法律翻译典籍的分析。通览全书，读者可以感受有关法律翻译的精到批讲和研判，还可领略有关清朝法律、外交、法律翻译组织和实践、中外文化交汇融合、法律文化碰撞与调适、社会变迁以及清朝统治走向没落的具体例证。

作者思前人之未思、做前人之未做，大胆开辟思路，从典籍中拮取例证，悉心论辩，将自己思想融于其中，左腾右挪，出入辗转，甚是自由。同时又不失系统性，保证读者能依据中国法律的历史演变主线，蔓引株求，融会贯通。

依靠来自语言学与法学两个学科的基本素养，作者又旁征博引，汲取多学科、多视角的学术精要，将研究对象深入解读、剖析。社会学视角是作者赖以研究的基本框架，可见作者甚能不拘一格，突破樊篱，求取根本。

著作中不乏对理论的剖析和引介，法学理论、语言学理论、翻译理论、社会学理论，一应纳入，构成全书的脉络，并融于案例分析之中。语言研究、法律语言研究等西方理论成果和要义亦均能信手拮来，为吾所用，可见作者对相关领域的广泛涉猎。而且能细心甄别，批判吸收，有效服务于对晚清法律翻译中权力博弈的解析。

作者表述个人观点直来直往、慷慨果断，即使读者不能苟同，也难以否定作者的良苦用心和入理的议论。为强调社会学视角，作者对"纯"语言学路径的法律翻译研究提出批评，期待文化研究者摆脱语言学思维模式的束缚，这对容易误入极端的译者来说，不啻是醒目的警示。中国法律翻译研究尚需置于中国法律语言研究的背景中，才能成为有源之水，作者虽无暇展开讨论，但据其引述大量国外研究成果判断，并未予以轻看。毕竟法律语言学已经成为一个专门的研究领域，系统理解尚需耗费时日。

有幸抢先拜读滕超的新作，倍感荣幸，也算是缘分使然。先前曾读过他撰写的《英汉法律互译：理论与实践》，为他年轻好学，勤恳耕作的进取精神所折服，曾向身边的年轻同好力荐，且引以为豪。相信他能在法律翻译研究的道路上勇往直前，为法律翻译及研究的持续推进贡献力量。

杜金榜

2013 年 9 月 15 日

于广州白云山下

目　　录

前　　言

　　随着全球经济一体化，中国大陆加入 WTO 后，与世界各民族在政治、贸易、科技等领域的对话日益纷繁。盛况空前的跨国交流只有并轨相关国家法律制度才能获得良性发展，这就要求我们深刻理解并恪守异国他乡的法治传统。在此形势下，很多有识之士已然意识到了法律翻译对促进国际交往的重要作用与地位。

　　迄今为止，语言学路径依然是法律翻译研究的主流。法律语言属特殊用途语言，法律翻译亦因此归属工具翻译，其理论探索长期停滞于文本类型、意义阐释等问题，且过度纠结词汇、句式方面的修辞特征及实用技能的条分缕析，甚至极少触及篇章层面，更未能透过复杂流动的现象，挖掘现象背后支配译者决策的深层原因。

　　有鉴于此，学者们开始将视野转向社会学领域，试图在文化交流、历史演进的框架下重塑法律翻译研究范式：法律翻译不只是法律机制内的交际行为，更是跨越法律文化的交际行为。然而新近文献虽已将影响交际的背景分析从直接情境拓展至宏观社会场域，浓墨重彩的笔触却依旧局限法文化比较及其对翻译行为的干扰，仍然热衷构建操作规范，奢求原文与译文能够达成某种程度的动态对等，令人颇感遗憾。

　　正本溯源，构成特定社会上层建筑核心的法律制度是历史发展的产物，不但集中体现所属社会群体的主流价值理念，还综合反映该社会的多元意识形态。就社会演进而言，成文法的字斟句酌既是现行权力关系的固化载体，亦将对未来权力博弈产生持久影响；就跨文化交际而言，法律翻译构成原法律文化对目标法律文化的侵蚀。

　　只有将已经发生的法律翻译行为视作理性的文化实践，才能洞悉译介活动的历史意义，这是毋庸置疑的。笔者选择晚清法律翻译活动作为研究对象，不仅因为它构成我国现代法制进程的起点，更重要的原因在于两次鸦片战争致使神州大陆逐渐沦为半殖民地，绵延数千年的封建法统暴露严峻危机，而救亡图存亟须的新兴法理思想尚未破茧，既柔弱且僻处边缘。恰是法律翻译得显身手之良机，社会文化系统内纵横交错的权力关系对译者决策的操纵亦必无限扩张。

综上所述，本书将从追溯西方法律语言学源流入手，通过概览法律翻译研究现状及其局限，阐明描写范式（descriptive paradigm）依托系统论的优越性，继而结合晚清法制转型期的多元文化特征（multiculturalism），考察鸦片战争前后、洋务运动及宪政革命等关键历史节点涌现的经典译著，以期重构西法东渐在我国近代内政外交博弈中留下的不可磨灭的印记。

（一）追溯西方法律语言学科源流，概览中外法律翻译研究现状

现代西方法律语言学研究是融合语言学、法理学、社会学等诸多领域的交叉学科。笔者主要关注法律书面语言的词汇特征、确定性幻象和平实化运动；法律程序语言的描写、分析与解释方法等焦点问题的最新成果，旨在由此揭示纯语言学路径的法律翻译研究，刻意简化多法域交际活动的复杂性，必然遭遇不可克服的缺陷，因而持续推进当前仍然稚嫩的历史文化转向势在必行。

（二）阐释系统描写翻译研究范式，融合法制转型时期文化特征

描述性翻译研究的流派繁芜庞杂，多元系统观、规范学派、改写范式等不一而足。他们将翻译描写成在权力博弈影响下受多元异质规范制约的改写行为，并与社会文化的动态演进密切联系。尽管其领军人物泰半以文学系统作为主要分析对象，却并未否认该研究路径对理解其他文化实践的有效性。实际上，这尤其适合探求晚清半殖民地半封建社会语境中法律翻译活动对我国内政外交近代化进程的影响。

清末西法东渐彰于修律，无论立法思想、编撰技术乃至遣词造句，无不笼罩着欧美法哲思想的渗透——"诸法合体"的传统形式终被抛弃，"依伦理而轻重其刑"的礼教特征亦受冲击。但其急遽变革，即便有随波逐流、水到渠成的点点滴滴，也万难摆脱国内外形形色色政治经济集团逐鹿中原的喧扰时局。士大夫墨守伦理纲常、殖民者鼓吹基督教义，本土核心意识形态与舶来边缘意识形态短兵相接，进退攻守间此消彼长的博弈态势，从来都是历史的必然性与偶然性交互作用的结果。

（三）从英译《大清律例》到西法东渐的历史转型与权力博弈

本书关注清季法律及其语言近代转型过程中光怪陆离的西法东渐现

象。虽则如此，笔者首先考察的却是小斯当东英译本《大清律例》，只因这部鸦片战争前夕出版发行的著作较为全面地反映了 19 世纪欧美列强对华夏传统理念有失偏颇的诠释。序幕既启，林则徐组织选译的《各国律例》；馆译《万国公法》及《公法便览》；局译《各国交涉公法论》与《各国交涉便法论》；翰墨林印书局编译的《英国国会史》等亦将相继粉墨登场。

这些极具代表性的译作都是权力场内意识形态博弈的产物，有的甚至某种程度上激化战争爆发或扭曲战争进程，也有丧权辱国后意欲推行和平外交、借法自强的策略考虑。囿于时代局限性的意识形态制约译者及其赞助人代表各利益集团的改写行为，实际折射的全然是争权夺利的尔虞我诈，当然折冲退让难以避免，否则亦不容合译的法律经典通行神州大地。故而首当其冲之要务就在于寻求公度性。如何沟通分属两个迥异世界本质上不可通约的社会价值体系，成为横亘在当时中外译员眼前几乎无法逾越的天堑。

遭逢乱世，如果说和风细雨般的文学翻译对目标文化变革的影响尚属潜移默化，那么胜似地震海啸的法律翻译无疑是东西方社会制度的直接碰撞与冲击。从公法到宪政、从欧美到日本、从华洋合译到独担重任，法律翻译实践的漫长变迁，非借助描述性研究路径不能剖析其中情非得已之尴尬窘境。

当然，本书勾勒晚清西法东渐的出发点和归依只能是译文本身及包括译者序言在内的规范申明（normative pronouncement）。尤须注意，历时性动态研究的特质要求旁征博引中外史料、名人典籍。唯其浩如烟海，笔者虽夙夜埋首，仍恐挂一漏万。

在本书的撰写过程中，深受浙江大学翻译学研究生导师、翻译学研究所所长陈刚教授的热情鼓励与悉心指导，谨此表示衷心感谢。

鉴于笔者水平有限，疏阔之处在所难免，还望广大读者不吝赐教。

滕　超

二零一三年十月

于西子湖畔

绪　论
——中国法律及其语言的历史演进与近代转型

法律语言缘何相对稳定？作为法律思想及法律信息的物化载体，法律语言折射的力量具有强制性，差之毫厘则谬以千里，动辄关乎个人生死荣辱、财产安全乃至国家主权。正是这种权力表象，使得法言法语更显威严神秘，令人顶礼膜拜，也因此赋予法律语言两项最基本的特征——权威性和约束力，同时亦造就了法律语言倾向保守、抗拒变革的惯性。

可正如高鸿钧、贺卫方教授在《比较法学丛书》总序中所言，"法，作为习俗结晶、文化符号之一种，其演进标志人类族群进化之轨迹：由隔离而接触，由孤立而群合，由独行而协作，由排斥而共存"（2002：1）。语言随社会文化制度的变迁而逐步演化，同样是任何壕沟壁垒都无法抗拒的常态，尤其在天翻地覆的清末民初转型期，除却跃进更难以形容。

第一节　中国法律及其语言的封建传统

我国古代法制至迟在夏禹时期便已揭开序幕，"从殷周起经过春秋战国秦西汉新莽东汉魏蜀吴晋宋齐梁陈隋唐宋至明都是汉族一系相传，循序进展，中间虽屡有北方野蛮民族的侵入：如晋末的后赵前秦后秦南燕北朝的后魏北齐后周五代的后唐，宋以后的辽金元清各朝虽立国的久暂不同，但都是努力汉化，而编纂法典，传播法律知识诸事，尤有可值得赞美的成就，因此中国法律系延四千年线不至中断，在世界五大法系中——罗马法系、英国法系、印度法系、回回法系——能独立自成一统"（杨鸿烈，1984：1—2）。

潘庆云教授着眼法律语言沿革，将传统法制发展过程划分成四个主要阶段（2004：33）：滥觞阶段（夏、商至春秋后期）、形成阶段（秦、汉）、发展阶段（唐、宋）和完善阶段（明、清）。不过，潘先生论述阶段特征的焦点似乎在诉讼文书特别是判词风格的变化。仅就成文法而言，从已知最早的郑刑书、晋刑鼎及现存较系统完整的《法经》到集大成的《大清律例》，"中国古代法律具有十分明显的内在发展的联系和因袭性"（陈炯，1998：22）。自唐朝起，"中华法系"甚至还影响到日本、越南、朝鲜等一衣带水的属国邻邦。

一 封建法制特征

1964 年，著名学者陈顾远教授在中国台湾地区出版了颇具学术影响的《中国法制史概要》，将我国封建时代的法律制度称作"固有法系"，主张传统农业社会以人文主义、民本思想为基础，因而除"国法"外，仍重视"天理"、"人情"。陈先生认为相关特征"不能完全以今日眼光批判其优劣，盖为适合当时之需要而产生耳"，故其描写虽简明扼要，言语间却频现溢美之词（2011：54—59）。

（甲）礼教中心	（乙）义务本位
（丙）家族观点	（丁）保育设施
（戊）崇尚仁恕	（己）减轻讼累
（庚）灵活其法	（辛）审断有责

时光流转半个多世纪，现代大陆法制史权威张晋藩教授（2005 年）的研究视野似乎更开阔，阐释也更客观全面。

1. 引礼入法、礼法结合	2. 以人为本、明德慎行
3. 权利等差、义务本位	4. 法尚公平、重刑轻民
5. 恭行天理、执法原情	6. 法自君出、权尊于法
7. 家族本位、伦理法治	8. 以法治官、明职课责
9. 纵向比较、因时定制	10. 统一释法、律学独秀
11. 诸法并存、民刑有分	12. 立法修律、比附判例
13. 援法定罪、类推裁断	14. 无讼是求、调处息争

纵观各家真知灼见，暂且不论立场如何，笔者以为诸要素当可大致归属法学哲理文化、法典编纂技术、法规适用原则等范畴。法学哲理文化坚守儒家礼教；法典编纂技术因循诸法合体；法规适用原则兼采比附推定。

凡此种种，体用参差固然有别，但在成文法传统绵延四千年之久的中国必然付诸律令典籍的篇章结构、字里行间。

二　封建法律语言

（一）律令典籍——法出多门，君权至上

南北朝时期著名文学理论家刘勰（约 465—520 年）在《文心雕龙·书记》中写道：

> 夫书记广大，衣被事体，笔札杂名，古今多品。是以总领黎庶，则有谱籍簿录；医历星筮，则有方术占式；申宪述兵，则有律令法制；朝市征信，则有符契券疏；百官询事，则有关刺解牒；万民达志，则有状列辞谚：并述理于心，著言于翰，虽艺文之末品，而政事之先务也。①

放之今日，所谓"律令法制"涵盖法律规章②，"状列辞谚"囊括诉讼书供；"符契券疏"仿佛协议凭证，"关刺解牒"无非政府公文。古人知此乃"政事先务"，仍难免屈居"艺文末品"。尤其明清以降，朝堂内外颇好程朱理学，鸿儒雅士不屑俯就，研究律法小道者日稀。

当然，刘勰是文学家而非法学家，其《书记》文笔优美，修辞典雅，与法律风格的严谨性要求自是风马牛不相及。狭义而言，中国封建时代法律的重要典籍包括三大类共九种：

（1）成文性典籍：律、令、典
（2）命令性典籍：敕、格、式
（3）伸缩性典籍：科、比、例

另据陈顾远先生所言，"律在中国法制史上，虽立于正统之地位；而在汉受制于比，在蜀吴受制于科，在唐受制于格，在五代及宋受制于敕，

---

① 详见《文心雕龙汇评》。黄霖编著，第 90—91 页。
② 刘勰云："律者，中也。黄钟调起，五音以正；法律驭民，八刑克平，以律为名，取中正也。令者，命也。出命申禁，自若有天，管仲下令如流水，使民从也。"同上书，第 91 页。

在明清又受制于例，其能卓然发展其效力，盖仅矣！所以然者，法为君主一人所立，纵不然，亦出自一二臣工之操纵，尽可另立名目以弁髦之"（2011：90—91）。这岂不是"法自君出，权尊于法"的最佳注脚？

法出多门的形成固有时代背景，但其弊端亦彰显无疑。譬如《清史稿·刑法志》便称：

> 盖清代定例，一如宋时之编敕，有例不用律，律既多成虚文，而例遂愈滋繁碎。其间前后抵触，或律外加重，或因例破律，或一事设一例，或一省一地方专一例，甚且因此例而生彼例，不惟与他部则例参差，即一例分载各门者，亦不无歧异。展转纠纷，易滋高下。①

（二）篇章结构——礼刑合一，诸法合体

诸法合体是我国传统法律典籍篇章结构的基本特征。"封建时代颁行的法典，基本上都是刑法典，但它包含了有关民法、诉讼法以及行政法等各方面的法律内容，形成了民刑不分、诸法合体的结构"（张晋藩，1982：16）。其他如汉朝的编令、宋朝的编敕、明清的编例，更是按时间先后而非调整对象加以编辑。

究其原因，脉络亦清。儒家以礼入法，苛求个体遵循社会礼仪道德；出礼入刑，即便民事纠纷仍用刑罚调整。封建王朝视律令等同刑法也就顺理成章，否则纪传体断代史中便无所谓《刑法志》，概括叙述的内容却覆盖国家全部立法与司法制度。实际上，自东汉班固在《汉书》中首辟"刑法志"体例以来，历朝相率沿用，如《晋书》、《魏书》②、《隋书》、《旧唐书》、《新唐书》、《旧五代史》、《宋史》、《辽史》、《金史》、《元史》、《明史》及民国初年编撰的《清史稿》等不一而足。

（三）字里行间——名教纲常，儒学思想

陈炯教授称我国古代法律词语的选用及其含义在很大程度上蕴含了中华法系的特征及其法学思想（1998：23）。这是确然无疑的，尤其不遗余力地固守礼教人伦、三纲五常。

---

① 详见《清史稿》卷一百四十二。赵尔巽等撰，第4186页。
② 详见《魏书·刑罚志》。

（1）"法"之渊源——效法自然、固守成规

据东汉许慎（约58—147年）的《说文解字》，"法"字古体写作
"灋"，"刑也"，属会意字——从"水"，表示法律制度"平之如水"；从
"廌"、从"去"，"所以触不直者去之"（2001：561）。

"廌"，《论衡·是应》篇释义："一角之羊也，性知有罪。皋陶治狱，
其罪疑者，令羊触之。有罪则触。无罪则不触。"① 这当然是远古凭天意
神权断案习俗的真实写照，及至唐宋尚有官吏借此震慑嫌犯。尽管如此，
中华法系的形成"源于神权而无宗教化色彩，源于天意而有自然法精神"
（陈顾远，2011：48—53）。

另有清末法学家沈家本在《历代刑法考》中旁征博引，凸显"法"
的稳定性（2011：25）：

> 《尔雅·释诂》："法，常也。"
> 《管子·法法篇》："不法法则事毋常。"
> 又《正篇》："制断五刑，各当其名，罪人不怨，善人不惊。曰
> 刑，如四时之不贷，如星辰之不变，如宵、如昼、如阴、如阳，如日
> 月之明。曰法，法以遏之，遏之以绝其志意，毋使民幸。当故不改
> 曰法。"
> 按：当故，不改常也。

由此可见，效法自然、固守成规的思想深入中华法系的骨髓，悠悠数
千年的漫长岁月，真正称得上变法的运动不过四次：秦代变法、新莽变
法、宋世变法、清末变法（陈顾远，2011：25）。秦代变法强国终能定鼎
天下，然商鞅车裂；王莽、安石难免背负骂名，为世人唾弃；即便清末立
宪修律，亦未能挽狂澜于既倒、扶危厦于将倾。

（2）儒家思想——礼教人伦，三纲五常

封建法律语言反映儒家思想及家族地位，笔者以为其核心乃"三纲
五常"，这也是名教纲常的基本架构。

所谓"三纲"，即"君为臣纲、父为子纲、夫为妻纲"。初见《韩非
子·忠孝》曰："臣事君，子事父，妻事夫，三者顺则天下治，三者逆则

---

① 详见《论衡校释（附刘盼遂集解）》卷第十七。黄晖撰，第760页。

天下乱。此天下之常道也，明王贤臣而弗易也。"① 所谓"五常"，指礼教人伦原则"仁、义、礼、智、信"。西汉儒学大师董仲舒（公元前179—公元前104年）的《春秋繁露·深察名号》中有"三纲五纪"之说②，而其渊源可上溯至孔子。三国魏何晏（？—249年）注《论语》，在《为政》篇"殷因于夏礼，所损益，可知也"句后引东汉经学家马融（79—166年）的话说："所因，谓三纲五常。"③ 这种名分与教化的观念是儒家政治思想的重要组成，通过上定名分来教化天下，以维护社会的伦理纲常。

知名法学家瞿同祖曾著《中国法律与中国社会》，从家族、婚姻、阶级的维度切入，论述了律法条例对父权、夫权和皇权的保护，及其对封建社会结构框架的巩固。"法律之所以特别着重上述两种身份，自是由于儒家思想的影响。在儒家心目中家族和社会身份是礼的核心，也是儒家所鼓吹的社会秩序的支柱。古代法律可说全为儒家的伦理思想和礼教支配"（瞿同祖，2010：375—376）。

套用社会语言学的理论，语言既是社会现实的反映，同时也改造着社会现实（language both reflects and shapes society）。"十恶"、"八议"、"七出"及容隐、代刑等负载着鲜明文化特色的法言法语，可说无一例外。

第二节　中国法律及其语言的近代转型

秦汉律令法家所定，"出礼入刑"、"明刑弼教"乃法律之儒家化。此过程渐次完结后，"中国古代法律便无重大的、本质上的变化，至少在家族和阶级方面是如此"（同上，376）。直到19世纪，欧美列强凭借坚船利炮，武装输出所谓西方文明。鸦片开埠、甲午割地、庚子赔款，深重灾难摩肩接踵，晚清社会急转直下，天朝上国竟为鱼肉，中华法系亦土崩瓦解。又历百余年的移植与融合，方才辗转而成近现代法律体系雏形。

一　近代法制转型维度

值此内忧外患交迫的近代转型期间，传统法制观念的改弦更张势在必

---

① 详见《韩非子集解》卷第二十。（清）王先慎撰，钟哲点校，第466页。
② 详见《春秋繁露义证》卷第十。苏舆撰，钟哲点校，第303页。
③ 详见《十三经注疏·论语注疏》卷第二。（魏）何晏注，（宋）邢昺疏，朱汉民整理，张岂之审定，第23页。

行。张晋藩教授（2005 年）将之归结为八个方面：

（一）由固守成法到师夷变法　　（二）由维护三纲到批判三纲
（三）由盲目排外到中体西用　　（四）由专制神圣到君宪共和
（五）由以人治国到以法治国　　（六）由义务本位到权利追求
（七）由集权统治到司法独立　　（八）由以刑为主到诸法并重

　　需要说明的是，固守成法、盲目排外，名虽有异，实则互为表里；其余皆是以"三纲五常"为核心的封建专制思想的体现，从正统沦为腐朽终被弃如敝屣，绝非一日之功，更非一人之力。期间，旷日持久的法律翻译不无潜移默化之微劳。上至洋务运动、下及宪政革命，既受其影响，亦收其效用。

二　法律翻译与现代法律术语体系及分支学科的构建

　　若认师夷变法策略与中体西用学说不可逆转地推动西法东渐的迅猛发展，那么反过来正是法律翻译催生近代法学思想指导下法律制度的激烈转型。这首先表现在蕴含法律意义的术语层面的渐变，特别是外来词汇的本土化。毋庸置疑，法律术语与法学学科，"二者成共生同构的关系"（俞江，2008：12）。现有相关研究尽管凤毛麟角，但的的确确已然稳步起航，且其演进历程呈现出三分法和五分法之各论。

　　（A）认知阶段三分法

　　华东师范大学俞江教授将晚清时期法学语词的生成与发展划分为三个主要阶段（2008：3—22）：

　　Ⅰ　感知阶段：1800 年至 1860 年的《五车韵府》与《各国律例》

　　Ⅱ　整合阶段：1860 年至 1900 年，以罗布存德氏（Wilhelm. Lobscheid）《英华字典》（*English and Chinese Dictionary*）为主线

　　Ⅲ　改造和平衡阶段：1900 年至 1911 年，中国第一批法律辞典及其他

（B）时代背景五分法

西川大学崔军民副教授则认定法律新词萌芽的主要来源包括借词①、新义词②和新创词③，并从五个时期分别进行考察（2001：4，15—16）：

Ⅰ 1840 年以前：传教士东来与法律新词

Ⅱ 鸦片战争前后：知西政之始与法律新词

Ⅲ 洋务运动时期：译介公法与法律新词

Ⅳ 甲午战争之后：师法东瀛与法律新词

Ⅴ 20 世纪初十年：清末修律与法律新词

乍看之下，貌似两位学者的视角大相径庭，实则认知阶段与时代背景完全是珠联璧合，相得益彰：

表1 晚清西法东渐的演进历程

认知阶段	感知洋传教士介绍的欧美文化	整合公法东渐输入的近代理念	改造和平衡阶段
时代背景	鸦片泛滥，白银外流	洋务运动	宪政革命
法律辞典	无专门法律辞典唯有《华英字典》④	无专门法律辞典 通常只能参考罗存德的《英华字典》⑤ 或麦都思的《英汉字典》和《汉英字典》⑥	《法律名词通释》等专门法律辞典

──────────

① 所谓借词，包括借音词和借形词，其中借音词又分为纯音译词、音兼意译词和半音译半意译词。

② 所谓新义词，包括形式改造的词和语义改造的词。

③ 所谓新创词，包括意译（含仿译）词和完全自创词。

④ 《华英字典》（*A Dictionary of the Chinese Language*）的编纂者是英国传教士马礼逊（Robert Marrison，1782 - 1834），他也是西方列强派驻中国大陆的首位基督教新教传教士。该字典由三部分组成：第一部分名《字典》（*Chinese and English, Arranged According to the Radicals*，1815），译自嘉庆十二年（1807年）刊刻的《艺文备览》；第二部分名《五车韵府》（*Chinese and English Arranged Alphabetically*，1819）；第三部分名《英汉字典》（*English and Chinese*，1822）。

⑤ 德国传教士罗存德（Wilhelm Lobscheid，1822 - 1893）编纂的《英华字典》（*English and Chinese Dictionary*）于 1866 年首次出版。

⑥ 英国传教士麦都思（Walter Henry Medhurst，1796 - 1857）曾经编纂《汉英字典》（*Chinese and English Dictionary*）和《英汉字典》（*English and Chinese Dictionary*）各两卷，皆以《康熙字典》为蓝本。前者初版于 1842—1843 年，后者初版于 1847—1848 年。

认知阶段	感知洋传教士介绍的欧美文化	整合公法东渐输入的近代理念		改造和平衡阶段
主持翻译	组织者：林则徐 实施者：伯驾 袁德辉	京师同文馆，美国传教士丁韪良主持	沪局翻译馆，英国基督徒傅兰雅主持	翰林院修撰张謇设翰墨林编译印书局
代表译作	《滑达尔各国律例》（法律本性正理所载）	《万国公法》《公法便览》	《各国交涉便法论》《各国交涉公法论》	《英国国会史》
选译意图	师夷长技以制夷	和平外交借法自强		尊英仿日立宪修律
译介特征	呈现早期文化接触的说明性翻译特征	文化上：秉承中体西用学说；形式上：难免"一词多译"、"多词一译"的混乱局面		法律术语概念：系统输入并固化；法律分支学科：逐渐形成并拓展

俞江教授认为我国现代法学的移植与本土化主要发生在 20 世纪最初十年，却也不能否认其与甲午战争的密切联系（2008：11—13）。大片国土割让、巨额白银赔款标志着洋务运动日渐式微，从而引发公车上书及其后的百日维新。与此同时，师法东瀛迅速形成热潮，尤其庚子事变后公法以外的其他法律移植活动更是上升至政府层面逐步展开。宪政特具提纲挈领之功效而备受重视，各部门法概念、规范、原则也随之井喷。近代中国法律术语的概念正是在此阶段相继固定并系统化，其巅峰即清末沈家本先生主持修订的各项法律草案，实质上效仿欧美统一规划了诸多法律分支学科的术语概念。

无论如何，学界对中国近代法制转型期西法东渐的翻译研究主要局限于词汇层面，尽管有意识地结合社会背景与文化交流（崔军民，2011），或试图从符号学角度解释早期法律翻译的说明性特征及"一词多译"、"多词一译"的混乱局面（俞江，2008），却未能将两者密切联系起来，探讨东西方文明碰撞过程中激烈的权力博弈对术语定名与译名歧出的影响。何况"怎么译"尚在其次，"译什么"岂不是更为重要？或者说，词汇层面的问题绝非问题的全部，篇章选择亦不容小觑。

三　东西方意识形态碰撞中的权力博弈

清末西法东渐之深远影响彰于修律。细察《钦定大清商律》（1903年）、《钦定宪法大纲》（1908年）、《大清法院编制法》（1909年）、《大清新刑律》（1911年）、《大清民律草案》（1911年）、《大清刑事诉讼律草案》（1911年）、《大清民事诉讼律草案》（1911年）等从立法思想、编撰技术乃至遣词造句，无不笼罩着欧美法哲思想的渗透——"诸法合体"的传统形式终被抛弃，"依伦理而轻重其刑"的礼教特征亦受冲击。但正如陈顾远先生所言，"万变仍有其宗，文化并未骤改，民俗依然如故"（2001：15）。本土核心意识形态的抵御与舶来边缘意识形态的侵蚀，进退攻守间此长彼消的博弈态势，自是历史的必然性与偶然性交相作用。

何况"为社会生活之规范，经国家权力之认定，并具有强制之性质者曰法"（陈顾远，2011：12），其急遽变革，即便有随波逐流、水到渠成的点点滴滴，也万难摆脱国内外形形色色政治经济集团逐鹿中原的喧扰时局。

尤其值得注意的是，我国近代法律翻译始自华洋合译或西译中述，首当其冲之要务就在于寻求公度性。如何沟通分属两个迥异世界本质上不可通约的社会价值体系，成为横亘在当时中外译员眼前几乎难以逾越的天堑。

（一）士大夫墨守伦理纲常

晚清政府师夷变法，皆因内外交困，亟欲救亡图存，日暮途穷方才两害相权取其轻。虽说"穷则变，变则通，通则久"，统治阶层依然固执"数千年相传之礼教民情"。无论倡导中体西用的洋务运动，还是"仿效外国资本主义法律形式，固守中国封建法制传统"的立宪修律，无有胆敢逾矩的莽撞举措。皓首穷经的士大夫们闭目塞听，内心深处仍视西洋诸邦为蛮夷，取"奇技淫巧"已属非分，更难接受耶稣基督的"异端邪说"，遑论容忍上帝凌驾伦理纲常。

（二）殖民者鼓吹基督教义

清末民初之际，热衷研究中华法系的英美学者能够辨识法典编纂体例，理解法规适用原则，却无从洞悉隐藏在字里行间的传统法律理念。譬如杨鸿烈在《中国法律发达史》的导言中引巴系佛尔特（Bp. James Whitford Bashford[①]）列举我国古代法律的十项特征，难觅只字片语涉及人伦礼教的核心价值[②]。即便为数不多通晓汉语言文字的欧美驻华传教士亦洋洋自得于西洋近代科技文明之昌盛，将儒家思想不分青红皂白，一概贬为束缚人性的封建专制糟粕，首译《大清律例》的小斯当东便是个中典型。

第三节　小结

晚清是一个异域文明企图颠覆传统的动荡时代，孕育新思想的阵痛牵动着华夏文明的亿兆生灵。欲捋顺其间来龙去脉，绝难凭今时今日之境况，臆造子丑寅卯，生搬硬套式地品评优劣，妄言先驱者的贤愚不肖。面对"千年未有之大变局"，我们应当以更为宏大的目光、更加宽广的胸怀，在悲壮的历史画卷上重温那些迷雾笼罩的往事。

有鉴于此，笔者将从追溯西方法律语言学源流入手，通过概览法律翻译研究现状及其局限，阐明描写范式（descriptive paradigm）依托系统论的优越性，继而结合晚清法制转型期的多元文化特征（multiculturalism），考察鸦片战争前后、洋务运动及宪政革命等关键历史节点涌现的经典译作，以期重构西法东渐在我国近代内政外交博弈中留下的不可磨灭的印记。

---

① 今译柏锡福（1849—1919 年），美国驻华传教士。

② 杨鸿烈转引巴系佛尔特在《阐述中国》（*China：An Interpretation*）中归纳的传统法律特征如下："第一，中国古代法律几乎对于每一种犯罪都规定有身体刑（corporal, or physical punishment）。第二，中国法律以科罚严厉著称，但在执行时又可减宥（leniency）。第三，中国法律条理异常清晰，如此则每一特别案情可得确切的判决（exact justice）。第四，中国法律在本国区域内有至高无上的权力。第五，中国司法的管辖是受流行全国的地方自治政府的限制。第六，中国立法制度是皇帝的敕令较一切地方规程为优越。第七，中国司法缺少辩护的规定（provision for litigation）。第八，中国司法管辖的特点即在诉讼程序的方法上。第九，中国立法最显著的地方是社会对犯罪须负责任。第十，中国司法机关最大的弊病便是司法权行政权为'同一的官吏所掌握'。"（1984：2—3）

第 一 章
普通法系法律语言学源流

第一节　学科研究范畴

遥想数百年前，苏格兰逻辑实证主义哲学家大卫·休谟（David Hume，1711－1776）就曾断言："法与法律制度是一种纯粹的语言形式，法的世界肇始于语言，法律是通过语词订立和公布的。"

尽管如此，法律语言学仍属新兴的国际性边缘学科，是法学界和语言学界共同聚焦的交叉学科热点。1993 年在德国波恩成立的国际法律语言学家学会（International Association of Forensic Linguistics，简称 IAFL）及其每两年举行一次的学术性会议为法律语言学的蓬勃发展构建起跨文化交流的国际化平台。法学界和语言学界对法律语言的探讨，从研究视角来说，有历史学、逻辑学、修辞学、心理学等；从研究重心来说，有立法语篇、法庭语篇等。时至今日，甚至出现了"法学的语言学转向"潮流。"法律与语言融合性交叉使法律语言学不再是法律事实的语言解释，而成为语言在法律问题中的直接实践。"（李振宇，2006：184）

一　法律语言学的英文名称及其研究范畴

法律语言学究竟如何命名？这个问题在英美国家未获得应有的重视，只能感谢致力于对比分析的欧洲学术界就此进行了追本溯源式的探求。

概括来说，大陆国家尤其法国和德国惯常使用术语"*linguistique juridique*"（法语）、"*Rechtslinguistik*"（德语），译入英文即"legal linguistics"或"jurilinguistics"；英美学者则倾向"law and language"或"forensic linguistics"——前者通行虽久，却难抵后来者居上之势（Mattila，2006：8）。

无论如何，法律语言学的研究范畴更为繁复，很多学者试图沿袭各自不同的路径给予独特诠释，大致可将其分作三支：语言学视角、司法学视角与社会学视角。

二 语言学视角

加利福尼亚州立大学（California State University）语言学荣誉教授杰拉德·R. 麦克梅纳明（Gerald R. McMenamin）是这方面当之无愧的领军人物。他在应用语言学（applied linguistics）的框架下研究法律语言学（forensic linguistics），并将之定义为"应用于法律目的及语境的语言学研究"（the scientific study of language as applied to forensic purposes and contexts）（McMenamin，2002：84）。

该研究路径偏重应用语言学的理论和方法，按照语言结构与功能划分法律语言学涵盖的领域①（同上，87—97）：

（1）听觉语音学（Auditory Phonetics）

（2）声学语音学（Acoustic Phonetics）

（3）语义学（Semantics：Interpretation of Expressed Meaning）

（4）话语分析与语用学（Discourse and Pragmatics：Interpretation of Inferred Meaning）

（5）文体学与作者归属（Stylistics and Questioned Authorship）

（6）法律语言（Language of the Law）

（7）法庭语言（Language of the Courtroom）

（8）口译与笔译（Interpretation and Translation）

麦克梅纳明教授的贡献还在于将自己所接触的法律语言学领域最具代表性的文献分门别类地归入相应的研究主题，为后学晚进理解此学科的来龙去脉提供了极大便利。

---

① 麦克梅纳明在《法律语言学：法律文体学的最新发展》（*Forensic Linguistics：Advances in Forensic Stylistics*）第4.2节中提出了语言学视角下法律语言研究领域的划分标准："The classification of areas in forensic linguistics evolves as the field develops. It usually follows existing classifications in the structure and function of language（see Chapter 1）as a basis for cataloging actual and potential subject areas."（McMenamin，2002：86）

三 司法学视角

约翰·奥尔森（John Olsson）也许是这方面走得最远的。他经营着全球知名的法律语言学咨询公司（forensic linguistics consultancy），丰富的实务经验使得多国大学争聘其为兼职教授（adjunct professor）或客座教授（visiting professor）①。

顺理成章的是，奥尔森的著作虽然也将法律语言学视作"语言学的应用分支（an application of linguistics）"，却着眼司法实践中亟须应用语言学的领域，开列法律语言学研究的子项目如表1—1 所示：

表1—1　法律语言学分支学科（Disciplines of Forensic Linguistics）

（Olsson，2004：4–5）

Category	*Description*
Authorship identification Mode identification	Identifying authors of texts Ascertaining whether a text was produced by speech，writing or some combination of both（e. g. part written，part dictated）
Legal interpreting and translation	Interpreting and translation in the courtroom，*viva* interpreting for police and defendants/witnesses；translating statements and other legal documents—issues of accuracy and fairness，the role of interpreters，their licensing，'control'，etc.
Transcribing verbal statements	In some legal systems statements are audio/video recorded and require transcription for courtroom use—issues of completeness and bias
The language and discourse of courtrooms	A study of the relationship between courtroom participants and the language they use—issues of power，prejudice，culture clashes，etc.

---

① Google 图书对奥尔森的介绍如下（引自 http：//books. google. com. hk/books？ id = i3399LFSzqQC&dq = forensic + linguistics&hl = zh-CN&source = gbs_ navlinks_ s）：Since 1996，John Olsson has operated a world-renowned forensic linguistics consultancy and training service at www. thetext. co. uk. He is an Adjunct Professor at Nebraska Wesleyan University，USA，where he teaches forensic linguistics online. He is also a Visiting Professor of Forensic Linguistics at the International University of Novi Pazar，Serbia，where he runs an annual summer school in Forensic Linguistics，and is a board member of the Language and Law Centre at the University of Zagreb，Croatia，where he is also a Visiting Professor.

续表

Category	Description
Language rights	These include: the language rights or minority groups in cultures dominated by other languages or other dialects of the same language, the linguistic rights of those without language, and the oppressiveness of bureaucratic language. Note that some of the other areas mentioned here are also concerned (sometimes indirectly) with language rights, e. g. interpreting, transcription of statements, courtroom discourse, etc.
Statement analysis	Analysing witness statements for their veracity
Forensic phonetics	Analysis of audio material for speaker identification and other purposes; voice line-ups
Textual status	Analysing texts and auditory material for their genuineness, e. g. genuine *vs* hoax emergency calls, genuine *vs* simulated suicide/ransom notes, etc.; assessing risk from text

尽管其书名为《法律语言学》（*Forensic Linguistics*），但副标题"语言、犯罪与法律导论"（An Introduction to Language, Crime, and the Law）明确指出作者关注的焦点是刑事司法领域。实际上，他常以专家证人（expert witness）的身份参与司法程序，因此主要探讨"作为证据的语言"（language as evidence）而无暇旁顾：

> In this book we will be discussing most of the above areas of forensic linguistics, except for language rights, courtroom discourse, and legal interpreting and translation. This is not because I view these areas as less interesting or important, but rather because they require a different approach from those areas that I will be dealing with. (Ibid. 3)

四 社会学视角

从社会学视角研究法律和语言（law and language）的流派起步亦不算晚，较为著名的包括华盛顿大学（University of Washington）英语教授盖尔·斯塔高尔（Gail Stygall）。她归纳了法律语言学的三个主要研究方向——作为对象的法律语言（language-as-object）、作为过程的法律语言

（language-as-process）和作为工具的法律语言（language-as-instrument）：

> In the first category, language-as-object, falls work focused on describing the phenomena of legal language or on applying a single element of theoretical linguistics, such as speech acts, to the occurrence of legal language. Language-as-process studies sketch issues of comprehension and differential understanding. Studies analyzing how jurors or mock jurors understand jury instructions, for example, might fall into this category, as would studies examining how language affects perception of attorneys or witnesses or as would studies examining criminal defendants' understanding of pleas in their cases. Finally, a category that I would propose as currently emerging, language-as-instrument, examines how legal language can function instrumentally, as an instrument of the law's own power, or an element of the maintenance of or resistance to institutional power. (Stygall, 1994: 7)

斯塔高尔的"三分法"在我国法律语言学界影响颇大，廖美珍教授（2004）、刘蔚铭教授（2009）等都曾有所论述。可正如其本人所言，上述路径之间相互重叠的领域颇多，特别是语言作为过程和工具的研究都发生在司法程序中，关系尤为密切，两者合而为一的著述亦层出不穷。另外，她强调社会学理论与话语分析法的结合，目光所至自然未及"作为证据的语言"研究。

有鉴于此，近年来阿斯顿大学（Aston University）法律语言学研究中心修正了"三分法"，将之变更为法律语言（language of the law）、司法程序中的语言（language in the judicial process）和语言学证据（linguistic evidence）：

> Forensic linguistics can be fairly characterised as taking linguistic knowledge, methods and insight, and applying these to the forensic context of law, investigation, trial, punishment and rehabilitation. It is not a homogenous discipline in its interest, methods or approach, but rather both involves a wide spectrum of practitioners and researchers applying

themselves to different areas of the field. There are perhaps three main areas of application for linguists working in forensic contexts; understanding language of the written law, understanding language use in forensic and judicial processes and the provision of linguistic evidence. ①

五　小结

综上所述，语言学和司法学视角下划分的研究方向不仅繁芜庞杂，也过分强调各自领域的特征，而未充分考虑法律语言学本身的固有属性。相比之下，社会学理论关照下的"三分法"更能超越狭隘的学科界限。

当然，阿斯顿"三分法"亦非横空出世。早在 20 世纪 90 年代，芝加哥洛约拉大学（Loyola University）法学院教授皮特·M. 梯尔斯马② （Peter M. Tiersma）就曾撰文《法律中的语言学问题》（"Linguistic Issues in the Law"），将法律与语言学的交叉领域一分为二，即语言学家"作为法律程序的观察者"（observers of the legal process）和"以专家证人的角色作为法律程序的参与者"（participants in the legal process in the role of expert witness）（Stygall，1994：21）。

时至今日，很多颇具影响力的法律语言学著作仍以此标准编写。譬如，阿斯顿大学法律语言学荣誉教授马尔科姆·库萨德③（Malcolm Coulthard）和利兹大学（University of Leeds）英语与语言学讲师埃里森·约翰逊（Alison Johnson）合著的《法律语言学导论：证据中的语言》（An Introduction to Forensic Linguistics: Language in Evidence，2007），便由"法律程序的语言"（The language of the legal process）和"作为证据的语言"（Language as evidence）两部分组成。数年后，他们又领衔编纂了《劳特利奇法律语言学手册》（The Routledge Handbook of Forensic Linguistics，2010），"法律及法律程序的语言"（The language of law and the legal process）和"法律程序中作为专家证人的语言学家"（The linguist as ex-

---

①　引自阿斯顿大学法律语言学研究中心对法律语言学的介绍（http://www. forensiclinguistics. net/cfl_ fl. html）。

②　梯尔斯马曾任国际法律语言学家协会主席（2005—2007 年）。

③　库萨德是国际法律语言学家协会首任主席，还曾担任阿斯顿大学法律语言学中心主任。

pert in legal processes）的划分标准亦相仿佛①。然而毋庸置疑的是，"法律语言"分支的地位正冉冉上升，终将与"司法程序中的语言"、"作为证据的语言"不分轩轾、并驾齐驱。

这使我们回想起美国西北大学（Northwestern University）语言学家朱迪思·N. 利维（Judith N. Levi），其视野更为宽阔，理论也更高屋建瓴。他主编了划时代的经典论文集《司法程序中的语言》（*Language in the Judicial Process*，1990）并亲自撰写提纲挈领的开篇第一章"司法程序中的语言研究"（The Study of Language in the Judicial Process），根据自己的理解与展望描述法律语言学（law and language）研究主题的分层结构②，包括"法律环境中的口语研究"（spoken language in legal settings）、"作为法律主题的语言研究"（language as a subject of the law）和"法律及其书面语研究"（law and its written language）。

表1—2   利维的法律语言学研究纲要（Levi's Law and Language：Outline for Research）（Levi, 1990：14）

Ⅰ. Spoken Language in Legal Settings

    A. Courtroom language：general

    B. Effects of language on eyewitness testimony

        1. Issues in memory acquisition，retention，retrieval

        2. Forms of questioning and their effects on memory

    C. Effects of language variation in the courtroom

        1. Language variation and witness credibility

        2. Language variation and attorney effectiveness

    D. Comprehensibility of jury instructions

    E. Semantic and pragmatic issues in legal discourse

        1. Courtroom discourse

        2. Discourse in other legal settings

    F. Communicative competence in legal settings

---

① 该手册总共三部分，但第三部分"新争论与新方向"（New Debates and New Directions）明显带有学科展望性质。

② 利维在《司法程序中的语言》（*Language in the Judicial Process*）第一章中将自己的研究领域称之为"the domain of social science research on language and law"（Levi, 1990：11）。

G. Storytelling as a model of courtroom testimony

H. The "verbatim" transcript: linguistic and legal issues

I. The language of plea bargaining

J. The language of lawyer-client interactions

Ⅱ. Language as a Subject of the Law

   A. Rights of language minorities

      1. In general

      2. In public education

      3. In legal proceedings

      4. As citizens (especially in regard to government services)

   B. Verbal offenses

      1. Taped conversations as evidence in trials

      2. Defining individual verbal offenses (e. g. , perjury, threats to the life of the President, defamation, libel and slander, solicitation to murder)

      3. Other

   C. Language issues in consumer protection

      1. Informed consent (e. g. , consent forms, retainer agreements, package inserts for pharmaceuticals)

      2. Products liability (e. g. , warning labels)

      3. Advertising language and the law (e. g. , trademarks and copyright infringement, regulation of advertising language by the Federal Trade Commission)

      4. Effect of (in) comprehensibility on legal adequacy of mandated notices

   D. Free speech, symbolic speech, and the First Amendment

   E. Legal and judicial notions of linguistic authority

Ⅲ. Law and Its Written Language

   A. Comprehensibility of written legal language

      1. What is and what is not "Plain English"

      2. Language in contracts

      3. Language in public documents and official notices

a. Issues of adequate legal notice

b. Issues of equal access to public services

4. Language of laws and statutes

B. Linguistic analyses （e. g., prosodic, semiotic, syntactic） of written legal language

C. Problems in legal drafting and interpretation/construction

D. Other issues （sce also topics in I-H and II-C）

间或有学者从书面语和口语研究的宽泛主题中抽取社会正义（social justice）、教学（teaching and learning）、翻译（translation and interpreting）等焦点问题单列，似乎亦无不可。

As the title of this collection implies, Forensic Linguistics, in its now widely accepted broader definition, has many aspects. Major areas of study include: the written language of the law, particularly the language of legislation; spoken legal discourse, particularly the language of court proceedings and police questioning; the social justice issues that emerge from the written and spoken language of the law; the provision of linguistic evidence, which can be divided into evidence on identity/authorship, and evidence on communication; the teaching and learning of spoken and written legal language; and legal translation and interpreting. （Gibbons & Turell, 2008: 1）

本书旨在考察法律翻译活动中的权力博弈问题，故而稍后将设专节探讨翻译研究的现状，但社会正义问题无法回避。接下来，笔者将从法律书面语言和法律程序语言两个维度回顾西方法律语言学发展现状。至于作为法律主题（包括证据）的语言研究，因其相关性较弱，而本书篇幅有限，请允许笔者暂且搁置。

第二节　法律书面语言

法律语言既是技术性机构语言（institutional language），也是普通人群了解法律的唯一途径。"不论喜欢与否，文字乃律师和法官的主要工具。它对于我们正如手术刀和胰岛素之于医生"① （Zachariah，1941：381 – 382）。

因此，法律写作大师研究语言强调实践性，目光所及无非专业领域的技能培养。尤其在英语国家，阐述如何起草法律文书的著作汗牛充栋。仅就管窥所见，试举其中较为典型者如下：

（1）《法律语言》（*The Language of the Law*）（Mellinkoff，1963）

（2）《法律语言》（*Legal Language*）（Tiersma，1999）

（3）《法律写作》（*Legal Drafting*）（Haggard，2004）

（4）《法律英语：中英双语法律文书制作》（*Legal English：Guidelines for Drafting Chinese-English Bilingual Legal Documents*）（陶博，2004）

（5）《现代法律写作——为使用更清晰的语言提供指南》（*Modern Legal Drafting：A Guide to Using Clearer Language*）（Butt & Castle，2001）

（6）《使用平实英语进行法律写作：附带练习》（*Legal Writing in Plain English：A Text with Exercises*）（Garner，2001）

（7）《法律风格要素》（*The Elements of Legal Style*）（Garner，2002）

（8）《法律英语》（*Legal English*）（Haigh，2009）

（9）《法律文件起草之道》（*Drafting*）（都南 & 福斯特，2006）

（10）《法律文书写作之道》（*Legal Writing*）（科斯坦佐，2006）

（11）《法律文书写作：步骤·分析·组织》（*Legal Writing：Process，Analysis，and Organization*）（Edwards，2003）

（12）《法律推理与法律文书写作：结构·策略·风格》（*Legal Reasoning and Legal Writing：Structure，Strategy，and Style*）（Neumann，2003）

（13）《法律检索、分析与写作》（*Legal Research，Analysis and Writing*）（Putman，2010）

---

① 英语原文："Words are the principal tools of lawyer and judges，whether we like it or not. They are to us what the scalpel and insulin are to the doctor."

上述作品都出自英美国家声名卓著的法学家。譬如，加州大学洛杉矶分校（UCLA）法学院教授大卫·麦林科夫（David Mellinkoff），可谓系统描述法律语言的鼻祖，开启了运用平实英语撰写法律文书（legal writing in plain English）的运动；还有业界公认的法律文献专家布莱恩·A. 加纳（Bryan A. Garner），亦即《布莱克法律辞典》（*Black's Law Dictionary*）主编，该辞典现已推出第九版，久享法律圣经的盛誉。

同样值得重视的是法哲学或法理学家如哈特、德沃金、摩尔、马默、帕特森、莱昂斯、鲍勃金、恩迪科特、比克斯等学术权威，他们跨越哲学、法学和语言学等诸多领域，试图洞悉语言在法律中的地位及其与法律解释的关系。

一 法律英语的定义

何谓法律英语？麦林科夫在半个多世纪前撰写的革命性专著《法律语言》（*The Language of the Law*）对此作过详尽论述，备受西方学者推崇：

> *The Language of the Law*, as described in this book, is the customary language used by lawyers in **those common law jurisdictions** where English is the official language. It includes distinct words, meanings, phrases, and modes of expression. It also includes certain mannerisms of composition not exclusive with the profession but prevalent enough to have formed a fixed association. [1] (Mellinkoff, 1963: 3)

作者选择中性术语"法律语言"（the language of the law）指称通常所说的"法律英语"，自然煞费苦心[2]。首先是考虑到"legal"多表示"合

---

① 粗体由本书作者添加。

② 以下解释均出自 Merriam-Webster Online Dictionary（http：//bbs. enfamily. cn/tools/dict. htm）。

法性"（lawful），极易导致混淆。而"lingo"①、"jargon"②、"argot"③ 等虽作"行话"解，但所指或者怪异，或者难以理喻，或者隐秘；"legal-ese"④ 则近似汉语八股文⑤。这些词汇不仅概念界定过分狭隘，且贬抑色彩溢于言表。相比之下，"the language of the law"涵盖的领域更为宽泛。

In the first decade of the century Sir William Holdsworth wrote of "the language, or rather languages, of the law," stressing a polyglot origin. Others have emphasized the relationship between language and the law. The language of the law is a convenient label for a speech pattern with a separate identity. *Law language* is sometimes used here as it shortener; *law words* for individual words in the *language of the law*. These expressions are preferred to *legal parlance*, *legal English*, and *legal language*, for the reason that *legal* is so frequently and properly used to mean *lawful* as to cause confusion at the outset. *Legal lingo*, *legal jargon*, and *legalese* are rejected on the additional grounds of being too sweepingly opprobrious and also too narrow. These objections apply equally to *legalistic jargon* and *argot of the law*.

---

① Definition of lingo: strange or incomprehensible language or speech as
a: a foreign language
b: the special vocabulary of a particular field of interest
c: language characteristic of an individual

② Definition of jargon:
1 a: confused unintelligible language
b: a strange, outlandish, or barbarous language or dialect
c: a hybrid language or dialect simplified in vocabulary and grammar and used for communication between peoples of different speech
2: the technical terminology or characteristic idiom of a special activity or group

③ Definition of argot: an often more or less secret vocabulary and idiom peculiar to a particular group

④ Definition of legalese: the specialized language of the legal profession

⑤ 麦林科夫认为"legalese"语带贬义，陶博持同样观点，故将之译成"法律八股文"（2004: 2）。但也有学者认为该术语属于中性词，与之意思相近的"legalspeak"方在特定语境中隐含否定态度（Stanojević, 2011: 66）。

Swift's acid phrase was "a peculiar Cant and Jargon of their own, that no other Mortal can understand." Bentham had a bag of phrases, applied with uncomplimentary impartiality: *law jargon*, *lawyers' cant*, *lawyers' language*, *flash language*. Opposed to these is the *language of jurisprudence*, dignified but confining. The *language of the law* partakes of some of the essence of all of these diverse characterizations. (Ibid. 3 – 4)

同时也请注意,麦氏定义中"普通法法域"(those common law jurisdictions)的曲折词缀为复数形态。毋庸置疑,"法律英语"涉及的并不只有英国,还包括美国、加拿大、澳大利亚、印度及其他以英文为母语的普通法系国家。这些日不落帝国曾经的殖民地(相当部分至今仍是英联邦成员)虽亦使用发端不列颠群岛的英语,但历经岁月洗礼,渐与各地区固有文明相互交融,折射在表达层面的细微差别难以斗量。

二　从历史演进角度谈法律英语的词汇特征

但正如芝加哥大学(University of Chicago)法学院客座教授普雷斯顿·M. 陶博(Preston M. Torbert)所言,"这些细微的差异实际上起到的作用是突出了在所有这些英语为母语的国家中所使用的法律语言的共同特征(并且在实际上,这些国家在使用各自的法律语言的过程中还存在着一些相互之间的法律语言的借鉴和移植)"(2004:3)。

陶博教授凭借自己长期从事国际法律事务的优势,在培训英汉双语律师的系列讲座中,将麦林科夫业已体系化的法律英语典型特征(characteristics of the language of the law)继续扩充为十项①(Mellinkoff, 1963:11;陶博,2004:3):

(1)经常使用常用词汇不常用的含义(Frequent use of common words with uncommon meanings)

(2)经常使用曾经常用但现在已很少使用的古代英语和中世纪英语的词汇(Frequent use of Old English and Middle English words once in common use, but now rare)

---

① 陶博教授不仅将麦氏著作的原文译入汉语,并补充了第十项特征。

（3）经常使用拉丁语单词和短语（Frequent use of Latin words and phrases）

（4）使用一般词汇表中不会有的古法语及法律法语中的词汇（Use of Old French and Anglo-Norman words which have not been taken into the general vocabulary）

（5）专门术语的使用（Use of terms of art）

（6）"行话"的使用（Use of argot）

（7）经常使用官样文章用语（Frequent use of formal words）

（8）刻意使用具有可变通含义的词汇和短语（Deliberate use of words and expressions with flexible meanings）

（9）力求表述准确（Attempts at extreme precision of expression）

（10）冗长性、保守性和精确性（Lengthiness, conservatism and accuracy）

威斯康星大学（University of Wisconsin）法学院副教授劳伦斯·M. 弗兰德曼（Lawrence M. Friedman）曾撰文评论这些特征可约略划分成两类：法律词汇（legal vocabulary）和法律风格（legal style）（1964：563）。实际上，正式性①、模糊性②、准确性③及"冗长性、保守性和精确性"等要素借用麦氏的话说，在某种程度上更接近"与职业表述相关的独特方式"（mannerisms associated with professional expression）（1963：11）。若将之暂时搁置，则不难发现其余各项针对的都是词汇层面的现象。

20 世纪初，英国著名法制史学家威廉·霍兹沃思男爵（Sir William Holdsworth）就有 "the language, or rather languages, of the law" 之说（同上，3），由此可见法律英语的"多元化渊源"（polyglot origin）。

现代法律英语的发展史漫长曲折，历经盎格鲁（Angle）、撒克逊（Saxon）、朱特（Jute）、弗里斯兰（Frisian）诸日耳曼民族融合；皈依基督教（Christianization）；维京海盗劫掠（Viking raid）等影响深远的事件

---

① 即经常使用官样文章用语（Frequent use of formal words）。

② 即刻意使用具有可变通含义的词汇和短语（Deliberate use of words and expressions with flexible meanings）。

③ 即力求表述准确（Attempts at extreme precision of expression）。

（Tiersma, 2012: 19 – 24）。而诺曼征服（Norman conquest）遗留的烙印更是永不磨灭，最终使之成为多种语言的混合体，尤其大量借用法语和拉丁词汇（Haigh, 2009: 2）：

> ... Following the Norman invasion of England in 1066, French became the official language of England, although most ordinary people still spoke English. For a period of nearly 300 years, French was the language of legal proceedings, with the result that many words in current legal use have their roots in this period. . .
>
> During this period, Latin remained the language of formal records and statutes. However, since only the learned were fluent in Latin, it never became the language of legal pleading or debate.

外来语和中古英语词汇频现，凸显了法律语言的保守性。加之术语、行话充斥，且刻意使用普通词汇的特殊含义及多义词汇，难怪非专业人士常作"法律语言不是英语"的感叹：

> But it is a commonplace that that which gives the language of the law its distinctive flavor issomething other than the King's or the commoner's English. Laymen are certain that law language is not English. Statutes make the distinction official. （Mellinkoff, 1963: 10）

尽管法律语言具有鲜明的保守性，但绝非一成不变。语言随社会文化的变迁而逐步演进，这是任何职业壁垒都无法抗拒的常态。有关这方面的探讨早已不限于现代达尔文主义（modern Darwinian theory）与人类集体道德（human group-level morality）等理论之争，渐次转向关注发展方式的实证研究。

当然，零星个案的新术语究竟如何融入普通法词汇，传播模型仍有待具体描述：

> Although judges introduce individual terms in discrete cases and those terms enter the common law lexicon through a process of information diffu-

sion that likely mirrors the spread of other memes, as both an empirical and theoretical matter, the model(s) by which these key phrases become dominant is still drastically underspecified. (Katz *et al.*, 2011: 1)

密歇根州立大学 (Michigan State University) 五位学者在第二十四届法律知识与信息系统国际大会 (The 24th International Conference on Legal Knowledge and Information Systems) 上宣读的论文《法律 N-Grams? 追溯法律语言 "进化" 的简易方式》("Legal N-Grams? A Simple Approach to Track the 'Evolution' of Legal Language", 2011), 利用 Google Books Ngram Viewer 软件①收集数据, 基于模因论 (memetics) 重构现代法律语言的形成, 其研究路径颇具启发性。

三　从逻辑修辞角度谈法律英语的行文风格

现代法律职业人士总将弗朗西斯·培根 (Francis Bacon, 1561 – 1626) 的至理名言奉为圭臬——"历史使人贤明, 诗文使人灵秀, 数学使人周密, 自然哲学使人深刻, 伦理学使人庄重, 逻辑学和修辞学使人能言善辩"②。

所谓修辞, 亚里士多德将之定义成 "可用于说服他人的手段"③ (Aristotle, 2007: 37); 埃里克·林德曼 (Erika Lindemann) 将之视为 "使用口语或者书面语与读者进行沟通的工具" (1982: 53)。它解决的 "不仅仅是文风的问题", "同时也涉及语法与句法" (科斯坦佐, 2006: 15)。但无论 "手段" 或者 "工具", 仅是达成目标的途径, 绝非特定体裁所固有。因此, 麦林科夫强调风格不同于其特征, 只因源远流长, 方被视为法律语言的组成部分:

The nine characteristics of the language of the law are of universal application, to the profession. Taken as a group, those characteristics

---

① http://books.google.com/ngrams/info.

② 英语原文: "History makes men wise; poetry witty; the mathematics subtle; natural philosophy deep; moral grave; logic and rhetoric able to contend. "

③ 英语原文: "Let rhetoric be [defined as] an ability, in each [particular] case, to see the available means of persuasion. "

mark off the language of the law from ordinary speech and from other specialized speech. In addition, widely associated with the language of the law are mannerisms, to which lawyers can claim neither priority nor monopoly. The profession's association with these mannerisms is sufficiently ancient and sufficiently close to justify considering them a part of the language of the law. (Mellinkoff, 1963: 24)

陶博教授着眼实务操作，糅合加拿大立法泰斗埃尔默·德力格尔（Elmer Driedger）等权威专家丰富的起草经验，描绘出文书写作的风格蓝图（2004: 50）：

(1) 确定性（Certainty）

(2) 明确性（Clarity）

(3) 复杂性（Complexity）

(4) 全面性（Comprehensiveness）

(5) 一致性（Consistency）

(6) 精确性（Precision）

(7) 简洁性（Simplicity）

(8) 普通含义（Ordinary Meaning）

(9) 模糊性（Vagueness）

(10) 细节描述（Detail）

纵观诸要素，虽称得上包罗万象、细致入微，词汇、句法与语义各层面无所不及，然首当其冲的仍是"确定性"。因为"确定性与民主控制的原则密切相关"（同上，51），除"模糊性"以外其余各项，归根结底皆为确定法律文本的意义服务，故不能也不应牺牲"确定性"换取行文的"清晰"或者"简洁"。

然而后者恰是当代很多推崇平实文风的法律英语写作大师关注的焦点。譬如加纳教授理想中的法律文体应力求"简洁"（brevity）和"清晰"（clarity）（Garner, 2005: 350）；鲁伯特·海埃（Robert Haigh）则将"清晰"（clarity）视作与"一致性"（consistency）及"法律效力"（effectiveness）相提并论的风格三要素（2009: 47）。

这实际上就触及了法律语言研究中的两大论题：确定性幻象与平实化运动。

四　法律语言的确定性幻象

（一）黄金原则与维特根斯坦遵守规则论

透视法律语言的确定性幻象，不妨从英美国家解释及起草法律的两项黄金原则（Golden Rule of Interpretation and Drafting），即普通含义原则（the "ordinary sense" of words）和术语一致性原则（consistent terminology）破题。

所谓普通含义原则，即"词语应赋予其一般含义。普通英文词语究为何意，这是事实问题而非法律问题，应根据个案的全部情节来认定"①；或者转引麦克米伦大法官（Lord Macmillan）的话说：

> The grammatical and ordinary sense of the words is to be adhered to unless that would lead to some absurdity or some repugnance or inconsistency with the rest of the instrument, in which case the grammatical and ordinary sense of the words may be modified so as to avoid that absurdity and inconsistency, but not further. (Butt & Castle, 2001：48)

所谓术语一致性原则，即"使用不同的词语指称不同的事物；使用相同的词语指称相同的事物"②，亦可作更具体的陈述：

> Never change your language unless you wish to change your meaning, and always change your language if you wish to change your meaning. (Ibid. 49)

陶博将之纳入法律文书的风格要素旨在竭力消除语言的模糊性，但考

---

① 英语原文："... words be given their ordinary sense. The meaning of an ordinary English word is not a question of law but of fact, to be found by taking all the circumstances of the case into consideration."

② 英语原文："Different words are taken to refer to different things, and same words to same things."

量词汇语境意义的规则适用势必牵涉拉特格斯大学（Rutgers University）法学院荣誉教授丹尼斯·帕特森（Dennis Patterson）称为"解释性转向"（interpretative turn）的"当代解释传统"（the current interpretation orthodox）①。相关命题的起源可追溯至路德维希·维特根斯坦（Ludwig Wittgenstein，1889－1951）在《哲学研究》（*Philosophical Investigations*）第143—242节中对规则及其适用与解释之间关系的思考②。

有意思的是，无论法律不确定性（legal indeterminacy）观点的支持者抑或反对者，都希望借重维特根斯坦的遵守规则论（rule-following consid-

---

① 帕特森在《法律与真相》（*Law and Truth*）中专节讨论了解释普适主义（interpretive universalism）及其代表学者罗纳德·德沃金（Ronald Dworkin）和斯坦利·费希（Stanley Fish），并认为当代解释传统存在无限放大的根本谬误："There is something fundamentally wrong with the current interpretive orthodoxy. The notion that every act of textual and verbal comprehension is a matter of some act or theory of interpretation is a deeply misconceived idea, one born of a lack of attention to some obvious features of ordinary understanding, coupled with an inordinate emphasis upon, and faith in, the power of theory as the genesis of expressive intelligibility. As we shall see, by making interpretation central to legal thought, the proponents of interpretive universalism have created nothing short of a philosophical hall of mirrors."（Patterson，1996：72）

② 著名分析哲学家葛丽泰·伊丽莎白·玛格丽特·安斯康姆（Gertrude Elizabeth Margaret Anscombe）师从维特根斯坦。她的英译本《哲学研究》（*Philosophical Investigations*）在英美国家流传甚广。就遵守规则论而言，尤其值得关注的是第201、242节，现将其译文摘录如下："201 This was our paradox: no course of action could be determined by a rule, because every course of action can be brought into accord with the rule. The answer was: if every course of action can be brought into accord with the rule, then it can also be brought into conflict with it. And so there would be neither accord nor conflict here. That there is a misunderstanding here is shown by the mere fact that in this chain of reasoning we place one interpretation behind another, as if each one contented us at least for a moment, until we thought of yet another lying behind it. For what we thereby show is that there is a way of grasping a rule which is not an interpretation, but which, from case to case of application, is exhibited in what we call 'following the rule' and 'going against it'. That's why there is an inclination to say: every action according to a rule is an interpretation. But one should speak of interpretation only when one expression of a rule is substituted for another. 204 It is not only agreement in definitions, but also (odd as it may sound) agreement in judgments that is required for communication by means of language. This seems to abolish logic, but does not do so. —It is one thing to describe methods of measurement, and another to obtain and state results of measurement. But what we call 'measuring' is in part determined by a certain constancy in results of measurement."（Wittgenstein，2009：84^e，94e－95e）

erations) 来提升自身观点的说服力①。请注意，他们之间旷日持久的抗辩正是理解法律和语言问题的基础，因为规则的适用问题即词汇的适用问题：

> Understanding of this debate is basic to understanding of the problem of law and language, because the philosophical question about what connects a rule with its applications amounts to the question of what connects a word with its applications (as both Kripke and the non-skeptical Wittgensteinians recognize). (Endicott, 2000: 23)

随后，笔者将考察两位权威学者的经典著述，借此勾勒当前西方法学界对法律语言确定性问题的研究现状。这两位代表性人物分别是牛津大学（Oxford University）法学院院长梯莫西·A. 恩迪科特（Timothy A. Endicott）教授和明尼苏达州立大学（Minnesota State University）法律与哲学弗雷德里克·W. 托马斯（Frederick W. Thomas）教席教授布莱恩·H. 比克斯（Brian H. Bix）。

在此之前，我们还有必要简单回顾新分析法学派开创者赫伯特·L. A. 哈特（Herbert L. A. Hart）教授影响深远的开放结构理论（open texture theory）及倡导建构性法律解释的罗纳德·德沃金（Ronald Dworkin）教授与其针锋相对的正解论题（right answer thesis）。事实上，正是哈特首先正视了语言在法律中举足轻重的地位，而让德沃金殚精竭虑的却是如何

---

① 梯莫西·A. 恩迪科特（Timothy A. Endicott）教授认为正是"什么将规则与其适用衔接在一起"（What connects a rule with its applications）？这一哲学思考引发了（不）确定性论战，故将之概述如下："On the skeptical interpretation, Wittgenstein is pointing out that, because there is no extra something, there is an unbridgeable gap between a rule and its applications... The skeptics deal with this paradoxical situation by saying that the consensus of a community licenses us to talk as if a rule existed: 'following a rule' is another way of saying 'doing what members of the community say is following a rule'. The non-skeptical interpretation claims that Wittgenstein was trying to dissolve a philosophical muddle rather than to generate one. The remarks on following rules are an articulation of the relation between meaning and use that Wittgenstein pointed out. On this view, he was not arguing that nothing bridges a gap between rule and application... So learning a rule is neither finding something to bridge the gap, nor merely happening to do the same thing as other people, but grasping a way of using the examples that the teacher gives." (2000: 22-23)

剔除这语义学之刺（semantic sting）。

（二）哈特的开放结构理论与德沃金的正解论题

1. 哈特的开放结构理论

1958 年，哈特在《哈佛法学评论》（*Harvard Law Review*，Vol. 71）上发表《实证主义及法律与道德的分离》（"Positivism and the Separation of Law and Morals"）一文，提出著名的"禁止车辆进入公园"假想（"Vehicles in the Park" Hypothetical）。他认为自然语言中的普通词汇均包含由确定意义构成的"核心"（core）和由不确定意义构成的"边缘"（penumbra）[①]：

> We may call the problems which arise outside the hard core of standard instances or settled meaning "problems of the penumbra". （Hart, 1958：607）

这令我们不由自主地联想起认知语言学中的典型理论（prototype theory），两者显然异曲同工。《法律的概念》（*The Concept of Law*，1961）以数个章节的冗长篇幅围绕"模糊性边缘"（a fringe of vagueness）诠释开放结构的理念[②]，并进而述及司法裁量权（judicial discretion）的性质与立法者的意图（lawmakers' intention）：

> In a system where *stare decisis* is firmly acknowledged, this function of the courts is very like the exercise of delegated rule-making powers by an administrative body. In England this fact is often obscured by forms: for the courts often disclaim any such creative function and insist that the proper task of statutory interpretation and the use of precedent is, respectively, to search for the 'intention of the legislature' and the law that already exists. （Hart, 1961：132）

[①] Hart says that any general term in a natural language has a central "core" of determinate meaning and a surrounding "penumbra" of indeterminate meaning （Lyons, 2000：2）.

[②] 诚如比克斯所言，"开放结构"的概念由弗里德里希·魏斯曼（Friedrich Waismann）首创，而魏斯曼的观点又以维特根斯坦的语言观为基础（Bix, 1993：7）。

（1）法庭行为的性质

既然法律文本中普通词汇的边缘意义存在开放性，这就需要法庭"根据个案的全部情节来认定"。问题是法庭确定词汇意义的自由裁量权究竟属于法律解释还是法官造法？

细察哈特的本意，似乎更倾向法官造法的观点。不过，当代很多学者却对其三段式推论颇有异议，譬如波士顿大学（Boston University）法律与哲学教授戴维·莱昂斯（David Lyons）。他认为"一般词汇的适用性取决于是否具备充分理由支持或反对其适用"①，故应纳入法律解释的范畴：

> This would explain why Hart neglects the topic of interpretation, although he comments on the assignment of meaning by courts. Attempts at interpretation are occasioned by the existence of non-negligible considerations on two sides of a legal question—reasonable grounds for more than one way of understanding and applying a law. If genuine interpretation of law is possible, it involves balancing conflicting legal considerations, and this does not fit Hart's syllogistic model. （Lyons, 2000: 6）

（2）立法者的意图

印第安纳州立大学（Indiana State University）法学院沃特·W. 福斯克特（Walter W. Foskett）教席教授威廉·D. 鲍勃金（William D. Popkin）概述法律与语言学的共通之处（1995），其中特别谈到作者意图（the author's intent）对确定语言含义的重要功能。仅制定法而言，所谓作者意图无疑就是立法者的意图。哈特将探求立法者的意图视为合理行使自由裁量权的目标，即要求法官在处理边缘情状（borderline case）时依据作者意图来解释语言中的开放结构。

2. 德沃金的正解论题

直接挑战哈特所谓部分不确定性（partial indeterminacy）推导的是德沃金早期著作提出的正解论题（right answer thesis）——即"绝大多数案件都有唯一正确的答案"（there is a unique right answer for the vast majority

---

① 英语原文："The applicability of a general term depends on whether there are good reasons for and against its application."

of legal cases)（Bix，1993：78）。尽管他晚近出版的《法律帝国》（*Legal Empire*）重新阐述了整体建构性法律解释方法（constructive interpretation of law as integrity）①，但仍固执地宣称："我未曾说过解决疑难案件只有不同方式而无唯一正确方式。"②（Dworkin，1986：412）

德沃金将模糊性视作"语义缺陷（semantic defect）"，并不无讥讽地嘲弄哈特式法学理论受制"语义学之刺（semantic sting）"的窘境③：

> Law's Empire presents an interpretive theory of law as an alternative to theories that suffer from a 'semantic sting'—theories, that is, that 'insist that lawyers all follow certain linguistic criteria for judging propositions of law'. Dworkin claims that legal theories like Hart's cannot explain theoretical disagreement in legal practice, because they suffer from this semantic sting: they think that lawyers share uncontroversial tests ('criteria') for the truth of propositions of law.（Endicott，2001：39）

他相信语言引起的任何问题都可通过创造性解释加以消除。或者说，"德沃金并不认为语言的有限性和复杂性构成其'正解论题'的障碍"④（Bix，1993：78）。

恩迪科特和比斯克两位教授都对德沃金的法律解释学及其规则适用的确定性观点持保留意见。事实上，法庭经常就不可通约的价值（incommensurable value）进行选择（同上，99），而他论证的基础却是非此即彼的司法裁判二价原则（juridical bivalence）：

> But the need for a decision cannot support an argument that the re-

---

① 德沃金在《法律帝国》第七章中对他所倡导的法律解释方法做出如下说明："It（Law as integrity）insists that legal claims are interpretive judgments and therefore combine backward and forward-looking elements；they interpret contemporary legal practice seen as an unfolding political narrative."（Dworkin，1986：225）

② 英语原文："I have not said that there is never one right way，only different ways，to decide a hard case."

③ 请参阅德沃金在《法律帝国》第一、第二章有关语义缺陷及语义学之刺的详尽论述。

④ 英语原文："Dworkin did not view the limitations and complexities of language as a serious obstacle to his 'right answer thesis'."

quirements of the law are determinate. *A duty to decide is a reason to give a decision , but is not a reason to conclude that the law requires one decision.* (Endicott, 2000: 167)

（三）法律语言的广义模糊性——无解的连锁推理悖论

近年来，语言学家对模糊性表述的兴趣尤为浓烈，并试图从不同视角界定其概念，可惜迄今尚无公论：

Vagueness, being an autological word, escapes a stable generally accepted definition. Most often it is defined through its antonymic relation to ambiguity, where vagueness suggests an unclear, underspecified reference while ambiguity is characterised by the presence of multiple reference. In a broader perspective vagueness can be understood as yet another type of modality, i. e. a (semi-) grammatical category which is able to modify the meaning of linguistic expressions. Vagueness has also been defined as an instance of "incomplete definition", which incurs an incomplete, imprecise acquisition of the meaning of a predicate. From a philosophical perspective it is most often presented as either "an epistemic phenomenon" or a semantic problem where, having accepted that statements are either true or false, vagueness corresponds to "cases of unclarity" in which language users are unable to determine the value of vague expressions. A related view suggests that vagueness emerges where there are "borderline cases", instances when people are unable to classify certain categories which are perceived as belonging to fuzzy sets. (Witczak-Plisiecka, 2009: 203)

上述引文出自语用学家伊沃娜·维特恰克—普利斯艾卡（Iwona Witczak-Plisiecka）于 2009 年发表的《浅析法律语境中语言的（不）确定性》（"A Note on the Linguistic(In)determinacy in the Legal Context"），笔者以为用于概括恩迪科特教授严密周致的模糊语言观真是恰如其分。

1. 与极端不确定性的语言观划清界限

《法律中的模糊性》（*Vagueness in Law*, 2000）是恩迪科特集大成的

杰作。为廓清探讨问题的平台，他首先鞭辟入里地驳斥法律语言具有极端
不确定性（radical indeterminacy）的激进理念。即便怀疑论者求助维特根
斯坦，并试图弥补解释主义（interpretation）与解构主义（deconstruction）
的理论空隙，但"无限语境"（boundless context）① 的概念是恩迪科特绝
对无法接受的：

> Context dependence does not necessarily lead to 'subjective interpre-
> tation', because context may give objective reasons for applying or not ap-
> plying an expression to something... It does not matter if an indefinite
> range of different contexts could be imagined for a particular use of a word,
> as long as there are reasons for deciding what contextual factors are relevant
> to applying the expression. （Endicott, 2000: 20–21）

2. 对边缘情状和容忍原则非哲学路径的解读

恩迪科特接受语言学家赫伯特·保罗·格赖斯（Herbert Paul Grice）
对"模糊性"的宽泛定义②，并认为其所谓"情状"（cases）即"边缘情
状"（borderline cases），继而指出"如果某种表述的适用存在边缘情状，
那么该表述就具有模糊性"③（同上，31）。

连锁推理悖论（the sorites paradox）及容忍原则（the tolerance princi-
ple）是其概念的核心要素，并由此推广广义上的"模糊性"及至颇具争

---

① 恩迪科特在《法律中的模糊性》第 2.4 节内引用了数位解构主义学者就意义对语境的依赖
（the context dependence of meaning）展开的论述："There are still rules. But there are no rules that can be
understood apart from the context... （Margaret Jane Radin）...if the meaning of a signifier is context
bound, context is boundless—that is, there are always new contexts that will serve to increase the different
meanings of a signifier. （J. M. Balkin）Deconstruction... stresses that meaning is context bound—a function of relations within or between texts—but that context itself is boundless: there will always be new con-
textual possibilities that can be adduced, so that the one thing we cannot do is to set limits. （Jonathan Cul-
ler）"（Endicott, 2000: 17–18）
② 格赖斯曾在《言辞用法研究》（*Studies in the Way of Words*）中约略论及模糊性表述的界
定："To say that an expression is vague （in a broad sense of vague） is presumably, roughly speaking,
to say that there are cases （actual or possible） in which one just does not know whether to apply the expression or to withhold it, and one's not knowing is not due to ignorance of the facts." （Grice, 1989:
177）
③ 英语原文："An expression is vague if there are borderline cases for its application."

议的范畴①，却又特别强调"模糊性"（vagueness）不同于"歧义"（ambiguity）（同上，33）。

或许正因为这样，他绝不认同哲学层面上否定容忍原则的认识论（the epistemic theory）或语义学理论（the semanticist theories）：

> The epistemic theory claims that, in every sorites series, there is a counter-instance to the tolerance principle. The semanticist theories claim that tolerance principle is false, or not altogether true, or that its truth is indeterminate, but they deny that there is generally any single counter-instance to the tolerance principle. I want to say that the tolerance principle can be true. Not that any tolerance claim is true, but that for the application of all ordinary vague expressions in most ordinary contexts, it is possible to come up with forms of the tolerance principle that are true. (Ibid. 78)

3. 模糊语言的不可消除性及其必要性

尤其值得关注的是，恩迪科特在对比"界限模型"（the boundary model）和"相似性模型"（the similarity model）的差异②后，明显倾向于

---

①　恩迪科特在《法律中的模糊性》第二章罗列了法律语言模糊性的各种表现形式，包括不精确性（imprecision）、开放结构（open texture）、不完整性（incompleteness）、不可通约性（incommensurability）、不可测度性（immensurability）、可争辩性（contestability）、家族相似性（family resemblance）等："I will start with imprecision, and then look at additional characteristics of expressions in virtue of which they might fit Grice's definition of vagueness. I will look at what various people have termed 'open texture', 'incompleteness', 'incommensurability' (and something I call 'immensurability'), 'contestability', and 'family resemblances', and ask how they differ from imprecision and, more importantly, how they are connected to imprecision. A brief look at 'dummy standards' will introduce a discussion of pragmatic vagueness. Ambiguity will be mentioned, because it might be viewed as a source of pragmatic vagueness; but I will try to distinguish it from vagueness." (Endicott, 2000: 33)

②　恩迪科特在《法律中的模糊性》第六、第七章深入透彻地比较了"界限模型"与"相似性模型"的差异："The boundary model is the framework of classical conceptions of vagueness. It represents the extension of a word as a geometrical figure, and represents vagueness either as a failure of language to draw a boundary to the figure, or as ignorance of the boundary that language draws. In the similarity model, vagueness is flexibility in the normative use of paradigms. The associated indeterminacy is not a deficiency or incoherent in the social facts that determine meaning, but is a feature of the creativity of language use." (Ibid. 137)

将模糊性表述视作麦氏所谓"刻意使用具有可变通含义的词汇和短语"（deliberate use of words and expressions with flexible meanings）。

模糊性是法律适用不确定性的根源之一①。模糊的法律语言有可能使司法裁判逸出法律约束，但这并不必然构成法律规则的缺陷（同上，4—5）。或者说，它也可以"渐进的方式"认定问题，同时赋予司法机关或者行政机关相应的自由裁量权，使制定法更能适应纷繁复杂的社会生活：

> Vagueness is an inescapable aspect of our language. . . vagueness is not always a hindrance to precise and effective communication. . . vagueness is sometimes an indispensable tool for the achievement of accuracy and precision in language, particularly in legal language. Vagueness in legal language has also given our law a much needed flexibility. At the same time, there are some jobs which our linguistic tools, partly even because of vagueness, cannot completely perform without the aid of other communication devices. The error to be avoided here, it has been submitted, is that of assuming that because general rules cannot do it alone the job cannot be done, or is not worth doing. That would be an error of the first magnitude. (Christie, 1964: 911)

（四）法律语言的相对确定性——语义、意图和目的

安德烈·马默（Andrei Marmor）在《解释与法律理论》（*Interpretation and Legal Theory*）中将其所讨论的"解释"界定为"把意义强加给某个对象的活动"（the imposition of meaning on an object）（2005：25），并从辨析意义的类型着手进行论证（同上，22）：

---

① 恩迪科特的模糊语言观从阐释"不确定性"和"模糊性"概念出发渐次展开。他在区分了"法律不确定性"（legal indeterminacy）和"语言不确定性"（linguistic indeterminacy）后，将"不确定性"概念视作特定情状下法律或语言适用的特征，而"模糊性"概念则是法律或语言本身的特征："I will generally treat 'indeterminacy' as a feature of the application of the law, or of an expression, to a particular case (or cases), and 'vagueness' as a feature of the law and of expression." (Endicott, 2000: 9)

Ⅰ　语义——依据规则或传统分配意义①

Ⅱ　意图——由说话者的意图分配意义②

Ⅲ　目的——为解释者的目的分配意义③

对此意图论题笔者不欲详尽展开，但这恰好为概览比克斯教授的法律语言观，提供了清晰的逻辑框架。实际上，比克斯撰写的专著《法律、语言与法律的确定性》（*Law，Linguistics and Legal Determinacy*，1993）及后续发表的两篇论文——《意义指称理论能否解决法律上的确定性问题？》（"Can Theories of Meaning and Reference Solve the Problem of Legal Determinacy?"，2003）和《法律理论中慎用维特根斯坦思想》（"Cautions and Caveats for the Application of Wittgenstein to Legal Theory"，2005）等相关研究成果的核心内容就在于通过解读维特根斯坦对遵守规则的思辨，揭示并批驳建构性解释理论（constructive interpretation）与形而上学实在论（metaphysical realism）的误区，强调语境特别是立法意图对意义的探求不可或缺。

1. 建构性解释理论——目的导向

德沃金演绎的法律解释是近似艺术阐释的创造性解释（creative interpretation）而非会话性解释（conversational interpretation），或者说他强调解释目的（the interpreter's purpose）胜于作者意图（the author's intention）。约略言之，"建构性解释就是将目的强加在某个对象或习惯上，从而把该对象或习惯描述成其所属形式或体裁的最佳可能实例"：

I shall defend a different solution: that creative interpretation is not conversational but constructive. Interpretation of works of art and social practices, I shall argue, is indeed essentially concerned with purpose not cause. But the purposes in play are not (fundamentally) those of some au-

---

①　马默称之为语义学上的意义（semantic meaning）："the meaning of an expression, which is, at least in the semantic context, basically determined by rules or conventions"。

②　马默在此强调的是说话者的意图（the speaker's intention）："someone meaning that such-and-such by an expression, which is normally defined in terms of communication intentions"。

③　马默在此强调的是解释者的目的（the interpreter's purpose）："formulations of the meaning of an object for the interpreter (or, for some particular community interested in the relevant object)"。

thor but of the interpreter. **Roughly, constructive interpretation is a matter of imposing purpose on an object or practice in order to make of it the best possible example of the form or genre to which it is taken to belong**... For the history or shape of a practice or object constrains the available interpretations of it, though the character of that constraint needs careful accounting view, as we shall see. Creative interpretation, on the constructive view, is a matter of interaction between purpose and object. ① (Dworkin, 1986: 52)

作为回应，比克斯引述拉利·亚历山大（Larry Alexander）的话说立法者并非阿波罗神庙中传达神谕者："在解释权威规则所包含的词语时，摒弃会话标准在道德上是不可取的，而道德上可取的是立法机关有能力通过制定权威规则来解决道德争议"② (Alexander, 1987: 424)。

实际上，"词语的重要性在于包含立法者的意图"③ (Bix, 1993: 131)。否则，法律解释就有可能沦为理查德·罗蒂（Richard Rorty）所谓的实用主义（pragmatism）④ 而陷入极端不确定性的危险境地：

It is true, as Alexander conceded, that following the (relatively) concrete intentions of rule-makers may mean ignoring their most abstract intentions (for example, 'to make the morally best choice'), intentions which might approximate to the result of a Dworkinian constructive interpretation of the texts. However, at that abstract level of intention—and with

---

① 粗体由本书作者添加。

② 英语原文："Abandoning conversational standards for interpreting the words of canonical rules is morally undesirable because it is morally desirable that legislative bodies have the ability to settle moral controversies through the enactment of canonical rules."

③ 英语原文："The words are important as embodying the rule-makers' intentions: whether as resolutions of disputes or as choices among possible co-ordination schemes."

④ 罗蒂在《实用主义的后果》（*Consequences of Pragmatism*）第八章中探讨 19 世纪唯心主义与 20 世纪文本主义时，曾有如下描述："The critic asks neither the author nor the text about their intentions but simply beats the text into a shape which will serve his own purpose. He does this by imposing a vocabulary—a 'grid,' in Foucault's terminology—on the text which may have nothing to do with any vocabulary used in the text or by its author, and seeing what happens." (Rorty, 1982: 151)

the variety of different readings it would inspire in different judges—the au-
thorities（and the authoritative sources）would then fail in their function
of making（largely）determinate and（largely）settled choices.
（Ibid. 131）

2. 形而上学实在论——语义导向

以迈克尔·摩尔（Michael Moore）、大卫·布林克（David Brink）和
尼科斯·斯塔弗洛普洛斯（Nicos Stavropoulos）为代表的唯实论者认为
"语言或是发现正确结果的途径；或是导向错误结果的诱惑，而错误结果
必须加以克服"①（Bix，1993：1），故主张运用克里普克—普特南因果指
称理论（Kripke-Putnam Causal Theory of Reference）阐释法律文本，借此
最大限度实现意义的确定性：

> Their semantic theories are tied to a particular approach to reference
> developed by Saul Kripke and Hilary Putnam（Kripke 1972；Putnam
> 1975）. Kripke and Putnam criticize theories which equate the extension of
> a name or term with the beliefs of speakers；they argue instead for an ap-
> proach that equates a term's reference with our best current theory of the
> person or category to which the term refers. In different terms，under this
> approach，meaning and reference are determined largely by the way the
> world is，not by what is in our heads（that is，reference or extension de-
> termines meaning；meaning does not determine reference or extension）.
> （Bix，2003：282 – 283）

这种形而上学的分析法亦遭遇比克斯的严重质疑。在法律解释过程
中，"语义学理论有时必须让位于其他因素的考虑"②，尤其立法者的意图
若被彻底排除，民主社会的权威亦将得不到体现（同上，286—287）。

---

① 英语原文："... language，alternatively，as a path to finding the correct result and as a tempta-
tion towards the wrong result that must be overcome."

② 英语原文："... semantic theories must sometimes yield in this area to other considerations."

那么"语义"（semantic meaning）与"立法意图"（legislative inten-
tion）究竟能否兼容？摩尔的观点是应当认定立法者"拥有与其他语言使
用者即（形而上学）实在论者相同的语言意图"①（1985：323），即"将
说话者的意图归结为简单的语义功能"②（Bix, 1993：153）。可事实上，
两者绝非总是并行不悖：

> Legal systems frequently need to choose between semantic content and
> lawmaker's intentions（and, where relevant, among the various levels of
> lawmaker's intentions）, and this choice may sometimes turn on political
> values or considerations of relative institutional competence.（Bix, 2003：
> 290）

3. 语义、意图与目的关系

比克斯并不否定"应当根据具体法律规则、学术领域或一般法律的
目的来'引申……规定或限制'该规则"的观点③（Bix, 1993：121），
但若认为"范式是任何可能的解释都必须与之相适应的具体事例"④
（Dworkin, 1986：72），这样的论断无疑是走得太远了。

另外，研究法律语言的确定性应当借鉴语义学理论，但纯粹沿袭语义
学路径的法律解释总难免差强人意（Bix, 1993：293）：

> Theorists like Michael Moore, David Brink, and Nicos Stavropoulos
> are correct in suggesting that theorists of law who offer claims about inter-

---

① 英语原文："... to have the same linguistic intentions as other language users, namely［meta-
physically］realist ones."

② 英语原文："... reducing it［speakers' meaning］to a simple function of semantic content."

③ 比克斯的原文如下："... a legal rule should be 'extended... or qualified or limited' according to some view of the purposes of that particular rule, that doctrinal area, or law in general"。其中引文
出自德沃金的《法律帝国》："The second is the further assumption that the requirements of courtesy—
the behavior it calls for or judgments it warrants—are not necessarily or exclusively what they have always
been taken to be but are instead sensitive to its point, so that the strict rules must be understood or applied
or extended or modified or qualified or limited by that point."（Dworkin, 1986：47）

④ 英语原文："For the paradigms will be treated as concrete examples any plausible interpretation
must fit..."

pretation and determinacy need to be more attentive to semantics...

... However, the role of authority (in the form of lawmaker choice) in law in general and democratic systems in particular requires that these realist prescriptions be seriously rethought, and their "solutions" to the problem of legal determinacy be rejected or at least significantly revised.

（五）关于法律语言确定性论题的小结

探讨法律语言的确定性，正是考虑到模糊表述的普遍存在及其必要性。哈特的开放结构理论立足语言有限精确（limited precision of language）的特征，并由此强调法律的确定性虽能增进，却无法完全消除其中隐含的模糊性。

可怀疑论者紧紧抓住与字面意思相悖却在法律上正确（counter-literal yet legally correct）的普通法先例，渲染法律起草过程中的局限性（drafting limits），主张合理的法律裁判即正确的法律信念（justified legal decisions as correct legal beliefs），从而将语言的不确定性推向极端，甚至宣称文本的"字面意思不可能决定法律上的正确含义"（literal meaning cannot be decisive of what's legally correct）：

> If the argument is sound, it follows that an enactment's literal meaning neither weighs in the determination of correct legal outcomes nor permits the application of a sequencing model, ie a non-monotonic logic, to its interpretation. （Flanagan, 2010: 255）

这与纯粹的语义分析或坚信存在鲜为人知的明确界限（sharp, unknown borderline）的哲学路径同样剑走偏锋。

毋庸置疑的是，学者们的讨论对法律翻译研究而言绝非全然无益。尽管语言很难避免由模糊表述导致的不确定性，但在某种程度上受制解释目的的译者至少应当在理解文本的过程中将立法意图等语境因素纳入视野。

> Suppose it is granted that linguistic expressions are "open textured" or unavoidably somewhat vague. It does not follow that there are determinate

facts only where our current linguistic resources enable us straight-forwardly to express them. The same applies to the law. Even if we assume that legal formulations are unavoidably somewhat vague, we cannot infer from this alone that the law is indeterminate whenever legal formulations have indeterminate implications. For this ignores the possibility that law has further resources which help to determine how to decide cases when the language of the law is unclear. (Lyons, 1993: 99)

五 法律语言的平实化运动

"平实英语"(plain English) 亦称"平实语言"(plain language) 或"现代英语"(modern English)、"标准英语"(standard English)。

澳大利亚维多利亚省法律改革委员会 (The Law Reform Commission of Victoria (Australia)) 在其 1 号会议文件《立法、法律权利与平实英语》(*Legislation, Legal Rights and Plain English*) 中称"平实英语"是"成年人使用的完整英语"(a full, adult version of English),并非仅仅"简单化"(simplified) 而已:

> Plain English is language that is not artificially complicated, but is clear and effective for its intended audience. While it shuns the antiquated and inflated word and phrase, which can readily be either omitted altogether or replaced with a more useful substitute, it does not seek to rid documents of terms which express important distinctions. Nonethelss, plain language documents offer non-expert readers some assistance in coping with these technical terms. To a far larger extent, plain language is concerned with matters of sentence and paragraph structure, with organization and design, where so many of the hindrance to clear expression originate. (Melbourne, 1986: 3)

2006 年 2 月,专门负责为苏格兰政府起草法律的议会顾问室 (Office of the Scottish Parliamentary Counsel) 制作了名为《平实语言与立法》(*Plain Language and Legislation*) 的手册,该手册也认同"平实语言"就是"直接明确的语言",能够"清晰、高效而无异议地向目标读者传递信息"①（OSPC，2006：1）。

法律英语平实化运动（plain English movement）旨在"简化法律英语，使之不再成为法律专家或职业人士等少数群体的特权，同时让普通人也能理解时常看似难以逾越的法律文本"②（Stanojević，2011：65 – 66），因为"人们有权利通过浅显易懂的语言了解自身享有的利益和负有的义务"③（OSPC，2006：1）。

麦林科夫教授是该运动的首倡者之一。他总结了传统法律文书写作方式存在的四大缺陷，即冗长（wordy）、模糊（unclear）、浮夸（pompous）和枯燥（dull），并由此提议使用"平实英语"（plain English），追求简洁（shorter）、准确（more precise）、可读性强（more intelligible）的文风，期待绕梁三日、余音不绝的效果（more durable）。

该运动发展至今声势日益浩大，在英国、美国、加拿大、澳大利亚等国家都已渐入人心。塞尔维亚法律语言学家斯坦诺捷维奇（Maja Stanojević）在《语言学与文学》（*Linguistics and Literature*）上发表的《法律英语——不断变化的视角》（"Legal English—Changing Perspective"）将相关理论与实践研究的路径描述如下（2011：68）：

　　Thus, initial research of legal language was carried out by Mellinkoff (1963), Crystal and Davy (1969) and Gustafsson (1975). They were concerned with common features of legal English, with the emphasis on style, syntax and terminology. This type of approach was followed by Hiltunen (1990). Subsequently Bhatia (1993) and Trosborg (1997) included discourse analysis and genre analysis of legal texts, focusing on lexico-grammatical and rhetorical features (Giannoni and Frade 2010：8).

---

①　英语原文："Plain language is language which is direct and straightforward. It is designed to deliver its message to its intended readers clearly, effectively and without fuss."

②　英语原文："The movement aimed to simplify legal English, prevent it from being the privilege of a small group of people who were either legal experts or legal professionals, and at the same time enable average people to come to grips with the task of comprehending legal texts which occasionally seemed insurmountable."

③　英语原文："People are generally considered to have the right to be informed of benefits they are entitled to, and of obligations imposed on them, in language which is self-evident to them."

Plain English movement exponents（Garner 1986，2002；Rylance 1994；Tiersma 2000；Butt and Castle 2001；Haigh 2004；Schneidereit 2004；Williams 2004），not only depicted the linguistic features of Legal English, but also gave concrete proposals regarding Plain English writing style, as they were seriously alarmed by the state of affairs in legal writing.

笔者将首先概览在法律英语平实化问题上产生的诸多争议，接着就平实写作的宗旨、策略与技巧等方面回顾当前的主要研究成果。

（一）争议与博弈

陶博在评述麦林科夫的法律语言观时，虽承认"应尽量更多地使用直白的英文"，但同时也指出"应当受到一些限制"（2004：40）。然而究竟存在哪些具体限制呢？

1. 针锋相对

美国杰出的平实语言写作专家之一约瑟夫·金伯尔（Joseph Kimble）教授将反对平实化运动的批评意见分为法律界内外新旧两派（1994/1995：51）：

Ⅰ 法律界内陈旧的批评意见（old criticism）

The old criticism is, in essence, that we either should not or cannot write in plain language：should not, because it debases the language; and cannot, because of the overriding demands of precision.

Ⅱ 法律界外新兴的批评意见（new criticism）

The new criticism is, in essence, that plain language doesn't matter：its approach to communication is too narrow, and there is no empirical evidence that it improves comprehension.

对于法律界内的批评，金伯尔旁征博引诸家学说，强调平实写作只为清晰有效地交流，绝不可武断地归入反文学（anti-literary）、反智主义（anti-intellectual）、不缜密（unsophisticated）、乏味（drab）、丑陋（ugly）、幼稚（babyish）或低俗（base）的实践；且多数情况下，"清晰"与"精确"乃互补的写作目标（同上，52—53）。

对于法律界外的批评，金伯尔更多地通过实证研究，借助数据和实例从以下六个方面进行论证（同上，62—80）：

1. There is long-standing evidence that plain language improves comprehension.

2. Plain language involves much more than just plain words and short sentences.

3. The plain-language movement definitely recommends testing documents on readers whenever possible.

4. When testing is not possible, plain language is more likely to be understood and appreciated than traditional legal writing.

5. Ultimately, you must use plain language to write clearly.

6. Plain language would reduce litigation by preventing the unnecessary confusion that traditional legal writing produces.

2. 各擅胜场

（1）传统风格根深蒂固

悉尼大学（University of Sydney）平实法律语言研究中心（The Center for Plain Legal Language）主任彼得·布特（Peter Butt）教授与新西兰律师理查德·卡瑟尔（Richard Castle）合著的《现代法律写作——为使用更清晰的语言提供指南》（*Modern Legal Drafting—A Guide to Using Clearer Language*）专门就传统法律写作风格难以被撼动的根源进行了迄今最为完整的综述（Butt & Castle，2001：5）：

1. 熟悉与习惯（familiarity and habit）

2. 保守性（conservatism）

3. 害怕疏忽大意的指控（fear of negligence claims）

4. 撰写工具（the means of production）

5. 职业压力（professional pressures）

6. 避免歧义的压力（straining to avoid ambiguity）

7. 多语言混合体（the mixture of languages）

8. 按篇幅计费（payment by length）

9. 按时间计费（payment by time）

10. 诉讼环境（the litigious environment）

而德克萨斯州立大学（Texas State University）法学院大卫·J. 贝克法律检索、写作与上诉辩护中心（The David J. Beck Center for Legal Research, Writing, and Appellate Advocacy）主任韦恩·希斯（Wayne Schiess）分析了律师因循守旧的心理状态，包括误解法官的期待（a misconception about what judges want）、惰性（inertia）、害怕（fear）及职业精神的误导（a misguided sense of professionalism）等（2008/2009：163—165），并不由自主地感慨墨守成规的陋习很难消除。但他也指出其让位于理智和权威的可能性：

Old ways die hard, but they may yield to good sense and good authority. (Ibid. 167)

（2）平实语言大势所趋

无论如何，使用平实英语撰写法律文书的优势是显而易见的。《现代法律写作》认为这至少表现在以下几个方面（Butt & Castle, 2001：86 – 95）：

1. 提升效率（increased efficiency）
2. 减少错误（fewer errors）
3. 改善法律职业形象（image of the legal profession）
4. 促进市场营销（marketing）
5. 遵循法律要求（compliance with statutory requirements）

为更好地说明问题，该书作者不仅逐个描述英国、澳大利亚、美国、加拿大等主要英语国家平实化运动的蓬勃发展，还不厌其烦地列举了这些国家要求使用平实英语撰写法律文书的现行规定，包括卡特和克林顿签发的总统令，以及牵涉消费者权益的各部门法规（同上，77—81，91—95）。

（二）写作准则——"为读者而写"

《联邦政府平实语言指南》（*Federal Plain Language Guidelines*）① 的封

---

① 该指南由平实语言行动与信息网（The Plain Language Action and Information：www. plainlanguage. gov）编写，初版于 20 世纪 90 年代中期发布。

面上印着："改善联邦政府与公众之间的交流"（Improving Communication from the Federal Government to the Public）。其撰写者强调平实语言写作的首要准则就是——"为读者而写"（write for your audience）。这与澳大利亚维多利亚省法律改革委员会和苏格兰议会顾问室的宗旨不谋而合。

正如布特与卡瑟尔所总结的，法律文书功能很多，最根本的当然是实现法律目的，但同时也有其他功能需要实现——交流、预测和说服等。"传统法律文书是律师之间的交流，而法律写作的改革运动提醒我们，这也是律师与客户之间的交流"[①]（Butt & Castle，2001：95）。无疑，清晰、高效地向非法律职业人士传递与之密切相关的信息，正是平实化运动的出发点和皈依。

（三）写作策略与技巧研究

多数致力于推进语言平实化运动的法律写作专家将讨论的焦点集中在谋篇布局、遣词造句乃至标点与排版的层面，并从整体概述延伸至各种具体文书的写作方法，包括预测与说服型文书（predicative and persuasive writing）以及立法文书（legal drafting）[②]/论述性法律文件（discursive writing）、涉诉性法律文件（litigation-related writing）和规定性法律文件（normative writing）[③]，希望借助语言层面的种种实用技巧，扭转传统文书"冗长"、"模糊"、"浮夸"的弊病（科斯坦佐，2003；都南、福斯特，2003；Butt & Castle，2001；Garner，2001；Haigh，2009；etc.）。

特别值得一提的是加纳教授的《法律风格要素》（*The Elements of Legal Style*，2005），从修辞角度比较了两种不同文学传统，即华丽的亚洲式风格（Asiatic prose）与朴素的阿提卡式风格（Attic prose）。他的结论是两者各有所长，法律职业人士应当量体裁衣，杜绝矫揉造作，"'用诚实来书写，用热情来表达'的文章都是好文章"[④]（Garner，2005：309）。作者还历数了法律写作中常见且行之有效的修辞手法，包括比较（com-

---

①　英语原文："The traditional legal document is a communication from lawyer to lawyer. The reform movement in legal drafting reminds us that it is also a communication from lawyer to client."

②　加纳教授在《使用平实英语进行法律写作》（*Legal Writing in Plain English*）中采两分法（Garner，2001：53，89）。他提出的"analytical writing"即通常所谓的"predicative writing"。

③　哈格德教授在《法律写作》（*Legal Drafting*）中采三分法（Haggard，2004：10 - 13）。

④　英语原文："Everything is good that is 'conceived with honesty and executed with communicative ardor'."

parison)①、巧妙用词（wordplay)②、句法安排（syntactic arrangement)③、重复（repetition)④ 四大类。

除此而外，另有文书写作方面的学者从法律分析（legal analysis）与法律推理（legal reasoning）角度出发，阐明法律解释原则，介绍法律检索及引用方法（legal research and citation），然后在此基础上论述法律文书的写作步骤（包括提纲、起草、定稿、修改四个环节）、逻辑结构、风格策略等（Neumann，2003；Edwards，2003；Putman，2009，2010）。

第三节　法律程序语言

美国北卡罗来纳大学（University of North Carolina）法学教授约翰·M. 康利（John M. Conley）和杜克大学（Duke University）文化人类学教授威廉·M. 奥巴尔（William M. O'Barr）在《法律，语言与权力》（*Just Words：Law，Language and Power*，1995）中勾勒了法律与语言研究的兴起——社会语言学和法律与社会运动的相互融合：

> Law and language emerged as a field ofscholarship in the 1970s as so-ciolegal scholars incorporated the language of the law into their studies and as linguists began to concern themselves with language in legal arenas. (Conley & O'Barr，2005：viii)

此类研究超越传统的静态结构决定论，聚焦法律程序，将斯特高尔教授所谓作为过程和工具的语言研究兼而论之。学者们立足法律语境，描写法官、陪审团、警察、律师、证人、当事人等参与者相互间的真实会话，

---

① 加纳列举的比较类修辞手法：暗喻（metaphor）、拟人（personification）、明喻（simile）。

② 加纳列举的巧妙用词类修辞手法：夸张（hyperbole）、反讽（irony）、间接肯定法（mei-osis）、双关语（paronomasia）。

③ 加纳列举的句法安排类修辞手法：倒装（anastrophe）、对比（antithesis）、省略连词（asyndeton）、递进（climax）、平行（parallelism）、圆周句（periodic sentence）、反问（rhetoric question）。

④ 加纳列举的重复类修辞手法：头韵法（alliteration）、联珠法（anadiplosis）、首语重复法（anaphora）、反向法（antanadasis）、交错法（chiasmus）、间隔反复（epanalepsis）、叠句（epis-trophe）、紧接反复（epizeuxis）、冗词法（pleonasm）、连词叠用（polysyndeton）。

分析话语结构、话语风格、话语策略，并试图解释法律话语折射的不平等权力关系。

澳大利亚新英格兰大学（University of New England）语言、文化与语言学学院（School of Languages，Cultures and Linguistics）的戴安娜·伊德斯（Diana Eades）教授著有《社会语言学与法律程序》（*Sociolinguistics and the Legal Process*，2010）一书，较为全面地综述了社会语言学视角下法律程序中的语言研究现状。笔者将以此为基础，概览普通法语境中的话语分析。

一 社会语言学与法律程序

所谓社会语言学，简而言之即在社会语境中研究语言的使用。如果说语言学主要分析的是语言结构，那么社会语言学分析语言的功能与用法。尽管如此，社会语言学研究通常要求理解语言学的原则和方法，且两者之间的界限并非截然分离。只不过社会语言学家讨论法律语言结构，更多地关注交际目的（Coulthard & Johnson，2007：55）：

> … when creating texts，the producer's lexical choice is a direct consequence of their communicative activity and purpose. This assertion makes *register* and *genre* inter-related aspects of textualisation. Lexical and grammatical choices，such as the use of a restricted set of reporting verbs in police statements and notes（*said*，*replied*），inclusive phrases and lists in legal texts（using *and* and *or*），passive constructions with *by* and phrases that contain the verbs *including* or *provided* in contracts，are made because of what needs to be communicated.
>
> 'Genre' can be defined simply：conventional，repeated and distinctive features of text that arise from its communicative purpose.

从方法论角度看，运用社会语言学理论进行现场研究（field study），早已成为法律语言学领域的主要潮流：

> … mainly refer to the legal process because the interest of sociolinguists is in what happens in the process，specifically what people do in in-

teractions that take place within the legal system. （Eades，2010：5）

二　程序语言的公理假设（axiomatic assumption）
（1）二元对立关系（the dichotomy）
Ⅰ　语言反映社会（language reflects society）

Such an assumption would view the hierarchical ways of addressing people in the courtroom—such as calling the judge *your honour*—as a reflection of the hierarchical authority structure of courtrooms.

Ⅱ　语言改造社会（language shapes society）

... the hierarchical authority structure in courtrooms would be seen partly as the effect of such language usage as calling the judge your honour.

（2）动态双向关系（the dynamic and reciprocal relationship）
Ⅲ　语言既反映也改造社会（language both reflects and shapes society）
正如伊德斯所言，认为语言和社会之间存在动态双向联系的观点，在更宽泛的层面上假设社会结构（social structure）与个体能动性（agency of individuals）密不可分，这特别适合法律程序中的语言研究：

This third view can be seen as part of the wider approach in the social sciences, in which the earlier dichotomy between social structure and agency is also rejected, in favor of an understanding that the two are inseparable：it is the agency of individuals in social groups which creates, shapes, maintains, reinforces and changes social structures, which in turn limit and enable the agency of individuals. This axiomatic understanding of society underpins the best sociolinguistic work on language in the legal process. Indeed, the legal process is an ideal institutional site for the examination of this dynamic interrelationship between social structure and agency, as we will see. To understand language usage in any specific legal context is impossible without an examination of structural institutional aspects of the legal system. On the other hand, sociolegal studies of the law can be greatly enriched by an examination of situated language practices in specific legal contexts. (Ibid. 5)

三　程序语言的研究方法

社会语言学视角下法律程序中的语言研究路径，包括描写（descriptive）、分析（analytical）与解释（interpretative）三个层面。焦点当然是真实参与者的语言互动，虽以共时性分析为主；但也关注历时性变化，譬如道恩·阿彻（Dawn Archer）的《英国法庭问答 1640—1760：社会语用学分析》（*Questions and Answers in the English Courtroom 1640 – 1760：A Sociopragmatic Analysis*，2005）。

适合法律程序语言研究的社会语言学分析工具包括（Eades，2010：14 – 15）：

（1）口语/交际民族志研究方法（ethnography of speaking/ethnography of communication）①：运用人类学民族志方法研究言语社群中的口语表达方式（或更宽泛的交际方式）。例如康利与奥巴尔合著的《规则与关系：法律话语的民族志研究》（*Rules Versus Relationships：The Ethnography of Legal Discourse*，1990）。

（2）话语分析（discourse analysis）②：研究超越句法层面的语言使用。

---

①　英语原文："Ethnography of speaking/ethnography of communication studies the ways of speaking (or more broadly ways of communication) in a speech community. It can be characterised as the study of who can talk to whom about what, where, when and how. It uses the anthropological approach of ethnography, in which researchers are interested in how members of a social group live, and in learning about their beliefs, values and practices from careful observation (rather than for example, interviews)."

②　英语原文："Discourse analysis studies language use beyond the sentence level, whether in face-to-face interactions such as conversations or interviews or public speeches, or written communication such as newspaper articles or codified laws. Analysis in this approach examines the details of actual talk, and is a type of microanalysis. It often uses audio- or video-recorded data, although it can use written data. The term 'discourse analysis' is used quite widely in the social sciences to refer to a range of approaches to the analysis of discourse. Sociolinguistic discourse analysis pays attention not just to the content of what is said but how it is said, examining linguistic dimensions, such as grammar, accent, word choice, turn-taking and context. Within sociolinguistic discourse analysis, there are several more focused traditions."

Ⅰ 会话分析（Conversation Analysis，CA）

Ⅱ 互动社会语言学（interactional sociolinguistics）

Ⅲ 批判话语分析（Critical Discourse Analysis，CDA）

（3）变体社会语言学（variationist sociolinguistics）①：通常运用数量分析研究语言变体的模型与结构。

（4）语言社会学（sociology of language）②：关注涉及语言的社会问题。

（5）批判社会语言学（critical sociolinguistics）③：运用各种（宏观和微观）社会语言学方法结合社会学分析，考察语言在权力关系中的作用。

（6）描写语言学（descriptive linguistics）④：研究语言结构，补充或伴随社会语言学分析。

四 法律语境与弱势群体

法律程序涉及的典型社会语境主要包括两类，即法庭（courtroom）与警察问询（police interview）。绝大多数相关著作论文都是在此背景下结合社会学理论展开话语分析的，譬如英国卡迪夫大学（Cardiff University）语言与交际中心讲师珍妮特·科特里尔（Janet Cotterill）编辑的《法律程

---

① 英语原文："Variationist sociolinguistics studies patterns and structures of language variation, often using quantitative analysis, e. g. to examine different ways of pronouncing the same word by a large number of speakers. Initially this approach correlated social variables such as age, gender and socioeconomic class with language variation. Increasingly this is being broadened to examine dynamic interactions between variations in ways of using language and ways in which speakers can actively fine-tune a wide range of aspects of their social identity."

② 英语原文："Sociology of language focuses on society-level issues involving language. Topics include language choice and language planning in multilingual contexts. Traditionally this kind of analysis has used macroanalysis."

③ 英语原文："Critical sociolinguistics typically uses a range of sociolinguistics approaches (both macro and micro) in combination with social theoretical analysis to examine the role of language in power relationships."

④ 英语原文："Descriptive linguistics studies the structure of language and it complements and accompanies much sociolinguistic analysis. It uses a number of analytical approaches: phonetics and phonology encompass the study of speech sounds and sound systems, morphology and syntax make up the study of the structure of words and sentences (and is sometimes referred to with the term 'grammar'); and semantics refers to the study of the meaning of words and expressions."

序中的语言》（*Language in the Legal Process*，2002）。

该论文集的最大特色就是撰稿人来自四大洲六个不同国家，包括美国、加拿大、英国、巴西、澳大利亚和南非，因而极具代表性。其中既有学者亦有律师，却都关注法律程序中可能出现的交际困难（communicative difficulties），尤其是非职业人士及非母语人士经常遭遇的语言障碍。

全书除第一部分"法律程序中的语言学家"（The Linguistic in the Legal Process）探讨作为证据的语言外，其余章节的组合恰恰反映了社会语言学视角下作为过程的法律语言研究方向：

（1）警察语言与警察问询（The Language of the Police and the Police Interview）。

（2）法庭语言Ⅰ：律师和证人（The Language of the Court Ⅰ：Lawyers and witness）。

（3）法庭语言Ⅱ：法官和陪审团（The Language of the Court Ⅱ：Judges and juries）。

（一）警察语言（language of the police）

严格而言，警察语言包括调查（investigation）、询问（interview）和审讯（interrogation）三个方面。根据《劳特利奇法律语言学手册》，相关研究主要聚焦以下主题（Coulthard & Johnson，2010：viii）：

1. 公民紧急求助电话（citizens' emergency calls）

2. 米兰达权利（Miranda rights）

3. 问询中的证人和犯罪嫌疑人（witnesses and suspects in interviews）

4. 问询中的律师（lawyers in interviews）

5. 司法程序中的警察询问（police interviews in the judicial process）

警察语言的研究同样关注弱势群体（minority group），诸如非母语人士（second language speakers）、未成年人（minor）、智障者（intellectually disabled people）等。

（二）法庭语言（language of the courtroom）

麦克梅纳明将法庭语言细分为证人、律师和法官语言，并收集现有文献研究的相关论题如下（McMenamin，2002：96－97）：

1. 证人语言（Language of Witnesses）
Ⅰ 证人质询（witness examination）
Ⅱ 性侵犯受害人（sexual assault victims）
Ⅲ 未成年受害人（child-victim witnesses）
Ⅳ 争议与调解（disputes and mediation）
Ⅴ 法庭中的语言与性别（language and gender in the courtroom）
2. 律师语言（Language of Lawyers）
Ⅰ 律师与语言学家（lawyers and linguists）
Ⅱ 审判语言（trial language）
Ⅲ 律师语言（language of lawyers）
Ⅳ 法律辩论语言（legal-debate language）
Ⅴ 总结陈词语言（language of closing arguments）
3. 法官语言（Language of Judges）
Ⅰ 法官语言（language of judges）
Ⅱ 陪审团指示语言（language of jury instructions）

毫无疑问，麦氏罗列的清单详则详矣，仍未能穷尽。此外，考察法庭参与者之间的语言互动，可以各有侧重不同，却绝对无法将法官、律师、证人等各自的话语方式与策略完全分离出来孤立研究。早期成果如约翰·麦斯威尔·阿特金森（John Maxwell Atkinson）撰写的《法庭秩序：司法环境中口语互动的组织》（*Order in Court：the Organisation of Verbal Interaction in Judicial Settings*，1979）、华盛顿大学交际学卢迪科·C. 劳伦斯（Ruddick C. Lawrence）教席教授兼政治学教授 W. 兰斯·贝内特（W. Lance Bennett）与加州大学（University of California）民政与公共管理约翰逊（Johnson）教席教授马瑟·S. 费尔德曼（Martha S. Feldman）合著的《重构法庭真实》（*Reconstructing Reality in the Courtroom*，1981）就很能说明问题。

（三）小结

尽管如此，我们已不难发现无论警察语言还是法庭语言的研究，全都关注法律专家与非职业人士的交流，特别是律师和证人、警察和犯罪嫌疑人、法官和陪审团之间的语言互动；弱势群体譬如女性[①]、未成年人[②]等更是分析的焦点。

本节开篇提及的《法律、语言与权力》可以说是对法律程序语言问题探究最为深入的专著之一。该书从性犯罪的审判、离婚案件的调解入手，通过微观话语分析，揭示了司法程序中存在的各种不平等的权力关系：

> 虽然法律的字面规定不再公然对人们实行歧视和区别对待政策，但是法律话语仍旧继续使不同种族、阶级和性别之间存在的各种不平等的权力关系正常化、合法化、永恒化。正是通过语言，尤其是通过法律交谈的微观话语，实际上的不平等才得以产生和存续。（程朝阳，2007：3—4）

---

① 研究法庭中性侵犯受害人作证情况的经典著作有两部，分别是：（1）苏珊·林恩·埃利希（Susan Lynn Ehrlich）的《再现强奸：语言与同意发生性关系》（*Representing Rape：Language and Sexual Consent*，2001）；（2）珍妮特·科特里尔的《性犯罪的语言》（*The Language of Sexual Crime*，2007）。

② 关注交叉质询中未成年人话语权利的代表学者是马克·布伦南（Mark Brennan），他曾撰写过两篇重要文献：（1）专著：《陌生语言：接受交叉质询的未成年受害人》（*Strange Language：Child Victims Under Cross Examination*，1988）；（2）论文：《否认话语：交叉质询未成年受害人作证》（"The Discourse of Denial：Cross-examining Child-Victim Witnesses"，1994）。

第二章
中外法律翻译研究现状概览

导　言

若说法律语言学的研究呈现出体系完整、成果丰硕的繁荣景象，那么法律翻译学亦非乏善可陈。中外学界孜孜以求者，实欲替翻译活动确立放之四海而皆准的应然原则，虽皓首穷经，仍无怨无悔。

时至今日，仅笔者管窥所见汉英文献已琳琅满目。论文专著固难尽数，但究其核心理念，或者沿袭纯语言学路径，或者顺应历史文化转向，这也是本章借以落笔处。请特别注意，如此截然切分，只求论述便捷。本质上，任何割裂语言与文化间伴生关系的企图都极其荒谬可笑。

语言既承载文化，又构成文化不可或缺的要件。所谓纯语言学路径，并非完全排除文化因素，只是套用语言学范式解析翻译实践问题；而历史文化转向，试图将语言现象置于更广阔的社会情境中进行考察。

千头万绪总有源，我们不妨从法律翻译学家苏珊·沙尔切维奇（Susan Sarcevic）首先提出后为世人普遍接受的著名观点开始概览：

> ... legal translation is no longer regarded as a process of linguistic transcoding but as an act of communication in the mechanism of the law. (Sarcevic，1997：55)

法律翻译是"法律机制内的交际行为"，此论断暗示法律翻译超越语言形式的转换，情境因素及目标读者的可接受性同在译者考虑之内。

第一节　纯语言学路径

迄今为止，语言学路径依然是法律翻译研究的主流。法律语言属特殊用途语言，法律翻译亦因此归属工具翻译，其理论探索长期停滞于文本类型、意义阐释等领域，且过度纠结词汇、句式方面的修辞特征及实用技能的条分缕析，甚至极少触及篇章层面，更未能透过纷繁流动的现象，挖掘现象背后支配译者决策的深层原因。此等规定性路径（prescriptive approach）既然试图简化多法域交际活动的复杂性，对理想与现实间的天壤之别自是漠然冷对。

一　文本类型——法理、语言、翻译

法律文本类型（text typology）分析是以实践为导向的翻译研究的起点，当前路径无非法理、语言、翻译三支。

（一）法理学主导的分类

1. 法律体裁

尽管我国传统法律语言学家聚焦立法文本和司法文本等书面语篇之余，还惯常游猎执法、普法与涉法语言（李振宇，2006：220），但翻译界普遍接受的却是通行英美的四分说，即立法文本（statutory text）、司法文本（judicial text）、私人法律文件（private legal document）及法学著作（legal scholarly works）（Cao，2008：83）。其中，私人法律文件备受关注，法学著作则罕有问津者。

2. 法律功能

这方面影响深远的是南卡罗莱纳大学（University of South Carolina）法学院教授托马斯·R. 哈格德（Thomas R. Haggard）的权威论述。他将狭义法律文书的范畴（法学著作除外）重组为三大板块："论述性法律文件"（discoursive writing）、"涉诉性法律文件"（litigation-related writing）和"规范性法律文件"（normative writing）（2004：10－13）；或亦可简化成"规范性法律文件"与"非规范性法律文件"①（滕超、孔飞燕，2008：40）。

---

① 非规定性法律文件包括论述性法律文件和涉诉性法律文件两大类，也有学者将之合称为法律文书。它们都是根据事实和法律，为了解决实际法律问题而制作的，因而主旨的实效性对其至关重要——"只有把主旨建立在解决具体案件的有效性上，才能充分发挥法律文书的作用"（刘国涛 & 范海玉，2005：27）。

（二）语言学主导的分类：言语行为理论（speech act theory）

尤令人瞩目的是，梯尔斯马教授划分"实施性法律文件"（operative legal document）、"阐述性法律文件"（expository legal document）和"说服性法律文件"（persuasive legal document）的独特视角（Tiersma, 1999：139 - 141）：

Basically, a **genre** refers to a category of composition; the members of the category usually share a particular structure as well as level of formality.

Some of the more common legal genres are pleadings, petitions, orders and statutes, and private legal documents like contracts and wills. As a class, there can be called **operative legal documents**, in that they create or modify legal relations. In linguistic terminology, they all contain **legal performatives**. Operative documents tend to have not only very formal and formulaic legal language, but they traditionally adhere to a very rigid structure. The most notorious attributes of legal English tend to occur in operative documents.

Another general class can be called **expository documents**. These typically delve into one or more points of law with a relatively objective tone. An office memorandum explaining a legal matter or letter to a client are examples of this category. Expository genres tend to conform to a traditional structure, but it is usually less rigid than that of operative documents. The style resembles formal everyday language, although use of legal terminology is almost unavoidable...

A final general category of legal genres is **persuasive documents**. This class includes briefs that are submitted to courts and memoranda of points and authorities. Like expository documents, they tend not to be especially formulaic or legalistic in language, although they do use fairly formal standard English.

毫无疑问，梯氏分类法沿袭了英国哲学家约翰·L. 奥斯汀（John L. Austin）首创并经美国语言学家约翰·R. 塞尔（John R. Searle）修正的言语行为理论①与间接言语行为（indirect speech act）② 概念。而我国法律语言学家刘红婴教授也曾探索以言行事与法律表达形态之间的关系，只不过目光所及仅限法律程序中的话语分析领域（2003：35—41）。

两位大师针对言外行为的精辟思考甚至引发后世学者就其典型形式展开旷日持久的讨论③，但这无法掩盖传统理论的最大缺陷表现在很大程度上忽略了自身的社会属性。有鉴于此，安娜·威尔日比卡（Anna Wierzbicka，1985）、雅各布·梅伊（Jacob L. Mey，2001）、耶夫·维索尔伦（Jef Verschueren，2000）等知名语用学家分别立足各自研究领域，全方位揭示并完善以言行事的文化机制，这对法律翻译研究亦不无启示（李健雪，2006：27）：

> 自 Searle（1976）就 Austin（1962）的言语行为进行修正后，对言语行为的批评已从单纯的分类标准问题转向了对言语行为理论自身不足的问题上去了。如言语行为理论缺乏文化依赖性（Wierzbicka，1985），言语行为理论没有考虑社会语境（Mey，1993）和语境顺应性（Verschueren，1999）等真实环境下语言使用的必要因素。因此，从语用行为（Mey，1993），从人类认知的、社会的和文化的综观（Verschueren，1999）的角度对言语行为的研究逐渐增多。随着认知语言学理论对语用研究的渗透，言语行为理论再一次受到了挑战。"把现实建构成有意义的经验"（Marmaridou，2000：63）的经验主义语用观在体验认知框架内把言语行为概念化为"以语言和社会文化惯例改变现实的力量"。（Marmaridou，2000：208）。

（三）翻译学主导的分类：语言功能模型（*organon* model of language）

译者研究文本类型学，应当以翻译为导向（translation-oriented），基

---

① 所谓言语行为，通常可在言内行为（the locutionary act）、言外行为（the illocutionary act）和言后行为（the perlocutionary act）三个层面上进行解析（Austin，1962：94 - 107）。

② 所谓间接言语行为，即"通过实施另一种言外行为来间接地实施特定的言外行为"（one illocutionary act is performed indirectly by way of performing another）（Searle，2001：31）。

③ 奥斯汀将言外行为划分为：（1）裁决（verdictives）；（2）执行（exercitives）；（3）承诺（commissives）；（4）阐释（expositives）；（5）表态（behabitives）（Austin，1962：150 - 151）。塞尔则将言外行为划分为：（1）断言（assertives）；（2）指令（directives）；（3）承诺（commissives）；（4）表情（expressives）；（5）宣告（declarations）（Searle，2001：12 - 20）。

于语言的交际功能（communicative function）对文本进行分类，方能促使我们有针对性地确定翻译策略。就此而言，德国目的论（*Skopostheorie*）学派倡导的翻译理念无疑最具开拓性。

起初，卡特琳娜·赖斯（Katharina Reiss）依据德国心理学家卡尔·布勒（Karl Bühler）的语言功能模型①将文本分为三大类型，并在此基础上提出了以文本为导向的翻译策略（text-oriented translation strategy）（Reiss, 2004：25 – 27）：

> Ⅰ 以内容为重的文本（content-focused text），其功能是符合理性逻辑的客观描述（objective representation）；
>
> Ⅱ 以形式为重的文本（form-focused text），其功能是展现审美趣味的主观表达（subjective expression）；
>
> Ⅲ 以诉情为重的文本（appeal-focused text），其功能是富有感染力的诉求（persuasive appeal）

基于导师的研究成果并借鉴俄国语言学家罗曼·雅各布逊（Roman Jakobson）的观点，克里斯蒂娜·诺德（Christiane Nord）不仅重新诠释语言交际功能对翻译策略的影响，而且以应酬功能（phatic function）作为补充：

> The phatic function aims at establishing, maintaining or ending contact between sender and receiver. (Nord, 2001：44)

但与同样试图融合布勒及雅各布逊语言功能理论的皮特·纽马克（Peter Newmark）六分学说有别的是，诺德将雅各布逊模型②中的另两种独特语言功能——元语言功能（metalingual function）和诗学功能（poetic function）的各种表现形式分别纳入描述（representative）、表达（expres-

---

① 布勒模型将语言功能划分为三类："representation"、"expression"、"appeal"（Nord, 2006：47）。

② 雅各布逊模型区别了六种语言功能："the referential function"、"the emotive function"、"the connative function"、"the poetic function"、"the phatic function"、"the metalingual function"（同上）。

sive）与诉求（appellative）的范畴（Nord，2006：47）。

无论如何，西方翻译学家们大都认为法律语篇注重内容的客观描述
（Snell-Hornby，2001：32），而我国法律翻译研究者在这方面仍有分歧。

（1）观点一：文本功能重在规范行为

持此观点的代表学者是李克兴和张新红博士。他们在《法律文本与
法律翻译》中坚决主张"法律文本的主要功能应当是呼吁、规范，提供
信息只是它的各种次要功能之一。法律文本具有规定、约束性功能以规范
和指导社会与个人之间、个人与个人之间在政治、经济和文化等领域的活
动和行为，其规范功能受到国家强制力的保护，具有强制性"（李克兴、
张新红，2006：10）。

他们引用沙尔切维奇的法律语言功能二分说作为关键性的支撑理据。
沙氏认为法律语言主要具有调节功能/规定功能（regulatory/prescriptive）
和信息功能/描写功能（informative/descriptive），并据以划分法律文本类
型如下：

> Generally speaking, legal texts can bedivided into the following three
> groups according to their function：1）primarily prescriptive，2）primarily
> descriptive but also prescriptive， and 3）purely descriptive. （Sarcevic，
> 1997：11）

需要指出的是，这两位学者也许无意间偷换了沙尔切维奇的观点，将
上述第二类文本的功能从"primarily descriptive but also prescriptive"改写
成"主要功能是规定性的但也有描写性的成分"，还由此顺理成章地提出
"第三类是描写性法律文本（如法律论文）……为了保证分类标准的一致
性，应当把它们划入其他文本类型（科研论文类），因为它们的主要功能
并非规范人们的社会行为"（李克兴、张新红，2006：11）。

（2）观点二：翻译目的旨在传递信息

实际上，沙尔切维奇主要研究权威翻译（authoritative translation）。所
谓权威翻译，即译文与原文具有同等法律效力：

> Vested with the force of law, authoritative translations enable the
> mechanism of the law to function in more than one language. （Sarcevic，

1997：20）

这是依据平等语言权利诉求应运而生的机制，常见于相同法域内数种官方语言之间的互译（请参阅本章§2—2）。与其相对应的非权威翻译（non-authoritative translation）则情势大相径庭。考虑到国家法律制度事涉主权，官方正式语言的主导地位绝不容妥协动摇，故而译入非官方语言的文本未被赋予任何法律效力。

须知以原文本为导向的翻译策略针对的是赖斯所谓正常的翻译（normal translation）；若是我们期望译文实现某种区别原文的特殊功能（special function），那么以目的为导向的翻译策略（goal-oriented strategy）显然更胜一筹（滕超、孔飞燕，2008：42—45）。有鉴于此，姑且不论原法律文本功能如何，目标语篇的文本功能显然更应强调忠实传递原法律文件所包含的信息，努力实现译文与原文在内容层面上的动态对等性（dynamic equivalence）。至于原文借以增加权威性的法言法语乃至固定格式，则应通过归化手段转换成目标法律文化中的相应表达形态，但前提是绝不可损害内容重现的准确性。

（3）小结

仔细审视沙尔切维奇的论述，不难察觉她也赞成汉斯·J. 弗米尔（Hans J. Vermeer）提出的目的论，因而将法律翻译视作交际行为，坚持意义取决于包括文化在内的情境因素，并由此反对凡特殊用途语言仅有指示功能的武断观点：

> ... texts of the humanities and the social sciences are exceptions. As for texts of the exact sciences, their content consists of factual information describing some state of affairs, i. e., referential meaning. More important, the referential meaning of such texts is based largely on a universal system of knowledge interpreted according to a common system of reference. (Sarcevic, 1997：66)

另外，沙氏明确指出准确性（accuracy）对于法律翻译的重要性至高无上，这也从某个侧面肯定了法律信息在翻译活动中的优先地位：

In legal translation, in which accuracy is of utmost importance, it is presumed that all the authentic texts of a single instrument have the same meaning. (Ibid. 67)

遗憾的是，所谓"相同含义"（the same meaning）不过是镜花水月似的假象，仅此而已。

二　意义阐释——解释与推定

规范性法律文件的解释（interpretation/construction）亦称推定（presumption）（Butt & Castle，2006：47），是法律语言学家与翻译研究者共同关注的焦点。仅就调节层面而言，普通法系的解释原则虽纷繁复杂，仍可辨识法律推定和语言推定两大范畴（滕超、孔飞燕，2008：84）。

（一）法律推定范畴

（1）严格解释规则（The Rule of Strict Construction）

（2）宽泛解释规则（The Rule of Liberal Construction）

（3）引文规则（The Borrowed Language Rule）

（4）单行法优于一般法规则（the Rule that Specific Statutes Prevail Over General Statutes）

（5）后法优于前法规则（the Rule *Lex Posterior Derogat Priori*）

（6）禁止默示废止规则（the Rule Disfavoring Repeals by Implication）

（7）采有效性解释规则（the Rule of Adopting a Construction that Favors Validity）

（8）不利起草者的解释规则（the Rule of Constructing a Document against the Drafter/the Rule of *Contra Proferentem*）

（9）支持符合公共政策的合同解释规则（The Rule Favoring the Construction of Contracts in a Manner Consistent With Public Policy）

（二）语言推定范畴

（1）一致表达规则（the Rule of Consistent Expression）

（2）文义解释规则（the Plain Meaning or Four Corners Rule）

（3）避免赘言规则（the Rule against Tautology）

（4）整体解释规则（the Rule that a Document Must Be Read as a Whole）

（5）否定解释规则（the Rule of *Expressio Unius Est Exclusio Alterius*）

（6）类别解释规则（the Rule of *Ejusdem Generis*）

（7）关联解释规则（the Rule of *Noscitur a Sociis*）

（8）对应解释规则（the Rule of *Reddendo Singula Singulis*）

（9）修饰最后先行词的规则（the Rule of Last Modification）

（10）支持行政解释的规则（the Rule Favoring Agency Interpretation）

（11）手写条款效力高于打印或印刷条款规则（the Rule that Handwritten Words Prevail Over Typed or Printed Words）

（12）大写数额效力高于阿拉伯数字规则（the Rule that Written Amounts Prevail Over Arabic Number）

较之语言推定原则，法律推定的解释方法虽有助法庭处理冲突法律规范或合同条款的适用问题，但泰半与翻译活动本身若即若离。有鉴于此，哈格德教授依据规则形成的渊源区分成文法规则（statutory rule）与判例法规则（case law rule）的路径好似无的放矢（Haggard，2004：85–113），不如陶博先生目光所及始终围绕语言问题（2004：103—105）。

判例法推定原则的核心要旨在于限制对法律文件起草者意图的过度解释，这也是哈格德教授将其置于诸项之首的关键。所谓意图控制（intent controls），由两项相互矛盾的规则协同构成：文义规则和危害规则。前者要求读者根据文件的字面意思解释文本；后者却敦促读者周全考虑一切情境因素（all the circumstances），而情境因素中至关紧要的无非是立法纠正或补救的危害行为。这便有可能导致解读者"越过直接目的，探求所谓法的精神"① （Haggard，2004：91）。

---

① 英语原文："... goes beyond the direct purpose and looks at the so-called *spirit* of the legislation."

实际上，布特与卡瑟尔在探讨了各项常见的法律解释原则后，亦不得不承认很多情况下语言模糊问题的解决必须求助语境（context），并引用英国上议院对合同解释原则根本变化（fundamental change）的最新重述如下①（Butt & Castle，2001：53－54）：

（1）Interpretation is the ascertainment of the meaning which the document would convey to a **reasonable** person having all the **background** knowledge which would **reasonably** have been available to the parties in the situation in which they were at the time of the contract.

（2）The **background** was famously referred to by Lord Wilberforce as the 'matrix of fact', but this phrase is, if anything, an understated description of what the **background** may include. Subject to the requirement that it should have been **reasonably** available to the parties and to the exception to be mentioned next, it includes absolutely anything which would have affected the way in which the language of the document would have been understood by a **reasonable** man.

（3）The law excludes from the admissible **background** the previous negotiations of the parties and their declarations of subjective intent. They are admissible only in an action for rectification. The law makes this distinction for reasons of practical policy and, in this respect only, legal interpretation differs from the way we would interpret utterances in ordinary life. The boundaries of this exception are in some respects unclear.

（4）The meaning which a document（or any other utterance）would convey to a **reasonable** man is not the same thing as the meaning of its words. The meaning of words is a matter of dictionaries and grammars；the meaning of the document is what the parties using those words against the relevant **background** would **reasonably** have been understood to mean. The **background** may not merely enable the **reasonable** man to choose between the possible meanings of words which are ambiguous but even（as occasionally happens in ordinary life）to conclude that the parties

---

①　粗体由本书作者添加。

must, for whatever reason, have used the wrong words or syntax.

(5) The 'rule' that words should be given their "natural and ordinary meaning" reflects the commonsense proposition that we do not easily accept that people have made linguistic mistakes, particularly in formal documents. On the other hand, if one would nevertheless conclude from the **background** that something must have gone wrong with the language, the law does not require judges to attribute to the parties an intention which they plainly could not have had.

南辕北辙的是为澄清语义模糊，我们又被强加了两个臭名昭著的不确定概念："理性"（reasonable）及"背景"（background）。本欲接近真理，哪曾想离得更远。

三　纯语言学路径的内在缺陷

实际上，本书开篇回顾的英美国家法律语言学研究成果，自身就对翻译的语言学路径构成挑战。已经浮现的关键性问题至少包括三个方面，均无法在纯粹语言学的范畴内彻底加以解决。

（一）普通法英语多样

麦林科夫曾经指出法律英语牵涉五湖四海诸多普通法法域（请参阅本书【1.2.1】）。尽管往昔的日不落帝国早已雄风不再，但英语依旧在全球范围内保持着超强地位，各种地区性变体更是层出不穷并持续相互影响。世界级权威专家戴维·克里斯特尔（David Crystal）在其著作《英语：全球通用语言》（*English as a Global Language*）中引用印度学者布拉杰·卡克鲁（Braj Kachru）的观点将英语方言按重要性划分为三个同心圆（concentric circle）（2003：60）：

● The *inner circle* refers to the traditional bases of English, where it is the primary language: it includes the USA, UK, Ireland, Canada, Australia and New Zealand.

● The *outer* or *extended circle* involves the earlier phases of the spread of English in non-native settings, where the language has become part of a country's chief institutions, and plays an important 'second language' role in a multilingual setting: it includes Singapore, India, Malawi and over fifty other territories.

- The *expanding* or *extending circle* involves those nations which recognize the importance of English as an international language, though they do not have a history of colonization by members of the inner circle, nor have they given English any special administrative status. It includes China, Japan, Greece, Poland and (as the name of this circle suggests) a steadily increasing number of other states. In these areas, English is taught as a foreign language. (The term 'expanding' reflects its origins in the 1980s: today, with English recognized virtually everywhere, a tense change to expanded circle would better reflect the contemporary scene.)

其中，仅内外层同心圆就包括将近七十五个国家和地区。从前备受推崇的伦敦音绝非如今的唯一标准，北美英语和澳新英语也是重要变体，其他譬如印度英语、东南亚英语、加勒比地区英语和非洲某些新兴国家的英语，亦受本土文化影响而各呈特色。这些方言发音迥然，词汇语法纷繁。

尽管学术或科技方面的英语文献倾向于遵循更具共性的正式文体要求，但企盼彻底剔除语言符号的社会属性，这是不可能完成的任务。正如潘·彼得斯（Pam Peters）所言，"英语的任何一种区域变体都承载着系统的政治、社会和文化内涵，即便是所谓的'标准'形式也无例外……区域联想的确可能令人误入歧途……"①（2004：286）

这就为译者（包括法律翻译工作者）设置了几乎难以逾越的障碍：究竟译入英语哪种方言变体才是最正确的选择？或许唯有国际英语（international English）尚可救我们于水深火热。遗憾的是，"国际英语"本身就包含着令人尴尬的双重概念②：

---

① 英语原文："Any regional variety of English has a set of political, social and cultural connotations attached to it, even the so-called 'standard' forms... Regional associations can indeed be quite distracting..."

② [2013/4/18] http://en.wikipedia.org/wiki/International_English. 粗体由本书作者添加。

International English is the concept of the English language as a global means of communication in numerous dialects, and also the movement towards an international standard for the language. It is also referred to as **Global English**, **World English**, **Common English**, **Continental English**, **General English**, **Engas** (English as associate language), or **Globish**.

Sometimes, these terms refer simply to the array of varieties of English spoken throughout the world.

Sometimes, "international English" and the related terms above refer to a desired standardisation, i. e. **Standard English**; however, there is no consensus on the path to this goal. There have been many proposals for making International English more accessible to people from different nationalities. **Basic English** is an example, but it failed to make progress. More recently, there have been proposals for **English as a lingua franca** (**ELF**). It has also been argued that International English is held back by its traditional spelling. There has been slow progress in adopting alternate spellings.

对于前一种定义，国际英语凸显的是本土特征的多样性（variety）；对于后一种定义，国际英语代表的却是标准化的中性特征（neutrality），它不应掺杂美国、英国、加拿大、澳大利亚或任何其他方言色彩：

What could be better than a type of English that saves you from having to re-edit publications for individual regional markets! Teachers and learners of English as a second language also find it an attractive idea—both often concerned that their English should be neutral, without American or British or Canadian or Australian coloring. (Peters, 2004: 286)

诚如上文所言，国际标准英语的发展活跃于学术界或科技界，因为相关领域通行正式英语用法，同时又不可避免地抹杀了语言运用的个性与创造力。然而即便这种所谓"中性"的标准英语传递的仍然是西方文化与价值观。原想消除英式殖民帝国主义（colonial imperialism）与美式文化帝国主义（cultural imperialism）深重痕迹的标准英语，结果却陷入企图抹杀一切区域差异的新语言帝国主义（linguistic imperialism）困境难以自拔：

> We may, in due course, all need to be in control of two standard Englishes—the one which gives us our national and local identity，and the other which puts us in touch with the rest of the human race. In effect，we may all need to become bilingual in our own language.（Crystal，1988：265）

鉴于国际英语的中性化进程尚无定论，方言干扰在未来可预见的时期内还是任何英译者都不得不直面的事实。选择不同普通法域英语的同时也意味着译文将或多或少被赋予该变体所属地区社会政治文化色彩，或者说译文读者很可能因此产生某种原文本没有的联想。仅此而言，单纯的语言学路径也是法律翻译研究所不可取的，当然更无法指导我们理解法律翻译特别是近代中国早期法律翻译活动的另类现象。

（二）确定性幻象破灭

尽管法律语言追求确定性，然而意义边界的相对模糊是符号体系保持弹性的本质特征。凡夫俗子既无力复起通天塔，唯有逢迎貌合神离的规范强加诠释。恩里克·阿尔卡拉兹（Enrique Alcaraz）和布莱恩·休斯（Brian Hughes）甚至将译者解读法律文本的行为与律师、法官等职业人士相提并论：

> Like translators，allpracticing lawyers，and judges most specifically and professionally engaged in the task of interpreting the meaning of texts，and of particular words in particular texts. **To interpret，in general，is to assign a meaning to a word，phrase，clause，sentence or utterance，and，where two or more meanings are possible，either to decide between them or to declare the utterance indeterminably ambiguous.** For the translator，the purpose of interpretation is to decide on the closest possible linguistic equivalent in the target language，while for the judge it is to match up the resulting propositions against the definitions established in ex-

isting law. The difference, of course, is that the translator's work is over once the semantic hurdle has been negotiated, whereas the judge must go on to apply the results of the linguistic analysis and announce a decision in accordance with the rules and principles of law.① (Alcaraz & Hughes, 2002: 24)

且勿论此说是否稍嫌太过，只看它将文本意义视作解读者的选择，便不能贸然地令之归属纯粹的语义问题。分配意义的基础究竟是什么？适法目的还是立法意图？若偏重立法意图，那又如何看待意图控制等南辕北辙的普通法解释传统？若偏重适法目的，莫非欲构陷法律于极端不可预测的深渊？法哲学家们喋喋不休几近半个世纪（请参阅本书【1.2.4】），自非笔者寥寥数语可解。但不言而喻的是，无论前述哪种因素均非语言系统内部所能独自判定。

（三）平实化运动坎坷

关于法律英语风格平实化的争议，前文已作详尽描述（请参阅本书【1.2.5】）。当然，纸上谈兵式的唇枪舌剑并不能迅速扭转平实语言虽大势所趋、传统风格仍根深蒂固的现实窘境。更何况从译者的角度出发，目标语篇的文体特征绝不是非此即彼般界限分明，只因这绝非法律体裁的固有属性，而是历史演进过程中的文化积淀。无论言语行为理论抑或语言功能模型，斟酌的只是具体翻译活动的直接情境，故均不足以说明译者行为的合理性，更不足以消融译者艰难抉择的矛盾心态。

正如切斯特曼所言，规范的合法性既可得益于权威，亦得益于公众的认可（Chesterman，2012: 56 – 57）。不幸的是，一方面，法律写作大师言之凿凿的权威论述，却未必符合社会公众长久以来形成的惯性思维，这让译者何去何从？另一方面，维护法律职业的精英性与推动法律知识的普及化，两者权衡利弊又是孰轻孰重？

第二节　历史文化转向

正是考虑到纯语言学路径已陷困境，学者们开始将视野转向社会学领

---

① 粗体由本书作者添加。

域，试图在文化交流、历史演进的框架下重塑法律翻译研究范式：法律翻译不只是法律机制内的交际行为，更是跨越法律文化的交际行为。尽管如此，现有文献关注的焦点依然囿于狭义的法律文化，特别是不同法系传统与制度的比较；罕有系统论述翻译对社会现实的影响。

一 翻译导向的法文化研究

尽管比较法律传统的研究及国际法的发展使得不同国家的法律制度正趋向融合，尤其在国际贸易（international trade）领域（Gotti，2009：55），但大陆法系与普通法系之间的差别仍昭然若揭。"一系列社会的、经济的、心理的、历史的和文化的因素以及一系列价值判断，都在影响着和决定着立法和司法"（博登海默，1999：199）。这使得现代法律工作者依旧备受语言与文化问题的困扰（Kischel，2009：7）。正是有鉴于此，翻译导向的法文化研究对跨法域交流的助益更显而易见。

（一）比较法律传统

总体而言，英美国家和地区（包括绝大多数前英国殖民地）的法律文化起源于诺曼底公爵威廉征服英格兰后推行的普通法制度。该制度的基石是独特的不成文宪法以及口口相传并最终记录下来的由才华横溢、备受尊重的法官们做出的判决（Glendon，Gordon & Carozza，2004：150）。这与欧洲大陆以罗马法传统（Roman tradition）为基础的民法制度截然不同，并称当今西方世界最具影响力的两大法系。为了建立与社会主义市场经济相适应的现代法治，中国大陆的立法主要借鉴了欧陆民法法系国家和地区的法律模式。

（二）比较法律风格

陶博教授在论述英美国家法律起草风格的过程中，曾经比较了普通法系与大陆法系立法技术方面的差异。这首先源自哲学层面的思考：如何才能更好地保护民众的利益？解决方案可能大相径庭——普通法强调"精确"（precision）；大陆法强调"简练"（conciseness）。

毋庸置疑，法系之间的立法差异是由传统造成的。大陆法系由拿破仑法典衍生而成并间接效仿罗马法，因此采用与普通法系截然不同的路径。另外，这种传统塑就的差异又反过来对当前社会制度产生深刻影响：

在普通法系的国家里，很多结论是由立法机构通过详细的法律得到的。在大陆法系的国家里，这些同样的结论则是通过行政机关发布规章制度或者通过法官作出裁决得到的。如果我们对大陆法系和普通法系的法律和辅助立法进行一个全面的审查，看上去似乎两者的详细程度是相同的。普通法系在法律的细节程度和民主控制上更胜一筹，而大陆法系的法律则更注重表述上的明确但又有更多的行政和司法控制的成分。（陶博，2004：62）

也许正因为如此，普通法系与大陆法系对待成文法字面意思（literal meaning/grammatical meaning）的态度迥异（Sarcevic，1997：61－61）。英美国家视文义解释优先，只有法条自相矛盾或可能导致荒谬结果时，才会基于公平考虑，适用其他各种复杂的推定原则；而在民法国家，语言的日常含义只能充当理解的起点，包括筹备立法的材料及其他补充规章细则均可借以作为推论依据。

（三）比较法律渊源

所谓法律渊源，指的是法律的形式渊源，即法的创制方式和表现形式（沈宗灵，2001：269）。它也是法官解决具体争议应当适用的法律规范的出处，拥有获取特定法律概念准确定义的最终权威性（ultimate authority）。

就英汉法律互译而言，我们有必要考察普通法国家与中国大陆在法律渊源方面的差异（滕超、孔飞燕，2008：51—52）。这也是法律文化交流的起点：因为术语即表达概念的语言形式（linguistic expression），而抽象的概念不仅是人类基于事物的特征和/或其关系将之范畴化的工具（Bussmann，2000：332），还是人类借以认识并理解周围世界的认知单位（cognitive unit）（Baker，2004：259－260）。

1. 普通法渊源

普通法传统中最引人注目的莫过于判例制度，即遵循先例（*stare decisis*）原则：法院判决，尤其是终审法院的判决，成为英美法律最主要的正式渊源。虽然这些国家也颁布了大量成文法，但奠定普通法制度基础的仍是先例（precedent）（Glendon，Gordon & Carozza，2004：262），且成文法（statute law）的适用同样离不开诠释立法文本的司法意见（Cohen & Olson，2004：139），尽管其效力高于包括判例法（case law）在内的其他法律渊源。

2. 中国法渊源

反观中国大陆自近代变法以来，立法参照欧陆民法法系的模式——"立法机关制订的法律乃是法官适用法律的主要依据"（王利明，2002：6）。鉴于成文法具有概括性、抽象性和滞后性的特点，有权机关对成文法做出的正式解释也被赋予法律上的约束力。此外，权威法律学说（legal doctrine）虽不属正式法律渊源，然而根据大陆法系的传统，立法者和法官制定、解释或适用法律都无法摆脱学说的指导，难怪成文法亦被视为学者制定的法律（scholar-made law）（Glendon，Gordon & Carozza，2004：90）。

3. 成文法与判例法概念之间的差别

法律渊源的差异决定了法官在适法过程中阐释法律概念的不同标准。"制定法①概念必须表明其出自制定法文本，由此才能证明制定法概念的正当性"，而"普通法概念也必须表明自己出自合理的公众政策，以此才能证明普通法②概念的正当性"（波斯纳，2002：314）。尽管波斯纳针对的仅仅是美国的成文法与判例法，然推而广之，这同样有助于译者把握一切成文法与判例法概念之间的差别（滕超、孔飞燕，2008：53）。

（四）介绍异域法文化

安立奎·阿尔卡拉兹（Enrique Alcaraz）和布莱恩·休斯（Brian Hughes）在其合著的《法律翻译解析》（*Legal Translation Explained*，2008）一书中简单勾勒了英国法律制度的独特性。英国是普通法系的发源地，而我国现代法律体制在很大程度上借鉴的是大陆法系。因此，理解英国的法律文化对于英汉法律互译的重要性不言而喻。

两位学者用了近三十页的篇幅，对英国的法律渊源、管辖权、法院系统及程序法中的特殊术语作了相对比较细致的描述（Alcaraz & Hughes，2008：47－76）：

---

① 制定法即成文法。

② 根据《布莱克法律词典》的定义，"common law"包含四层意思："1. The body of law derived from judicial decisions, rather than from statutes or constitutions; case law. 2. The body of law based on the English legal system, as distinct from a civil-law system; the general Anglo-American system of legal concepts, together with the techniques of applying them, that form the basis of the law in jurisdictions where the system applies. 3. General law common to the country as a whole, as opposed to special law that has only local application. 4. The body of law deriving from law common as opposed to those sitting in equity."（Garner，2004：293）由此可见，波斯纳所谓的普通法即判例法。为免歧义，本章以术语"判例法"指示上述第一层含义，而术语"普通法"则用于指示上述第二层含义。

（1）法律渊源（the source of English Law），包括普通法（common law）、衡平法（equity）、成文法（statute law）。

（2）管辖权（jurisdiction），主要区分民事管辖权（civil jurisdiction）和刑事管辖权（criminal jurisdiction），至于行政纠纷管辖权及雇佣纠纷管辖权通常归属基层法院或半司法性质的机构。

（3）民事法院系统（the English Civil Courts），包括郡法院（County Court）、高等法院（the High Court of Justice）、民事上诉法院（the Court of Appeal（Civil Division））、上议院（the House of Lords）。

（4）刑事法院系统（the English Criminal Courts），包括治安法院（Magistrates' Court）、巡回刑事法院（Crown Court）、高等法院（the High Court of Justice）、刑事上诉法院（the Court of Appeal（Criminal Division））、上议院（the House of Lords）。

（5）民事和刑事程序法中的诸多法律术语。

尽管介绍普通法文化的文献多如牛毛，比照不同法系制度差异的研究亦不可胜数，但如同这两位学者那样以翻译为目的，考察异域法律传统的却是难能可贵。尤其该书着墨最多的正是程序法方面的迥异特征。这显然是考虑到现代社会发展日新月异，全球一体化进程迅猛，调整对象的多样性及其跨法域的相似性，使得追溯实体法术语的流变，既无可能也无必要。

（五）法律翻译的文化制约

华东政法大学外语学院马莉教授曾有专著，全面论述法律翻译牵涉的文化问题。书名很有意思——《法律语言翻译的文化制约》（2009），似乎是在刻意强调"语言转换与文化转换"的对立。无论如何，这是笔者所见唯一专门探讨广义法律文化的文献。

所谓广义上的法律文化，"指与法律有关的历史、传统、习惯、制度、学理和其他任何东西"（马莉，2009：前言001）。马教授认为"在法律语言学中探讨文化对翻译的制约性，正是语言工作者为促进不同法律文化的理解、交流和合作所做出的贡献"（同上，前言002），因而按语言学的标准从词汇、句法、语用修辞三个层面揭示法律语言的文化特征，并概括总结了八项翻译补偿策略（同上，151—157）：

　　（1）整合补偿；（2）分立补偿；（3）同类补偿；（4）异类补偿
（5）原位补偿；（6）异位补偿；（7）同步补偿；（8）差异补偿

　　值得注意的是，运用文化补偿策略的最终目标旨在实现法律文本的语用等效翻译。由此可见，笔者虽立足文化研究，却未能完全摆脱语言学的思维模式，严格意义上还不能算是在宏观社会情境中探索法律翻译现象。

二　法律领域的翻译史研究

　　当前，法律翻译研究引人注目的另一重要领域就是历时性维度的开拓。有的学者着眼宏观层面，追溯社会变迁对法律翻译发展的影响；有的学者着眼微观层面，关注法律翻译在社会转型时期的表现。

　　（一）宏观层面

　　沙尔切维奇在其影响深远的著作《法律翻译新路径》（*New Approach to Legal Translation*）中从直译（literal translation）与意译（free translation）之争入手，将西方国家法律翻译策略的演进过程划分成六个主要阶段：严格直译（strict literal）、直译（literal）、适当直译（moderately literal）、近似地道翻译（near idiomatic）、地道翻译（idiomatic）及共同起草（co-drafting）（Sarcevic，1997：24）。

　　1. 拉丁文语言霸权：字字对应的严格直译

　　追溯法律翻译史的起点被定位于查士丁尼（Justinian）时代。这位雄伟君主编纂的《民法大全》（*Corpus Juris civilis*）记载着现存最早有关立法文本翻译的钦定规则。作为罗马皇帝，查士丁尼坚决捍卫拉丁文至高无上的地位。他禁止对自己颁布的法律进行任何评注，并明确规定只可译成希腊语，且翻译方式仅限字字对应（word for word），以免其神圣的拉丁文法典遭遇扭曲误解。

　　尽管中世纪早期，罗马帝国的权威就已难及西欧，但继之而起的罗马天主教庭（Roman Catholic Church）仍竭力保存拉丁文明。由于各国民族语言尚未得到充分发展，记载书面法律离不开拉丁文，而立法者与法官却常使用民族口语。唯有严格直译方可确保"回译"（back translation）最大限度的准确性。

2. 各民族语言崛起：更为自由的翻译策略

随着拉丁文的统治渐次瓦解，民族意识日趋觉醒，更为自由的翻译策略方始流行，语境亦将发挥作用，可接受性成为译者必须考虑的重要因素，故而不得不向目标语言规范退避三舍。

沙氏考察了 20 世纪以来多语言法域内立法与司法过程中的翻译问题，分别以瑞士、加拿大、比利时为例，探讨法律文字（letter）与法律精神（spirit）、平等语言权力（equal language right）等命题。他认为正是少数民族追求平等语言权力，最终对法律语篇的直译传统构成严峻挑战。

（二）微观层面

在很大程度上，历史发展制约法律翻译，但法律翻译亦不可避免地影响历史进程。这方面案例以有关苏联解体的研究最为典型。

20 世纪 90 年代中期，正在俄罗斯从事法律翻译工作的柯妮丽娅·E. 布朗（Cornelia E. Brown）深有感触地发表了论文《驾驭命运：译出原苏联加盟共和国的法律》（"Riding the Waves of Fortune：Translating Legislation of the Successor Soviet Republics"），由美国翻译工作者协会（American Translators Association）收录至学术论文集第八卷（*Scholarly Monograph Series Volume VIII*，1995）。

布朗女士敏锐地注意到，这些新兴国家急不可耐地重建法律制度，某种程度上正是为了鼓励欧美投资，因而聘请西方律师事务所翻译乃至起草法律文件，旨在寻求有关资本主义经济模式的专业知识。其间，译者通过传递欧美法律术语推广西方法律文化的作用极其关键：

> These law firms translate legislation, advise Western businesses about it, and may also help the republic draft new laws. Clearly translators play a large role in this enterprise as experts who can, perhaps, bridge the gaps between English, European languages, and Russian. Indeed "translation" is taking place on a cultural level, as the independent states consider reshaping their political and economic structures on Western models. To do so, the states experiment with Western legal terminology and practices, including conventions for writing the laws intended to implement and guarantee new structures. To a great extent, the impulse to change encourages a focus on legal writing, the very stuff of a translator's job. (Brown, 1995：68)

　　显然，作者所谓"发生在文化层面"的翻译，更多指向政治、经济因素。这在新颁布法律的风格上亦有体现：

　　Stylistically, the new laws retained much from the Soviet period but increasingly showed the influence of Western concepts and drafting conventions. （Ibid.）

　　法律翻译既要充分传递原文信息，又需确保目标读者群能够顺畅理解。不过，当时的宏观社会语境迫使译者更多考虑的是文本的可接受性而非准确性，与之相契合的策略亦应运而生：

　　In conjunction with the Russian and American lawyers in our joint venture, I end up producing translations, perhaps better called commentaries, where footnotes and text would work in dialogue, the text typically veering far towards the target language （the language into which a translation is done）, and then the footnotes, correctively, veering back towards the original. （Ibid.）

　　形成鲜明对比的是爱尔兰。正如克尼瓦·昆斯（Keneva Kunz）在《争锋相对：爱尔兰与欧共体法律》（"Where the Devil Meets his Grandmother: Iceland and European Community Legislation", 1995）中所论证的，爱尔兰人竭力维护本国语言与法律的纯洁性，反倒成为其加入欧共体的障碍：

　　... the problems faced by Iceland translating European Community legislation and subsequently adapting its own laws, and especially its own language, to the requirements of semi-membership of the European Community. （Kunz, 1995：85）

　　发人深省的是作者在文末引用 H. C. 格特里奇（H. C. Gutteridge）的话说，尽管独立的法律思想乃民族自尊精神的源泉之一，但法律与人类文明的其他领域同样需要自由地交流知识和观念：

> The isolation of legal thought in national watertight compartments has
> always seemed to me to be one of the factors which is most prolific in pro-
> ducing that frame of mind which leads to a spirit of national egotism. We
> have much to learn from one another in legal as well as other departments
> of human activities, and it is, in a sense, a reproach to the lawyers of all
> nations that they have been unable, up to the present, to arrive at the free
> interchange of knowledge and ideas which has been attained in other
> branches of learning. (Ibid. 92)

三 焦点问题研究

（一）多语言法域的困境

Doczekalska 曾将"法律上的多语制"（legal multilingualism）描述成"多语言国家、国际及超国家组织的重要特征，它以法律文件全部语言版本同等真确原则为基础。该原则意味着经确认的各语言版本都具有法律效力，法庭在解释过程中探求法律文件的意义时都必须加以考虑。该原则假定各语言版本包含相同意义，因而具有相同的法律效果，旨在确保各语言版本都被平等地视作真确，并不得出于解释目的而以任何单独语言版本为准"①（2009：116）。这就不可避免地导致官方语言多样性与法律解释一致性之间的矛盾，其中最突出的核心问题表现在术语和风格两个层面。

1. 术语问题

（1）"标准化"解决方案——以欧盟为例

欧洲联盟（European Union）是以《马斯特里赫特条约》（*Maastricht Treaty*）为基础成立的、承载政治实体和经济实体双重身份的重要区域一

---

① 英语原文："Legal multilingualism—characteristic of multilingual states, international and su-pranational organizations—is based on the principle of equal authenticity of all language versions of a legal act. The principle means that each of the authenticated language versions has the force of law and must be considered by a court during the interpretation process when the meaning of a legal act is sought. In order to assure that all language versions are treated as equally authentic and none of them prevails for interpretation purposes, the principle presumes that all language versions have the same meaning and consequently the same legal effect."

体化组织。该组织现有 27 个会员国，通过协调法律制度整合市场，确保货物、服务、资本和劳动力的自由流动（freedom of movement for goods, services, capital and labor）。

欧盟尊重平等语言权力，因而规定其法律由全部官方语言起草，且各版本享有同等的法律效力。多种语言版本共存，当然便于法官发现立法意图，促进法律规范实现其调整目标：

> Whatever problems face Europe and the EU, statutory interpretation is not high on the list. On the contrary, the European Court of Justice resolves disputes among member states in what appears to be a routine manner. In this chapter, I argue that the proliferation of languages actually assists the interpretation of statutes by the ECJ. To the extent that the goal of the court is to construe statutes to effectuate the intent of the legislature and to further the goals of the enacted directive or regulation, the existence of so many versions of the law makes this task easier. In other words, my argument is that the Babel of Europe facilitates communication. (Solan, 2009: 35 - 36)

无论如何，相同法律效果的假定难以掩盖不同版本术语使用方面存在的深刻差异，这始终是欧洲一体化进程中最令人棘手的实际问题。有鉴于此，欧盟委员会制定了《合同法实施方案》（*Action Plan on European Contract Law*），旨在构建"共同参照框架"（Common Frame of Reference），以便确立跨语言与法域的规则和术语。

正如前文所述，沙尔切维奇认为法律翻译不同于数学、化学、物理等自然学科的严谨翻译，原因就在于人文学科的语言受特定社会文化的制约，未能"使构成学科知识基础的概念实现高度国际标准化"①（Sarcevic, 1997: 66）。故而有学者建议多语言法域，应当推进法律语言的通用性：

---

① 英语原文："... a high degree of international standardization of the concepts (definitions) constituting the knowledge base of such disciplines..."

In my understanding of European legal integration there must be a place for interaction between different groups. Within different groups I mean between lawyers and non-lawyers, and, on another level, even between consumers and professionals. To reach this common use of language we need to develop a curriculum for a more coherent linguistic and terminological use inside the European Union... In my opinion legal harmonisation can only be attained by standardising legal terms within the European Union. (Heutger, 2003: 1 - 2)

（2）"法系化"解决方案——以香港为例

香港是世界上唯一以中英文实施普通法的地区。借香港回归祖国为契机，逐步确立并完善双语化，旨在实现双重历史使命：维持现有法律制度，兼顾民族文化意识（严元浩，2004：2）。

2004年，曾任基本法咨询委员会秘书处高级翻译主任的陆文慧女士邀请多位法律领域卓有建树的官员、专家、学者集成《法律翻译——从实践出发》（Legal Translation in Practice）。诚如编者所言，该书希望着眼不同视角探讨法律翻译方面的实践问题，然而参与人员的观点与立论虽有参差，却都认同法律翻译是构建双语法制的必由之路（陆文慧，2004：vii—viii）。

值得注意的是，尽管真确中文本法律与英文本的地位相同，但用中文表述普通法概念绝非易事。实际上，双语立法机构早已接受原文与译文无力实现完全对等的事实，因而《释义及通则条例》预设了方便消除分歧的条款①：

第10B条两种法定语文本条例的释疑
（1）条例的中文本和英文本同等真确，解释条例须以此为依据。
（2）条例的两种真确本所载条文，均推定为具有同等意义。
（3）凡条例的两种真确本在比较之下，出现意义分歧，而引用通常适用的法例释义规则亦不能解决，则须在考虑条例的目的和作用后，采用最能兼顾及协调两文本的意义。

---

① 援引自香港律政司双语法例资料系统（http://www.legislation.gov.hk/chi/index.htm）。

Section 10B Construction of Ordinances in both official languages

(1) The English language text and the Chinese language text of an Ordinance shall be equally authentic, and the Ordinance shall be construed accordingly.

(2) The provisions of an Ordinance are presumed to have the same meaning in each authentic text.

(3) Where a comparison of the authentic texts of an Ordinance discloses a difference of meaning which the rules of statutory interpretation ordinarily applicable do not resolve, the meaning which best reconciles the texts, having regard to the object and purposes of the Ordinance, shall be adopted.

第 10C 条普通法词句

(1) 凡条例英文本内使用普通法词句，而中文本内使用对应的词句，则条例须依该词句在普通法上的意义解释。

Section 10C Expressions of common law

(1) Where an expression of the common law is used in the English language text of an Ordinance and an analogous expression is used in the Chinese language text thereof, the Ordinance shall be construed in accordance with the common law meaning of that expression.

以上所引法条出自香港法例首章。其中，第 10B 条陈述的解释规则并无甚特异之处，值得关注的是第 10C 条。它要求依托普通法的语境，解释中文本术语，这是典型的"法系化"解决方案，其目的在于确保现行制度不受外来文化的侵扰：

> 即使中英文术语在字面上意义不同，但借着上述条文，便可确保有关词汇在普通法及法例上的意义得以保持。我们大可视之将普通法"移植"至中文本内，因此，我们亦可以说：纵然是"双语"，但仍属"一法"。（严元浩，2004：4—5）

2. 风格问题——共同起草 (co-drafting)

所谓共同起草，若望文生义，可能被过分解读为运用数种官方语言共同起草法律文件（multilingual legal drafting）。尽管全部语言版本享有同等的法律效力，但在各份法律文本经法定程序确认通过前，或具体地说即起草行为本身，依然牵涉诸多可以适用翻译理论进行研究的棘手问题，故称翻译过程是恰当的，只不过翻译产品在法律上被赋予了原文的地位（Doc-zekalska，2009：132 – 133）。

那么我们引入"共同起草"术语，对于解决法律翻译中的风格问题又有什么特殊贡献呢？毋庸置疑，衡量法律文件的可信度（reliability）通常依据该文件各平行版本在语言方面的一致程度（concordance）：

> It is necessary to follow the standard format prescribed for a particular instrument, thus preserving the organizational plan, division into parts, etc. It is well known the plurilingual communication could not function without a method of guaranteeing uniform citation of the provisions of the parallel texts of a given instrument. (Sarcevic, 1997：181)

考虑到上述形式制约的压力，多数机构遵循的起草原则是："同项文件、同种版式、同样风格"（one instrument, one format, one style）（同上）。

而沙尔切维奇创设"共同起草"的概念，正欲摆脱平行文本间近乎严苛的传统束缚，并由此提倡创造性的法律翻译，优化译入文本风格，增进目标读者的可接受性。他还列举了五个方面的具体措施，包括抛弃单句规则（disregarding one-sentence rule）、删节标准配置（deleting standard equipment）、构建宽松结构（creating a looser texture）、分段区别主从（paragraphing to distinguish between the main and dependent clauses）和重新组织文本（restructuring the text）（同上，182—191）。

（二）国际仲裁的全球化与协调一致

国际仲裁是法律翻译研究者关注的另一重要领域。仲裁法律文件（arbitration document）具有特殊性——虽由国际组织制定，却在特定国家实施。这方面有三篇经典论文值得特别关注，即《仲裁话语中的文化制约》（"Cultural Constraints on Arbitration Discourse"）、《仲裁话语中的术语翻译》（"Translating Terminology in Arbitration Discourse"）和《国际仲裁中的翻译》（"Translation in International Arbitration"），均收录在国际著名语篇分析专家维杰·巴提亚（Vijay Bhatia）教授等主编的论文集《跨文化与制度的法律话语》（*Legal Discourse across Cultures and Systems*，2008）。

考察仲裁程序（arbitration procedure）与仲裁文本（arbitration text）牵涉的各类文化制约，我们不难发现本土特征正是导致各国仲裁法律制度千差万别的深层原因：

> In spite of the growing efforts of the international arbitration community to guarantee even more harmonization in legislation and in procedures, local constraints and specific cultural aspects still represent relevant conditioning factors. （Gotti，2008：247）

就因为如此，仲裁虽已成为国际化的法律领域，但术语转换仍是译者面临的焦点问题：

> Although arbitration is by now an internationalized legal topic, there are still many lexical and terminological issues which are treated differently in different national legal systems. Extensive conceptual analysis of key, as well as collateral, terms needs to be undertaken so as to avoid the potential risk of choosing translational equivalents which would not be adequate in the target legal system and, in consequence, misleading or incomprehensible for the ultimate recipients. （Chroma，2008：325 - 326）

但也只有通过翻译才能穿越文化障碍，使操持不同语言的当事人得以通过仲裁解决国际纠纷：

> ... despite the growing use of English, translation continues to make a significant contribution not only to the globalization but also to the harmonization of international arbitration. （Sarcevic，2008：291）

四 历史文化转向的局限

法律翻译的历史文化转向单就时间来看，萌芽至今亦有数十年之久。然而，相关研究虽将影响交际的背景范畴从直接情境拓展至宏观社会语境，涉足的领域却依旧局限法文化的比较及其对翻译行为的制约，仍热衷于构建规范，假想原文与译文能够达成某种层面上的对等（equivalence）。或者借马歇尔·莫里斯（Marshall Morris）的话说，学者们坚信准确与公平都是可以实现的：

> Given the range of contributors, it is worthy of note that they share at least these two qualities: a clear concern for the common plight of individuals under the sharp scrutiny of a court, and a radical faith in the value of straining for both exactitude and fairness in this most fluid and uncertain world. (Morris, 1995: 5)

但现代社会语言学家早已普遍公认，语言与社会的关系双向互动。只关注社会架构在语言中的折射，却无视语言对社会架构的改造，这般思维即便可行亦算不得全面周致。仅此而论，跨法域交际尤其值得我们探讨。因为无论译者多么倾心归化策略，多么重视目标读者的可接受性，最终产品必定包含相当程度的异质文化元素。正如乔治·斯坦纳（George Steiner）所言：

> But whatever the degree of "naturalization", the act of importation can potentially dislocate or relocate the whole of the native structure. (Steiner, 2001: 315)

这方面，社会学视角下围绕法律程序展开的批判话语分析已经为我们树立了丰碑。譬如斯塔高尔教授就主张法律语言作为工具，发挥着维护或抵御制度权力（the maintenance of or resistance to institutional power）的重要作用（Stygall, 1994: 7）。承载前述功能的并非只有程序语言，书面语言亦不外如是。

正本溯源，构成特定社会上层建筑核心的法律制度是历史演进的产物，不但集中体现所属社会群体的主流价值理念，还综合反映该社会政治、经济、文化等各方面的意识形态。就社会演进而言，成文法的遣词造句既是现行权力关系的固化载体，亦将对未来的权力博弈产生影响；就跨文化交际而言，法律翻译构成原法律文化对目标法律文化的侵蚀。

这与斯坦纳将翻译视作目标文化对原文化的掠夺并行不悖。只是视角有异，主客之势自然易位：欢迎异质文化的，必定愿意"掠夺"，譬如前苏联加盟共和国；排斥异质文化的，必定警惕"入侵"，譬如爱尔兰。无非一个问题的两个方面，程度或者参差，却没有可能将之断然割裂。

无论如何，只有将已经发生的法律翻译活动视作理性的文化实践，才能深刻理解译介行为背后所蕴含的权力博弈，这是毋庸置疑的。换言之，规定性研究（prescriptive studies）遭遇瓶颈之际，改弦易辙势在必行。故而本书另循描述性路径（descriptive approach），依托系统理论，透过动态视角，追溯西法东渐在中国近代转型期留下的足迹。

最后，请允许笔者引用密西根大学哈特法学教授兼英语语言与文学教授詹姆斯·博伊德·怀特（James Boyd White）的警世箴言结束我们对法律翻译研究现状的概览：

> Our deepest obligation and highest hope is to create a world in which each person is fully recognized, in which each may achieve the realization of his or her capacities for life. That is easy to say and has often been said. The major difficulty is to give it meaning not at the level of concept or theory but in literary and intellectual practice, in our speech and conduct. This is the task of the art that unites justice and translation. (1990:269)

第 三 章
西法东渐:系统、规范与权力

导　言

描述性翻译研究（Descriptive Translation Studies：DTS）的理念源自半个多世纪前约翰·麦克法兰（John McFarlane）在《杜伦大学学报》（*The Durham University Journal*）上发表的名作《翻译模式》（"Modes of Translation"）。

麦克法兰教授有感意义的复杂性和模糊性（complexity and elusiveness）及其对受众个体解读的依赖，认为无须苛求原文与译文的全方位等值（equivalence in all aspects），因为这是译者不可能完成的任务。相反，研究翻译应当"本着就事论事的精神"[①]：

> ... to underline the need for some new, provisional theory of translation— 'new' in the sense that it should be diagnostic rather than hortatory, that it should be concerned not with unreal ideals and fictional absolutes but actualities, and that it should not hesitate to use the instruments of modern semantic theory; and 'provisional' in the sense that it should not so much attempt to impose a rigid pattern on the facts as we at present see them but rather serve as a device for the better understanding of them. (McFarlane, 1953：92 – 93)

尽管这篇颇具创见的文章预设了描写范式（descriptive paradigm）的诸多关键要素，唯其名称的确定尚待翻译研究学派的杰出先驱詹姆士·霍姆斯（James Stratton Holmes, 1924—1986）在哥本哈根举行的第三届国际

[①]　英语原文："... in the belief that translation is as translation does..."

应用语言学大会翻译分会（the Translation Section of the Third International Congress of Applied Linguistics）上宣读具有划时代意义的论文《翻译研究的名与实》（"The Name and Nature of Translation Studies"）[1]。

鉴于"围绕翻译行为和翻译作品产生的诸多复杂问题"[2]（Holmes, 2007：67），霍姆斯主张新学科的创设顺理成章，并建议将之定名为翻译研究（translation studies），包括纯翻译研究（pure translation studies）与应用翻译研究（applied translation studies）。

所谓纯翻译研究，又分描述性翻译研究和理论性翻译研究（theoretical translation studies）两支：

> As a field of pure research-that is to say, research pursued for its own sake, quite apart from any direct practical application outside its own terrain—translation studies thus has two main objectives： (1) to describe the phenomena of translating and translation(s) as they manifest themselves in the world of our experience, and (2) to establish general principles by means of which these phenomena can be explained and predicted. The two branches of pure translation studies concerning themselves with these objectives can be designated *descriptive translation studies* (DTS) or *translation description* (TD) and *theoretical translation studies* (ThTS) or *translation theory* (TTh). (Holms, 2007：71)

毫无疑问，翻译研究属实证学科（empirical discipline）。相应的，翻译现象的经验主义描写涵盖翻译作品（product-oriented DTS）、翻译功能（function-oriented DTS）及翻译过程（process-oriented DTS）三个主要方向（同上）。但若就此认为上述领域的探索得以截然分离且能自给自足，则必使描述的笔触流于肤浅。实际上，社会预期的翻译功能决定翻译作品的表现形式，并由此不可避免地掌控翻译过程的策略选择

---

[1]　该文后经修订扩充并有英文、荷兰语等多个版本问世，霍姆斯去世后终被收录至《译稿杀青! 文学翻译与翻译研究文集》（*Translated ! Papers on Literary and Translation Studies*, 2007）。

[2]　英语原文："... the complex of problems clustered round the phenomenon of translating and translation..."

（Toury，2001：12）：

the（prospective）systemic position & function of a translation

determines

its appropriate surface realization（=textual-linguistic make-up）

governs

the strategies whereby a target text（or parts thereof）is derived from its original, and hence
the relationships which hold them together

图3—1 翻译功能、作品与过程之间的关系（同上，13）

"因此可以说，无论译者怎样设想译入文化的福利，他们的活动首先都是为此服务"①（同上，12）。不经意间，翻译研究的重心逐渐从源语文本转向译入文化，进而开启了目标导向（target-oriented）的系统论时代。

时至今日，描述性翻译研究的流派日益纷繁，伊塔马·埃文—佐哈（Itama Even-Zohar）的多元系统观；以吉恩·图里（Gideon Toury）、安德鲁·切斯特曼（Andre Chesterman）和西奥·赫曼斯（Theo Hermans）为代表的规范学派；及安德烈·勒菲弗尔（Andrew Lefevere）倡导的改写范式，等等，不一而足。他们将翻译描写成在权力博弈影响下受多元异质规范制约的改写行为，并与社会文化的动态演进密切联系。在很大程度上，翻译活动被视作社会文化活动（social-cultural activity）的组成部分，翻译研究亦理所当然地升华为社会文化研究，即巴斯内特和勒菲弗尔所谓的"文化转向"（cultural turn）（Bassnett & Lefevere，2001）。

尽管诸多学派的领军人物泰半以文学系统作为主要考察对象，却并未否认该研究路径对理解其他文化实践的有效性。或者借用赫曼斯的话说，

---

① 英语原文："Consequently，translators may be said to operate first and foremost in the interest of the culture into which they are translating，however they conceive of that interest."

文学翻译的研究"可以衍生出更广泛的适用领域"① （Hermans，2004：124）。笔者以为这尤其适合探求晚清半殖民地半封建社会背景下西法东渐活动对我国内政外交近代化进程的影响。

遭逢乱世，如果说和风细雨般的文学翻译对目标文化变革的影响尚属潜移默化，那么胜似地震海啸的法律翻译无疑是东西方社会制度的直接碰撞与冲击。从公法到宪政、从欧美到日本、从华洋合译到独担重任，缠绕法律翻译实践的漫长变迁，种种光怪陆离的现象相继粉墨登场，非借助描述性翻译研究的路径不能洞悉其中情非得已之尴尬窘境。

第一节　虚拟文化系统

毋庸赘言，描写本身并非自给自足，却是另有其服务的目标，这就要求将翻译现象放置具体情境（context）内进行考察。而虚拟的系统（system）概念之所以能在翻译研究的描写范式中居于核心地位，正因为它扮演的角色近似法国社会学家皮埃尔·布迪厄（Pierre Bourdieu，1930 – 2002）的术语"场域"（field）（Hermans，2004：131），且由探求相互关系的功能路径（functional approach）取代收集分析数据的实证主义（positivistic）传统：

> ... the positivistic collection of data, taken *bona fide* on empiricist grounds and analyzed on the basis of their material *substance*, has been replaced by a functional approach based on the analysis of *relations*. （Even-Zohar，2010：40）

一　动态功能主义：调节性平衡与历时性演进

佐哈标新立异地创设"多元系统"（polysystem）概念，旨在与瑞士语言学家费尔迪南·德·索绪尔（Ferdinand de Saussure，1857 – 1913）的"静态系统理论"（the theory of static system）相区别，凸显系统的动态功能主义（dynamic functionalism）属性，并由此导入描写范式的关键要

---

① 英语原文："... broader applications can be derived from it［the frame of reference which is primarily literary］."

素之一："时间序列"（time-succession）或"历时性"（diachrony）。

简明扼要地说，多元系统内各子系统的地位存在层级差异（hierar-chized）。层级之间的永恒张力（permanent tension）构成系统的共时状态（synchronic state）；层级之间的离心（centrifugal）或向心（centripetal）运动则顺应系统的历时轴（diachronic axis）方向。

若将特定社会文化视作多元系统，那么正是包括翻译在内的子系统间动态张力的调节性平衡（regulating balance）有效维护了该系统，并确保其持续演进：

> ... the dynamic tensions which operate within the culture for its effi-cient maintenance. This regulating balance is possibly manifested in the stratificational oppositions... guarantees the evolution of the "system," which, paradoxical as it may sound, is the only means of its preservation. (Ibid. 46)

反之，缺乏足够弹性和包容力的系统譬如晚清法律制度，便因竭力抗拒近代政治思潮而难免彻底崩溃，这同样体现在封建统治阶级对翻译活动所持的极端保守态度。

二 系统描写参数：二元对立概念的利弊权衡

故而研究者考察系统内部的运行机制，终南捷径便是借助佐哈提出的三组备受争议却依然令人难以割舍的对立概念（binary opposition），即经典化（canonized）与非经典化（non-canonized）、中心（center）与边缘（periphery）及"主要类型"（primary type）与"次要类型"（secondary type）。

（一）经典化与非经典化、中心与边缘

"经典化"与"非经典化"的划分，涉及相关形式库（repertoire）是否由特定社会文化的统治阶级接纳为合乎正统。因此，"经典性（canon-icity）并非任何层面上任何活动的本质特征，而是系统内部权力关系的产物"[1]（Even-Zohar，2010：46）。

---

① 英语原文："... canonicity is therefore no inherent feature of any activity on any level, but the outcome of power relations within a system. "

佐哈认为,"多元系统整体的中心等同于最具权威性的经典化形式库,因此最终决定特定形式库经典性的是掌控多元系统的群体。但凡其经典性得到确定,上述群体或坚守或修正已被经典化的属性,旨在维护自己的控制权。另外,如若两策尽皆失利,其他群体将通过经典化不同形式库,走向系统中心取而代之"①(同上,47)。尽管如此,我们仍需谨记经典化与否和中心或者边缘并非平行术语:

> While repertoire may be either canonized or non-canonized, the system to which a repertoire belongs may be either central or peripheral. (Ibid. 48)

譬如欧美国家虽然视华夏封建法制为没落的边缘系统,仍争相转译《大清律例》(详见第三章),只因它是该系统毋庸置疑的经典化形式库;馆译《万国公法》(详见第五章)和局译《各国交涉公法论》与《各国交涉便法论》(详见第六章)选择的亦是正在19世纪中国社会努力向心运动的近代西方法制系统中的权威文本。

(二)"主要类型"与"次要类型"

某种意义上,"主要类型"与"次要类型"的二元对立在描写范式中的有效性颇为可疑,甚至佐哈本人修改后于2004年再次发表的《多元系统理论》("Polysystem Theory")亦未重新提及。或许是因为类似划分很难摆脱"研究者自证预言"(the researcher's self-fulfilling prophecy)的嫌疑:

> Primary (i. e. innovative) is what the benefit of hindsight permits us retrospectively to label as primary. (Hermans, 2004: 119)

---

① 英语原文:"Accordingly, the center of the whole polysystem is identical with the most prestigious canonized repertoire. Thus, it is the group which governs the polysystem that ultimately determines the canonicity of a certain repertoire. Once canonicity has been determined, such a group either adheres to the properties canonized by it or alters the repertoire of canonized properties in order to maintain control. On the other hand, if unsuccessful in either the first or the second procedure, both the group and its canonized repertoire may eventually be pushed aside by some other group, which makes its way to the center by canonizing a different repertoire. "

即便如此，赫曼斯亦认可这组术语为系统注入了"推进历史发展的动力"（historical dynamism）（同上，118），因为它们专指"形式库里革新与保守的对立"（opposition of innovativeness vs. conservatism in the repertoire）（Even-Zohar，1990：21）。

然而具体到自成子系统的翻译活动，何种境遇下方能在文化多元系统的演进过程中发挥革旧鼎新的作用？佐哈曾就文学现象述及三种特殊情形：

> It seems to me that three major cases can be discerned，which are basically various manifestations of the same law：（a）when a polysystem has not yet been crystallized，that is to say，when a literature is "young," in the process of being established；（b）when a literature is either "peripheral" （within a large group of correlated literatures）or "weak," or both；and（c）when there are turning points，crises，or literary vacuums in a literature. （Ibid. 47）

显然，事后追溯式的价值判断亦有其特殊作用，只需将上述论断稍加拓展，即可用于说明笔者选择晚清法律翻译现象作为研究焦点的合理性：两次鸦片战争致使神州大陆逐渐沦落半殖民地，延绵数千年的封建法统暴露严峻危机，而救亡图存亟须的新兴法理思想尚未破茧，既柔弱且僻处边缘。恰是法律翻译得显身手之良机，社会文化系统内纵横交错的权力关系对译者决策的操纵亦必无限扩张。

三 综述

尽管多元系统下的"翻译被视为历史连续体中与其他实践相互作用的一种文化实践"①，但此研究路径"不仅过分抽象与非人格化，而且存

---

① 英语原文："Translation is recognized as a cultural practice interacting with other practices in a historical continuum. "

在极端确定性的危险倾向"① （Hermans，2004：118）：

> One is that polysystem theory is aware of the social embedding of cultural systems but in practice takes little heed of actual political and social power relations or more concrete entities such as institutions or groups with real interests to look after... The other reason follows from this. Polysystem theory invests heavily in classifications and correlations but shies away from speculating about the underlying causes of such phenomena as changes in genres, norms, and the concepts and collective practices of translation.

有鉴于此，笔者将随后探讨另两种更具操作性的描写范式：规范理论 （the norm theory） 和改写理论 （the rewriting theory）。

第二节 重构翻译规范

何谓规范？图里立足规范化行为的规律性 （regularity） 表象 （2001：55）；切斯特曼强调规范化行为的正确性 （correctness） 理念 （2012：54）；赫曼斯则更关注解释行为规范的深层机制 （underlying mechanism）：

> The mechanism is a psychological and social entity. It mediates between the individual and the collective, between the individual's intentions, choices and the interaction between people, more especially on the degree of coordination in a group, as the Venson case illustrate. （Hermans，2004：80）

换言之，规范承担着社会调节功能 （socially regulatory function），即增进行为的可预测性，从而稳定人际关系。因此，学者们普遍认同规范表现出人际间性 （intersubjectivity）。

---

① 英语原文："... studies of this nature are not only ferociously abstract and depersonalized, they also run the risk of being ultimately deterministic."

一　规范概念的折中性质

社会学领域的规范理论之所以吸引翻译研究者的目光，在于它的相对可选择性。无论图里的**规则**（rule）－规范－个人风格（idiosyncrasy）**模型**还是切斯特曼的**法律**（law）－规范－习惯（convention）**模型**，都尝试借助渐变的等级连续体（graded continuum）凸显规范概念的独特性。

就强制力而言，规范虽较法律（law）及规则（rule）逊色，却又不似习惯那般武断或随心所欲如同个人风格。法律规则必须遵循，习惯或个人风格却可任意抛弃。唯独规范作为正确性理念的社会现实（social reality），涉及交际参与者对重复情境（recurrent situations）下行为规律性的期待，故而既非绝对强制，更不是完全随意。

社会语境中的翻译活动需要调用规范来解决频繁发生的人际协调问题。或者顺延利维（Jiří Levý）将翻译视作决策过程的观点（2000：148—159），那么影响译者决策的重要因素就是行为规范。当然，规范的折中性质注定永远存在译者违背行为要求的可能性，只不过如此选择必有其特殊原因方为合理。

二　规范研究的描写特征

请特别注意，虽称规范性翻译研究（normative translation studies），其路径却是描述性的而非规定性（prescriptive）。依据 *Random House Compact Unabridged Dictionary* 提供的解释，"规范性"（normative）的含义如下（Flexner，1996：1322）：

1. of or pertaining to a norm, esp. an assumed norm regarded as the standard of correctness in behavior, speech, writing, etc.

2. tending or attempting to establish such a norm, esp. by the prescription of rules: *normative grammar.*

3. reflecting the assumption of such a norm or favoring its establishment: *a normative attitude.*

尽管上述引文中的第二项近似"规定性"，但该术语采纳的却是第一项定义，即"与规范相关的"（of or pertaining to a norm）。换言之，笔者探讨翻译规范,并无意为将来的翻译行为设定应然原则,而是通过描述特定历史时期的翻译现象,推定存在可供解释的规范,即所谓的"解释性假设"(explanatory hypothesis)(Toury,2001:59)。

也正因为如此,图里依据规范介入翻译过程的阶段差异及其在产品层面的折射划分类型,较之切斯特曼套用技术性框架的过程——产品标准,更符合笔者研究清末西法东渐的需要。毕竟,译者脑海中的认知机制在很大程度上仍然藏在深闺人难知,而最便于直接观察的基本信息来源还是作为产品的译文。唯虑图里单纯着眼译者决策的视角似乎有失偏颇,若能仿效切斯特曼引进其他交际参与者对翻译行为的期待,无疑能使翻译规范理论更臻圆满。故本节后续诠释的翻译规范,主要沿袭图里的理论模式,同时融合切斯特曼不乏真知灼见的观点。

三　规范调节的翻译范畴

探求描述性翻译研究路径,应首先界定研究对象,即翻译的范畴。就此而言,图里构建的"假定翻译"(assumed translation)概念无疑深具启发性。既称"假定翻译",自当包含假设条件(Toury,2001:33-35):

(1)原文本条件(The Source-Text Postulate)

"在其他文化/语言中存在另一文本,具有时间上和逻辑上的双重优先性,即不仅假定此假定文本在时间上先于被视作其翻译的文本,还假定它充任了后者的出发点和基础"[1]。

(2)转移条件(The Transfer Postulate)

"假定译文的形成过程涉及从假定原文本中转移特定特征,该特征现为两者所共享"[2]。

(3)关系条件(The Relationship Postulate)

"某文本是译文,还意味着存在将之与其假定原文联结在一起的

---

[1]　英语原文:"... the assumption that there is another text, in another culture/language, which has both chronological and logical priority over it: not only has such an assumed text assumedly preceded the one taken to be its translation in time, but it is also presumed to have served as a departure point and basis for the latter."

[2]　英语原文:"... the process whereby the assumed translation came into being involved the transference from the assumed source text of certain features that the two now share."

可以解释的关系，存在两个文本声称共有的显著功能，并认为该功能跨越文化符号（语言）的界限发生了转移"①。

值得注意的是，译文与原文之间所谓"可以解释的关系"（accountable relationships）本质上存在难以消除的模糊性，这进而促使切斯特曼转向更简捷的方案——"最低限度仅要求某文本被称作译文，且该文本在目的文化中被（客户和/或读者）认定为译文：即被认定符合通行翻译规范"②（Chesterman，2012：62）。

仅凭字里行间仿佛绕口令的繁复措辞，便不难觉察研究者们正竭力与按照预设的应然原则对译文属性进行价值判断的传统路径保持距离。描述性研究立足目的文化对译者的信任，假设特定文本属翻译作品，即假设该文本符合相关先决条件。如此倒置逻辑关系，极大地拓展了承载社会文化意义的翻译范畴，伪翻译（pseudo-translation）等边缘情状亦可囊而括之。

基于上述理念，笔者在本书的讨论中毫不犹豫地将魏源的《海国图志》（1842）、梁廷枏的《海国四说》（1846）、徐继畲的《瀛寰志略》（1848）及王韬的《法国志略》（1871）等纳入考察西法东渐的视野范围。上述著作虽由国人编撰成册而后通行海内，所涉内容多数无法考证源语资料的详尽出处，却仍可推定必有先行原文、必有特征转移、必有相似关系，立足接受文化进行描写正可谓恰如其分。

或许更进一步，晚清时期恰逢东西方法律文化碰撞的初始阶段，借调华夏传统法言法语表述欧美近代资本主义法律思想，其结果在现代学者看来必然粗鄙疏阔。比比皆是增删并改的早期译作，难免与主流翻译的典型形象大相径庭。不过，既然无须斤斤计较译文与原文的相关性（relevance）或近似性（similarity）程度，又何必分门别类？大可以改写的名目，统而视之，坐而论道。

---

① 英语原文："... the assumption that a text is a translation also implies that there are accountable relationships which ties it to its assumed original, an obvious function of that which the two texts allegedly share and which is taken to have been transferred across the cultural-semiotic (and linguistic) border."

② 英语原文："The minimum requirement is simply that a text is claimed to be a translation, and that it is accepted (by the client and/or the readers) as a translation in the target culture: it is accepted as conforming to the prevalent translation norms."

四　翻译规范的类型划分及其多重变异

图里按照翻译过程中规范发挥调节功能的阶段差异及其在产品层面上的反映将之划分成预备规范（preliminary norm）和操作规范（operational norm），辅之以起始规范（initial norm）充当解释性工具（explanatory tool）。而切斯特曼的翻译规范体系，依据过程—产品标准将预备阶段以外的其他规范重组为期待规范（expectancy norm）与职业规范（professional norm）。

实际上，过程与产品是密不可分的，任何过程都将导向产品，任何产品均由过程造就。仅此而言，起始规范与期待规范构成整体层面的过程——产品关系，职业规范与操作规范则构成细节层面的过程——产品关系。抽象层面的规范解释并决定细节层面的规范。简言之，翻译规范的功能无非是为"翻译什么"（what to translate）和"怎么翻译"（how to translate）的问题提供"解释性假设"。

（一）翻译什么（what to translate）

图里将有关翻译什么的规范称为预备规范，主要由相互联系的两类因素构成（Toury，2001：58）：

> （1）翻译政策（translation policy）
> 规范特定时期文本类型乃至个体文本的选译。
> （2）翻译的直接性（directness of translation）
> 规范直接从原文翻译抑或从另一种语言间接转译。

（二）如何翻译（how to translate）

1. 整体层面：起始规范与期待规范

鉴于典型的翻译行为至少牵涉两种语言、两种文化传统，或者说两套规范系统（norm-system），译文体现的价值亦具有双重性（同上，56）：

> （1）being a text in a certain language，and hence occupying a position，or filling in a slot，in the appropriate culture，or in a certain section thereof；

（2）constituting a representation in that language/culture of another, pre-existing text in some other language, belonging to some other culture and occupying a definite position within it.

尽管对应价值体系的亲缘关系远近有别，差异却是普遍存在的，并由此导致兼容性的相对缺失。译者必须作出抉择：或遵从源语文化规范；或遵从目的语文化规范，而影响译者决策的因素即构成起始规范。这与发端德国哲学家弗里德里希·施莱尔马赫（Friedrich Schleiermacher，1768 - 1843）的异化（alienation）/归化（familiarization）翻译方法，名虽不同，理则近似：要么尽量不打扰作者，而将读者移近作者；要么尽量不打扰读者，而将作者移近读者。

图里称前者为"充分性"（adequacy），称后者为"可接受性"（acceptability），但更常见的翻译策略是游移两极之间进行适当调和。当然，即便是最极端的充分翻译也难免对原文本的变动。或许正是在此意义上，勒菲弗尔称一切翻译无非改写。

若将观察的视角转换成目标文化接受者，那么切斯特曼的期待规范概念便有用武之地。期待规范属产品规范（product norm），即目的语读者群期待的译文应当是怎样的：

Expectancy norms are established by the expectations of readers of a translation (of a given type) concerning what a translation (of this type) should be like. (Chesterman, 2012: 64)

期待形成的基础是文本类型（text type），由此朱丽安·豪斯（Juliane House）对"隐性翻译"（covert translation）和"显性翻译"（overt translation）的功能区分（1981）亦被再次提及：特定时期特定社会文化中的读者是否期待特定类型的译文与本国非翻译形成的同类文本之间存在差异，构成了隐性与显性的界限。

那么我们是否可以继续推断，正是译文潜在读者群的期待影响译者对翻译策略的抉择？换言之，起始规范与期待规范是相同问题的两个方面：前者调节过程，后者掌控产品；规范化的过程必然导向规范化的产品，译者的决策与读者的预期遥相呼应。

2. 细节层面：操作规范与职业规范

图里定义的操作规范，"指导翻译行为实施过程中的决策"[①]（Toury, 2001: 58 – 59）：

（1）结构规范（matricial norm）

调控译文的宏观层面，涉及翻译的完整程度（the degree of full-ness of translation）、实际分布形式（the form of actual distribution）和文本章节安排（textual segmentation）。

（2）文本—语言规范（textual-linguistic norm）

调控译文的微观层面，涉及遣词造句、修辞格乃至斜体、黑体、大小写等表示强调的方式。

显然，其论述着眼规范在译入文本宏观或微观层面的折射。至于特定时期特定社会文化中的操作规范究竟包含哪些内容，则属解释性假设的范畴，正是运用规范理论分析具体翻译作品的研究者所要探求的。切斯特曼在这方面做出了初步努力。他于职业规范的概念下提出三项高阶过程规范，或者说"调节过程，指出实施行为的正确或优越方法"[②]（Chesterman, 2012: 55, 68 – 69）：

（1）责任规范（the accountability norm）：译者的行为应适当地满足忠实性要求，忠实于原著作者、翻译委托人、译者本人、预期读者及任何其他相关当事人。[③]

（2）交际规范（the communication norm）：译者的行为应根据情景的要求优化所有相关当事人之间的交际活动。[④]

（3）关系规范（the relation norm）：译者的行为应构建并维持原

---

① 英语原文："... directing the decisions made during the act of translation itself."

② 英语原文："... regulate processes, specifying correct or good methods for doing something."

③ 英语原文："The *accountability norm*: a translator should act in such a way that the demands of loyalty are appropriately met with regard to the original writer, the commissioner of the translation, the translator himself or herself, the prospective readership and any other relevant parties."

④ 英语原文："The *communication norm*: a translator should act in such a way as to optimize communication, as required by the situation, between all the parties involved."

文本与目的文本之间适当的相关性和近似性。①

3. 综述

图里定义的起始规范只是"解释性工具（explanatory tool）"：取归化策略提升翻译的可接受性；取异化策略提升翻译的充分性。因其逻辑上的先在性，足以指导译者选择具体的操作规范，进而掌控译文的宏观与微观层面。换言之，译者遵循特定操作规范改写原文，正是为了实现翻译行为的可接受性或充分性，或者加以折中妥协。

（三）多重性与变异性

无论图里抑或切斯特曼，都承续了佐哈的多元系统观。他们认为翻译规范同样具有多重性（multiplicity）的普遍特征，并借用系统描写参数阐释"主流（mainstream）/时髦（trendy）"、"先前（previous）/过时（old-fashioned）"、"新潮（new）/先进（progressive）"三类规范同时并存的现象：

> Therefore, it is not all that rare to find side by side in a society three types of competing norms, each having its own followers and a position of its own in the culture at large: the ones that dominate the center of the system, and hence direct translational behavior of the so-called *mainstream*, alongside the remnants of *previous* sets of norms and the rudiments of *new* ones, hovering in the periphery. This is why it is possible to speak—and not derogatorily—of being 'trendy', 'old-fashioned' or 'progressive' in translation (or in any single section thereof) as it is in any other behavioral domain. (Toury, 2001: 62 – 63)

上述概念本身就暗示了语境化（contextualization）的异质规范存在历时轴方向的动态转变：往日流行的规范也许现在已经过时，眼前新潮的规范也许将来成为时髦。

---

① 英语原文："The *relation norm*: a translator should act in such a way that an appropriate relation of relevant similarity is established and maintained between the source text and the target text."

五　重构规范对晚清法律翻译研究的作用

图里不仅立足规范在译作各层面的反映划分其类型，而且视翻译行为的产品是可直接加以观察的主要信息来源，并据此重构翻译规范，为现象提供解释性假设（同上，65）：

（1）textual：the translated texts themselves，for all kinds of norms，as well as analytical inventories of translations（i. e.，'virtual'texts），for various preliminary norms；

（2）extratextual：semi-theoretical or critical formulations，such as prescriptive'theories'of translation，statements made by translators，editors，publishers，and other persons involved in or connected with the activity，critical appraisals of individual translations，or the activity of a translator or'school'of translators，and so forth.

本书描写晚清法律翻译的历时性演变正是沿袭此思路推进，选择各重要历史节点的经典作品，着眼"翻译什么"和"怎样翻译"两个问题展开研究。而笔者引作依据的当然只能是译文本身及包括译者序言在内的规范申明（normative pronouncement）。

预备规范的多重性和变异性是探求的重要焦点。19 世纪中期的清王朝在国家层面上确立了译介公法的政策，西法东渐毫无争议地构成主流预备规范（详见第五、六章）；及至 20 世纪初的黄金年代，翻译对象逐步过渡至宪政方面的著作，且多从日文转译欧美法学典籍，此变化与其背后隐藏的社会文化制约因素显然值得我们思考（详见第七章）。

同样进入视野中心的还有寻求迥异文化公度性的翻译规范。譬如袁德辉受林则徐所托摘译《万民法》时为何只选商品进口例禁与违禁、外商属地管辖原则（第一百七十二条）、战争的发动及其决定权（第二百九十二条）等寥寥数款（详见第四章）？《各国交涉公法论》又为什么被指割裂原文卷帙（详见第六章）？

目标文本的宏观结构及微观表述当然是归化或异化决策的体现，但动态流转的规范体系究竟如何操纵译者貌似自由的行为？仅从规律性、正确性、读者期待或增进可预测性加以解释，似乎仍是隔靴搔痒。只有继续深入社会文化场域,方能追溯权力博弈关系。

第三节　追溯权力关系

在描述性研究框架中,规范被设定为解释现象的假设。这并不意味着规范内容虚无缥缈,只是其表现形式未曾如同法律那般明确成文。有鉴于此,我们必然要追问,规范既非率性武断,那又因何成型?又因何流变?为什么往日流行的现已过时?为什么眼前时髦的转眼消逝?究竟是哪些要素共同作用,决定了边缘与核心形式库的此长彼消?

欲探求上述问题的答案,我们很有必要将规范放置系统中整体考察它们之间的关系。然而恰如赫曼斯所言,多元系统的理论架构为实现普遍适用性的目标,刻意抽象文化行为,尽量使之非人格化(Hermans,2004:118)。毋庸置疑,人是一切社会文化活动都不可或缺的重要因素,因而任何脱离人的考察,都不可能深刻洞悉社会现象的本质。

正是在此背景下,勒弗菲尔的改写范式应运而生。他试图从意识形态(ideology)和诗学形态(poetology)的双重维度完善系统的控制机制(control mechanism)或文化逻辑(logic of culture)——意识形态制约系统外部的互动;诗学形态制约系统内部的组织:

> One control factor belongs squarely within the literary system; the other is to be found outside of that system. The first factor tries to control the literary system from the inside with the parameters set by the second factor. (Lefevere,2004:14)

诗学形态受制意识形态,正如专业人士亦受赞助人掣肘。更兼本书主要关注晚清法律翻译活动折射的权力博弈轨迹,旨在洞悉法律系统与其他社会系统之间的关系变迁,因而下文着重意识形态方面的论述,这也是勒弗菲尔案例分析的核心。

一　社会文化意识形态

(一)社会文化环境

宽泛意义上,"社会可以被视作各种系统的组合,文学只是其中

之一"① （Hermans，2004：126），法律亦无例外。借鉴俄国形式主义
（Russian formalism）层级观，包罗万象的社会文化正位于结构顶端，而文
学、法律等皆为其子系统（subsystem）：

> Literature，to go back to the description of the Russian formalist theo-
> rists，is one of the systems that constitute the "complex 'system of sys-
> tems'" know as a culture. Alternatively，a culture，a society is the envi-
> ronment of a literary system. （Lefevere，2004：14）

显然，翻译学家眼中的文化常与社会同行，或者说承载着人类学意
义，指向人类生活受社会调节的各个方面。至于其具体范畴，玛丽·斯内
尔—霍恩比（Mary Snell-Hornby）更有鞭辟入里的评述：

> ...firstly，the concept of culture as a totality of knowledge，profi-
> ciency and perception；secondly，its immediate connection with behaviour
> （or action）and events，and thirdly，its dependence on expectations and
> norms，whether those of social behaviour or those accepted in language us-
> age. （Snell-Hornby，2001：40）

（二）意识形态制约

特定社会乃文化实践的环境，而调节子系统与其环境之间关系或子系
统间动态张力的机制主要是通过"意识形态"发挥作用的。

所谓"意识形态"，即"关于社会应当（允许社会）是怎样的主流概
念"② （Lefevere，2004：14）。它是子系统外部对具体文化实践的制约，
因此可以从规范力（modality of normative force）的角度进行理解。而潜藏
在意识形态背后的则是各种权力关系的博弈，这种权力关系的一端联结着
赞助人；另一端则联结着译者等专业人士。当然，勒弗菲尔的权力观应当
从迈克尔·福柯（Michel Foucault，1926–1984）的视角加以理解。

---

① 英语原文："The broad idea is that society can be viewed as a conglomerate of systems，of
which literature is one."

② 英语原文："...of what society should （be allowed to）be—ideology."

What makes power hold good, what makes it accepted, is simply the
fact that it doesn't only weigh on us as a force that says no, but that it trav-
erses and produces things, it induces pleasure, forms knowledge, produces discourse. (Foucault, 1980: 119)

二　赞助人与译者

(一) 赞助人 (patron)

勒弗菲尔在文学系统的框架下研究翻译，故将特定社会文化视作文学
系统所处的环境，而赞助人被理解为 "能够促进或妨碍文学阅读、创作
和改写的权力主体（个人、机构）"① (Lefevere, 2004: 15)，他们关注文
学系统的意识形态多过诗学，并依靠专业人士使文学系统符合自己的意识
形态（同上）。

其理论架构显然具有更宽泛的适用性 (Hermans, 2004: 124)。为
此，我们不妨对 "赞助人" 作如下界定：掌握权力的个人 (person) 或团
队 (group of persons)，试图调节构成社会文化的子系统之间的关系。

尽管赞助人最感兴趣的是意识形态，但经济利益 (economic component) 与社会地位 (status component) 也是重要的制约因素。三者总是以
某种形式的组合相互作用 (interact in various combinations)，或者说它们
可能是无差别的 (undifferentiated) 也可能是有差别的 (differentiated)：

Patronage is undifferentiated when its three components, the ideol-og-
ical, the economic, and the status components, are all dispensed by one
and the same person... Patronage is differentiated, on the other hand,
when economic success is relatively independent of ideological factors, and
does not necessarily bring status with it... (Lefevere, 2004: 17)

在无差别赞助的系统中，赞助人主要致力于维护社会系统整体的稳定
性；但若赞助有差别，文化产品的受众亦将相应地分裂成具有不同需求的
群体。尽管系统倾向保守，可很多情况下环境促成变革的发生。

---

① 英语原文："... it (patronage) will be understood to mean something like the powers (persons, institutions) that can further or hinder the reading, writing, and rewriting of literature."

Change is a function of the need felt in the environment of a... system for that system to be or remain functional... If a... system resists change altogether, it is likely to collapse under growing pressure from its environment as soon as a differentiation of patronage sets in, usually under social conditions analogous to those prevailing in the West European Enlightenment state or when a certain type of patronage is superseded by another one, radically different in nature. (Ibid. 23 – 24)

然而无论保守抑或变革,其目标都是一致的——"掌握权力的阶层想要控制特定文化建构的权威神话,因为这是他们的权力基础"① (同上,17)。

若以晚清法律翻译为例,皇朝集权统治看似波澜不惊。实际上,统治阶层内部亦有保守与改良的派别之争,只瞧官方主要翻译机构京师同文馆与沪局翻译馆的筹建过程之曲折便可知端倪。华洋合译使得问题更为复杂,中方译员的意识形态、经济利益乃至社会地位当然与朝廷休戚相关;然而英美译员虽接受我国政府的薪金,知识结构却深受西方世界的影响,权势地位更在两可之间。这无疑就牵涉译者本人的选择。

(二) 译者

赫曼斯认为译者代表权力关系的另一方面 (Hermans, 2004: 130)。"事实上,赞助人依靠这些专业人士使……系统符合其意识形态"② (Lefevere, 2004: 15 – 16)。有鉴于此,译者的政治可靠性与忠诚度 (political reliability and loyalty) 至关重要。无论在社会系统发展的任何历史阶段,专业人士只有亲近占据主导地位的赞助人的意识形态才可能代表"现行正统"(reigning orthodoxy)(同上)。

这在直接交流途径有限时表现得尤为突出。毫无疑问,正是改写决定了异域文化的"面貌"(image)(Hermans, 2004: 128);或者说译者自

---

① 英语原文:"... 'the authoritative myths of a given cultural formation' with which those in power want to control because their power is based on them."

② 英语原文:"In fact, the patron(s) count on these professionals to bring the... system in line with their own ideology."

愿或被迫接受的意识形态影响其交际策略：

> . . . the translator's ideology（whether he/she willingly embraces it, or whether it is imposed on him/her as a constraint by some form of patronage）. . . The ideology dictates the basic strategy the translator is going to use and therefore also dictates solutions to problems concerned with both the "universe of discourse" expressed in the original（objects, concepts, customs belonging to the world that was familiar to the writer of the original）and the language the original itself is expressed in.（Lefevere, 2004：41）

无论怎样，翻译系统只是一系列针对读者、作者、改写者的"制约因素"（constraint），仅起调节作用，而非绝对不可挑战：

> Lefevere emphasizes that constraints are conditioning factors, not absolutes. Individuals can choose to go with or against them. Translators, too, can decide to defer to the powers that be, or foment opposition, be it poetic or political. Because translation means importation of goods from beyond the system's boundaries, it is always potentially subversive, which is why it tends to be heavily regulated.（Hermans, 2004：128 – 129）

若恰逢罕有人精通外语之际，譬如十八九世纪之交的英国、晚清时代的中国等，控制译者的活动，也就意味着信息与知识的垄断。官方译书机构如京师同文馆、沪局翻译馆等的设立，重要意义还在钳制思想，其作用已不仅限于出版审查，而是直接掌控信息来源、操纵知识传递。

三　替换视角：布迪厄社会学理论

皮埃尔·布迪厄（Pierre Bourdieu, 1930 – 2002）的社会学理论日益引起翻译学家的瞩目，只因其术语体系特别是"场域"（field）和"惯习"（habitus），与描述性翻译研究路径颇有契合之处，可借以加深我们对系统、规范及权力等概念的把握。

（一）场域

何谓"场域"？编辑出版布迪厄论文集《文化生产场域》（*The Field of Cultural Production*）的兰德尔·约翰逊（Randal Johnson）曾有以下评述①（1993：6）：

> According to Bourdieu's theoretical model, any social formation is structured by way of a hierarchically organized series of fields (the economic field, the educational field, the political field, the cultural field, etc.), each defined as a structured space with its own laws of functioning and its own relations of force independent of those of politics and the economy, except, obviously, in the cases of the economic and political fields. Each field is relatively autonomous but structurally homologous with the others. Its structure, at any given moment, is determined by the relations between the positions agents occupy in the field. A field is a dynamic concept in that a change in agents' positions necessarily entails a change in the field's structure.
>
> The formulation of the notion of field also represented an attempt to apply what Bourdieu, borrowing from Cassirer, calls a relational mode of thought to cultural production. This requires a break with the ordinary or substantialist perception of the social world in order to see each element in terms of its relationships with all other elements in a **system** from which it derives its meaning and function.

上述引文至少说明了"场域"概念的数项核心特征：

（1）场域作为结构化的空间，拥有独立的功能法则与力量关系；

（2）场域间层级组织，共同构成社会形态；

（3）场域间相对独立，又存在结构性相似；

（4）关系决定结构；关系变更决定结构演进。

尽管布迪厄自称并非系统论者（Hermans，2004：131），有关"场域"属性的简单勾勒，足以表明其与"系统"之间的亲缘关系，难怪约

①　粗体由本书作者添加。

翰逊解析"场域"概念时，最终还是不自觉地借助"系统"术语。

（二）惯习：规范

至于"惯习"，则指"持久的、可转换的潜在行为倾向系统"①（Bour-dieu，1990：53）：

> The *habitus*, a product of history, produces individual and collective practices—more history—in accordance with the schemes generated by history. It ensures the active presence of past experiences, which, deposited in each organism in the form of schemes of perception, thought and action, tend to guarantee the '**correctness**' of practices and their constancy over time, more reliably than all formal rules and explicit norms. This system of dispositions-a present past that tends to perpetuate itself into the future by reactivation in similarly structured practices, an internal law through which the law of external necessities, irreducible to immediate constraints, is constantly exerted—the principle of the **continuity** and **regularity** which objectivism sees in social practices without being able to account for it; and also of the regulated transformations that cannot be explained either by the extrinsic, instantaneous determinisms of mechanistic sociologism or by the purely internal but equally instantaneous determination of spontaneist subjectivism. ②（Ibid. 54）

布迪厄将"惯习"理解成历史的产物，按照历史生成的图式，产生个人与集体的实践。它能够确保实践的"正确性"（correctness），遵循"持续性"（continuity）与"规律性"（regularity）的原则。仅此而言，"惯习"与"规范"的差异似乎仅限于运行机制：

> Being a 'subject-grounded category', the habitus idea should prove useful to researchers interested in the translation process as such and to those in favour of paying more attention to real-life translators and their

──────────

① 理查德·奈斯（Richard Nice）英译本："...a system of durable, transposable dispositions..."

② 粗体由本书作者添加。

working environments than to impersonal norm systems...they（norms）
may be better suited to explain how translations fare once they leave the
translator's desk and, more broadly, to explicate historical concepts of
translation.（Hermans，2004：135）

值得一提的是，布迪厄的"惯习（habitus）"术语还可用于解释译者
的自主性——翻译行为的惯习具有"建构"（structuring）与"被建构"
（structured）的双重属性：

Just as following a norm reinforces that norm, submissive translators
play into the hands of custom and order. The reverse side of this coin is that
translators can govern norms as much as they are governed by them.
（Ibid. 134）

四　小结

比利时鲁汶天主教大学（Catholic University of Leuven）的何塞·兰博
特（Jose Lambert）曾在《法律翻译的身份与地位：社会话语构建的重要
篇章》（"The Status and Position of Legal Translation：a Chapter in the Discursive Construction of Societies"）中提出一系列相关问题发人深省（Lam-
bert，2009：78 – 79）：

On the basis of the paradox（es）noted so far, I would like to list additional questions that deserve to be part of any research（programme）on
law and language：

● what kind of language register is selected/in use/accepted as the
language of legal discourse, in any constitutional environment（and
where, when exactly；why, etc.）？

● to what extent is the language of legislation the result of translation
（and can it be recognized as translated discourse or not？）？ Is it 'visible'
（Venuti 1995）？

● to what extent are given legislations（in any society）dependent on
import/export operations, and how/why exactly？

● are the visible features of imported/translated texts experienced as part of the political power games, as part of colonial planning and organization (Lambert 1995), either at the very moment of their distribution (in synchronic terms) or afterwards (in diachronic terms)?

● how parallel was the dissemination of legal texts into a large number of languages in Central Europe, first in the case of Marxist models (from the Soviet Union), then in the case of the EU?

● to what extent are constitutions worldwide (now) submitted to international innovation and to globalization, how exactly does this work, and is this verbal internationalization experienced by the user as a chapter of another colonization?

兰博特教授批评传统研究总是千方百计地将工具性翻译行为简化成大多仅与译者相关的数量有限的问题。事实恰恰相反，法律翻译甚至经常就社会规划承担着积极的组织功能。这无疑是对笔者沿描述性研究路径探讨晚清西法东渐现象的最佳注脚：

The question of translation is well known to lawyers and theoreticians, it is even part of the curriculum, the training package of future lawyers. However it tends to be approached in a strongly reductionist way, it is generally speaking approached as a 'tool', as a service. And scholars dealing with translation as part of the (very young) discipline called 'translation studies' often tend to do the same: having entered translation studies via translation training (hence via business entries), as happens to be the case, they also tend to reduce 'the question' of translation to a few limited questions, mainly linked with the perspective of the translator. It will be shown that the translation issue (and the language issue) cannot be reduced to a few limited perspectives, neither in modern times nor in the study of the past. And it will become clear that translation often plays an active and organizational role in the planning of societies. Societies often seem to start first as 'discourse', and in the planning of new discursive communities, translations seem to have often played a central role from the very beginning. This may tend to be more the case in modern times and in the era of communication societies and global/virtual societies. (Ibid. 76 – 77)

五　权力博弈中的晚清法律翻译研究纲要

本书关注晚清法律及其语言近代转型过程中光怪陆离的西法东渐现象。虽则如此，笔者首先考察的却是小斯当东英译本《大清律例》，只因这部鸦片战争前夕出版发行的著作较为全面地反映了 19 世纪欧美列强对华夏传统理念有失偏颇的诠释。序幕既启，林则徐组织选译的《各国律例》；馆译《万国公法》及《公法便览》；局译《各国交涉公法论》与《各国交涉便法论》；翰墨林印书局编译的《英国国会史》等亦将相继粉墨登场。这些极具代表性的译作都是权力场内意识形态博弈的产物，有的甚至在某种程度上激化战争爆发或扭曲战争进程，也有丧权辱国后意欲和平外交、借法自强的策略考虑。囿于时代局限性的意识形态制约译者及其赞助人代表各利益集团的改写行为，实际折射的全然是争权夺利的尔虞我诈，当然折冲退让难以避免，否则亦不容合译的法律经典通行神州大地卷起千层浪。

第 四 章
开启序幕:英译《大清律例》

导 言

乔治·汤姆司·斯当东从男爵（Sir George Thomas Staunton, 2nd Baronet，世人常称"小斯当东"）的英译本精装巨著《大清律例》（*Ta Tsing Leu Lee*; being the fundamental laws, and a selection from the supplementary statutes, of the penal code of china），是西方最早最完整的中华成文法译作。1810 年（嘉庆十五年）在伦敦出版后，立即引起欧美诸国朝野轰动，不久便转介法、德、西班牙等多种语言，成为当时研究满清社会政治经济制度的最佳文献。

《大清律例》乃我国封建时代最后一部传世法典，其编撰工作始于满洲贵族定鼎中原之初。顺治三年（1646 年）五月，即秉承"详译明律，参以国制，增损剂量，期于平允"① 的原则，修成《大清律集解附例》，次年刊布中外。

康熙十八年（1679 年）九月十四日，又以"律例繁简"须"因时制宜"② 故，"特谕刑部将定律之外所有条例，应去应存，详加酌定"③，纂修刊刻《现行则例》。康熙二十八年（1689 年）载入大清律条例内。

雍正元年（1723 年），"念律例一书为用刑之本，其中条例繁多，如不校订画一，有司援引断狱，得以意为轻重"④，复命"于应增应减之处再行详加分析"⑤。雍正三年（1725 年）奏定，五年（1727 年）刊成，

---

① 详见《钦定四库全书·大清律例·世祖章皇帝御制大清律原序》。
② 详见《钦定四库全书·大清律例·圣祖仁皇帝上谕》。
③ 详见《钦定四库全书·大清律例·律例馆总裁臣三泰等谨查》。
④ 详见《钦定四库全书·大清律例·世宗宪皇帝上谕》。
⑤ 详见《钦定四库全书·大清律例·律例馆总裁臣三泰等谨查》。

六年（1728 年）颁行《大清律集解》。

高宗即位后，特命三泰为律例馆总裁，对顺治、康熙、雍正各朝原有律文"逐条考证，重加编辑"，"又详校定例"，折中损益，并"亲加鉴定"[①]。乾隆五年（1740 年）揆成新律，定名为《钦定大清律例》，正式"刊布内外，永远遵行"[②]。

《钦定大清律例》修订律文四百三十六门，作为"祖宗成宪"，不可变动，只可酌改条例。至此，清代最系统、最具代表性的基本法典方才定型。

小斯当东所译《大清律例》，选用的虽是嘉庆初年颁行的中文原版，但这些后续重订的版本均以《钦定大清律例》为底本。

第一节　主题与文本

透过多元系统的视角，描写《大清律例》的英译过程及其折射的权力博弈，应首先考察主题的确定与文本的甄选，即分析究竟是哪些社会文化因素综合决定了"翻译什么"（what to be translated）。笔者以为，这个问题的探讨绝不能脱离英国争夺海外贸易霸权的时代背景，然后结合赞助人的超商业意图解读译者序言（Translator's Preface），必将赋予我们相当启示。

一　译入文化的主导意识形态
——光荣革命以来英国社会经济面貌及其对海外市场的需求

1688 年的光荣革命在英国近代史册中具有继往开来的划时代意义：上承源自 17 世纪中叶的政治革命；下启始于 18 世纪中叶的工业革命。

（一）自由市场思想与海外贸易霸权

议会君主制度最终得以确立，奠定资产阶级的法治基石。牛顿代表的科学运动则催生瓦特等发明家不断技术创新，通过机器生产推进纺织、造船等行业蓬勃发展。

---

① 详见《钦定四库全书·大清律例·律例馆总裁臣三泰等谨查》。

② 同上。

图4—1　小斯当东译《大清律例》所附插图

即便如此，"英国经济的特征仍然是贸易而不是工业"（摩根主编，1993：445）。至少某种程度上，这应归因于倡导新重商主义的苏格兰经济学家亚当·斯密（Adam Smith）在《国民财富的性质和原因的研究》①（*An Inquiry into the Nature and Causes of the Wealth of Nations*）中充分缜密地论证了低关税自由贸易思想，令名流政要尽折腰。

疆域狭窄的不列颠群岛为寻觅工业产品的倾销地，亟须开拓海外市场。战争亦是欲达目标不可或缺的手段。尤其17世纪以来绵延至18世纪末的历次英荷战争，逐渐摧毁素有"海上马车夫"之称的传统殖民强国荷兰的航运业，其东方贸易霸权地位也只能拱手让予大英帝国。

重新划分欧洲列强在亚洲的势力范围已在所难免——荷属东印度公司日益丧失主导地位，取而代之的是英属东印度公司（British East India Company，以下简称BEIC）。从此，英国将长远目光投向中国。英国渴望广袤的市场，而中国正符合其理想：

Translator's Preface

The communications between European states and the dominions of China, which a spirit of commercialenterprise gave rise to, although they have been, at times, of considerable importance to several of the Continental nations, and are at present, with respect to Great Britain, of such a nature and extent, as to be very essentially contributive to her national prosperity... (Staunton, 1810: vii)

（二）中英贸易摩擦

出乎英国人意料的是，清政府不仅长期严控对外贸易，至乾隆年间由于中欧贸易经常诉诸武力，更逐渐演变成主要针对英、荷等国的闭关政策。乾隆二十二年十一月初十日（1757年12月20日），撤宁波、泉州、

---

①　郭大力、王亚南译。1930年初版译名为《国富论》，1972年再版时更名《国民财富的性质和原因的研究》。

松江三海关，晓谕"番商将来只许在广东收泊交易"①。乾隆二十四年
（1759 年），又准两广总督李侍尧进呈的《防范外夷规条》，全面管制
外商。

　　"一口通商"的局面使得英国输出的羊毛、呢绒等工业制品因缺乏有
效的销售渠道而无法融入中国市场。此外，中国还向英国商品抽取百分之
二十的高昂税率，海关官僚的腐败又滋生大量难以预料的额外费用，此所
谓"听税关人员随意估价"（马戛尔尼，2006：156），遂导致双边贸易巨
额逆差。

　　不列颠人认为他们的地位受到歧视，"毫无自由贸易可言"（马士，
1991：99），要求清政府增开商埠、减免课税，这也成为英国朝野的普遍
共识。于是，就有了 1793 年乔治·马戛尔尼伯爵（George Macartney，1st
Earl Macartney）率团访华之举，其用意在英王乔治三世（King George Ⅲ）
致马戛尔尼特使的私人指示内表露无遗，即恳请中国皇帝保护英商的
利益②。

---

　　① 出自《乾隆二十二年丁丑十一月戊戌》，详见《高宗纯皇帝实录》卷五五〇。《清实录》
第一五册，中华书局影印，第 1023 页。

　　② 据《英使谒见乾隆纪实》（*An Authentic Account of and Embassy from the King of Great Britain
to the Emperor of China*）第一卷第二章记载，英王乔治三世遣国务大臣向马戛尔尼特使转达的私
人指示原文如下："... a greater number of his subjects，than of any other Europeans，had been
trading，for a considerable time past，in China；that the commercial intercourse between several other nations and that great empire had been preceded，accompanied，or followed，by special communications
with its sovereign. Others had the support of missionaries，who，from their eminence in science，or inge-
nuity in the arts，had been frequently admitted to the familiarity of a curious and polished court，and
which missionaries，in the midst of their cares for the propagation of their faith，were not supposed to have
been unmindful of the views and interest of their country；while the English traders remained unaided，
and as it were，unavowed，at a distance so remote as to admit of a misrepresentation of the national character and importance；and where，too，their occupation was not held in that esteem，which might be
necessary to procure them safety and respect... under these circumstances，it become the dignity and character of his Majesty to extend his paternal regard to these his distant subjects，even if the commerce and
prosperity of the nation were not concerned in their success；and to claim the Emperor of China's protection
for them，with that weight which is due to the requisition of one great sovereign from another..." （Staun-
ton，1797：（V1）53 - 54）。

（三）英国使团访华

乾隆五十八年八月初十日（1793 年 9 月 14 日），马戛尔尼在承德避暑山庄万树园觐见皇帝。据其日记①陈述，"吾等曲一膝以为礼"（马戛尔尼，2006：100）。至十三日乾隆皇帝 83 岁万寿之期，马戛尔尼及其随从"仍依往例曲一膝为礼"，"其余大小华官咸向乾隆皇帝行叩首之礼……凡三跪九叩而礼毕"（同上，120）。

皇帝启跸回銮后，马戛尔尼代表英国提议互派使臣，并向清廷转呈六事（同上，155—156）：

第一，请中国允许英国商船在珠山、宁波、天津等处登岸，经营商业。

第二，请中国按照从前俄国商人在中国通商之例，允许英国商人在北京设一洋行，买卖货物。

第三，请于珠山附近划一未经设防之小岛归英国商人使用，以便英国商船到彼即行收藏，存放一切货物且可居住商人。

第四，请于广州附近得一同样之权利，且听英国商人自由往来，不加禁止。

第五，凡英国商货自澳门运往广州者，请特别优待赐予免税。如不能尽免，请依一千七百八十二年之税率从宽减税。

第六，请允许英国商船按照中国所定之税率切实上税，不在税率之外另行征收。且请将中国所定税率录赐一份以便遵行。

乾隆皇帝则以不合天朝体制为由，赐英王敕书拒绝所请，反严旨督促马戛尔尼一行由钦差大臣松筠陪同于五十八年（1793 年）九月初离京。

为改善贸易关系到访的英国使团，自认有别朝鲜、安南、缅甸等前往

①　马戛尔尼的访华日记经刘半农翻译出版名为《1793 乾隆英使觐见记》，其中有关觐见礼仪的细节描述与中国第一历史档案馆所纂《英使马戛尔尼访华档案史料汇编》（1996 年）影印的汉语文献不尽相同。详见黄一农撰《印象与真相——清朝中英两国的觐礼之争》（载《中央研究院历史语言研究所集刊》2007 年第 78 期）。

贺寿的属邦，既盼能在西方逐渐成形之国际法精神下平行相见①，却又毫无保留地接受贡船才拥有的免税待遇，并对易货、购物等无关外交的事务，提出许多违背使节身份的要求（黄一农，2007：37），最终招致皇帝愤懑，所请通商诸事一概回绝，此所谓"觐礼之争"。

如今看来，这不止缺乏沟通导致的文化碰撞而已，更深层次地折射了新旧帝国构建间权力和利益的冲突（何伟亚，2002：26—27）。何况马戛尔尼的门户开放要求隐含殖民扩张的野心，被清廷严拒亦理所当然。

但无论怎样，影响决策的重要因素仍是自恃"天朝物产丰富、无所不有，原不籍外夷货物以通有无"②的傲慢心态：

Translator's Preface

This Great Empire, **too well assured of the competence of its own natural and artificial resources**, to be induced to seek, and, **if not too powerful, at least to distant and compactly united**, to be liable to be compelled to enter into alliances and close connections with the Powers of

---

① 据《英使谒见乾隆纪实》第二卷第四章记载，当时马戛尔尼提交的照会原文如下："[H]is Majesty the King of Great Britain in sending an Embassy to his Majesty the Emperor of China, fully intended to give the strongest testimony of particular esteem and veneration for his Imperial Majesty; that the Embassador entrusted to convey such sentiments was earnestly desirous of fulfilling that object of his mission with zeal and effect; that he was ready likewise to conform to every exterior ceremony practiced by his Imperial Majesty's subjects, and the tributary princes attending at his court, not only to avoid the confusion of novelty, but in order to show, by his example on behalf of one of the greatest as well as most distant nations on the globe, the high and just sense universally entertained of his Imperial Majesty's dignity and transcendent virtues; that the Embassador had determined to act in that manner without hesitation or difficulty, on this condition only, of which he flattered himself his Imperial Majesty would immediately perceive the necessity; and have the goodness to accede to it, by giving such directions as should be the means of preventing the Embassador from suffering by his devotion to his Imperial Majesty in this instance; for the Embassador should certainly suffer heavily if his conduct on this occasion, could be construed as in any wise unbecoming the great and exalted rank which his master, whom he represented, held among the independent sovereigns of the world: that this danger could be easily avoided, and the satisfaction be general on all sides, by his Imperial Majesty's order that one of the officers of his court, equal with the Embassador in rank, should perform before his Britannic Majesty's picture at large, in his royal robes, and then in the Embassador's possession at Pekin, the same ceremonies which should be performed by the Embassador before the throne of his Imperial Majesty."（Staunton, 1797：（V2）318 - 319）。

② 详见《己卯赐英吉利国王敕书》（乾隆五十八年八月）。《续修四库全书·史部·编年类·东华续录》乾隆卷一百十八，（清）王先谦，《续修四库全书》编纂委员会编，第6页。

Europe, has never as yet, except in a precarious and limited degree, ad-mitted of any species of intercourse.[1]（Staunton，1810：iii）

特别值得警惕的是，在小斯当东的言辞中已隐隐透露出英国人并非不想武力征服华夏，唯恐相去路途遥远且其辖地联系紧密，只能对清廷无视欧洲列强的现状深感愤愤不平：

Translator's Preface

It continues to this day wholly regardless and independent of those na-tions of the West，whose general superiority in policy and in arms has tri-umphantly extended their power and influence over almost every other ex-citing society of mankind.（Ibid. iii）

（四）司法考察与律例研究

鉴于潜在的巨大商业利益，英国政府极其看重对华关系。然而，贸易摩擦导致司法纠纷频发，其裁判结果又时常不可估量，崇尚约翰·洛克（John Locke）和弗朗西斯·培根（Francis Bacon）的不列颠人偏好经验主义实证分析，他们急切想要了解的就是规范清朝社会生活的具体律令条例。正如《大清律例》英译本序言所述：“一个国家的法律构成其历史中最富教益的组成部分”[2]（同上，xv）。

为此，英国遣华的外交贸易使团不惜招揽众多法学专家。马戛尔尼伯爵本人就曾在伦敦学习法律，秘书乔治·伦纳德·斯当东从男爵（Sir George Leonard Staunton, 1st Baronet）[3] 则是牛津大学名誉法学博士。使团虽未达成通商之目的，却在访华过程中详细考察了当时清朝的司法活动，因而被西方社会普遍誉为获得史无前例的成功。

远航结束后，斯当东基于马戛尔尼伯爵及使团指挥官伊拉斯马斯·高厄爵士（Sir Erasmus Gower）的私人文件，撰写并出版正式报告《英使谒

---

[1]　粗体由本书作者添加。

[2]　英语原文："It has justly been observed by Mr. Gibbon, that 'the laws of a nation form the most instructive portion of its history'."

[3]　即乔治·汤姆司·斯当东从男爵（小斯当东）的父亲。

见乾隆纪实》（*An Authentic Account of and Embassy from the King of Great Britain to the Emperor of China*），由英国皇家学会主席约瑟夫·班克斯从男爵（Sir Joseph Banks，1ˢᵗ Baronet）亲自选配插图。

毫无疑问，他们已经发现清朝通行的"家长制原理"迥异欧洲诸国依法裁判的习惯（田涛、李祝环，2007：78）。紧接着，研究编撰成册的基本法典便提上议事日程，需要克服的只是语言障碍。

二 译介活动的实施者及其赞助人

早在马戛尔尼筹备访华期间，译员难觅的困扰就已经凸显[①]。幸而使团逗留中国之际尚有其他意外收获——孕育了一位杰出的汉学家，那就是《大清律例》的英文版作者小斯当东。

小斯当东（1781—1859 年）出生于英格兰威尔特郡的索斯贝里（Salisbury），年仅十余岁便以侍童身份伴随时任外交官的父亲前往谒见乾隆皇帝并接受赏赐。这次游历使他接触大量汉语知识，对中国文化亦产生浓厚兴趣。

自 1798 年开始，小斯当东常期任职英属东印度公司驻广州代理处，并着手完成《大清律例》的传译，前后共耗时八年。毋庸置疑，东印度公司正是此项浩瀚工程的幕后赞助人。

（一）赞助人的殖民倾向：英属东印度公司超商业性质

英属东印度公司又称可敬的东印度公司（the Honourable East India Company，简称 HEIC），有时也称约翰公司（John Company），以区别于荷兰等国的东印度公司。

其历史可追溯至 1600 年 12 月 31 日，英国女王伊丽莎白一世（Queen Elizabeth I）正式将为期十五年的皇家特许状（Royal Charter）授予富有创业心和影响力的伦敦商人，以"伦敦商人与东印度贸易总督及公司"

---

① 据《英使谒见乾隆纪实》第一卷第二章记载："One office more was still vacant, which was as necessary, as it was difficult to fill up; that of Chinese interpreter and translator. No man, capable of that employment, then existed throughout the British dominions... Recourse, therefore, was rather to be had to a search upon the continent of Europe, for such trustworthy persons, returning from China, as had happened to acquire the language of the mandarins, during their residence in that country; or for the few Chinese who had left it, and had since learned any of the European languages; if either such were, anywhere, to be found." (Staunton, 1797: (V1) 43 – 44).

(Governor and Company of Merchants of London Trading with the East Indies)
名义，独占好望角以东、麦哲伦海峡以西地区的贸易垄断权。鉴于伦敦商
人的东印度公司利润丰厚，詹姆士一世（King James I）又于 1609 年重新
颁发了不设期限的特许状，除非连续三年没有盈利才会被撤销。

最初，这只是家私营股份公司，董事会由持股人大会（the Court of
Proprietors）选举的一名总督和 24 位董事组成，并定期向持股人大会汇报
业务形势。尽管如此，东印度公司并非普通的商贸企业，它同时享有在其
独占区域内制定法律规章、实施行政管理并建立贸易据点的特权（汪熙，
2007：25）。随着时间变迁，公司还组建了雇佣军，成为殖民印度的真正
统治者。

东印度公司与中国的贸易往来虽始于明末清初，但每年经由英国船舶
运销广东的商易总额极其有限，即便 18 世纪中叶亦不过数万镑。直到
1784 年方才出现转机，英国议会通过《交易法案》（*Commutation Act*），
将茶叶的从价税自 119% 降为 12.5%，有效打击了走私活动。此后，公司
出口额逐年递增，至马戛尔尼访华时期已接近百万镑，但距离实际可能达
到的最高额相去仍远①。

东印度公司期待继续扩大对华贸易，难免频繁接触风俗迥异的清朝官
吏，因而有必要尽可能通晓关于中国政治经济文化等各方面信息。事实
上，谒见乾隆皇帝的英国外交贸易使团就是由东印度公司赞助的，其收集
情报的范围及规模远远超越单纯商业需要，仅《英使谒见乾隆纪实》的
附录部分就涵盖了《长城以内中国本部的人口和面积统计表》（Table of
the Population and Extent of China proper, within the Great Wall）、《中国本
部各省缴交北京国库的款项统计表》（Account of Revenue received into the
Imperial Treasury at Peking, from the different Province of China Proper）、
《主要文官职别、数目和薪俸表》（A List of the Chief Civil Officers of Chi-
na, Distinguishing Their Number, Station, and Salaries）、《主要武官职别、
数目和薪俸表》（A List of the Chief Military Officers of China, Their Num-

---

① 据《英使谒见乾隆纪实》第三卷附录五 "英国及其他欧洲各国同中国的贸易"（Trade of
the English and other Europeans to, and from, China）记载："Since the Commutation Act, the exports
have been gradually rising, but are yet far from having reached their highest point."（Staunton, 1797：
（V3）471）。

ber, Rank, and Salaries) 等翔实资料 (Staunton, 1797: (V3) 467 – 470)。

满怀觊觎之心的不列颠商人意欲洞悉华夏社会全貌，而小斯当东所译《大清律例》(*Ta Tsing Leu Lee*, 1810) 则正好提供了 "更加简明扼要又令人满意的诠释"：

Translator's Preface

... a faithful version of the Fundamental Laws of the Penal Code of China might, with the addition of some supplementary matter, not only prove interesting as far as regards its immediate subject, but likewise afford a more compendious and satisfactory illustration, than any other Chinese work that could have been selected, the peculiar system and constitution of the Government, the principles of its internal policy, its connection with the national habits and character, and its influence upon the general state and condition of the people in that country. (Staunton, 1810: i)

(二) 译者的政治忠诚度：文化学者小斯当东身份特殊

维基百科介绍小斯当东的身份是英格兰旅行家及东方文化研究者 (English Traveler and Orientalist)[1]，但其实际背景绝非如此单纯。

小斯当东出身外交官世家，他父亲是马戛尔尼伯爵的至交好友，曾被荐任 1793 年访华使团秘书，并获授权在必要情形下继任特使职位[2] (Staunton, 1797: (v1) 36)。小斯当东本人则长期效力于东印度公司驻广州代理处。甚至于 1816 年，还以东印度公司驻广州特别委员会主席名义与正使威廉·皮特·阿美士德伯爵 (William Pitt Amherst, 1st Earl Amherst)、副使亨利·埃利斯爵士 (Sir Henry Ellis) 出使中国，再次敦请清廷废除公行制度、多开商埠、允许自由贸易。返回不列颠后的小斯当东还数任不同地区的国会议员 (1818—1852 年)。

正因其身份的特殊性，小斯当东影响最为深远的译著除《大清律例》

---

① 引自维基百科 [2012/5/1] (http://zh.wikipedia.org/wiki/%E5%B0%8F%E6%96%AF%E7%95%B6%E6%9D%B1)。

② 英语原文："his Majesty's Secretary of the Embassy and eventual successor to the Embassador"

(*Ta Tsing Leu Lee*，1810) 外，就是《异域录》（*Narrative of the Chinese Embassy to the Khan of the Tourgouth Tartars*，1821）；其他知名作品则包括《中国与中英商业关系杂评》（*Miscellaneous Notices Relating to China and our Commercial Intercourse with that Country*，1822）；《阿美士德勋爵使华记》（*Notes of Proceedings and Occurrences during the British Embassy to Peking*，1824）；《对华商务观察报告》（*Observations on our Chinese Commerce*，1850）等。

所有这些著作皆表明小斯当东主要关注的无疑就是与中国相关的政治、经济问题，尤其是外交和贸易关系。即便涵盖部分汉语言文学研究成果的《中国与中英商业关系杂评》也以商业考虑为重，该书序言对此给予明确说明①。

另外，小斯当东的商业政治背景还决定了他的立场和看待问题的角度与以往在中国生活的西方传教士截然不同。这是因为传教士总以无比神圣的态度看待其宗教事业：

Translator's Preface

. . . persons thus situated should be, generally speaking, under the influence of a strong pre-disposition in favour of a people, for the sake of whose conversion they had renounced their country, and devoted their lives; and of a government, from whom, at one period, they had received extraordinary kindness and indulgence, and upon the continuance of whose protection the success of their future undertakings was foreseen almost entirely to depend. (Ibid. v – vi)

有鉴于此，传教士介绍中国文化的原作及译著即便汗牛充栋，依然"欠缺客观性与鉴别力"②，并"极度渴望以最讨人喜欢、最令人愉悦

---

① 据《中国与中英商业关系杂评》的序言记载："The latter and principal part of the present volume, has little connection with Chinese literature, being almost wholly devoted to considerations of a commercial nature."（Staunton，1822：iv）

② 英语原文：". . . a want of substantial impartiality and discriminating judgment in their writings. . ."

的角度"① 解读中国最古老的诗人、历史学家和哲学家的晦涩作品（同上，vi）。

长久以来，中国人总是自诩较其他"蛮夷之邦"拥有知识与道德方面的优势，欧洲历史学家们对此也是深信无疑。但曾经跟随马戛尔尼伯爵访华的小斯当东却不以为然，只留下帝国迟暮的印象：

Translator's Preface

... their knowledge was perceived to be defective in those points in which we have, in Europe, recently made the greatest progress, and to which we are therefore proportionately partial. Their virtues were found to consist more in ceremonial observances, than in moral duties; more in profession, than in practice; and their vices, when traced and discovered upon occasions where they were the least expected, seemed to deserve a more than ordinary degree of reprobation. (Ibid. ix)

上述论断当然有失偏颇，却也包含部分事实真相。更重要的是，小斯当东的观点增强了不列颠人的自信，为中英之间平等通商建交提供理据：

Translator's Preface

... a considerable proportion of the opinions most generally entertained by Chinese and Europeans of each other was to be imputed either to prejudice, or to misinformation; and that, upon the whole, it was not allowable to arrogate, on either side, any violent degree of moral or physical superiority. (Ibid. ix – x)

小斯当东坚信，唯本民族自己撰写的文献才更能反映该国真实状况，而这些文献中最具分量的就是国家基本法典。

---

① 英语原文："... an extreme anxiety to place these productions in the most favourable and pleasing light..."

Translator's Preface

After making every allowance for national partialities, prejudices, and defects, whatever they may be, it will generally be found, that the best and most authentic information of the state of any country, having pretensions to civilization, is contained in the works of the natives, and in the vernacular language. (Ibid. xii)

因此，无论从主题的重要性而言，还是着眼法令编纂机关的权威地位，经典化的《大清律例》都完全符合小斯当东研究中国社会制度的根本意图。

Translator's Preface

Among the multifarious publications of the Chinese, ancient as well as modern, which are still extant, and hitherto untranslated into any European language, the *Ta-Tsing-Leu-Lee*, or Imperial Code of Penal Laws, certainly ranks with those of the first class, in respect to the importance of the subject of which it treats, and the pre-eminence of the authority by which it was originally established, as well as, at different periods down to the present time, successfully sanctioned and confirmed. (Ibid. xv)

第二节　策略与技巧（一）
——提升英译本实用性

引言

上节中，我们讨论了影响小斯当东选定《大清律例》作为翻译对象的各种宏观及微观意识形态因素。需要强调的是，这些因素操纵的不只是主题的确定与文本的甄选，还无孔不入地渗透到更为具体的表述层面——特别是通过翻译策略的调整来实现文本以外权力博弈的其他意图。

* * *

为赢得围绕中英贸易展开的权力博弈，不列颠人首先想到的是知己知彼——探究规范清朝社会生活的基本法律制度，既可借此了解异域政治经济运行的普遍原则，更可在贸易引起"华夷纠纷"时，以彼之道，还施其身。

实际上，译者本人便坦言，选择《大清律例》最初就是为有效避免英商因误解中国法制精神导致"不必要的挑衅、无谓的忧虑及令人尴尬的议论"：

Translator's Preface

It first occupied his attention in consequence of his having been personally a witness to **many of the unnecessary provocations, groundless apprehensions, and embarrassing discussions, of which, since the first commencement of our present important commercial and national intercourse with the people of China**, false or imperfect notions of the spirit of their laws have been, but too often, the occasion: and although the translation of every part of the work did not promise, in this point of view, to be of equal utility, he always found it, at the least, a gratification to curiosity, and a not uninteresting employment of leisure hours: it is only, however, very recently, and in compliance with the perhaps too partial suggestions of those to whose perusal the Translator has had the pleasure of submitting the manuscript, that he has allowed himself to believe it might prove not altogether unworthy of the attention of the Public at large. [1] (Staunton, 1810: xxxiii)

有鉴于此，我们不难理解小斯当东的翻译活动绝非纯粹的东方文化研究，而是明确指向直接的实用意图。相应的，目标语篇期待的读者群亦主要涵盖关注对华贸易却对中国文明完全陌生的政客、商人。这都促使译者对原文进行多方面的改写，旨在尽可能增进译语的可读性。

Translator's Preface

Throughout the work, the Translator's first object, and that which he has endeavoured to keep constantly in view, has been to convey the full

---

① 粗体由本书作者添加。

meaning of each article or paragraph successively，**in appropriate，and，at the same time，intelligible language；in other words，to draw as justly as possible，the middle line between the unfaithfulness and inaccuracy of a free，and the ungracefulness and almost ungrammatical obscurity of a close version.** ①（Ibid. xxxi）

一　比较版本

现有资料表明，小斯当东了解《大清律例》存在数个前后衔接的不同版本（请参见图4—2），并在一定程度上进行相互比较。其中，能够确定无疑的就包括译者引作原文主要来源的嘉庆四年（1799年）刻本（请参见图4—3），及时而参考的嘉庆六年（1801年）奉部颁行的《大清律例重订辑注通纂（比引条例督捕则例附后）》。

小斯当东选用嘉庆初年的《大清律例》，绝不仅仅因为其版本最新，囊括了续纂并增修的近年条例，具有无与伦比的时效性。

事实上，译者非但未将律例中所包含的例文完整译出。恰恰相反，真正传译的条例只占原书所附极小部分。至于律文，《钦定四库全书·大清律例·凡例》已经说明"历代相因，至雍正五年删改增并，定为四百三十六门，今仍其旧"，并将其规定为"圣朝成宪"②。换言之，雍正五年（1727年）以后各版《大清律例》的律文内容再无更动。对于这个问题，小斯当东是有所察觉的：

Translator's Preface

The *LEU*，or Fundamental Laws，are those of which the Penal Code，upon its formation soon after the accession of the present dynasty，appears originally to have consisted，and which，being，at least nominally，permanent，are reprinted in each successive edition，without either alteration or amendment.（Ibid. xxix – xxx）

---

①　粗体由本书作者添加。
②　详见《钦定四库全书·大清律例·凡例》。

TA TSING LEU LEE;

BEING

THE FUNDAMENTAL LAWS,

AND A SELECTION FROM THE

SUPPLEMENTARY STATUTES,

OF THE

PENAL CODE OF CHINA;

ORIGINALLY PRINTED AND PUBLISHED IN PEKIN,
·IN VARIOUS SUCCESSIVE EDITIONS,
UNDER THE SANCTION, AND BY THE AUTHORITY, OF THE SEVERAL
EMPERORS OF THE TA TSING, OR PRESENT DYNASTY.

TRANSLATED FROM THE CHINESE;
AND ACCOMPANIED WITH AN APPENDIX,
CONSISTING OF AUTHENTIC DOCUMENTS, AND A FEW OCCASIONAL NOTES,
ILLUSTRATIVE OF THE SUBJECT OF THE WORK;
BY SIR GEORGE THOMAS STAUNTON, BART. F.R.S.

Mens, et animus, et confilium, et fententia civitatis, pofita eft in LEGIBUS.
CICERO PRO CLUENTIO.

LONDON:
PRINTED FOR T. CADELL AND W. DAVIES, IN THE STRAND.
1810.

图4—2　小斯当东译本《大清律例》的标题页①

---

① 黑框由本书作者添加。

[lxiii]

I.

TA TSING LEU LEE;

OR

THE LAWS AND STATUTES

OF

THE DYNASTY OF TSING,

A NEW EDITION,

PRINTED AND PUBLISHED IN THE FOURTH YEAR OF THE REIGN OF *KIA-KING,*

OF

THE ENTIRE CODE OF FUNDAMENTAL LAWS AND SUPPLEMENTARY STATUTES ;

WHICH, AFTER HAVING BEEN REVISED AND COMPLETED, WAS, IN THE SIXTIETH YEAR OF THE REIGN OF *KIEN-LUNG,* PROMULGATED IN ITS PRESENT FORM, BY THE SUPREME COUNCIL OF STATE IN THE DEPARTMENT OF PUBLIC JUSTICE.

TO WHICH IS ADDED,

THE EXPLANATORY COMMENTARY ANNEXED TO THE FUNDAMENTAL LAWS, BY THE EMPEROR *YONG-TCHING*; AN EXTENSIVE COLLECTION OF ADJUDGED CASES AND A VARIETY OF USEFUL NOTES AND OBSERVATIONS DERIVED FROM THE MOST APPROVED SOURCES.

NOTE.—The above is an Abſtract of the Title-Page to the Edition of the original Chineſe Work, printed in the Year 1799, from which the Fundamental Laws, tranſlated in the following Pages, have been extracted. — A ſtill later Edition, exactly ſimilar in reſpect to the Fundamental Laws, but containing a greater Number of Supplementary Statutes, and a different Selection of illuſtrative Notes, has likewiſe been occaſionally conſulted.

The Title-page of the later Edition may be tranſlated as follows : " Recently engraved " in the 10th Year of *KIA-KING*, a new Edition of the Laws and Statutes of the great " Dynaſty of *TSING*; compriſing, agreeably to the univerſal Compendium promulgated " by the Supreme Court of Judicature on the 6th Year of *KIA-KING*, all the Additions " and Alterations which have been made of late Years in the ſupplementary Statutes ; " alſo compendious Abſtracts from the various Commentaries, and an Appendix, con- " ſiſting of two Books of additional ſupplementary Statutes.　The whole carefully " reviſed and examined ; and each Copy ſold for three *leang* ſix *tſien* of ſilver."

图 4—3　Abstract of the Title-page of the Edition of the Penal Code

printed and published in China in 1799, the 4th year of the

Reign of the present Emperor Kia-King (Ibid. lxiii)

尽管如此,以《钦定四库全书·大清律例》为底版的嘉庆初年刻本,其最大优势在于纂修新例时,废弃了按时间顺序开列的传统模式,改为依具体例文的内容与性质分类附入律条。律例合编不但解决了清初法典中律、例相抵触的弊端,更重要的是方便理解并参照适用。这也许是促使小斯当东作出抉择的另一重要因素①。正如《钦定四库全书·大清律例·凡例》第四条所言:

> 雍正五年刻本,于每条之上,分列原例、增例、钦定例各名目,既以时代为先后,势必不能依类编辑。今将原例、增例等名目,概不登载,如钱粮则由仓库,而次及杂项;侵挪、贼盗则由正犯,而次及搜赃、举首,庶几条分缕析,次序秩然。

二 损益内容

前文已经谈及小斯当东的译本只涉猎极少数条例。对此,译者的解释是为了确保目标作品的形式"简明扼要",同时又可尝试令"结构安排更系统化、风格更宜人、措辞更融洽":

Translator's Preface

If, in order to reduce the work into **a compendious form**, the Translator had permitted himself the liberty of making an abstract or abridgment of the text, he might, at the same time have endeavoured to have adopted **a more systematic arrangement, a more pleasing style, and a more harmonious phraseology**...② (Ibid. xxix)

毋庸置疑,小斯当东也敏锐地意识到内容的删节不应亦不能率性而为,否则极易危及《大清律例》值得翻译的核心特征——权威性与独创

---

① 尽管小斯当东译出的条例数量很少,但在各项律文之后均注明了原版所附条例数目(请参阅图4—5),方便目标读者群查阅:"The number of supplementary clauses annexed to each section in the original is regularly noticed, and will enable the student of the Chinese language, if desirous of investigating the subject of any particular section more closely, to judge how far a reference to the original text is likely to afford him satisfaction." (Staunton, 1810: 488)。

② 粗体由本书作者添加。

性。因此，他决定依据中文原版法典划分律、例的标准进行选择：保留律文（基本规范），放弃条例（补充规范）。

Translator's Preface

... but he was sensible that he should in the same proportion have impaired the two recommendations most essential to the value of the work, **its authenticity and its originality**. He, therefore, determined upon a selection, not, indeed, according to any conjectural estimate of the superior importance of any particular part of the Code over another, but **according to the rule, which, by the division of the laws into fundamental and supplementary, the Code itself afforded.** ① （Ibid. xxix）

保留律文，这是着眼基本规范的重要性和稳定性；放弃条例，也不仅因为补充规范只是律文的修正、延伸或限制，还考虑到其时常处于变动之中。按照《清会典》的规定："条例五年一小修，十年一大修。"②

Translator's Preface

The *LEE*, or the Supplementary Laws, are the modifications, extensions, and restrictions of the Fundamental Laws, which, after undergoing a deliberate examination in the Supreme Councils, and receiving the sanction of the Sovereign, are inserted in the form of clauses, together with the Fundamental Laws, be equally known and observed. They are generally, however, revised every fifth year, and subjected to such alterations as the wisdom of government determines to be expedient. （Ibid. xxx）

值得研究者推敲的是，小斯当东对译出例文别具匠心的安排：这些条例并未如原版那样编入律文，而是集中开列于附录。因其量少，尤其瞩目（同上，lviii – lxi）：

① 粗体由本书作者添加。
② 详见田涛、郑秦点校本《大清律例》（1999）之点校说明，第6页。

（1）Translation of the Supplementary Clauses to Section I, entitled *"Description of ordinary Punishments"*

（2）Translation of an Extract from the Clauses annexed to Section LXXVIII, entitled *"Rules of Succession and Inheritance"*

（3）Abstract of some of the principal Clauses annexed to Section XCV, entitled *"Law of Mortgages"*

（4）Translation of two of the Clauses annexed to Section CCXXV, entitled *"Illicit Exportation of Merchandize"*

（5）Translation of the Clauses annexed to Section CCLIV, entitled *"High Treason"*

（6）Translation of the Clauses annexed to Section CCLV, entitled *"Rebellion and Renunciation of Allegiance"*

（7）Translation of the Clauses annexed to Section CCLVI, entitled *"Sorcery and Magic"*

（8）Translation of the most material among the Clauses annexed to Section CCLIII, entitled *"Stealing Timber from a Burying-ground"*

（9）Translation of the first seven Clauses annexed to Section CCLX-IV, entitled *"Embezzlement of public Property"*

（10）Translation of the Clauses annexed to Section CCLXV, entitled *"Theft of public Property"*

（11）Translation of the Clauses annexed to Section CCLXVI, entitled *"Robbery—Highway Robbery"*

（12）Translation of the Clauses and Commentary annexed to Section CCLXXXII, entitled *"Preconcerted Homicide—Murder"*

（13）Translation of the Clauses annexed to Section CCCLXVI, entitled *"Criminal Intercourse in general"*

从内容上分析，小斯当东选译的十三处例文除第（1）项出自名例律、第（2）和第（3）项出自户律、第（4）项出自兵律外，其余绝大多数都属刑律。再者，户律例文选译的是嫡子继承与典买田宅条款，兵律例文选译的是边境走私条款，而刑律例文则以贼盗、人命为主。据此，译者侧重的焦点似乎是中国社会普通民众的生活规范。

从形式上考察，选译的例文并非单列，而是与典型案例并置文末。这些案例大致可分为两类：

（一）本朝内政要案，主要包括嘉庆皇帝神武门遇刺、乾隆朝军机大臣和珅革职赐死、镇压川楚白莲教起义等震惊全国的重大事件。

（二）涉欧外交成例，主要针对通商和传教事务，关注在华英商及英国海员、定居澳门的葡萄牙人、欧洲传教士等。

中文原版律书未曾附录上述典型案例，完全是小斯当东自主决定增添了部分皇帝圣旨（Imperial Edict）、督抚谕令和京城邸报（Pekin Gazette）。尤其圣旨，在译者看来虽无法律之虚名，却有法律之实效：

Translator's Preface

... but the number of documents which possesses the force of laws without the name, must, under a government in which every authenticated expression of the will of the Prince bears that character, necessarily be un-limited. (Ibid. xxx)

选译的例文与典型案例，按照相关律条的顺序混编。这无疑说明小斯当东损益内容的标准同样出于实用性意图，期望促进目的语读者更深刻地理解他认为属核心范畴的基本规范：本朝内政要案足以反映当前满清统治是否稳定；涉欧外交成例自然关乎中英通商；至于了解普通华人的独特生活方式也是适应开拓海外市场的需要。

三　甄别注释

嘉庆初年版《大清律例》除律、例外，还包括小注，一般以小字夹编在律或例条相应的行文之间，主要起疏通或阐明的作用①。换言之，小注本身虽非法律条文的固有内容，不具法律效力，但对律例的诠释至关重要。

小斯当东处理夹编注释的策略亦甄别功能：疏通文义的小注，大都直接融入译本；阐明实施细则的小注却可能有所不论，尤其是对特殊情形的列举等多被剔除。请看以下图示：

---

① 详见孙家红撰《〈大清律例〉百年研究综述》［2012/4/29］（http：//blog.sina.com.cn/s/blog_ 4b862b3e01009ymb.html）。

徒流人又犯罪

凡犯罪已發決未論又犯罪者從重科斷已徒已流

而又犯罪者依律再科後犯之罪科斷不在從重之限其

重犯流者三流並決杖一百於配所拘役四年

若又徒而犯徒者依後所犯杖數該徒年限

決訖令應役前通亦總不得過四年三年已役四年若先犯徒年未滿其又犯流者亦

一年又犯徒三年止加杖一百徒一百俱役四年三年之類明白議擬

則應徒不得過四年若先犯徒年未滿其又犯流者又犯杖罪以下者亦

照數決訖應役

钦定四库全书

各依笞杖數決之罪亦准此其應加杖者亦如充軍又犯杖罪以下者亦

大清律例

之犯者亦依律科之　謂天文生及婦人

條例

一先犯雜犯死罪納贖未完及准徒年限未滿又

犯雜犯死罪者決杖一百除杖過數目准銀七

分五釐再收贖銀四錢五分又犯徒流笞杖罪

者決其應得杖數五徒三流各依律收贖銀數

仍照先擬發落若三次俱犯雜犯死罪者奏請

图4—4　《钦定四库全书·大清律例·卷四名例律上》截图

SECTION XXI. — *Offences of Perſons already under Sentence of Puniſhment.*

When any perſon, after having been charged with an offence, commits another offence before the infliction of the puniſhment due to the former, the puniſhment of the greater offence ſhall always ſuperſede that of the leſſer.

But if the offender had been already ſent into baniſhment for the former offence, the puniſhment of the latter offence ſhall be inflicted according to the law in the uſual manner, except in the caſe of a ſecond ſentence of perpetual baniſhment, when the latter ſhall be commuted for a ſentence of extra-ſervice for four years.

In like manner, a ſecond ſentence of temporary baniſhment ſhall prolong the period of ſervice, but it ſhall never exceed four years on the whole.

When, after ſentence of baniſhment or of corporal puniſhment, a further offence puniſhable with blows of the bamboo is committed, a proportionate puniſhment ſhall be inflicted to the full extent directed by law, in the uſual manner.

Ten clauſes.

图4—5　小斯当东译本《大清律例》第 XXI 条截图（Staunton, 1810: 23）

比较上述两幅图例，我们不难发现"未论决"（before the infliction of the punishment）、"不在从重科断之限"（in the usual manner）、"徒而又（犯徒）"（a second sentence of temporary banishment）、"仍令"（in like manner）、"通前"（on the whole）、"徒流人又犯"（after sentence of banishment or of corporal punishment）、"（杖罪以下）者"（when）、"后犯笞杖"（a further offence punishable with blows of the bamboo is committed）等旨在使语篇含义更为圆满流畅的注释，均在译文中与律条本身所含信息天衣无缝地合为一体。

至于"谓先犯徒三年已役一年又犯徒三年者止加杖一百徒一年之类则总徒不得过四年三流虽并杖一百具役四年若先犯徒年未满者亦止总役四年"、"充军又犯罪亦准此"、"谓天文生及妇人犯者亦依律科之"等篇幅较长的注释，原为说明特殊情形下律条的具体适用，消除执行过程中可能出现的犹疑，然而英文版的字里行间却完全不见其踪迹。

译者这样煞费苦心的安排，无非考虑到汉英语言文字系统的实质差异：汉语强调意合，英文注重形合。如果置疏通性质的小注不顾，遵循形式逻辑的英文句法将无法连贯表达凭借意义贯通的汉语律条。但若小注仅具列举性质，涉及的又是执行律例的冗长细节，除非特别紧要（请比较图4—6/4—7①），其余本就对英国人了解清朝统治制度的总体状况助益甚微，倘使无法简洁明快地并入律文，频繁使用脚注必然失之累赘，以致妨碍目标读者对语篇整体的顺畅理解。

四　调整体例

小斯当东译本对原文的另一显著改写，就是在所有律条前添加罗马序数编号。不注条文序号本是中国传统法典编撰技术的明显缺陷，但英译版弥补了这并非无关紧要的检索障碍，为目标读者群的研究参证提供难以估量的便利条件。

如图4—8所示，中文原版《大清律例》的目录卷既不序律条编号，也未标明相应页码，较之英译本（图4—9）编号、页码分列左右的体例，孰优孰劣，不言而喻。

---

①　图4—6所引"给没赃物"条律文中夹编的小注"谓官物还官私物还主又若本赃是驴转易得马及马生驹羊生羔畜产蕃息皆为见在其赃"由译者择要译入图4—7末段"...when of a productive nature, with all its produce..."。

給沒贓物

凡彼此俱罪之贓　謂犯受財枉法　計贓與受同罪者　及犯禁之物　謂如應禁兵器　及禁書之類　則入官若取與不和強生

事逼取求索之贓並還主　謂恐嚇詐欺強買賣　有餘利科欽及求索

○其犯罪應合籍沒財產赦書到後罪人雖　在敕產而家　未曾抄割入官者並從赦免其

已抄割入官守掌及犯謀反叛逆者　坐家口不　分已未入官　並不放免若　除謀反罪未處決之　籍沒物

欽定四庫全書　　大清律例

雖已送官　但　與人者猶為未入其緣　未經分配　守掌者

坐流人犯及本　家口雖已入官　若已　者亦從免放○若以贓入罪正贓見在者還官主　人犯　見在者還官　罪人赦得免　罪

謂官物還官私物還主又若本贓是驢轉易得　馬及馬生駒羊生羔富產蕃息皆為見在其贓

已費用者若犯人身死勿徵　若不因贓罪而犯　別罪身死者亦同

私理罪亦有應追物　如埋葬銀兩之類　餘皆徵之若計雇工賃錢

官車船之類　為贓者　死　亦勿徵○其估贓者

皆據犯處　方當時　地　時犯　中等物價估計定罪若計

图4—6　《钦定四库全书·大清律例·卷四名例律下》截图

SECTION XXIV. — *Restitution and Forfeiture of Goods.*

In any cafe of an illegal transfer of property, in which both parties are guilty, or when any perfon is convicted of poffeffing prohibited goods, fuch goods or property fhall be forfeited to the ftate :—But when any article of property has been obtained from an individual by violence, injuftice, extortion, or falfe pretences, it fhall be reftored to the owner.

In all cafes wherein the offender is liable to be punifhed in his property as well as in his perfon, if a pardon arrives after the execution of corporal punifhment, but before the confifcation has taken place, or before the fine has been levied, the latter part of the fentence fhall be remitted.—If however the amount to be levied by fine or confifcation, is actually received and appropriated before the notice of the general act of pardon arrives ; or if the

E　　　　　　　　　　　　　　　　offence

图4—7　小斯当东译本《大清律例》第 XXIV 条部分截图
（Staunton，1810：25－26）

offence is connected with circumſtances of a treaſonable nature, the general act of pardon ſhall, in that particular caſe, have no effect.

Moreover, in any caſe of an available pardon arriving before the execution of corporal puniſhment, the property ſequeſtrated on account of government, if not ſpecifically appropriated, ſhall be reſtored, and the family of the offender, who may have been likewiſe held bound to government, ſhall be releaſed from their reſponſibility.

If the offence ariſes from the unlawful poſſeſſion of any property, and the property, the reſtitution of which is conſequently claimed by government or by an individual, is ſtill in exiſtence, it ſhall be duly transferred, and, when of a productive nature, with all its produce. If, however, the unlawful poſſeſſor had waſted it, and afterwards died, his heirs ſhall not be compelled to make up the deficiency.

欽定四庫全書
大清律例卷一
名例律目錄 共四十六條 附例一百八十四條
五刑　十惡
八議　應議者犯罪
應議者之父祖有犯　職官有犯
文武官犯公罪　文武官犯私罪
犯罪免發遣　軍籍有犯
欽定四庫全書　大清律例
犯罪得累減　以理去官
無官犯罪　除名當差
流囚家屬　常赦所不原
流犯在道會赦　犯罪存留養親
天文生有犯　工樂戶及婦人犯罪
徒流人又犯罪　老小廢疾收贖
犯罪時未老疾　給沒贓物
犯罪自首　二罪俱發以重論

图 4—8　《钦定四库全书·大清律例·卷一》截图

xviii TABLE OF CONTENTS.

FIRST DIVISION, — *General Laws.*

BOOK I.

PRELIMINARY REGULATIONS.

XXII. In-

图 4—9 小斯当东译《大清律例》名例律目录截图（Staunton，1810：xxxviii）

第三节 策略与技巧（二）
——力争中英地位平等

颇令人玩味的是，小斯当东归化英文版《大清律例》语言表述的努力不单欲增进可读性，更具其他深刻用意，即尽量改写原文尊卑殊异的措辞所反映的话语霸权，争取实现中英地位平等。这在译者序言内亦有明示：

Translator's Preface

... they might even have at last determined, that a considerable proportion of the opinions most generally entertained by Chinese and Europeans of each other was to be imputed either to prejudice, or to misinformation; and that, upon the whole, it was not allowable to arrogate, on either side, any violent degree of moral or physical superiority. (Staunton, 1810: ix - x)

一 谕旨体例
（一）自"奉天承运"至"钦此"

作为事实上的律法，清代的诏书是以皇帝名义发布臣民周知的文书（雷荣广 & 姚乐野，1990：224）。凡属重大事件，均向全国昭告。通篇常由"奉天承运皇帝诏曰"起始，最后则归结成类似"布告天下咸使闻知"或"布告中外咸使闻知"等语及"钦此"。

所谓"奉天"，即尊奉上天意旨；所谓"承运"，即继承五德气运。前者盛行春秋战国，假借天命统治臣民；后者按《史记·封禅书》记载："秦始皇既并天下而帝，或曰：'黄帝得土德，黄龙地螾见。夏得木德，青龙止于郊，草木畅茂。殷得金德，银自山溢。周得火德，有赤乌之符。今秦变周，水德之时。昔秦文公出猎，获黑龙，此其水德之瑞。'于是秦更命河曰'德水'，以冬十月为年首，色上黑，度以六为名，音上大吕，事统上法。"①

---

① 详见《史记》卷二十八。（西汉）司马迁撰，（宋）裴骃集解，（唐）司马贞索隐，（唐）张守节正义，第1168页。

汉承秦制，兼容并蓄两种理论，虚构君权神授幻象，自称"奉天承运皇帝"，并逐步建立起完备的皇帝制度。"诏曰"最初就出现在汉代文书，为后世历代帝王沿用。

但"奉天承运皇帝诏曰"真正完整套用于帝王诏书，却起自明朝。据明万历年间天文学家沈德符所言："太祖初，定大朝会正殿曰奉天殿，门名亦如之……以故《祖训》中云：'皇帝所执大圭，上镂"奉天法祖"四字，遇亲王尊行者，必手秉此圭，始受其拜。以至臣下诰、敕命中，必首云"奉天承运皇帝"……'"①。

小斯当东对圣旨开篇八字套语的处理，特别是"奉天承运"的传译相对程式化。请看以下图例：

ON the seventh day of the second moon of the fourth year of KIA KING †, is recorded the testamentary edict of His late Majesty, by the grace and appointment of Heaven, THE MOST HIGH EMPEROR, in these words.

图4—10 小斯当东译本《大清律例》嘉庆四年正月初三日太上皇帝诰书截图
(Staunton，1810：477)

HIS Majesty the Emperor, by the grace and appointment of Heaven, issues this Edict extraordinary.

图4—11 小斯当东译本《大清律例》嘉庆四年正月初三日皇帝诏书截图
(同上，483)

其中，"by the grace and appointment of Heaven"的固定搭配，诱使目标读者群不由自主地联想起英文尊崇王室的惯用语"by the Grace of God"，譬如乔治三世致乾隆皇帝国书的开场白：

His Most Sacred Majesty George the Third, by the Grace of God King of Great Britain, France and Ireland, Sovereign of the Seas, Defender of the Faith and so forth, To the Supreme Emperor of China KIEN-LUNG worthy to live tens of thousands and tens of thousands thousand years,

---

① 详见《万历野获编·更正殿名》。《万历野获编》卷二，（明）沈德符撰，（清）钱枋编，第46页。

sendeth Greeting.

　　不言而喻，英译本有效调动了译入文化语境，巧妙利用信息接收者预设的知识结构，迎合主流社会意识形态主张中英平等对话的权力建构模式。

　　与之形成鲜明比照的是，小斯当东对篇末"钦此"却采用音译法（请参见图4—12①）。学者们理解其含义即钦定此文，转换成现代汉语就是"皇帝同意这样办理"。古时公文制度对君王的决定、命令或所作所为冠以"钦"字表示异常尊崇，譬如"钦此钦遵"。当然，也有研究者认为该词专用于上谕圣旨，表示恭敬地引文至此，亦起到替代句号与后引号的功能（雷荣广、姚乐野，1990：247—248）。故帝王面谕，从未添足；钦差宣旨，则势必申明。

　　或可将其译成"That's all（for the Imperial Edict）"。但平心而论，直接取音当然便捷，更何况还能悄无声息地擦除汉语原文无处不笼罩的君权神圣光环。

This edict and notification extraordinary we now publish for general information and obedience. *Khin-tse.*

图4—12　小斯当东译《大清律例》嘉庆四年正月初三日皇帝诏书截图
（Staunton，1810：486）

（二）"朕"≠"we"

　　按《说文解字》："朕，我也。"（许慎，2001：489）先秦时期，贵族庶民皆可用"朕"作单数第一人称代词。及至始皇奋六世之余烈，横扫列国，统御宇内，王绾、李斯等议君主称号"天子自称曰'朕'"②，自此方成帝王的专属尊号。察其含义，与周天子自称"予一人"及诸侯南面称孤道寡本出同源，无非是为凸显唯我独尊的心态，天下莫有能与之比肩者。

---

　　①　原文请参见图4—15。
　　②　出自《史记·秦始皇本纪》。详见《史记》卷六。（西汉）司马迁撰，（宋）裴骃集解，（唐）司马贞索隐，（唐）张守节正义，第168页。

小斯当东版《大清律例》共译清代顺治、康熙、雍正、乾隆、嘉庆五朝皇帝的十六份谕旨。其中,"朕"的出现频率可谓比比皆是。

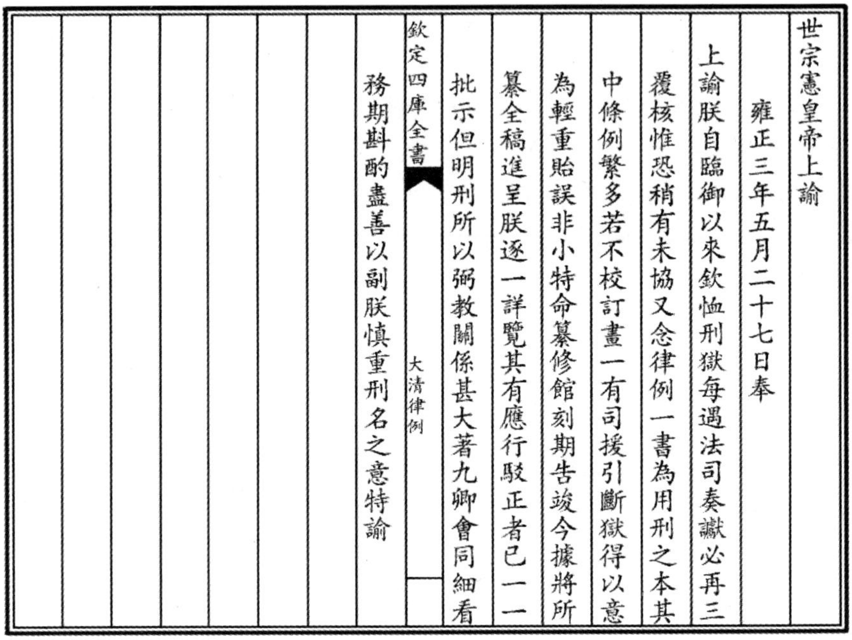

务期斟酌尽善以副朕慎重刑名之意特谕

批示但明刑所以弼教关系甚大著九卿会同细看

纂全稿进呈朕逐一详览其有应行驳正者已一一

为轻重贻误非小特命纂修馆刻期告竣今据将所

中条例繁多若不校订畫一有司援引断狱得以意

覆核惟恐稍有未协又念律例一书为用刑之本其

上谕朕自临御以来钦恤刑狱每遇法司奏谳必再三

雍正三年五月二十七日奉

世宗宪皇帝上谕

钦定四库全书

大清律例

图 4—13 《钦定四库全书·大清律例·世宗宪皇帝上谕》截图

仅以图 4—13 所引《钦定四库全书·大清律例·世宗宪皇帝上谕》为例,短短六行文字就三次使用"朕"。小斯当东将所有这些圣谕中的"朕"字,全部译入英文第一人称复数代词"we"或其宾格"us"或其所有格"our"(请参见图 4—14)。对此种处理方式,他通过附录"I:TRANSLATION of the Testamentary Edict of KIEN-LUNG, the late Emperor of China"(乾隆皇帝遗诏译文)的脚注补充说明如下:

> *The plural is here introduced, not solely in conformity to European usage, but also the nearest approximation to the pronoun exclusively appropriated in the Chinese language to sovereignty. The phrase "I the Emperor" might perhaps be more strictly correct, but its adoption would have been in many places very inconvenient. (Ibid. 477)

PREFATORY EDICT

OF

THE EMPEROR *YONG-TCHING*,

THE THIRD OF THE PRESENT DYNASTY.

SINCE the period of our Acceſſion to the Imperial Throne of our ·Anceſtors, the criminals who, at different times, have been awaiting their ſentence in confinement, have not failed to ſhare our Royal compaſſion and conſideration. — The reports of all the caſes adjudged by the provincial magiſtrates, and requiring our ſanction to their deciſion, have been examined by us with the moſt ſcrupulous attention, leſt they ſhould contain any flaw or incongruity which might invalidate the reſults. — We have alſo conſidered that among our various inſtitutions, the Code of Penal Laws is the moſt varied and complicated in its conſtruction ; and that, therefore, unleſs clear and invariable rules are pointed out, the magiſtrates muſt, in ſome inſtances, unavoidably take upon themſelves to aggravate or mitigate the puniſhment due to criminals, according to their own diſcretion ; in which caſes, they muſt conſtantly be liable to commit great errors, and even flagrant injuſtice.

With the view of preventing as much as poſſible, all ſuch abuſes, we ſubmitted the Penal Code to the reviſion of the members of our Imperial college, and have ſince attentively conſidered their written obſervations thereon, annexing, at the ſame time, to each article, the mark of our approbation or diſſent. In conſideration, however, of the vaſt mportance of a work which is to guide and inſtruct the magiſtrates in all judicial

proceedings,

lxx PRELIMINARY MATTER.

proceedings, it is our pleaſure, that the nine principal officers of ſtate, reviſe, examine, and correct the reſults of all theſe operations, ſo as moſt effectually to fulfil our deſign of adapting the penalties of the laws in a juſt proportion to the crimes againſt which they are ·denounced.

Dated the 27th of the 5th moon, of the third year of *Yong-tching*, A.D. 1725*.

图4—14 小斯当东译本《大清律例》世宗宪皇帝上谕（Staunton，1810：lxix – lxx）

译者的上述解释似有欲盖弥彰之嫌。难道说仅仅为方便，就连乾隆遗诏中追忆昔日传位承诺（【例1】）、允准九旬万寿庆典（【例2】）等如此切近个人心路历程的片段亦可以"we"敷衍塞责？特别是其中有关皇帝自陈年龄、自上尊号等细节描述，若非视之代词的特殊用法，则尤令译文读者大惑不解。

【例1】①

……上帝若能仰邀眷命在位六十年即当传位嗣子不敢有逾皇祖纪年之数其时朕春秋方二十有五……爰于丙辰正旦亲授玺皇帝自称太上皇……

... **our** intention to resign to **our** son and successor the sovereignty of the realm, if the Divine Will should grant to **our** reign a sixty years continuance; forasmuch as **we** were unwilling to exceed in any case, the duration of **our** Imperial grandfather's government.

Our years had indeed already amounted to twenty five...

Accordingly, on the first day of the year *Ping-shin*, **we** transferred to

---

① 详见《嘉庆四年正月初三日太上皇帝诰》。《嘉庆道光两朝上谕档》第四册，中国第一历史档案馆编，第2—3页。粗体及下划线由本书作者添加。乾隆遗诏原文完整片段如下："……回忆践祚之初曾默祷上帝若能仰邀眷命在位六十年即当传位嗣子不敢有逾皇祖纪年之数其时朕春秋方二十有五预计六十年时日方长若在可知不可知之数乃荷昊慈笃佑康疆逢吉年跻望九亲见五代元孙周甲纪元竟符初愿抚衷循省欣感交加爰于丙辰正旦亲授玺皇帝自称太上皇遂初元告天之本志……"小斯当东版译文："Ultimately, however, we recalled to our recollection the mental prayer which we had addressed to the Supreme Being on our accession to the Imperial dignity and in which we had made a solemn intimation of our intention to resign to our son and successor the sovereignty of the realm, if the Divine Will should grant to our reign a sixty years continuance; for as much as we were unwilling to exceed in any case, the duration of our Imperial grandfather's government. Our years had indeed already amounted to twenty five, when we thus provided for the event of a sexagenary reign, as if we were gifted with a prescience to enable us to anticipate so protracted a period; it is under the guardian auspices of our Imperial progenitors that this inestimable favor of a reign so glorious, and so happily prolonged, has been extended to us. While surrounded with numerous relations, and witnessing at once five generations of our family and descendants, we finally observed the progressive revolution of a cycle to be accomplished since the empire had been committed to our hands; and when we then reflected on our original wishes and designs, the contemplation of the corresponding event impressed us with the warmest sensations of joy and gratitude. Accordingly, on the first day of the year *Ping-shin*, we transferred to our son the present Emperor, the seals of the sovereign authority, reserving to ourselves the title of MOST HIGH EMPEROR, as a distinctive appellation, thus accomplishing in the end, what in our solemn invocation to Heaven we had originally proposed." (Staunton, 1810: 480)

our son the present Emperor, the seals of the sovereign authority, reserving to **ourselves** the title of MOST HIGH EMPEROR, as a distinctive appellation... (Ibid. 480)

【例2】①

越岁庚申为<u>朕</u>九旬万寿……夫以朕年跻上耄诸福备膺……然朕之本衷实不欲侈陈隆轨过滋劳费……今<u>朕</u>已登八十有九……

As upon the year *Keng-shin*, which is the next following to the present, would occur the ninetieth anniversary of **our** age, last year, the Emperor, our son, in concert with the princes and great officers of state...

Viewing, indeed, the advanced age of upwards of fourscore years, which **we** had then attained in the full enjoyment of every prosperity, the Emperor, our son, and the inhabitants of our vast domains...

The grandeur, however, and profusion attendant on a general rejoicing were by no means the objects of **our** desire...

---

① 详见《嘉庆四年正月初三日太上皇帝诰》。《嘉庆道光两朝上谕档》第四册,中国第一历史档案馆编,第2—3页。粗体及下划线由本书作者添加。乾隆遗诏原文完整片段如下:"……越岁庚申为朕九旬万寿昨冬皇帝率同王公内外大臣等预请举行庆典情词恳求实出至诚业降敕旨俞允夫以朕年跻上耄诸福备膺皇帝合万国之欢申亿龄之祝固为人子为人臣者无穷之愿然朕之本衷实不欲侈陈隆轨过滋劳费每思洪范以考终列福之五从古帝王恭享遐龄史册相望终归有尽且人生上寿百年今朕已登八十有九即满许期顺亦瞬息间事……"小斯当东版译文:"As upon the year *Keng-shin*, which is the next following to the present, would occur the ninetieth anniversary of our age, last year, the Emperor, our son, in concert with the princes and great officers of state, was desirous of determining upon the celebration of that event b a congratulatory festival, and earnestly requested our consent to the carrying the same into effect; to which we, shortly after, in consideration of the meritorious motives which actuated them in their proceedings, replied by an edict expressive of our approbation and concurrence. Viewing, indeed, the advanced age of upwards of fourscore years, which we had then attained in the full enjoyment of every prosperity, the Emperor, our son, and the inhabitants of our vast domains, were naturally filled with joy and exultation: no event could certainly have been more ardently desired by our son and the great officers of the empire, then an opportunity of celebrating such an anniversary. The grandeur, however, and profusion attendant on a general rejoicing were by no means the objects of our desire; we were satisfied with the contemplation of the maxim of antiquity, which enumerates a life prolonged to an advanced age amongst the five instances of human felicity: for although among our ancient monarchs, some have likewise attained a very advanced period of life according to the testimony of the annals of the empire, yet it may be observed, that within the full period of an hundred years, the longevity to which they had aspired has in every instance received its termination. We have already attained the eighty-ninth year of our age; therefore but a few short years are wanting to complete the utmost period of longevity..." (Staunton, 1810: 481–482)

We have already attained the eighty-ninth year of **our** age...
(Ibid. 481 – 482)

需要追问的是，不列颠君主果有自称第一人称复数代词的行文习惯吗？*Random House Compact Unabridged Dictionary* 中词条"we"的确包含相近的用法：

Also called the royal we. (used by a sovereign, or by other high officials and dignitaries, in place of *I* in formal speech)... (Flexner, 1996: 2152)

笔者还在英皇室官网（the Official Website of the British Monarchy①）上查阅到与乾隆皇帝同时代的乔治三世（King George III, r. 1760 – 1820）的一封亲笔信函②，表示对丧失美洲殖民地深感痛心疾首。此函就是通过"we"贯穿始终，但信的内容明显止于宣泄情绪，哀叹国事不顺。

尽管如此，国王的私人通信或日记③也常使用第一人称单数代词，即便正式演说中"I"和"we"的交替出现同样司空见惯。譬如伊丽莎白一世（Queen Elizabeth I, r. 1558 – 1603）挑战西班牙无敌舰队（the Spanish Armada）前夕向其军队发表的著名讲话，便以"I"自称：

My loving people, we have been persuaded by some that are careful of our safety, to take heed how we commit ourselves to armed multitudes for fear of treachery; but, I do assure you, I do not desire to live to distrust my faithful and loving people. ④

又譬如 1798 年乔治三世在国会开幕时演讲⑤的结束部分（George III,

---

① http: //www. royal. gov. uk.

② *A Letter by George III on the loss of America* (1780s)。原载于 http: //www. royal. gov. uk/HistoryoftheMonarchy/ KingsandQueensoftheUnitedKingdom/TheHanoverians/ GeorgeIII. aspx，全文详见附录 1。

③ *Extracts from Victoria's Diaries*。原载于 http: //www. royal. gov. uk/HistoryoftheMonarchy/ KingsandQueensof theUnitedKingdom/TheHanoverians/Victoria. aspx，全文详见附录 2。

④ *A Speech by Elizabeth I Addressing her Troops at Tilbury* (1588)。原载于 http: //www. royal. gov. uk/ HistoryoftheMonarchy/KingsandQueensofEngland/TheTudors/ElizabethI. aspx，节选部分仅为讲话的首段，全文详见附录 3。

⑤ THE KING'S SPEECH, AS IT MIGHT HAVE BEEN, AND AS IT IS.

1798：7 - 8）：

> *My Lords and Gentlemen*,
>
> I rely with confidence on the continuance of your exertions, to enable Me ultimately to conduct the great Contest in which we are engaged, to a safe and honourable conclusion.
>
> We have surmounted many and great difficulties—our perseverance in a just Cause has been rewarded with distinguished Success, and our present situation, compared with that of other Countries, sufficiently proves how much, in a period of general danger and calamity, the Security and Happiness of the British Nation have depended (under the blessing of Providence) on its own Constancy, its Energy, and its Virtue.

　　仔细揣摩相关历史文献后不难发现，若国王意欲宣示个人权威、阐明个人观点、付出个人承诺等，此类言语行为的实施，很多时候还是离不开第一人称单数代词，以区别于上下文中"you"所代表的广大特定或不特定的信息接收者。唯有需要感染并同化听众之际方才借助泛指的"we"，以便削弱他们可能对异质内容产生的排斥，从而唤起共鸣，使演讲者娓娓动听的雄辩说辞更易为人接受。换言之，"we"的这种用法，与其认定为指代帝王主权的"Royal We"，倒不如视作交流的艺术。

　　综上所述，小斯当东对"朕"译入"we"的托词很难自圆其说。笔者以为汉语尊称遭遇改写的根源还在于权力博弈的渴求。实际上，从马戛尔尼访华时坚持平行相见并因此产生觐礼之争，便可隐约查察端倪。工业革命中日渐富强的不列颠人早已凭借坚船利炮纵横四海，当然不愿对固步自封的大清皇帝致以较本国君主更高的崇敬。又何况英国资产阶级近代民主意识高涨，平等观念也渐趋深入人心，代表上层贵族精英的小斯当东不能亦不可能效仿中华子民对帝王卑躬屈膝式的盲目顶礼膜拜，嗤之以鼻是必然的。

　　故而译者毅然决然地摒弃"I（the Emperor）"，选择所谓的"（Royal）We"，至少在某种程度上有利于剥离"朕"字本身所固有的君权至上理念及其隐含的神秘光环。毋庸置疑，泛指的复数代词更能磨平单数特指或许张扬的棱角。且既无君臣之别，又何来夷夏之分？何来"普天之下，莫非王土；率土之滨，莫非王臣"的霸气？更不必提什么"四夷共主"！

小斯当东力争维持中英地位平等，真可谓苦心孤诣，正如 1793 年 8 月 6 日马戛尔尼首次拜见直隶总督梁肯堂时所宣称："敝国皇帝，为西方第一雄主；贵国皇帝，则为东方第一雄主"（马戛尔尼，2006：27）。

（三）抬头格式

被译文消磨殆尽的不止"朕"字，还有贯穿原谕旨始终的繁复格式，特别是抬头制度。

所谓抬头制度，指"缮写公文时，凡遇到皇帝或特定的尊贵字样，均不得紧接上文，而须另起一行或空格后书写，以示尊敬与别异"（雷荣广、姚乐野，1990：13）。

据王国维先生言，"平阙之制自秦以来然矣"（1961：907）。至清代，抬写格式规定之复杂、要求之苛刻，俨然是愈演愈烈。且根据字样的尊贵程度，抬头高度亦有差异：空抬、平抬、单抬、双抬、三抬、四抬等诸多形式迭出，等级制度森严蔚为可观。

图 4—15 所引诏书是嘉庆皇帝在其皇父太上皇帝驾崩之际昭告天下，为示尊敬不敢妄署"朕"字而谦称"予"，其中借抬写展露谦逊之意自然更甚。纷繁复杂似此的严谨格式在英文版中却绝无分毫蛛丝马迹可寻（请参见图 4—16）。

嘉慶四年正月初三日
5
皇帝詔曰予以薄德寅紹
丕基自丙辰初元
皇父太上皇帝親授大寶夙夜祗栗乾乾深以不克負荷是
懼仰賴
天
祖垂佑我
皇父康彊純固
訓政彌勤于日侍
聖顏時聆
恩誨事事得有稟承每歲披
肇巡方萬衆歡欣同殷瞻就予問
安視
膳之下竊幸
皇父精神愈鍊不減平時愛日寸忱於焉稍慰昨以庚
申年恭值
皇父九旬萬壽予躬率王公大臣等臚誠籲請舉行慶
典欣荷
慈俞率土歡天同伸舞蹈敬念

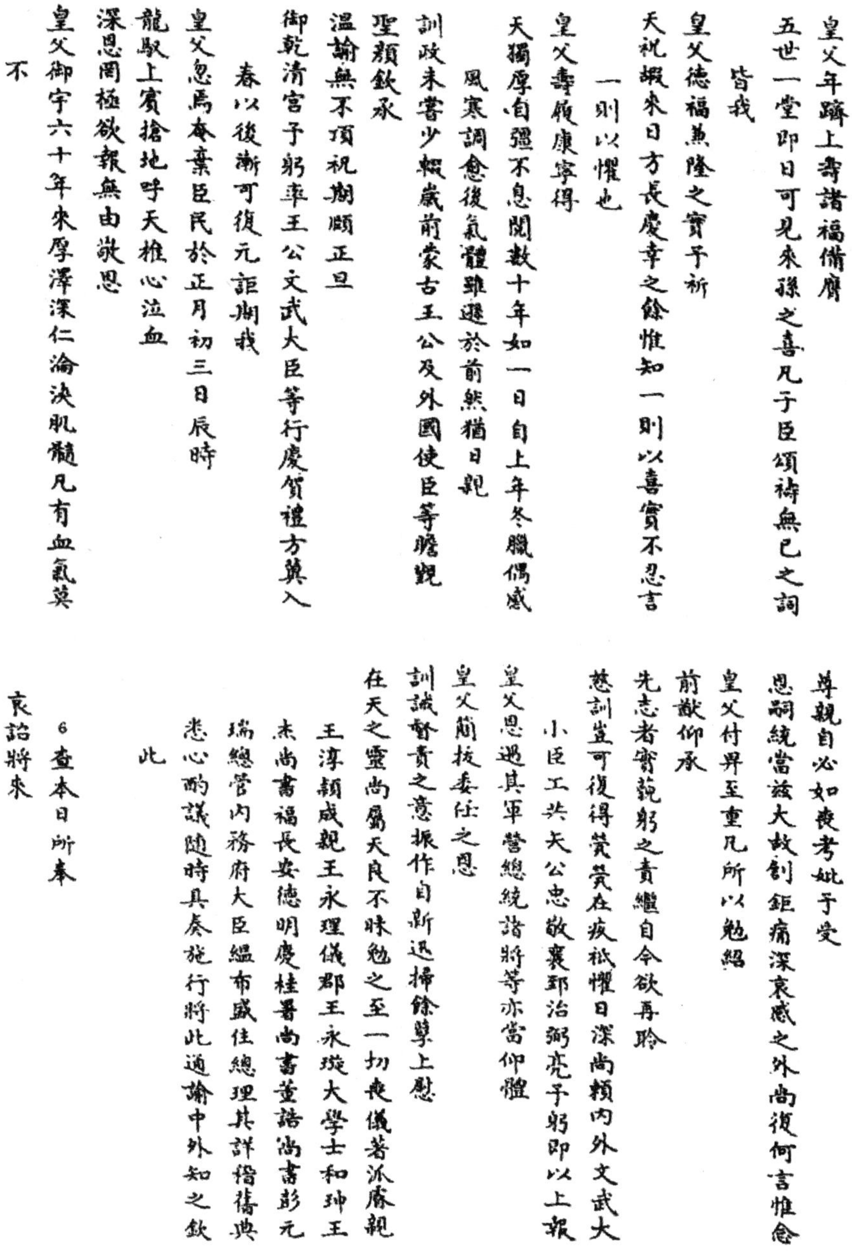

皇父年躋上壽諸福備膺

五世一堂即日可見來孫之喜凡于臣頌禱無已之詞

皆我

皇父德福熙隆之實予祈

天祝蝦米日方長慶幸之餘惟知一則以喜實不忍言

一則以懼也

皇父壽頤康寧得

聖顏欽承

訓政未嘗少輟歲前蒙古王公及外國使臣等瞻覲

風寒調念後氣體雖退於前然猶日覲

天獨厚自彊不息閱數十年如一日自上年冬臘偶感

溫諭無不頃祝期顒正旦

御乾清宮予躬率王公文武大臣等行慶賀禮方冀入

春以後漸可復元詎期我

皇父忽焉棄臣民於正月初三日辰時

龍馭上賓捨地呼天椎心泣血

深恩罔極欲報無由欲思

皇父御宇六十年宋厚澤深仁渝決肌髓凡有血氣莫

不

尊親自必如喪考妣予受

恩詞統當該大故剖鉅痛深衷感之外尚復何言惟念

皇父付畀至重凡所以勉紹

前歡仰承

先志者實可復償荷之責繼自今欲再聆

慈訓當可復得荷賞在疚祇懼日深賴內外文武大

小臣工共矢公忠敬襄郅治弼亮予躬即以上報

皇父恩遇其軍營總統諸將等亦當仰體

皇父簡拔委任之恩

訓誡督責之意振作自新迅掃餘孽上慰

在天之靈尚屬天良不昧先之至一切喪儀著沐廉親

王淳頴成親王永理儀郡王永璇大學士和珅王

未尚書福長安德明慶桂普尚書董誥尚書彭元

瑞總管內務府大臣綰布盛住總理其詳擅舊典

悲心酌議隨時具奏施行將此道諭中外知之欽

此

6 查本日所奉
哀詔將來

图4—15 嘉庆四年正月初三日皇帝诏书截图①

① 《嘉庆道光两朝上谕档》第四册，中国第一历史档案馆编，第2—3页。

　　也许有人认为译文首字母大写亦是表示敬意的变通方式，但笔者难以为然。且不说首字母大写的缘由多样，或为句首或为特指，无法逐项而论。更可虑者，并非全部抬头字样均被译入大写单词。譬如"仰赖天祖垂佑"句，"天"译入"Heaven"，"祖"却成为"our illustrious ancestors"（请参见图4—16）。即便是皇帝年号等专有名词的大小写也未完全统筹划一[①]，这足可说明两者之间绝无常例可循。若还需其他佐证，那么小斯当东本人的日记就常有将小写字母大写的现象（黄一农，2007：50）。

With feeble virtues, and infpired with awe by a fenfe of our own infufficiency, we have held the vaft inheritance of thefe dominions, fince it pleafed our Imperial Father, THE MOST HIGH EMPEROR, on the firft day of the year *Ping-fhin*, (the 8th of February 1ˉ96,) to transfer the feals of the empire to our charge.

We applied with unremitting diligence and attention to the difcharge of the high duty then impofed on us, that we might not fruftrate the gracious defigns that were executed in our favour, though our firmeft reliance was placed in the protection of Heaven and of our illuftrious anceftors.

图4—16　小斯当东译本《大清律例》嘉庆四年正月初三日皇帝诏书截图
（Staunton，1810：483）

　　英文版剔除抬头格式的意图是明显的。好似当初由广东巡抚郭世勋觅行商及中国通事翻译英属东印度公司董事会主席百灵（Francis Baring）呈送两广总督告知马戛尔尼使华事宜的文件，亦经逆向添附"天朝体例"[②]。清廷君臣总拟夷狄能效恭顺之心，而英国方自强盛，又岂甘久居人下？

────────────

① 请参阅本章【4.4.21】之一音译。
② 请读者比较图4—17/4—18。

The Honorable the President and Chairman of the Honorable the Court of Directors under Whose orders and authority the Commerce of Great Britain is carried on with the Chinese Nation at Canton to the High and Mighty Lord the Tsontock or Viceroy of the Provinces of Quantong and Kiang-Si Greeting.

These are with our hearty commendations to acquaint you that Our most Gracious Sovereign His most Excellent Majesty George the Third King of Great Britain France and Ireland Ve². Ve². whose fame extends to all parts of the World having heard that it had been expected his Subjects settled at Canton in the Chinese Empire should have sent a Deputation to the Court of Pekin in order to congratulate The Emperor on his entering into the Eightieth year of his age, and that such Deputation had not been immediately dispatched His Majesty expressed great displeasure thereat. And being desirous of cultivating the friendship of the Emperor of China and of improving the connection intercourse and good correspondence between the Courts of London and Pekin, and of increasing and extending the commerce between their respective subjects resolved to send his wellbeloved Cousin and Counsellor The Right Honorable George Lord Macartney Baron of Lissanoure one of his most honorable Privy Council of Ireland and Knight of the most honorable Order of the Bath and of the most ancient and royal Order of the white Eagle, a nobleman of high rank and quality, of great virtue wisdom and ability who has already filled many important offices and Employments in the State as his Ambassador Extraordinary and Plenipotentiary to the Emperor of China to represent his Person and to express in the strongest terms the satisfaction he shall feel if this mark of his attention and regard serves as a foundation to prove the sincerity of his sentiments and of his earnest wishes to promote the advantage and interest of the two Nations of Great Britain and China, and to establish a perpetual harmony and alliance between them.

The Ambassador with his attendants will very soon set out on his Voyage and having several Presents for the Emperor of China from the King of Great Britain which from their size nice mechanism and value could not be conveyed through the interior of the Country to so great a distance as from Canton to Pekin without the risk of much damage and injury will proceed directly and without delay in one of His Majesty's Ships properly accompanied to the Port of Tien-Sing, in order to mark his particular respect by approaching in the first instance, as near as possible to the residence of the Emperor of China. We request therefore that you will please to convey this information to the Court of Pekin, trusting that the Imperial Orders and Directions will be issued for the proper reception of the King of Great Britain's Ships with his Ambassador and his attendants on board them as soon as they shall appear at Tien-Sing or on the neigbouring Coasts. And so praying the Almighty God to grant you all happiness and long life and to take you under his heavenly protection we bid you heartily farewell.

Given at London the 27th day of the month of April in the year 1792 of the Christian Æra.

FRANCIS BARING.

图4—17　英使马戞尔尼来聘案截图①

---

① 《掌故丛编》，故宫博物院掌故部编，第621—622页。

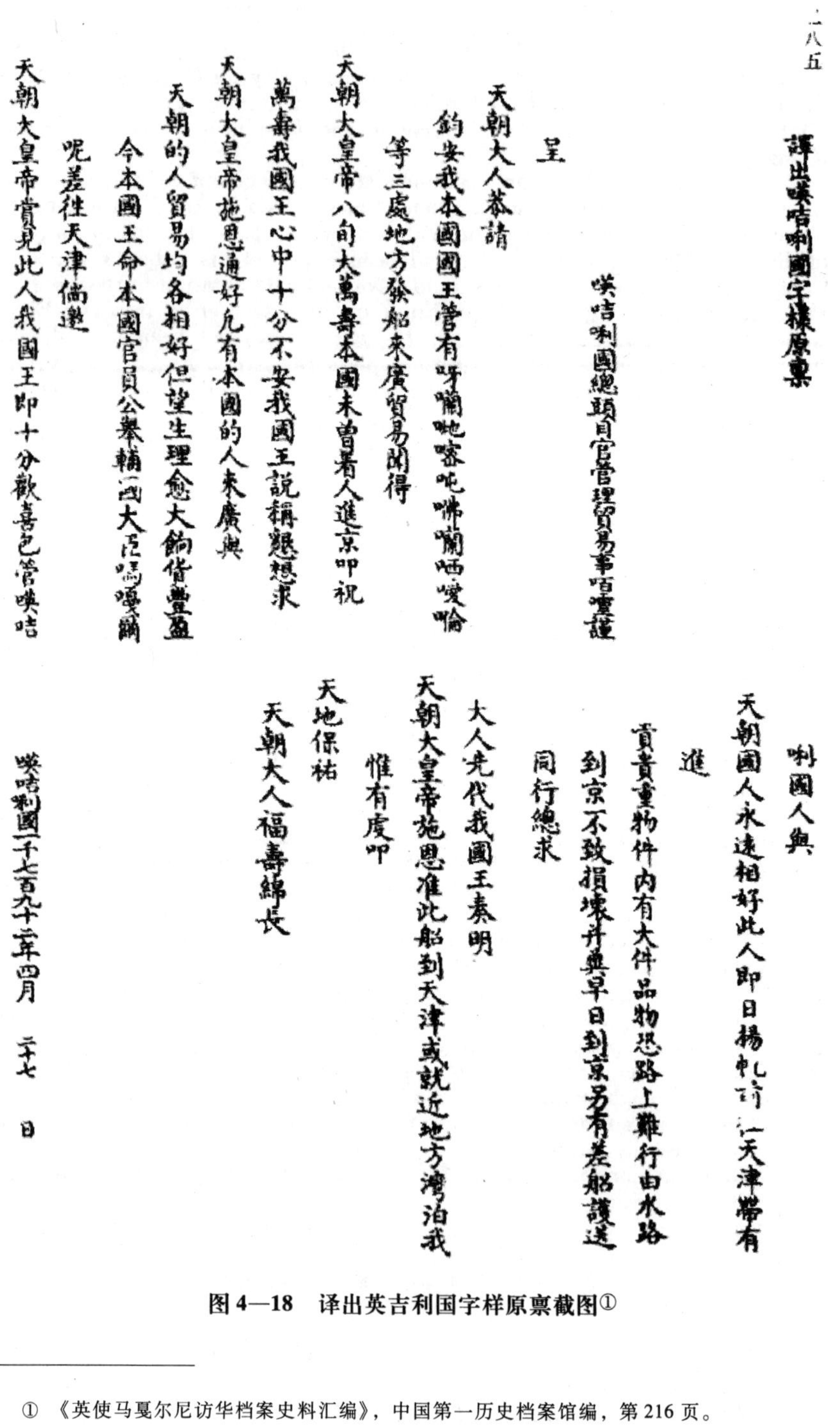

一八五

譯出喫啥唎國字樣原稟

喫啥唎國總頭目官管理貿易事喏嗹謹

進

唎國人與

天朝國人永遠相好此人即日揚帆行往天津帶有

貴貴重物件內有大件品物恐路上難行由水路
到京不致損壞并要早日到京另有差船護送

進

大人先代我國王奏明

天朝大皇帝施恩准此船到天津或就近地方灣泊我

惟有虔叩

天地保祐

天朝大人福壽綿長

呈

天朝大人恭請

鈞安我本國國王管有呼嚙呢嗹吪咈嘣哂覺嚧
等三處地方發船來廣貿易開得

天朝大皇帝八旬大萬壽本國未曾着人進京叩祝

萬壽我國王心中十分不安我國王說稱懇求

天朝大皇帝施恩通好凡有本國的人來廣興

天朝的人貿易均各相好但望生理慾大鋪貨豐盈

今本國王命本國官員公舉輔一四大臣嗎嘮嚩

呪差往天津備邀

天朝大皇帝賞見此人我國王即十分歡喜包管喫啥

喫啥唎國一千七百九十二年四月　二十七　日

图4—18　译出英吉利国字样原禀截图①

① 《英使马戛尔尼访华档案史料汇编》，中国第一历史档案馆编，第216页。

再比较以下图示所引敕谕国书，更能展现王朝衰微、权力倾颓所致文书体例的变换：乾隆末年尚属盛世，勉能居高临下；鸦片战争后残喘至光绪年间能以平等姿态为他国接纳已然不易，岂敢奢望他求。

奉　二二三四

天承運

皇帝勅諭噯咭唎國王知悉咨爾國王遠在重洋傾
心向化特遣使恭齎表章航海來庭叩祝萬壽並
備進方物用將忱悃朕披閱表文詞意肫懇具見
爾國王恭順之誠深為嘉許所有齎到表貢之正
副使臣念其使遠涉推恩加禮已令大臣帶領
瞻觀錫予筵宴疊加賞賚用示懷柔其已回珠山
之管船官役人等六百餘名雖來來京朕亦優加
賞賜俾得普沾恩惠一視同仁至爾國王表內懇
請派一爾國之人住居天朝照管爾國買賣一節
此則與天朝體制不合斷不可行向來西洋各國
有願來天朝富差之人原准其來京但既來之後
即遵用天朝服色安置堂內永遠不准復回本國
此係天朝定制想爾國王亦所知悉今爾國王欲
求派一爾國之人住居京城既不能若來京富差
之西洋人在京居住不歸本國又不可聽其往來

图4—19　乾隆皇帝敕谕英吉利国王截图①

图4—20　光绪二十八年二月初六日致比利时国王书

① 《英使马戛尔尼访华档案史料汇编》，中国第一历史档案馆编，第165页。

反之，体例的刻意变换亦能体现译者操纵文本以适应权力需求的心态。否则，又怎会出现将乔治三世致乾隆皇帝平等建交的国书篡改成向天下共主进贡祝寿的表文（请参见图4—21）如此深远影响历史进程的误会？小斯当东绝非始作俑者，至多不过是萧规曹随罢了。

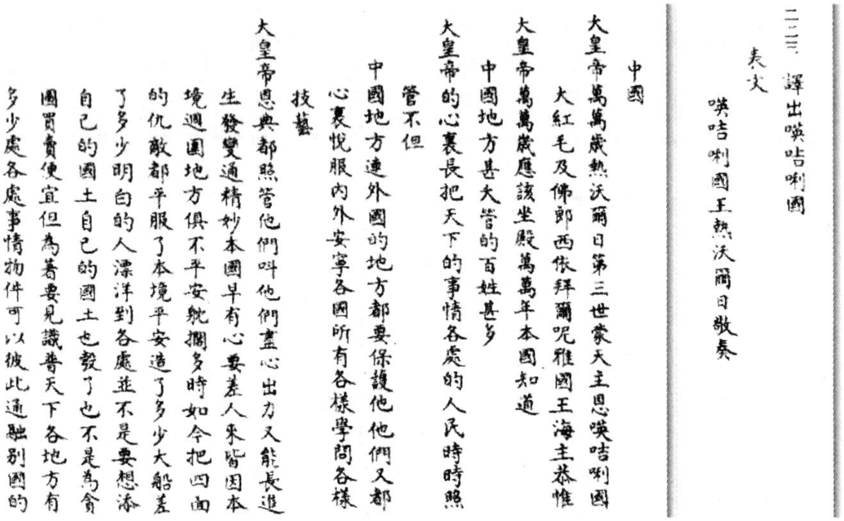

多少处各处各样事情物件可以彼此通融别国的
国贾贵便宜但为着要见识普天下各地方有
自己的国土也就了也不是为贪
了多少明白的人漂洋到各处并不是要想添
的仇敌都平服了本境平安适了多少大船差
境通圆地方俱不平安就拥多时如今把四面
生发贯通精妙本圆早有心要差人来的圆本
中国地方连外国的地方都要保护他他们又都
心裏悦服内外安宁各圆所有各样学问各样
技艺
大皇帝恩典都照管他们叫他们盡心出力又能长进
管不但
中国地方甚大管的百姓甚多本圆知道
大皇帝的心裏长把天下的事情各处的人民时时照
大皇帝万万岁应该坐殿万万年本圆知道
大红毛及佛郎西依拜兰呢雅圆王海主恭惟
大皇帝万万岁热沃尔日第三世蒙天主恩喚咭唎圆
中国

二二三 译出喚咭唎圆
表文
喚咭唎圆王热沃尔日敬奏

图4—21 译出英吉利国表文截图①

二 "化外人"与"外国人"

据沈家本考证，清代的"化外人有犯"条（请参见图4—22）"本《唐律》。唯唐有同类、异类之分，明删之，则同类相犯亦以法律论矣。今蒙古人自相犯，有专用蒙古例者，颇合《唐律》，各依本俗法之意"（2011：783）。另按《唐律疏议·名例律》之"化外人相犯"条规定："诸化外人，同类自相犯者，各依本俗法；异类相犯者，以法律论。"②

所谓"化外人"，"谓蕃③夷之国，别立君长者，各有风俗，制法不同。"④ 对此，钱大群所撰《唐律疏议新注》解释说，古代统治者相信只

---

① 《英使马戛尔尼访华档案史料汇编》，中国第一历史档案馆编，第162页。
② 详见《唐律疏议》卷第六。(唐) 长孙无忌等撰，刘俊文点校，第133页。
③ "蕃"同"藩"。
④ 详见《唐律疏议》卷第六。(唐) 长孙无忌等撰，刘俊文点校，第133页。

有中国人才受"王道教化"，故贬称外国人为"化外人"（2007：208）。需要说明的是，唐朝人心目中的"国"并非现代意义上的主权国家，将"化外人"等同"外国人"也不甚准确。实际上，"华夷之辨"无非有二：文化标准和族群标准。

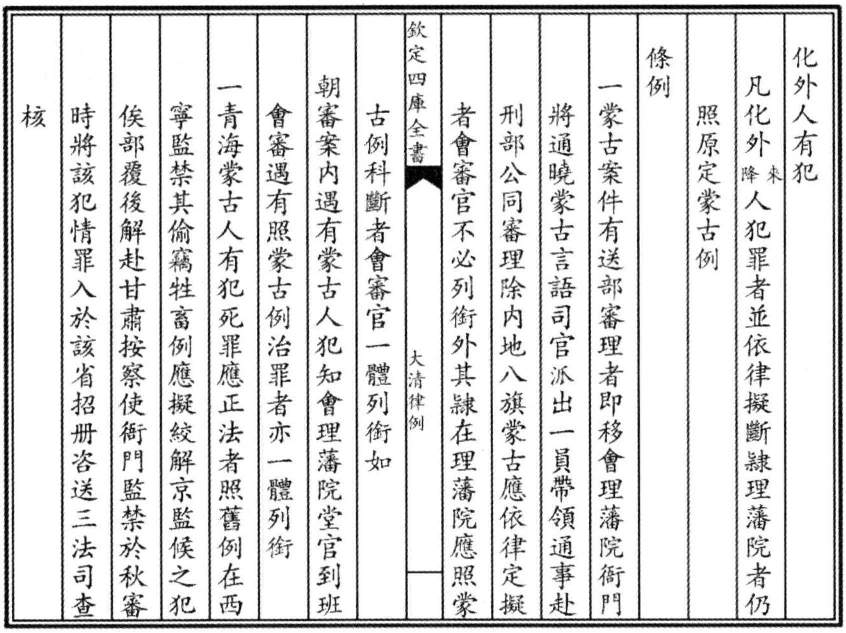

化外人有犯

凡化外（未）降人犯罪者並依律擬斷隸理藩院者仍

條例

照原定蒙古例

一蒙古案件有送部審理者即移會理藩院衙門

將通曉蒙古言語司官派出一員帶領通事赴

刑部公同審理除內地八旗蒙古應依律定擬

者會審官不必列銜外其隸在理藩院應照蒙

欽定四庫全書　大清律例

古例科斷者會審官一體列銜如

朝審案內遇有蒙古人犯知會理藩院堂官到班

會審遇有照蒙古例治罪者亦一體列銜

一青海蒙古人有犯死罪應照正法者照舊例在西

寧監禁其偷竊牲畜例應擬絞解京監候之犯

俟部覆後解赴甘肅按察使衙門監禁於秋審

時將該犯情罪入於該省招冊咨送三法司查

核

图4—22　《钦定四库全书·大清律例·卷五》截图

查《辞海》可知"化外"这个词，"旧时统治者称政令教化所达不到的地方"，即文明地区以外（夏征农，1999：589）。其中"化"字包含"教化"、"开化"之意。教化者，即"政教风化或教育感化"；开化者，则为"启蒙、教化"。显然，依文明程度识别"化外人"乃其本义，深谙中国传统社会以儒家学说为基底的"天下性"结构（曹全来，2005：22）。只因欠缺可操作性，又考虑到不同民族间文化迥异，方才引入易于区分的"族群标准"。故虽怀"戎狄同文则华夏，蛮夷同道亦华夏"之大同理想，贯彻的却是"内其国而外诸夏，内诸夏而外夷狄"[1] 的

---

[1]　出自《隐公元年》，详见《十三经注疏·春秋公羊传注疏》卷第一。（汉）公羊寿传，（汉）何休解诂，（唐）徐彦疏，浦卫忠整理，杨向奎审定，第5页。

隔离政策。

SECTION XXXIV. — *Offences committed by Foreigners* *.

In general, all foreigners who come to fubmit themfelves to the government of the empire, fhall, when guilty of offences, be tried and fentenced according to the eftablifhed laws.

The particular decifions however of the tribunal *Lee-fan-Yuen* † fhall

* This fection of the code has been exprefsly quoted by the provincial government of Canton, and applied to the cafe of foreigners refiding there and at Macao for the purpofes of trade. The laws of China have never, however, been attempted to be enforced againft thofe foreigners, except with confiderable allowances in their favour, although, on the other hand, they are reftricted and circumfcribed in fuch a manner that a tranfgreffion on their part of any fpecific article of the laws, can fcarcely occur; at leaft not without, at the fame time, implicating and involving in their guilt fome of the natives, who thus, in moft cafes, become the principal victims of offended juftice.—The fituation of Europeans in China is certainly by no means fo fatisfactory on the whole as might be defired, or even as it may be reafonably expected to become in the progrefs of time; unlefs fome untoward circumftance fhould occur to check the gradual courfe of improvement; it muft be admitted, however, that the extreme contrariety of manners, habits, and language, renders fome fuch arrangement, as that now fubfifting for the regulation of the intercourfe between the Europeans and the natives, abfolutely indifpenfable, as well as conducive to the interefts of both parties.—A tranflation of fome Chinefe official documents of a recent date, illuftrative of the above remarks, is inferted in the Appendix, No. XI.

† This tribunal might be styled the office or department for foreign affairs, but its chief concern is with the tributary and the fubject ftates of Tartary.

图 4—23 小斯当东译本《大清律例》第 XXXIV 条截图
（Staunton, 1810: 486）

换言之，"化外人"不仅指"夷国"、"藩国"，还包括王朝域内治下的少数民族，这一点在特别提及蒙古人的《大清律例》中更是毋庸置疑。无论如何，小斯当东还是果断地将之译入中性的"foreigners"，并音译处理与其相关的"理藩院"。

清代的"理藩院"是掌管内外蒙古、青海、新疆、西藏各地少数民族事务的机关，并负责与部分属国及其他国家的交往（马建石 & 杨育裳，1992：296）。不列颠人当然耻于屈就藩属之列，但译者也知道仅凭读音是无法使信息接收者了解此官署职能的，只能以脚注形式（请参见图 4—23）补明它就相当于西方国家的外交部（office or department for foreign affairs），却又强调其管理的主要是少数民族部落及臣服属国。

小斯当东还在另一条注释中提及清朝官衙处理定居广州及澳门的欧洲人的商业案件时明确引用"化外人有犯"条。这也说明按照大清体制，英、荷、葡等西方国家无疑也是"夷狄"，应当适用该款规定。只是自乾隆以来，但凡涉及欧洲商贾伤害大清子民的人命案，不论情节轻重，概循"一命抵一命"的恶例。难免致使不列颠人忧虑在华英商的处境，也为后来不平等条约中"治外法权"的提出埋下祸根。

三　"贡"抑或"使"？

小斯当东版《大清律例》附录 XXI：Translation of two of the Clauses annexed to Section CCXXV. entitled "*Illicit Exportation of Merchandize*" 中包含如下译文：

> 2. In general, only a limited number of persons shall be admitted into the empire in the suite of foreign embassies, excepting in the instance of the embassy from Corea. —The embassy from Siam shall be limited to twenty-six persons; those of European nations, in general, to twenty-two persons; and those of any other nation, to twenty only. (Staunton, 1810: 544)

尽管此例原文在《钦定四库全书·大清律例·卷二十兵律关津》之"私出境及违禁下海"条后并无记载，其出处尚有待确切考证①。不过，汉语律条所附相关例文亦牵涉朝贡制度：

---

①　据笔者考证，小斯当东英文本中所称暹罗（Siam）、西洋等国入京员役人数的限制应当出自康熙朝《大清会典·礼部·主客清吏使》："凡进贡员役，每次不得过百人，入京员役，止许二十人，余者留边听赏，其进贡船，不得过三，每船不得过百人。【暹罗国】……三年，暹罗国具表进贡，正贡二船，令员役二十名来京，补贡一船，令六人来京。四年，暹罗进贡至京，礼部题定，贡期三年一次，贡道由广东。六年，暹罗进贡，正贡船一，护贡船一，载象船一，续发探贡船一，礼部覆准，进贡船不许过三，每船不许过百人，来京员役二十二名，其接贡船，探贡船，概不许放入。【西洋国】康熙六年，广东巡抚奏称西洋国遣官入贡，正贡船一，护贡船三。七年题准，西洋进贡，以后船不许过三，每船不许过百人。八年题准，令正副使及从人二十二名来京。"详见《清代档案文献数据库·大清五部会典》之康熙朝《大清会典》卷七十二，王光越总编，第 2、16、18 页。

一凡外国贡船到岸未曾报官盘验先行接买番货及为外国收买违禁货物者俱发近边充

一凡外国差使臣人等朝贡到京与军民人等交易止许光素纻丝绢布衣服等件不许买黄紫黑皂大花西番莲缎疋并不得收买史书及一应违禁军器硝黄牛角铜铁等物如有将违禁货物图利卖与进贡外国者为首依私将应禁军器出境因而走泄事情律斩监候为从发近边充军

再比照乾隆朝《钦定大清会典·礼部·主客清吏司·宾礼·朝贡》对赴京觐见贡使人数的详细规定：

凡从人朝鲜贡使从书状官一人大通官三人护贡官二十四人有赏从役三十人无赏从役无常数琉球西洋暹罗苏禄贡舟无过三每舟人无过百赴京无过二十安南缅甸南掌入贡人无过百赴京无过二十其不赴京者留于边境边吏廪气之竢使回至边率之归国①

译文"foreign embassies"（外国使节）指向的源语词汇应为"外国贡使"，已可确定无疑。然而，两者包含的概念实质上风马牛不相及。所谓互派使节，这是近代西方列强在渐趋成熟的国际公法指导下平等建交的产物，完全不同于大清国旨在宣扬天朝上国威加海内、四夷来归的朝贡制度。须知纳贡便是称臣，必有宗主国与藩属国之分。

英文版改写的根源在于"朝贡觐见"、"遣使访问"之辨，孰是孰非可追溯至马戛尔尼访华。乾隆五十八年癸丑六月辛卯皇帝谕军机大臣不许称英使为"钦差"，应正名为"贡使"：

该国遣使入贡安得谓之钦差此不过该通事仿效天朝称呼自尊其使臣之词原不必与之计较但恐照料委员人等识见卑鄙不知轻重亦称该使臣为钦差此大不可著徵瑞豫为饬知无论该国正副使臣总称为贡使以符

---

① 详见《清代档案文献数据库·大清五部会典》之乾隆朝《钦定大清会典》之卷五十六，王光越总编，第3页。

体制①

当时,英国使团搭乘的舟船均分插"英吉利国贡舡"的旗帜,甚至在其携带的每箱礼物上亦标有"英吉利国贡物"等字样。马戛尔尼伯爵虽不满"tribute"(贡)字所蕴含的贬义,但为避免不必要的纷争,只好视若无睹。使团秘书斯当东从男爵在其归国后撰写的报告中记录下当时情形:

> In this spirit, care had been taken, in consequence, no doubt, of superior orders, to write in large Chinese characters upon the flags pendent from the yachts and land carriages of the Embassy, EMBASSADOR BEARING TRIBUTE FROM THE COUNTRY OF ENGLAND. As it was possible that the meaning of those characters might not have been mentioned to his Excellency, he did not think himself bound to make a formal complaint about them; especially as a failure of redress, which he had reason to judge by no means impossible, must have at once a stop to his proceeding: thus giving an abrupt, as well as unsuccessful termination to his mission... (Staunton, 1797: (II) 303 – 304)

事实上,清廷官员同样意识到操纵译文措辞的重要意义,所以才将不列颠国王乔治三世的国书说成"英吉利国表文"、"英吉利国王热沃尔日敬奏"(请参见图4—21),乾隆皇帝回复的谕旨则采用敕书形式,这都是符合贡使身份的体制要求、权力象征。

其时,《大清律例》的译者正当幼年,作为使团成员之一,亲身体验到强盛的英国为谋求商业利益不得不隐忍耻辱的艰难。直至1821年,小斯当东仍愤愤不平地在英译本《异域录》的序言内严词抨击中国朝贡式的外交政策,视其为文明低下的表现:

> It may readily be admitted that, considered in this point of view only,

---

① 详见《内阁档案·乾隆五十八年癸丑六月辛卯谕军机大臣等》。《英使马戛尔尼访华档案史料汇编》,中国第一历史档案馆编,第40页。

the Chinese would rank very low indeed in the scale of civilized nations.
(Staunton, 1921: vi)

他还指出清王朝毗邻野蛮部落，又长期借由自然地利，阻隔夷狄入侵，故而对国际法的原则一无所知，外交理念远远滞后于近代欧洲列强。在他眼里，中国人对和平与战争的理解无疑是荒唐可笑的：

> With them (the Chinese), there is no peace which does not, in some measure, imply submission: there can be no war, which does not at the same time savour, in some degree, of rebellion. (Ibid. vii)

四 综评

英国人欲与大清朝平等交往的意愿由来已久，特别是在他们发现即便屈从中国传统礼仪及朝贡制度，亦不能获得任何商贸优惠后更是怏然不乐。操纵《大清律例》中某些牵涉国家尊严的敏感体例、礼仪术语不过是牛刀小试，至多只能使译文读者略感宽慰而已。除非扭转华人根深蒂固的民族优越感，迫使其接受国际法原理，否则还是掩耳盗铃。

正是有鉴于此，两次鸦片战争结束后中英签订的不平等条约专门规定官方外交文书必须废止"禀"、"藩"、"夷"等歧视性用语：

(1)《南京条约》（*Treaty of Nanking*, 1842）第 11 款规定①：

英文版

ARTICLE Xl.

It is agreed that Her Britannic Majesty's Chief High Officer in China shall correspond with the Chinese High Officers, both at the Capital and in the Provinces, under the term "Communication" 照会. The Subordinate British Officers and Chinese High Officers in the Provinces under the terms "Statement" 申陈 on the part of the former, and on the part of the latter

---

① 详见《中外旧约章大全（第一分卷）》上册，海关总署《中外旧约章大全》编纂委员会编，第 73 页。

"Declaration" 札行, and the Subordinates of both Countries on a footing of perfect equality. Merchants and others not holding official situations and, therefore, not included in the above, on both sides, to use the term "Representation" 禀明 in all Papers addressed to, or intended for the notice of the respective Governments.

中文版

议定英国住中国之总管大员,与大清大臣无论京内、京外者,有文书来往,用"照会"字样;英国属员,用"申陈"字样;大臣批复用"札行"字样;两国属员往来,必当平行照会。若两国商贾上达官宪,不在议内,仍用"禀明"字样为著。

(2)《天津条约》(*Treaty of Tientisn*,1858)第51款进一步规定①:

英文版

ARTICLE LI.

It is agreed, that henceforward, the character "I" 夷 [barbarian], shall not be applied to the Government or subjects of Her Britannic Majesty in any Chinese official document issued by the Chinese Authorities either in the Capital or in the Provinces.

中文版

嗣后各式公文,无论京外,内叙大英国官民,自不得提书"夷"字。

第四节 策略与技巧(三)
——贬抑华夏传统文明

更有甚者,为敦促不列颠政府对清廷采取更为积极主动的外交措施,协助东印度公司开拓中国市场,小斯当东还充分利用自己的译介身份,通过改写《大清律例》,贬低华夏传统文明,一定程度上奠定了英国对华殖

---

① 详见《中外旧约章大全(第一分卷)》上册,海关总署《中外旧约章大全》编纂委员会编,第310页。

民输出的舆论基础。

一 序言直击弊端

英文版《大清律例》的译者序言貌似客观公允，主张中英两国均无理由自恃道德或身体上的优越性（Staunton，1810：x），实则通过冗长篇幅多角度立场鲜明地揭示华人观念之陈腐。

（一）科技滞后，道德低俗

序言伊始，小斯当东便毫不讳言，彻底颠覆数百年来驻华欧洲传教士塑造的东方古国的浪漫主义形象。

就知识传播而言，清朝未有机遇孕育出自己的牛顿、洛克或培根等现代文明先驱，实用科技水平当然远远落后于欧洲列强：

> **Translator's Preface**
>
> In regard to the diffusion of knowledge among the natives, they might not indeed meet with such illustrious instances as those of a Newton, a Locke, or a Bacon; nor even, perhaps, generally, find any tolerable proficiency in the sciences, which in Europe the writings ofthose great men have contributed to much to advance and to establish; but, nevertheless, such a sufficiency, in all ranks and conditions, of the information essential or most useful to each; such a competency and suitableness of the means to the end, as might, upon a general view of the whole population, fairly entitle the Chinese to be put in competition with some, at least, of the nations of Europe, in respect to all the essential characteristics of civilization. (Ibid. x)

就道德修养而言，小斯当东同样认为中国人非但远逊欧洲精英阶层，较之深受基督教影响的普通民众亦是不如。虽然他承认中国人较少表现出残暴自私的劣性，却又将此归结为未经西方启蒙思想运动的洗礼：

> **Translator's Preface**
>
> The virtues of the Chinese, although very inferior, no doubt, to their professions, and of a lower order than those which Christianity has happily

implanted, or invigorated, in the European world, they might also have found as little alloyed, either with the sanguinary or the selfish vices, as among any people for whose guidance the salutary light of revelation has not yet penetrated. （Ibid. x）

（二）法制思想原始

小斯当东指出清朝的刑法体系即使不能视为全世界最公正平等, 至少也是有史以来最全面统一的制度, 最适应其所针对的民族天赋（同上, xi）。即便如此, 他更孜孜以求、严厉抨击的是中国法制的缺陷。

1. 因循守旧, 固步自封

成文法难以克服的弱点之一就是无法自觉地与时俱进。尤其是在敬奉祖宗成制的中国, 修改《大清律例》以适应新形势的需要绝非易事:

Translator's Preface

... although the structure is comparatively of a recent date, it is often rendered intricate and inconvenient from an adherence to a plan, which, owing to its antiquity, is in some places altogether inapplicable to the state of things as they are present exit; and yet, out of respect to its origin, is only cautiously and perhaps awkwardly, modified, instead of being wholly set side or fundamentally altered, as often as new circumstances and events had rendered it expedient. （Ibid. xxiii－xxiv）

2. 单纯追求实质正义（substantial justice）

自古以来, 华人只看重朴素的实质正义。对此, 小斯当东毫不客气地批评《大清律例》中找不到任何程序条款能确保以最简单便捷的方式达到此目标。至于英国法中早已确立的无罪推定、不强迫认罪等先进理念, 更是传统封建体制所不容的:

Translator's Preface

... We shall look in vain, for instance, for those excellent principles of the English law, by which every man is presumed innocent until he is proved guilty; and no man required to criminate himself. Such maxims the

Chinese system neither does nor indeed could recognize. （Ibid. xxiv）

3. 荣誉感与宗教意识缺失

小斯当东认为清朝法律涵盖的行为规范之所以延伸到本应留待习俗或个人感受自决的领域，原因在于其未能体现对荣誉感及宗教意识的积极响应：

Translator's Preface

The acts which the laws of China enforce, and those which they prohibit, are indeed, in some cases, such as are more usually left in Europe to the decision of custom and individual feeling; but, in a country in which **the laws have not in any considerable degree, the active concurrence, either of a sense of honour, or of a sense of religion**, it may perhaps be absolutely requisite that they should take so wide a range. [1] （Ibid. xxvii）

4. 量刑复杂胜似数学计算

小斯当东发现，除十恶不赦的条款外，其余律例的执行远较其文义解释（*prima facie* interpretation）宽松。据此量刑所涉计算之复杂，致使中国法典条文看似如同一连串数学题。

Translator's Preface

... One considerable inconvenience, indeed, results form this system: in consequence of its adoption, although the place intended to be assigned to each transgression against the laws, in the general scale of criminality, is certainly very readily discoverable by the number of blows of the bamboo, or by the extent of the punishment, in other respects, nominally denounced against the transgressor, the punishment which he is in any particular case actually liable to suffer, is rarely if ever to be ascertained without various references and considerable research. （Ibid. xxviii）

----

[1]　粗体由本书作者添加。

5. 贪污腐败行为屡禁不止

小斯当东还发现，尽管中国人普遍对《大清律例》引以为豪，唯愿"王子犯法与庶民同罪"，然而贪官污吏徇私枉法之举虽难免严惩，却仍层出不穷：

Translator's Preface

That the laws of China are, on the contrary, very frequently violated by those who are their administrators and constitutional guardians, there can, unfortunately, be no question; but to what extent, comparatively with the laws of other countries, must at present be very much a matter of conjecture; at the same time, it may be observed as something in favour of the Chinese system, that there are very substantial grounds for believing, that neither flagrant, nor repeated acts of injustice, do, in point of fact, often, in any rank or station, ultimately escape with impunity. (Ibid. xxviii)

（三）综评

综上所述，小斯当东撰写的序言固然也简单介绍了华夏文明的一些基本情况，特别是有关清朝政府组织形式、法律传统等方面信息，但其主要精力还在于片面贬低中国传统体制的相对合理性，竭力暴露科技滞后、道德低俗、法律发展水平原始的现状，见缝插针地给目标读者群留下先入为主的烙印。

即便偶尔提及中华民族值得效仿的优异之处，小斯当东非但语焉不详，且不忘及时显摆西方列国开明富强仍不耻下问的姿态，其构建欧洲文化优越感的用意昭然若揭。以下引文可窥一斑：

Translator's Preface

But it will scarcely escape observation, that there are other parts of the code which in a considerable degree, compensate these and similar defects, are altogether of a different complexion, and are perhaps not unworthy of imitation, even among the fortunate and enlightened nations of the

West. (Ibid. xxiv)

二 译文暗示鄙陋

中国传统法律长期独立发展、历久自成体系，富含文化底蕴的特有术语繁杂，构成英译的严重障碍。

对此，小斯当东认为保留汉语原文的表述对译者而言当然最易卸责，但考虑到欧洲人既感中文发音陌生，借助字母注音也欠完善，故不足为常例。更值得推荐的通用策略是，以之类比英国法律中的近似术语，间或添加脚注解释说明。

Translator's Preface

In regard to terms, more or less peculiar to the Chinese, such as in a work of this nature would necessarily be of constant occurrence, the Translator might easily have relieved himself from every responsibility, by retaining in each case the original Chinese expression; but, considering that the very sounds of the language are strange and unpleasing to European ears, and, in fact, but very imperfectly capable of being represented by any European alphabet, he has conceived it would on every account be most desirable to reduce the untranslated words into as small a compass as possible, explaining the remaining few in notes in the margin; and remarking generally, with regard to the rest, that, as in the case of the words *Emperor*, *Tribunal*, and the like, they are approximations to the truth, whose ambiguity, if any, the context is generally fully sufficient to remove. (Ibid. xxxii – xxxiii)

（一）术语传译五法

具体说来，《大清律例》英文版传译术语的方法分五类：

1. 音译

皇帝年号、王公封号、臣民姓名、地理名称等专有名词，在《大清律例》正文特别是律条中出现的频率较低，但小斯当东选译的皇帝谕旨涉及相当数量的此类词汇，按惯例当然是音译为便，但在标注方式上并不完全统一。

（1）皇帝年号：标题正文以小型大写字母注音，仅脚注以斜体注音
　　　且（或首词或各词）首字母大写，各词以连字符相接。

　　　顺治　SHUN-CHEE
　　　康熙　KAUNG-HEE/*Kaung-hee*　雍正　YONG-TCHING/*Yong-tching*
　　　乾隆　KIEN-LUNG/KIEN-LUNG/*Kien-lung*
　　　嘉庆　KIA-KING/KIA-KING/*Kia-king*

（2）王公封号：斜体注音，首字母大写，各词以连字符相接。[①]

　　　睿亲王（醇颖）（*Chun-ying*）prince of *Rui-ching*
　　　成亲王（永瑆）（*Run-sing*）prince of *Ching-ching*
　　　仪郡王（永璇）（*Rung-siun*）prince of *Ree-Kiun*

（3）臣民姓名：斜体注音，首字母大写，各词以连字符相接。

　　　和中堂（和珅）*Ho-chung-tong*（*Ho-quen*）[②]
　　　魁伦　*Quay-lung*

（4）地理名词：斜体注音，首字母大写，各词多以连字符相接，省
　　　名偶有直接连写。[③]

---

　　① 本条数例皆摘自小斯当东译本《大清律例》附录 II：Translation of the Edict of the reigning Emperor KIA-KING, by which the Death of his Father, the Emperor KIEN-LUNG, was first officially made public（Staunton, 1810：486）。该附录选译了《嘉庆四年正月初三日皇帝诏书》，原文见《嘉庆道光两朝上谕档》第四册，第4—5页。小斯当东似乎不太理解"亲王"、"郡王"是两种不同等级的爵位，误将"亲"、"郡"二字音译。

　　② 译者将"和中堂"误作和珅的姓名，也许是因为先前马戛尔尼的日记、斯当东的正式报告均如此称呼，但小斯当东译本《大清律例》附录 VIII 说明"和中堂（*Ho-chung-tong*）"即"和珅（*Ho-quen*）"（Staunton, 1810：491）。

　　③ 省名音译偶有不使用连字符的，但并无确定标准，譬如小斯当东译本《大清律例》附录 I：TRANSLATION of the Testamentary Edict of KIEN-LUNG, the late Emperor of China 便将四川译作"*Se-chuen*"（同上，479，481）。该附录选译了《嘉庆四年正月初三日太上皇帝诰》，原文见《嘉庆道光两朝上谕档》第四册，第2—3页。

北京	*Pekin*	四川	*Sechuen/Se-chuen*		
山西	*Shan-see*	广东	*Quang-tung*	广西	*Quang-see*
湖广	*Hou-quang*	云南	*Yun-nan*		

圆明园　the palace of *Yuen-ming-yuen*

乾清宫　the palace of *Kan-tsing-kung*

正大光明殿　the great hall of *Ching-ta-quang-ming*

神武门　the gate of *Shin-vu-men*

2. 音译加注释

部分类别的专有名词譬如干支纪年、度量单位①等，仅凭音译对促进目标读者群的理解而言显然毫无意义，必须借助脚注方可与英文世界的时空观念建立联系。

（1）干支纪年：正文斜体注音，首字母大写，各词以连字符相接，脚注西元纪年。

丙辰年正旦　the first day of the year *Ping-shin**

英译本脚注内容：* The eighth of February 1796.

庚申年　the year *Keng-shin**

英译本脚注内容：* The year 1800.

（2）度量单位：正文斜体注音，首字母或大写，脚注相关单位与英式度量之间大致的换算关系。

里　*lee**

英译本脚注内容：* Ten *lee* are usually estimated to be equal to three geographical miles, but the proportion varies a little in the different provinces of the empire. ②

---

① 《大清律例》中有关五刑及纳赎的具体规定，涉及流放距离、刑具重量及尺寸、纳银数额等度量单位。

② 摘自小斯当东译本《大清律例》第 I 条：*Description of the Ordinary Punishments*（Staunton, 1810: 2）。

斤 *Kin* *

英译本脚注内容: * The *Kin* exceeds the British pound by one-third. ①

原文:夹棍,中梃木长三尺四寸,两旁木各长三尺。上圆下方,圆头各阔一寸八分,方头各阔二寸。

译文:The instrument for compressing the ancle-bones, shall consist of a middle-piece, 3 *Che* 4 *Tsun* * long, and two side-pieces, 3 *Che* each in length; the upper end of each piece shall be circular, and 1 *Tsun* 8 decimals in diameter; the lower ends shall be cut square, and 2 *Tsun* in thickness...

英译本脚注内容: * The *Che* exceeds the British measure of a foot by about half an inch; the *Tsun* is its decimal part. ②

原文:若计雇工钱者,一人一日为银八分五厘五毫。

译文:The wages of labour shall be extimated at 8 *fen* 5 *lee* and 5 *hao* *, for each man *per* day...

英译本脚注内容: * That is to say, 0855 decimal parts of a *lean* or Chinese ounce of silver, whose estimated value is 6*s*. 8*d*. sterling... ③

3. 混合音译、意译

作为脚注音译的替代方式,混合译法在《大清律例》英文版中并不常见。两者的显著差异是,前者通过脚注诠释音译的实际所指;后者则突出意译,音译仅为添附在后的补充说明而已。

---

① 摘自小斯当东译本《大清律例》附录 V: Translation of the Supplementary Clauses to Section I, entitled "*Description of ordinary Punishments*" (Staunton, 810: 489)。

② 摘自小斯当东译本《大清律例》附录 V: Translation of the Supplementary Clauses to Section I, entitled "*Description of ordinary Punishments*" (同上, 488)。该附录选译了《钦定四库全书·大清律例卷四·名例律上》五刑条所附例文,其中刑具尺寸单位似乎只有"分"意译成"decimal","厘"则意译为"寸"的百分数,例如"45/100 *Tsun*"。

③ 摘自小斯当东译本《大清律例》第 XXIV 条: *Restitution and Forfeiture of Goods* (同上, 26)。银钱数额的度量单位唯"两"有所不同:或意译成"Chinese ounce"(缩写 oz);或音意混合为"*lean* or Chinese ounce"。另外,译者还特意通过脚注说明:"The general currency in China is restricted to copper, but all accounts are kept in ounces, and the decimal parts of ounces, of silver"。

刑部　the supreme court for the execution of public justice (*Hing-Poo*)①

寿山口　the bottom of the mount called *Sheu-shan*②

4. 意译加注释

意译加注释的传译方式在《大清律例》英文版中也罕有出现，只对某些按原文字面意思直译可能与目标文化近似术语发生明显混淆的概念，小斯当东才以脚注进行澄清。

文武官犯公罪　Offences committed by Officers of Government in their public Capacity *

文武官犯私罪　Offences committed by Officers of Government, of a private and personal Nature *

英译本脚注内容：* The titles of this and the succeeding section would bear no other translation than that which has been given to them, and it is therefore requisite to add in explanation, that it appears from the notes in the original that the offences denominated *private*, in fact comprehend almost all cases of direct criminality, whereas those denominated *public*, are cases of liability to punishment, solely from the official responsibility of the party implicated. ③

吏律 *Civil Laws* *

英译本脚注内容：* Laws relating to the administration of the civil

---

① 摘自小斯当东译本《大清律例》附录 III：Note of the Translator; containing the Titles of omitted Articles of Preliminary Matter (Staunton, 1810：486)。

② 摘自小斯当东译本《大清律例》附录 VIII – 1：*Translation of an Imperial Edict, containing the Articles of Impeachment exhibited against Ho-chung-tong (otherwise Ho-quen) Minister of China, by the Emperor* KIA-KING, *in the* 4th *Year of his Reign* (同上，495)。该附录选译了《嘉庆四年正月十六日上谕》，原文见《嘉庆道光两朝上谕档》第四册，第 25—27 页。

③ 摘自小斯当东译本《大清律例》第 VII 条：*Offences committed by Officers of Government in their public Capacity* (Staunton, 1810：10 – 11)。清代律例中所谓"公"和"私"的划分，与欧洲传统的"公法"、"私法"概念没有丝毫共通之处。若单纯直译成"public"、"private"又不加解释，无疑是有欠考虑的。为此，译者插入了脚注，类似原文小注的内容："凡一应不系私己而因公事得罪者曰公罪"、"凡不因公事己所自犯皆为私罪"（详见《钦定四库全书·大清律例卷四·名例律上》)。

government. ①

5. 意译

正如前文所引译者序言的剖析,小斯当东最青睐的还是所谓比附说明原则,即套用英文近似术语来传递中国法律概念。这一倾向在很大程度上深刻影响了英美读者对融合儒学思想的《大清律例》质的认识。以下仅是数例官名意译:

> 大学士　the ministers of state
> 尚书/署尚书　the presidents of tribunals
> 总管内务府大臣　the great officer of state

(二) 独钟意译之法

小斯当东的父亲是牛津大学的名誉法学博士,家学渊源深厚。正因为如此,我们才不难理解译者可能立足英美法的理念,解析《大清律例》的建构。换言之,独钟意译之法只是表象,更值得我们考察的是中华传统礼法如何被西方资产阶级法律术语粗暴侵入的深层实质。

请看以下所列《大清律例》各律目、篇名的中英文对照表:

> 名例律　*General Laws*
> 吏律　*Civil Laws*
> 　职制　SYSTEM OF GOVERNMENT
> 　公式　CONDUCT OF MAGISTRATES
> 户律　*Fiscal Laws*
> 　户役　ENROLMENT OF THE PEOPLE
> 　田宅　LANDS AND TENEMENTS
> 　婚姻　MARRIAGE
> 　仓库　PUBLIC PROPERTY

---

① 摘自小斯当东译本《大清律例》第 XLVII 条:*Hereditary Succession*(Staunton,1810:49)。小斯当东将"吏律"处理成"*Civil Laws*"不能算直译,而是认为其内容主要针对文官体制。同时,他也意识到此译文极易被读者混同欧洲大陆源自罗马帝国的"民法",所以添加脚注说明。

　　课程　DUTIES AND CUSTOMS

　　钱债　PRIVATE PROPERTY

　　市厘　SALES AND MARKETS

礼律　*Ritual Laws*

　　祭祀　SACRED RITES

　　仪制　MISCELLANEOUS OBSERVANCES

兵律　*Military Laws*

　　宫卫　PROTECTION OF THE PALACE

　　军政　GOVERNMENT OF THE ARMY

　　关津　PROTECTION OF THE FRONTIER

　　厩牧　MILITARY HORSE AND CATTLE

　　邮驿　EXPRESS AND PUBLIC POSTS

刑律　*Criminal Laws*

　　贼盗　ROBBERY AND THEFT

　　人命　HOMICIDE

　　斗殴　QUARRELLING AND FIGHTING

　　骂詈　ABUSIVE LANGUAGE

　　诉讼　INDICTMENTS AND INFORMATION

　　受赃　BRIBERY AND CORRUPTION

　　诈伪　FORGERIES AND FRAUDS

　　犯奸　INCEST AND ADULTERY

　　杂犯　MISCELLANEOUS OFFENCES

　　捕亡　ARRESTS AND ESCAPES

　　断狱　IMPRISONMENT JUDGMENT AND EXECUTION

工律　*Laws relative to Public Works*

　　营造　PUBLIC BUILDINGS

　　河防　PUBLIC WAYS

1. 割裂传统

　　英文版《大清律例》割裂中国法律传统的效果自始便已显现。且看居诸律首位的《名例律》，合晋朝《刑名》、《法例》辗转演化而成，其本源"即李悝之《具法》也"（沈家本，2011：12）。所谓《具法》，"相当于现代刑法中的总则部分"(张晋藩,1998:11)。

小斯当东将《名例律》译成"*General Laws*",若细究含义,当然再恰当不过。可他紧接着毫无来由地插入了原版所未见的篇名"PRELIMINARY REGULATIONS"。上下标题文字叠加岂不就是"General Regulations"?

FIRST DIVISION,
General Laws.

BOOK I.
PRELIMINARY REGULATIONS.

图4—24 小斯当东译本《大清律例》第一部分首页截图(Staunton,1810:1)

这样排版仅视觉印象而言,于有意无意间,势必唤醒目标信息接收者脑海中潜伏的用以解读欧洲近代法律文件的格式塔图像。换言之,引导读者立足资产阶级法律的意识形态,剖析《大清律例》所隐含的礼法思想已然无法逆转。

如果说这还是偶合造就的负面影响,那么随后小斯当东以"*Civil Laws*"传译"吏律",生搬硬套英文民法术语的痕迹更跃然纸上。其意图自是要与"*Fiscal Laws*"(字面直译:财政法规,用以指《户律》)、"*Military Laws*"(字面直译:军事法规,用以指《兵律》)、"*Criminal Laws*"(字面直译:刑事法规,用以指《刑律》)等纵横交织严密的近现代法典框架。尽管译者试图以脚注形式添加模糊的说明①,但这并不能消除其背弃华夏传统律书编纂指导思想的事实。

须知除《名例律》外,《大清律例》分六部,盖因政归吏、户、礼、兵、刑、工六部之故(沈家本,2011:18)。其中,《吏律》针对的绝不止文官体制,而是吏部典掌执事,乃规范文武百官的行为准则。有鉴于此,将"*Civil Laws*"解释为"Laws relating to the administration of the civil government"实属牵强。既然"工律"可译作"*Laws relative to Public Works*",将"吏律"译成"*Laws relative to Officers*"又有何不妥呢?

译者之所作所为仿佛削足适履,偏将东方文明挤入西方模式。其间

---

① 请参阅本节【4.4.21】之四意译加注释。

"礼"的传译尤为突出。中华民族冠以礼仪之邦由来已久，直可追溯至周公制礼，向被视为"人兽之别"及"夷夏之辨"的文明标志：絮乱人伦、捐弃礼仪，无异禽兽夷狄。

以"尊尊"、"亲亲"为出发点和归宿的礼仪制度旨在"序尊卑、贵贱、大小之位，而差外内、远近、新故之级者也"①，故瞿同祖认为礼的正确含义是"异"（2010：313），正所谓"礼不同"②。这也体现了人有智愚贤不肖的儒学思想，坚持社会分工，维护社会秩序，然后才能"固国家、定社稷"。因此，孔子有言："为政先礼，礼其政之本与！"③

引礼入法、礼法结合始于两汉（张晋藩，2005：1），追求的是明德慎刑：礼则导人向善，积极的"禁于将然之前"；法则罚人为非，消极的"禁于已然之后"。④ 上自"君臣朝廷尊卑贵贱之序，下及黎庶车舆衣服宫室饮食嫁娶丧祭之分"⑤ 皆有规矩。

《名例律》中陈列"十恶"、"八议"、"犯罪存留养亲"、"亲属相为容隐"等特殊条款；《户律》又设置了婚姻嫁娶等方面的专门禁忌；《刑律》之《人命》、《斗殴》、《骂詈》等篇也对良贱尊卑间的冲突另行规范。这都是定罪量刑"于礼以为出入"的典型表现（张晋藩，2005：25）。

正因为"礼"的概念至关重要且博大精深，现代法学家译"礼"多采其音，然后配以诠释⑥。尽管《说文解字》亦有"履也。所以事神致富也"之说，单凭此理解清代礼制仍似太过简陋。须知"礼"固"肇于'俗'而生于'祭'"，但实"别于'仪'而归于'法'"（陈顾远，2011：324，327）。小斯当东译"礼律"为 *Ritual Laws*，视其完全等同

---

① 出自《奉本第三十四》，详见《春秋繁露义证》。苏舆撰，钟哲点校，第276页。

② 出自《礼记·礼器》，郑注："不同言异也。"详见《十三经注疏·礼记正义》卷第二十三。（汉）郑玄注，（唐）孔颖达疏，龚抗云整理，王文锦审定，第732页。

③ 出自《礼记·哀公问》，详见《十三经注疏·礼记正义》卷第五十。同上书，第1376页。

④ 出自《汉书·贾谊传第十八》，详见《汉书》卷四十八。（东汉）班固撰，（唐）颜师古注，第1729页。

⑤ 出自《史记·礼书第一》，详见《史记》卷二十三。（西汉）司马迁撰，（宋）裴骃集解，（唐）司马贞索隐，（唐）张守节正义，第1023页。

⑥ 譬如张晋藩著《中国法律的传统与近代转型》（2005年），英文目录中有"Inserting Li into Law，Integrating Li and Law"；瞿同祖所著《中国法律与中国社会》（*Law and Society in Traditional China*，2011）英文版，也将礼写作"*Li*"。

宗教礼拜仪式,岂非南辕北辙?难怪他添附"祭享"律文后的注释颇具微词:

> * The code of ritual regulations which, in this division of the Penal Laws, is frequently referred to, is, as might be expected from the national character and peculiar habits of the Chinese, extremely voluminous; and the subject likewise occupies a very considerable portion of the great Chinese work already noticed under the title of *Ta-tsing-hoey-tien*. (Staunton, 1810: 171)

《仪制》篇只能将就成杂糅的"miscellaneous observances",触动译者敏感神经的反倒是《祭祀》篇末条"禁止师巫邪术"的规定[①]。

表面平凡的概念替换,带来的后果却极其恶劣,小斯当东的序言甚至直陈华人虚伪,专好繁文缛节:

> **Translator's Preface**
>
> Their virtues were found to consist more in ceremonial observances, thanin moral duties; more in profession, than in practice... (Ibid. ix)

皮之不存,毛将安附焉?脱离儒家礼法合一的哲学思想,还想探求《大清律例》的精神实质,何异缘木求鱼?不幸的是,英文版读者纯以资

---

① 小斯当东异常关注欧洲传教士在华的境遇,故于该条律文下添加了冗长的脚注:"* As the Catholic Christians in China have been estimated at upwards of 200, 000, and have been very frequently objects of the attention of the government, sometimes encouraged, but much oftener severely persecuted, some specific notice in this place of the Christian sect, might naturally have been expected: but, whether on account of its comparatively small importance in the eyes of the Chinese, or from some hesitation which may still exist about pronouncing on its character a decisive and irreversible judgment, the subject is in this code entirely passed over in silence. —To make up in some degree for this defect of information on the interesting question of the present disposition of the Chinese government towards the Christian religion (at least in the form and under the appearance given to it by the Roman Catholic missionaries), a translation has been inserted in Appendix, No. XVIII. of two Imperial Edicts, which are expressly declaratory of the law on this subject, and were issued to the public as late as the year 1805. " (Staunton, 1810: 176)

产阶级法治理念看待中国律书，当然只见糟粕，全无可取处。

2. 变乱体例

此外，篇名术语的英文改写还可能破坏《大清律例》原有体例的内在逻辑性，致使其上不应律名，下难符罪条。

（1）不应律名：举"邮驿"为例。

《大清律例》中《邮驿》篇属《兵律》，因自明季以来，驿站向由兵部车驾清吏司统辖（马楚坚，1997：122）。据乾隆年间法学家吴坛考证："秦有厩置、乘传、副车、食厨。汉初承秦不改。后汉但设骑置，而除厩律，此后无考。唐律皆散见于各条。至明始类为一篇，曰邮驿。我朝因之。"① 继而，清末法学集大成者沈家本又详考得 "《邮驿》之名始于魏，《唐律》在《职制律》中，《元律》亦然。明始分立此篇"（2011：14）。

无论唐、元的《职制律》，还是明、清的《兵律》，规范的都是国政，完全不涉民事。故此，中国古代邮驿官办专用的性质确凿无疑，图4—25所列《邮驿》篇下的律例条目便是明证。

这与欧洲近代始于17世纪的国家专营邮政事业存在本质差异：后者专营仅为国家安全，既不隶属军队，满足的也绝非只是政府通信的需要，更多为公众提供服务②。

以"EXPRESS AND PUBLIC POSTS"（字面直译：快递及公共邮局）偷换传统"邮驿"概念，仍置于"*Military Laws*"（即《兵律》）之下，极易误导英文读者错判原版律文的编纂逻辑，特别是小斯当东仅添注官办专用的说明，始终未提及其军管的特征：

> *The government-post in China, which is the subject of the several sections of this book of the Penal Code, though not professedly open to the people in general, is an establishment of considerable utility and importance, and carried to a degree of perfection, which in an empire so extensive, as well as so ill adapted, from the inequalities and intersections of the surface of the country, to an expeditious mode of internal communica-

---

① 详见《大清律例通考校注》卷二十二。（清）吴坛著，马建石、杨育棠主编，第641页。

② 《邮政发展史》［2012 - 5 - 5］（http：//www.chinabaike.com/article/sort0525/sort0557/2007/20070803157395_ 3. html）。

tion, could scarcely have been expected. (Staunton, 1810: 252)

(2) 难符罪条:举"贼盗"为例。

《大清律例》中《贼盗》篇位列《刑律》之首。古文"贼"、"盗"两字的含义原本不同。按《说文解字》:"贼,败也,从戈则声。"(许慎,2001:742)"败,毁也。"(同上,180)"盗,私利物也。从次,次欲皿者。"(同上,502)

《周礼·士师》亦有"邦贼"、"邦盗"之说。所谓"邦贼"即"为逆乱者";所谓"邦盗"即"窃取国之宝藏者"。故战国魏相李悝首制《法经》六篇,以《盗法》、《贼法》居前。自秦汉至后魏,皆名《盗律》、《贼律》:盗则盗窃劫略之类,贼则叛逆杀伤之类。南朝梁武帝将其更名《盗劫》、《贼叛》二律。北齐始合为一,唐宋后不再分。而元代于《盗贼》外别立《杀伤》之目,明清又改为《人命》。[①] 据《大清律例通考》卷二十三所言:"我朝厘定律书,虽有损益而篇名不改。"(马建石 & 杨育裳,1992:657)换言之,叛逆、盗窃、劫略类罪名均属此篇。

反观译者比附的英美法术语"ROBBERY"和"THEFT",其实仅是涵盖财产犯罪的概念。譬如《布莱克法律辞典》给出如下定义(Garner,2004:1354,1516):

Robbery, n. The illegal taking of property from the person or another, or in the person's presence, by violence or intimidation; aggravated larceny.

Theft, n. 1. The felonious taking and removing of another's personal property with the intent of depriving the true owner of it; larceny.

2. Broadly, any act or instance of stealing, including larceny, burglary, embezzlement, and false pretense.

而《牛津法律大辞典》(*The Oxford Companion to Law*) 的解释也与之相仿佛(Walker,1980:1075,1215):

---

① 详见沈家本《历代刑法考》,第3—4页。

Robbery. In English law, an offence at common law and under statute; since 1968 it consists of stealing and, immediately before or at the time of doing so and in order to do so, using force on any person or putting or seeking to put any person in fear of being then and there subjected to force.

In Scots law, it is, at common law, theft accomplished by means of personal violence or intimidation, and the requirements for theft apply to it also.

Theft. In English law, the statutory offence of dishonestly appropriating property belonging to another with the intention of permanently depriving the other of it whether for gain or not. In 1968 it replaced larceny, embezzlement, and fraudulent conversion.

In Scots law theft is criminal at common law and may be constituted by unlawfully appropriating to oneself possession of goods belong to another, or by finding and appropriating to oneself. Theft by housebreaking is an aggravated form of theft.

In both systems the thing must be capable of removal, and be owned by another. To catch a trout in a river is not theft, but to catch it in another's fishpond is. Akin to theft are blackmail, burglary or housebreaking, cheating, embezzlement, fraud, and robbery.

将之用于指涉《贼盗》篇所隶"盗内府财物"、"监守自盗仓库钱粮"、"常人盗仓库钱粮"、"强盗"、"白昼抢夺"、"窃盗"、"盗马牛畜产"、"盗田野壳麦"、"亲属相盗"、"盗贼窝主"、"共谋为盗"、"公取窃取皆为盗"、"起除刺字"等款算是恰如其分①；用于指涉"恐吓取财"、"诈欺官私取财"、"发冢"、"夜无故入人家"、"略人略卖人"等或明文规定"计赃准窃盗论"或与"强窃盗"相关的律条亦不谓无因；但用于指涉"谋反大逆"、"谋叛"、"造妖书妖言"、"盗大祀神御物"、"盗制书"、"盗印信"、"盗城门钥"、"盗军器"、"盗园陵树木"、"劫囚"等

---

① 其中后四款律条分别是与盗窃罪相关的窝藏赃物、共同犯罪、犯罪构成、后续刑罚等补充规定。

叛逆罪名则无疑太滥。在欧洲人的逻辑思维中，"ROBBERY"和"THEFT"又如何能与分裂背叛、犯上作乱等而论之？

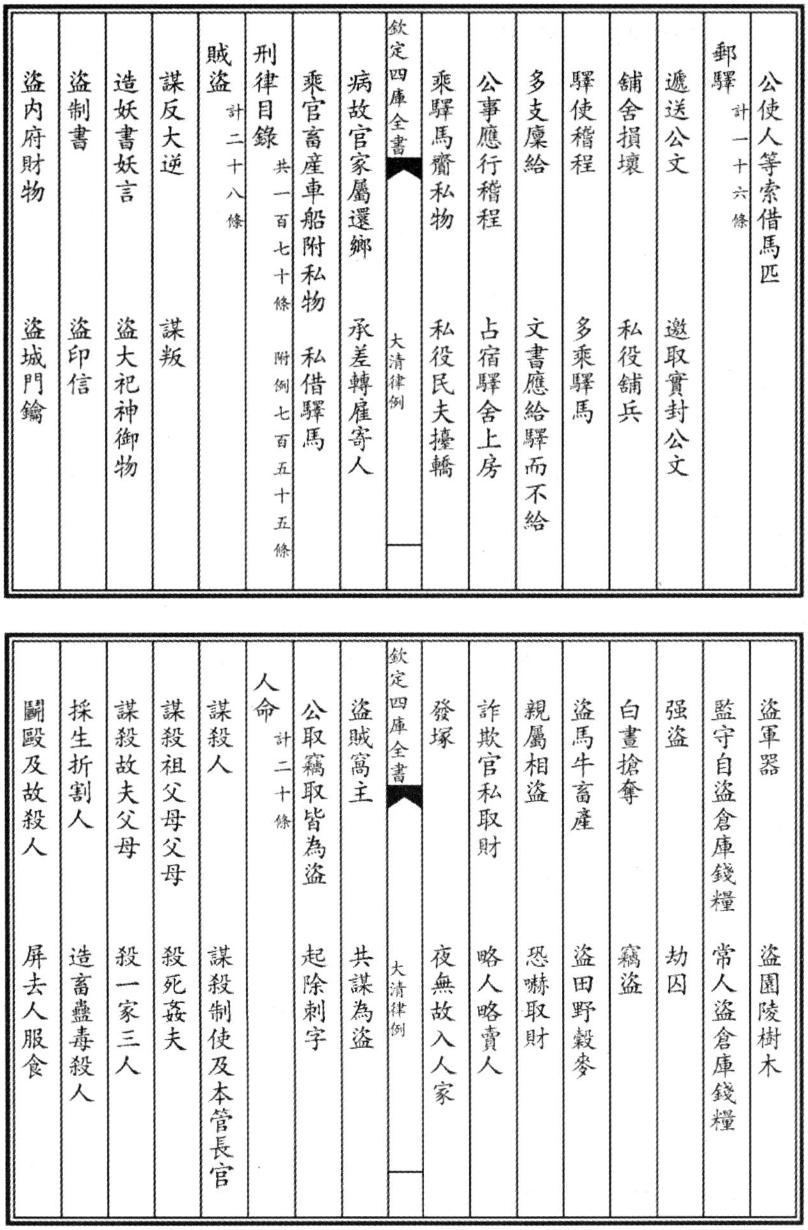

〔上表〕欽定四庫全書 大清律例

公使人等索借馬匹

郵驛 計一十六條 | 邀取實封公文
遞送公文 | 私役舖兵
舖舍損壞 | 多乘驛馬
驛使稽程 | 文書應給驛而不給
多支廩給 | 占宿驛舍上房
公事應行稽程 | 私役民夫擡轎
乘驛馬齎私物 | 私借驛馬
乘官畜產車船附私物 | 承差轉雇寄人
病故官家屬還鄉

刑律目錄 共一百七十條 附例七百五十五條
賊盜 計二十八條

謀反大逆 | 謀叛
造妖書妖言 | 盜大祀神御物
盜制書 | 盜印信
盜內府財物 | 盜城門鑰

〔下表〕欽定四庫全書 大清律例

盜軍器 | 盜園陵樹木
監守自盜倉庫錢糧 | 常人盜倉庫錢糧
強盜 | 劫囚
白晝搶奪 | 竊盜
盜馬牛畜產 | 盜田野穀麥
親屬相盜 | 恐嚇取財
詐欺官私取財 | 略人略賣人
發塚 | 夜無故入人家

盜賊窩主 | 共謀為盜
公取竊取皆為盜 | 起除刺字

人命 計二十條
謀殺人 | 謀殺制使及本管長官
謀殺祖父母父母 | 殺死姦夫
謀殺故夫父母 | 殺一家三人
採生折割人 | 造畜蠱毒殺人
鬥毆及故殺人 | 屏去人服食

图4—25 《钦定四库全书·大清律例·刑律目录》截图

（三）综评

小斯当东曾在序言中为其意译的归化策略进行辩护：

Translator's Preface

He is, at the same time, not unconscious, that the preservation of the style and form of expression observed in the original, is in itself, in this case, of little importance: that it is the nature and principles of the laws, not those of the language of the Chinese people, which it is properly the object of his work to illustrate. Under this impression, he has readily submitted to the necessity, whenever itoccurred, of altering the order of words, and the construction of sentences; he has seldom scrupled to supply the want of a synonymous expression, by a definition; he has even ventured to embody in words those ideas which, though forming an integral part of the sense of the text, were yet left, by a sort of ellipsis, to be understood by implication and inference. (Staunton, 1810: xxxi – xxxii)

或许是文言文的深奥晦涩，或许是东西方文化的形同陌路，某种程度上早已注定异化策略的不可沟通性。然而难以否认的是，小斯当东本有童年短暂游历华夏后留下的先入为主的藐视之心，且贯穿其翻译活动的始终。过度同化的倾向则加剧了英文读者以资产阶级近代法理为鉴，于割裂传统儒学的基础上苛责《大清律例》的内在合理逻辑。

如今看来，结果肯定是灾难性的。小斯当东的译本与英国拓展殖民霸权的渴求高度吻合，刚出版便获得《爱丁堡评论》（*Edinburgh Review*）等英国主流期刊的好评。譬如弗朗西斯·杰夫瑞（Francis Jeffrey）① 就认为他的翻译很有贡献，使不列颠人能从《大清律例》条文烦琐的特征中，判断"中国社会的文明程度不高"（1810：476—499）。

自此以后，华夏帝国的律令条例在西方社会长期被看成是野蛮与落后的象征，他们从内心深处愿意相信"这些法律在一些重要的方面是残酷

———————————

① 《爱丁堡评论》的主编。

的、不合理的",因而对执法的公平正直毫无信任可言(威罗贝,1957:368)。倏忽三十年后,东印度公司悍然挑动鸦片战争的爆发,并竭力鼓吹治外法权的确立,可谓当时已种其因。

第 五 章

鸦片战争时期:林则徐摘译《万民法》

第一节 影响《万民法》源语文本选择的
权力因素

瑞士法学家德·瓦泰尔 (Monsieur de Vattel[①], 1714—1767) 所撰《万民法》(*Le droit des gens. Ou Principes de la loi naturelle*, *appliqués à la conduite & aux affaires des nations & des souverains*, 1758) 被誉为 18 世纪最重要的国际法专著。"尤其在 19 世纪上半叶,它成了外交官特别是领事官必读的经典……在英语国家,特别是美国,瓦泰尔获得的威望更高"(Nussbaum, 1947: 160 – 161)。问世近百年间数度译入英文,其中影响至为深远的是 1834 年首版于伦敦的约瑟夫·切第 (Joseph Chitty, Esq.) 注释本《国际法,或运用在行为和民族与主权事务的自然法则的原则》(*The Law of Nations*, or, *Principles of the Law of Nature*, *Applied to the Conduct and Affairs of Nations and Sovereigns*)。

道光十九年 (1839 年),林则徐在两广总督任内为办理禁烟等涉外事宜选择该书部分文本[②],分别由美国医务传教士伯驾 (Peter Parker) 译成《滑达尔各国律例》、幕僚理藩院通事袁德辉译成《法律本性正理所载》,两者皆收录魏源编著的六十卷本《海国图志》卷五十二夷情备采之译出

---

① 又名 Emer de Vattel,旧译"滑达尔"。"Emer"是瓦泰尔的教名,很多现代作者将之误作"Emerich"(Kapossy & Whatmore, 2008: 555)。

② 据王维俭教授所言,"将《海国图志》保存的伯驾和袁德辉数段译文同英译本滑氏国际法著作对照,发现至少有两段译文译自英译本英译者的注释,而且其中一段为奇蒂所译(J. Chitty)的英译本奇氏所加的注释,为法文原著所未有"(1985: 63);挪威学者鲁纳 (Rune Svarverud) 亦认为他们"依据的是瓦泰尔著作的英文本,且以 1834 年切第版本最为可能"(2000: 302)。本书所引《国际法》原文,除非特别说明,均出自 1834 年切第英文注释本。

夷律及百卷本《海国图志》卷八十三夷情备采三①。

一　译入文化的意识形态
——19 世纪上半叶清代外交焦点：防夷与禁烟

（一）防范夷患，限制通商

乾隆初年加强海外贸易管制以来，各项防夷章程规条日益齐备：《管理澳夷章程》（乾隆九年海防同知印光任等）、《澳夷善后事宜条议》（乾隆十四年澳门同知张汝霖等）、《缉私章程》（乾隆十四年闽浙总督臣喀尔吉善等）、《防范夷商规条》（乾隆二十四年两广总督臣李侍尧等）、《民夷交易章程》（嘉庆十四年两广总督百龄与粤海关监督常显等）、《酌筹整饬洋行事宜》（嘉庆十九年两广总督蒋攸铦与广东巡抚董教增等）、《防范外夷章程八条》（道光十一年两广总督李鸿宾与粤海关监督中祥等）及《防范贸易洋人章程增易规条》（道光十五年两广总督卢坤与粤海关监督中祥等）相继颁布施行。

"一口通商"等限夷措施相当程度上加剧了英华贸易逆差。直至 19世纪二三十年代，清朝仍保持每年出超数百万两白银。眼见外交途径无济于事②，东印度公司为扭转局势不惜铤而走险，策划将鸦片大量输入中国。这被西方国家普遍视为减少白银储备外流的有效手段（Morse, 1910：175）。

（二）走私鸦片，扭转逆差

英属东印度公司虽自 1773 年就已取得孟加拉（Bengal）、柏哈（Behar）和奥理萨（Orissa）所产罂粟的贸易独占权（同上，174），但考虑到清廷严厉禁烟，公司商船遵照嘉庆五年（1800 年）谕旨停止直接输送鸦片至广州，只能在加尔各答先行出售然后转运澳门或伶仃岛（马士，1991：335）。

尽管如此，随着 18 世纪末单纯吸食鸦片法的传入，清朝社会消费毒品的恶习还是泛滥成灾（张馨保，1989：17），致使不列颠冒险家趋之若

---

①　《海国图志》于道光二十七年（1847 年）增补刊刻为六十卷，又于咸丰二年（1852 年）补成百卷本刊行。

②　1793 年马戛尔尼伯爵、1816 年阿美士德伯爵分别率团访华，但在平等通商建交的问题上均因清廷坚守朝贡体制无功而返。

鹜。正如1818年5月威廉要塞管理委员会副主席致总办事处商务部提请采取步骤保护加尔各答鸦片销售的信函中指出："至今获得鸦片的数量，比政府和贵部通常认为是市场的正当需求普遍降低……这种物品的性质，或它受到中国及东方民族居民中流行的特别嗜好，可以任何价钱都能获得相当数量的消费……"（马士，1991：336）

（三）流失白银，动摇国本

无论如何，1821年前输入中国的鸦片数量至多每年五千箱，发展到鸦片战争前夕已猛增至每年四万箱以上（贺力平，2007：78）。

道光十年（1830年）颁布施行的《查禁纹银偷漏鸦片分销章程》①皆因封疆大吏及海关官员的腐化堕落而收效甚微。屡禁不止的鸦片走私彻底逆转中英贸易态势，清朝输出的茶叶、丝绸和瓷器再也无法阻止白银源源流失。这引起诸多官员的高度警惕，他们认为长此以往必将扰乱帝国的经济稳定，动摇府库的财政基础。

鸿胪寺卿黄爵滋在其脍炙人口的《严塞漏卮以培国本折》②（1830年）中明言："近年银价递增，每银一两，易制钱一千六百有零，非耗银于内地，实漏银于外夷也。盖自鸦片流入中国，我仁宗睿皇帝知其必害也，故告诫谆谆，例有明禁……故自道光三年至十一年，岁漏银一千七八百万两。自道光十一年至十四年，岁漏银两千余万两。自道光十四至今，渐漏至三千万两之多。此外，福建、浙江、山东、天津各海口，合之亦数千万两。以中国有用之财，填海外无穷之壑，易此害人之物，渐成病国之忧，日复一日，年复一年，臣不知伊于胡底。"

（四）派遣钦差，厉行禁烟

道光皇帝为此特发谕旨，"著盛京、吉林、黑龙江将军，直省各督抚，各抒己见，妥议章程，迅速具奏"③，一时反响强烈。尤为强硬者如

---

① 详见《李鸿宾等奏呈查禁纹银偷漏鸦片分销章程清单（六月十七日）》。《鸦片战争档案史料Ⅰ》，中国第一历史档案馆编，第68—70页。

② 详见《鸿胪寺卿黄爵滋奏请严塞漏卮以培国本折（闰四月初十日）》。同上书，第254—255页。

③ 详见《著各地将军及各省督抚议奏黄爵滋奏请严塞漏卮以培国本折上谕（闰四月初十日）》。同上书，第258页。

湖广总督林则徐，奏复之余还提出禁烟章程六条①，并于十八年八月初二日（1838年9月20日）再上《钱票无甚关碍宜重禁吃烟以杜弊源片》痛陈利害："鸿胪寺卿黄爵滋原奏所云岁漏银数千万两，尚系举其极少之数而言耳……若犹泄泄视之，是使数十年后，中原几无可以御敌之兵，且无可以充饷之银"②。

当然，亦有相当部分官吏质疑其现实性，故持"变通"或"弛禁"的观点。早在道光十六年四月二十七日（1836年6月10日），太常寺少卿许乃济便呈递《鸦片烟例禁愈严流弊愈大应亟请变通办理折》③，同时奏请驰内地人民栽种罂粟之禁④。这虽得两广总督邓廷桢等认同并拟定章程九条⑤，却因皇帝倾向禁烟而未获真正施行。

迁延至道光十八年九月十一日（1838年10月28日），上谕严责太常寺少卿许乃济妄请弛禁鸦片，"著降为六品顶戴，即行休致"⑥，朝野舆论已达成禁烟共识。同年十一月十五日（12月31日），著颁给林则徐钦差大臣关防，"驰驿前往广东，查办海口事件。所有该省水师，兼归节制"⑦，正式开启驻洋守堵鸦片缉私的序幕。

（五）余论

不列颠政府默许东印度公司贿买满清官吏，偷运鸦片毒害华民，其用意在弥补茶叶贸易所致逆差，自是毫无疑问。难怪英国议院讨论鸦片问题

---

① 详见《湖广总督林则徐奏复黄爵滋塞漏培本之折并酌议禁烟章程六条折（五月十九日）》。《鸦片战争档案史料Ⅰ》，中国第一历史档案馆编，第270—274页。

② 详见《钱票无甚关碍宜重禁吃烟以杜弊源片》。《林则徐全集》第三册，林则徐全集编辑委员会编，第78页。

③ 详见《太常寺少卿许乃济奏为鸦片烟例禁愈严流弊愈大应亟请变通办理折（四月二十七日）》。《鸦片战争档案史料Ⅰ》，中国第一历史档案馆编，第200—202页。

④ 详见《太常寺少卿许乃济奏请弛内地人民栽种罂粟之禁片（四月二十七日）》。同上书，第202—203页。

⑤ 详见《两广总督邓廷桢等奏复应准许乃济所奏弛鸦片之禁并拟章程九条折（七月二十七日）》。同上书，第205—209页。

⑥ 详见《太常寺少卿许乃济妄请弛禁鸦片著即休致事上谕（九月十一日）》。同上书，第391页。

⑦ 详见《著颁给林则徐钦差大臣关防驰赴广东查办海口事件事上谕（十一月十五日）》。同上书，第424页。

后得出结论："放弃这一个重要的税源是不妥当的"①。

　　尽管现代经济学家认为黄爵滋、林则徐等主张严禁者缺乏金融常识，误将鸦片进口量或国内消费量等同货币外流数额，极大地扭曲了烟土泛滥影响帝国财政的规模及危害（贺力平，2007：64），但走私鸦片直接推动白银价格持续攀升，这是谁也无法回避的事实。

　　何况清代中晚期上层统治阶级闭目塞听的普遍心态，仍以为天朝原不过对英夷小邦"柔远绥怀，倍加优礼，贸易之利垂二百年，该国所由以富庶称者，赖有此也"②。林则徐虽是华夏睁眼看世界的第一人，亦难免囿于时代局限，并造就其摘译《万民法》的功利主义选择性——"以夷制夷"无非弹压外商的权宜之计。

二　发起人兼组织者
——主张以夷制夷的禁烟大员

（一）刺探夷情

林则徐（1785 年 8 月 30 日③—1850 年 11 月 22 日④），福建侯官人（今福建省福州市），字元抚，又字少穆、石麟，晚号竢村老人、端村退叟、七十二峰退叟、瓶泉居士、栎社散人等，卒谥文忠。嘉庆九年（1804 年）中举，嘉庆十六年（1811 年）进士，殿试第二甲第四名，初选翰林院庶吉士，从此仕途坦荡。嘉庆二十五年（1820 年）起外放浙江、江苏、陕西、湖北、河南等省任职，先后办理民事、漕务、盐政、河工、水利等，"勇于任事，勤政务实，清廉正直，治绩卓著"⑤，由道台累擢至巡抚。道光十八年十一月（1838 年 12 月）在湖广总督任上受命为钦差大臣。

　　林则徐驰赴广东，肩负的首要重任就是杜塞鸦片来源。故于道光十九年二月初四日（1839 年 3 月 18 日）示谕洋商及各国夷人呈缴烟土，并

---

　　① 详见《伦敦东印度与中国协会致巴麦尊子爵（一八三九年十一月二日）》。《中国近代史资料丛刊·鸦片战争》第二册，中国史学会主编，第 645 页。

　　② 详见《致英国国王檄谕稿（六月二十四日）》。《鸦片战争档案史料Ⅰ》，中国第一历史档案馆编，第 644 页。

　　③ 乾隆五十年七月二十六日。

　　④ 道光三十年十月十九日。

　　⑤ 详见《林则徐全集》第一册前言，林则徐全集编辑委员会编，第 1 页。

"签名出具夷字汉字合同甘结，声明'嗣后永不敢带鸦片，如再夹带，查出，人即正法，货尽入官'"①，矛头直指逡巡伶仃洋面藏匿烟土的趸船。

为更好地实现魏源所谓"师夷长技以制夷"②的策略，主张经世致用的林则徐认为"防夷吃紧之际，必须时常探访夷情，知其虚实，始可定控制之方"③。翻译西方书报亦是当务之急，因此派专员潜入澳门收集资料，"能中其款要，而洋人旦夕所为，纤悉必获闻"④。

驻粤期间，他不仅主持汇编《广州纪事报》（Canton Registers）、《广州周报》（Canton Press）和《新加坡自由报》（Singapore Free Press）等西方报刊有关中国的时事报道及评论，合成循时间顺序排列的《澳门新闻纸》⑤，后又按专题归类为《澳门月报》；此外还选译了《四洲志》⑥、《华事夷言录要》⑦等。这些书稿均被其幕僚兼好友魏源收入百卷本《海国图志》。与此种种，即便是英国人亦承认颇具成效：

中国官府全不知道外国之政事，又少有人告知外国事务，故中国官府之才智诚为可疑……然林行事全与上相反，他自己先预备几个最善翻译之本地人，他就指点奸细打听事件、法子……官府在四方各处打听，皆是有些才能之人，将打听出来之事，写在日记上，按日期呈递登于簿上，有几个夷人，甘心情愿广中国之知识，将英吉利好书卖

---

① 详见《谕洋商责令外商呈缴烟土稿（道光十九年二月初四日行）》、《谕各国商人呈缴烟土稿（道光十九年二月初四日行）》。《林则徐全集》第五册，林则徐全集编辑委员会编，第114—118页。

② 魏源在《海国图志》的序言中明确指出"是书何以作？曰：为以夷攻夷而作，为以夷款夷而作，为师夷长技以制夷而作。"详见《海国图志原叙》。《魏源全集》第四册，魏源全集编辑委员会编，第1页。

③ 详见《两广总督林则徐奏为澳门葡人驱逐英人片（道光二十年二月初四日）》。《鸦片战争档案史料Ⅱ》，中国第一历史档案馆，第30页。

④ 详见金安清撰《林文忠公传》。《清代传记丛刊·综录类·续碑传集》卷二十四，缪荃孙纂录，周骏富辑，第305页。

⑤ 据戴学稷先生考证，《澳门新闻纸》并非译自美国人裨治文（Elijah Coleman Bridgman）主编的《中国丛报》（Chinese Repository）（2006：138）。详见《林则徐译编西方书报述要》（载《闽都文化研究》2006年第1期）。

⑥ 摘译自幕瑞（Hugh Murray）所著《地理大全》（The Encyclopedia of Geography，1834）。

⑦ 摘译自德威时（John Francis Davis）所著《中国人》（The Chinese：A General Description of the Empire of China and its Inhabitants，1836）。

与中国，俾有翻译人译出大概之事情，有如此考究，并添许多知识，于今有何应验？林系聪明好人，凡有所得，不辞辛苦，常时习用，记在心中。于今观其知会英吉利国第二封信，好似初学知识之效验。①

(二) 摘译夷律

《万民法》是林则徐组织翻译的仅有的国际法书籍，显然与其办理鸦片事宜不无联系。据史学家考证，瓦泰尔著作的英文注释版极可能由幕僚袁德辉在澳门探访所得。

至于选择瓦泰尔而非其他国际法学作品的直接原因，挪威学者鲁纳（Rune Svarverud）的观点是瓦泰尔"以多元主义的视角看待国际社会的每一个体成员，认为国际社会是由对其成员的最低限度的约束而得以规制的"，这对"亟须国际组织在国际事务中接受其为独立的和具有平等法律地位的成员"的中国是有利的；且"瓦泰尔对国际社会成员国权利多元主义的阐释使林则徐相信中国在国际贸易问题上可以主张自己的主权和防卫权"（2000：302 - 303）。此说貌似有些道理，但笔者更赞同北京大学法学院赖骏楠博士的看法，无论袁德辉还是林则徐，身处19世纪30年代末"止有'国'而无'际'"的传统儒学语境，恐怕都很难领悟瓦泰尔作品体现的西方近代政治理念（2011：88）。与其说《万民法》适合译介是由于该书思想倾向有利清廷，毋宁说因之当时备受欧美世界推崇，故更易在澳门等地求购。

另外，很多学者误以为禁烟钦差只关注"战争及伴随的诸如封锁、禁运等敌对措施"，这也许是受伯驾在《一八三九年广州眼科医院第十次报告》（TENTH REPORT of the Ophthalmic Hospital, Canton, being for the year 1839）中病案6565号记录的影响②：

> His first applications, during the month of July, were not for medical relief, but for translation of some quotations from Vattel's Law of Nations,

---

① 详见《澳门十二月十四日新闻纸即中国十一月初九日》。《林则徐全集》第十册，林则徐全集编辑委员会编，第213—214页。该报道译自当时英国人办的《广州周报》（Canton Press）。

② 摘自 The Chinese Repository，Vol. VIII, p. 635。

with which he had been furnished: these were sent through the senior hong-merchant; they related to war, and its accompanying hostile measures, as blockades, embargoes, &c.; they were writing out with a Chinese pencil.

实际上，将《海国图志》收录的《滑达尔各国律例》和《法律本性正理所载》稍加比较，便很容易发现林则徐选择的文本既不限"战争"，也不包括"伴随的诸如封锁、禁运等敌对措施"。除战争的发动及其决定权（第二百九十二条）外，还牵涉商品进口例禁与违禁、外商属地管辖原则（第一百七十二条）等。

尽管林则徐选译前述国际法片段达到的实际效果，研究者依然争论不休①。可他了解西洋惯例的直接目的或多或少旨在为处理烟土走私问题及随后发生的林维喜案收集情报甚至增添理据，这是毋庸置疑的。

第二节　影响《万民法》译入文本表述的权力因素

综合前文所述，伯驾和袁德辉翻译《万民法》的活动是在中英两大帝国攫取对外贸易管理权的金融战争语境下展开的，深受权力博弈因素的干扰，因而不可避免地具有其局限性。

一　断章取义

（一）组织者难免成见

林则徐身为钦差，日处旋涡核心，必然着眼当前利益诉求的实现。故在组织翻译国际法时，他只策略性地摘选其中有关涉外急务的部分片段，绝未将之"视为普遍真理，而是把它当作一种以理服人的方法来使用，这个方法使他能够用一种他认为英国人能够理解的语言来证明鸦片贸易的

---

① 相关学者的争论请参阅王维俭撰《林则徐翻译西方国际法著作考略》（载《中山大学学报》（社会科学版）1985 年第 1 期），鲁纳撰、王笑红译《万民法在中国——国际法的最初汉译，兼及〈海国图志〉的编纂》（载《中外法学》2000 年第 3 期），陆玉芹撰《林则徐与〈滑达尔各国律例〉》（载《盐城师范学院学报》（人文社会科学版）2006 年第 3 期），韩琴撰《论林则徐摘译国际法的选择性》（载《福建师范大学学报》（哲学社会科学版）2008 年第 4 期）及赖骏楠撰《林则徐与国际法：虚构的与真实的》（载《北京大学研究生学志》2011 年第 1 期）。

危害"（刘禾，2000：72）。

但那不过断章取义之一端，同样难以避免的是林则徐还秉承清代贵族精英的传统，对欧美远夷深怀戒心。他遣人接触美国医生伯驾，间接委托这位传教士翻译瓦泰尔著作时，送去的只是毛笔抄写的数个片段并非整书，又令幕僚袁德辉别述原文，方便相互印证。相关情节不仅有伯驾本人撰写的医院报告为证①，更能说明问题的是译者竟然令人难以置信地将转录原书第 37 条注释的文本误作"第三十七章"②，摘自原书第 292 页的段落亦被误作"第二百九十二条"。顺便指出，袁德辉也未能纠正此处谬误，显见是参考了前者的译文③。

（二）译者的专断取向

比照伯驾和袁德辉的译作，首先激发我们探究兴趣的就是两篇文本截然不同的标题。伯驾译文的名称是《滑达尔各国律例》，明显取自英文注释本的正标题——*The Law of Nations*；袁德辉的译文名称则为《法律本性正理所载》，其含义类似英文注释本副标题的前半部分——*Principles of the Law of Nature*。

不同译者各取所需的做派实是颇具玩味。伯驾采直译之法，将语篇命名《各国律例》，深合原文"Law of Nations"的本来面目。该英文术语最早出现在牛津大学苏世教授撰写的《万国法的解释和一些有关的问题》，相对应的拉丁术语 *Jus inter gentes* 源自罗马时期的 *Jus gentium*，即万民法（刘达人 & 袁国钦，2007：14）。

---

① 请参阅本章【5.1.22】所引《一八三九年广州眼科医院第十次报告》（TENTH REPORT of the Ophthalmic Hospital, Canton, being for the year 1839）的片段。

② 请比较切第英文注释本《国际法》第 38 页末所载注释"（37）When such a prohibition has been established, any violation of it in general subjects the ship and goods to seizure and confiscation, as in case of smuggling, whether by exporting or importing prohibited goods, or permitted goods without paying imposed duties."（Vattel, 1834: 38），与伯驾译文"第三十七章 一禁立之后，如有犯禁船货物夹带出口，或夹带入口，或带货漏饷，则变价充公。"后者详见《海国图志》第八十三卷《夷情备采三·滑达尔各国律例》。《魏源全集》第七册，魏源全集编辑委员会编，第 1979 页。

③ 王维俭认为"袁氏翻译在伯驾之后，已有参考修正之依据"（1985：65）；鲁纳博士也认为"袁在有伯驾译文以资参照时，他很少会偏离原过远"，同时又推测"最初的翻译是袁德辉做的，伯驾的翻译只对袁的工作起辅助作用而非作为独立的译文……袁搞错了原作的结构，而他只给了伯驾含有这些错误的手书文本。一位像伯驾这样受过教育的西方人若是看过原文的话，是不可能犯这样的错误的。因而最可能的是，除了袁手书的段落外，伯驾根本没见过原作"（2000：308，303）。

　　作为美国传教士，伯驾虽只是医生，但对国际法调整不同国家之间关系的宗旨也有所了解。顾名思义，《各国律例》自是欲将清朝纳入"各国"体系，希望促其行事遵循惯例，客观上也能对译者自身肩负的传教使命给予方便。

　　若伯驾的遣词造句皆存此心，那么注定将会遭遇失望。魏源编辑《海国图志》已在鸦片战争过后，仍将所涉片段收入夷情备采篇就是明证①，足以反映林则徐译国际法时绝无令天朝降尊纡贵、俯从夷律之意。

　　比较而言，袁德辉的归化译名更符合清廷官吏坚守儒家学说的心理需求。尽管瓦泰尔阐述国际法规则实质上依托的是折中主义的自然法思想，可正如鲁纳博士所指出的，原作者坚持国际关系基于"国家的自然自由"观念对试图禁绝鸦片贸易的大清王朝乃至林则徐并不具吸引力（2000：303）。袁译借用"本性"、"正理"等传统儒学术语改写"Law of Nature"，无疑具有劝导科举出身的衮衮诸员接受崭新理念的便利优势。

二　术业不专

　　林则徐本人并不通晓英文或任何其他外语，无法亲自处理完全陌生的西方语言符号系统，只能聘用或委托他人完成具体翻译任务。其中，承担瓦泰尔国际法摘译工作的主要是美国人伯驾和华人袁德辉。对于此二人的译文质量，学者们历来颇有微词：伯驾的文笔生硬与袁译的履失要旨同样刺眼。

　　尽管如此，笔者不敢苟同张锡彤先生全面否定其历史意义的结论②。若以 20 世纪现代汉语的标准来衡量，晚清时期的译文当然是对瓦泰尔简洁明晰、逻辑缜密的语言风格过分粗糙的扭曲。但考虑到两位译者所面临的任务几乎史无前例，没有任何可资借鉴的现成标准或模式，因而必须独创性地探索"从西方到中文语义情境跨文化地传达国际法术语和哲学的途径"（鲁纳，2000：305），他们的贡献已属难能可贵。须知当时"在天

---

　　①　详见《海国图志》第八十三卷《夷情备采三》。《魏源全集》第七册，魏源全集编辑委员会编，第 1979—182 页。

　　②　Chang Hsi-t'ung（张锡彤）. *The Earliest Phase of the Introduction of Western Political Science into China*（1820 – 1852）[J]. *Yenching Journal of Asian Studies*（《燕京学报》），5. 1：13（July 1950）.

下万国中，惟英吉利留心中国史记言语，然通国亦不满十二人"①。

　　在复杂的语际转换过程中，伯驾和袁德辉的个人经历及其文化意识必将发挥深远影响，这也是本节考察的焦点所聚。

　　（一）伯驾生平与《滑达尔各国律例》

　　据《伯驾生平、书简和日记》（*The Life, Letters, and Journals of Rev. and Hon. Peter Parker, M. D. , Missionary, Physician, and Diplomatist, the Father of Medical Missions and Founder of the Ophthalmic Hospital in Canton*, 1896）、《伯驾与中国的开放》（*Peter Parker and the Opening of China*, 2008）等文献记载，伯驾出生于新英格兰的基督教家庭，是中国第一位新教医务传教士。

　　1834 年，伯驾修完耶鲁大学医学院和神学系的研究生课程，获医学博士学位及牧师资格。同年 6 月 4 日受美国公理会（Congregational Church）派遣来华，10 月 26 日抵达广州后不久前往新加坡学习汉语，并于次年 9 月返回。1835 年 11 月 4 日，创办颇著声名的广州博济医院，求医问药者络绎不绝，甚至包括很多清廷地方官员。1838 年 2 月，会同郭雷枢（Thomas R. College）、裨治文（Elijah Coleman Bridgman）等人成立"在华医务传教会"（Medical Missionary Society in China），还被誉为 19 世纪 30 年代中国新教传教会"最有希望的一部分"（Fay, 1971：153）。

　　1844 年作为美国特使顾盛（Caleb Cushing）的中文秘书参与《望厦条约》的谈判，从此揭开伯驾直接参与外交活动的生涯。1845 年至 1855 年期间任美国驻华使馆头等参赞并三次代理公使职务，1855 年开始正式成为美国政府驻华全权公使，直至 1857 年卸任回国。

　　上述史料记述伯驾的生平事迹，至少说明了三个问题，严重影响其国际法译文的表述：

　　1. 疏于文言

　　伯驾仅粗通汉语而已，修习中文的时间才断断续续数年。且因官府禁止华民教授外国人，只能在远离儒家文化中心的新加坡接受启蒙教育。更糟糕的是，他聘请的老师说闽南语，还不会书写，返回广州后又被迫重学粤语（吉利克，2008：34）。换言之，伯驾的艰难历程始于方言口语，对

---

① 详见《澳门月报·论中国（道光十九年及二十年新闻纸）》。《林则徐全集》第十册，林则徐全集编辑委员会编，第 326 页。

官话及文言文始终是陌生的。也正因为如此，他从事外交活动期间翻译正式文件时总是口译，再让中国助手负责整理最终稿件（赖骏楠，2011：89）。

考虑到伯驾处理的仅为手写转述的片段，既无从了解委托其翻译的真实意图，译文竟被刊录《海国图志》公开发行更是出乎意料，又怎会特意聘请华人协助削改汉语文本？这就注定他译介的国际法必然佶屈聱牙，词不达意。也难怪张锡彤先生会得出这样的评价：

> The rendering is thus a mockery of Vattel's precision and clearness, and a few notes added to make it more intelligible only serve to increase the confusion. One is forced to conclude that Parker did the work by himself, without seeking counsel from any Chinese. （Chang, 1950：13）

2. 未识法律

伯驾接受的高等教育主要是神学与医学方面的技能。1827 年，他在戴伊学院（Day's Academy）和弗雷明汉学院（Framingham Academy）完成预科，直接进入宗教氛围浓郁的阿莫斯特学院（Amherst College）进修，继而转往耶鲁大学（Yale University）。因宗教复兴运动的鼓舞及美部会（the American Board of Commissioners for Foreign Mission，简称 ABCFM）的影响，伯驾开始参与新教传教计划，并于本科毕业后继续攻读神学系及医学院的研究生课程，刚结束学业即由美国公理会派遣来华。由此可见，他从未有过研习法律知识的经历，因而在理解措辞严谨、自成体系的法言法语时遭遇巨大困难。

值得指出的是，鲁纳博士认为伯驾"运用了西方式的语法和论证技术"（2000：307），这亦构成汉语读者的接受障碍。试阅以下译文，便不难想见缺乏专业素养的伯驾在运用其生疏的中文书面语传递原著信息时是如何捉襟见肘。

伯驾、袁德辉所译第二百九十二条部分原文（Vattel, 1834：293）：

*I here speak of the right considered in itself. But as a king of England cannot, without the concurrence of parliament, either raise money or compel his subjects to take up arms, his right of making war is, in fact, but a slender prerogative, unless the parliament second him with sup-plies. ①

（**今译**：我这里说的是权利本身。但是像英吉利国王没有取得议会的同意，既不能筹集钱款，亦不能强迫其臣民去打仗，他发动战争的权利事实上仅仅是一种微不足道的特权，除非议会拨款支持他。——王维俭译②）

伯驾译文：今我说此，应想一想于自己。但如英吉利国王，不与大臣同行事，虽用钱粮，不逼迫百姓守兵械。他们为打仗，据实是必议大臣同行，与索军粮。③

3. 关注中外交往

伯驾在广州不仅行医传教，亦留意中外关系的发展。他曾于 1839 年六七月间撰写了致林则徐的倡议书④，称"反对罪恶的鸦片贸易"，"向上帝做最为热情的祈祷，希望钦差大人能够克服困难，圆满完成任务"，但又同时婉言提醒清廷官吏"对外国的法律及其发展程度尚无了解，并无意中采取了一些与友好国家的惯例不相一致的措施"，"已经在很大程度上冒犯了英国"。他认为妨碍中外交往的"祸根"是"各国相互之间的误解"，而"治疗的良方"是签订"共同遵守的条约"（honorable treaty），"并搁置那些'强硬的表述'"，以便促成"和平的氛围"。鸦片战争后，伯驾更是直接插手中美外交事务，常年担任美国驻华外交官员。

徐中约（Immanuel Hsu）教授认为伯驾的译文没有能够再现瓦泰尔的

---

① 切第英文注释本关于英王权力的脚注。

② 详见王维俭撰《林则徐翻译西方国际法著作考略》（载《中山大学学报》（社会科学版）1985 年第 1 期）。

③ 详见《海国图志》第八十三卷《夷情备采三·滑达尔各国律例》第二百九十二条第二段后半部分。《魏源全集》第七册，魏源全集编辑委员会编，第 1979 页。

④ 详见《伯驾致林则徐的倡议书，1839 年 6 月或 7 月》。摘自爱德华·V. 吉利克（Edward V. Gulick）所著《伯驾与中国的开放》（*Peter Parker and the Opening of China*）的附录"伯驾文献选译"（董少新译），第 269—270 页。原文收集在《伯驾生平、书简和日记》（Stevens & Mark-wick, 1896），只是未注明具体日期。考虑到信中既没有提及他与林则徐有何联系或交往，也没有提及翻译国际法之事，估计写在受托前夕。至于伯驾是否另用中文致函林则徐，林则徐是否收到此信或给予答复，据王维俭所见资料，无从查考。但笔者以为即便林则徐读了倡议书，亦很难接受平等建交的言论，或者了解外国法律的提议可能对其有所启发。

简明风格（1960：123）：

> The translation was not literal but paraphrastic, and the translator's comments were in a labored and unliterary style, which is a travesty of Vattel's perspicuity.

这正是由于他对如何维护国际惯例存有自己的独特见解，因此翻译过程中改写痕迹明显，时常删并增改、渗以个人评论。

伯驾、袁德辉所译第二百九十二条部分原文（Vattel，1834：291）：

> War is *that state in which we prosecute our right by force*. We also understand, by this term, the act itself, or the manner of prosecuting our right by force：but it is more conformable to general usage, and more proper in a treatise on the law of war, to understand this term in the sense we have annexed to it.
>
> *Public war* is that which takes place between nations or sovereigns, and which is carried on in the name of the public power, and by its order. This is the war we are here to consider：—*private war*, or that which is carried on between private individuals, belongs to the law of nature properly so called.

伯驾译文：打仗者，是我们出于不得已，强逼而应有此事也。盖打仗者，有公私之分，或两国交战，或二主相争，所事皆出于公，而兵权亦出于公，此是也。私自两人相敌，此是性理之常，此之谓也。

予详审有应战，有不战者。若情有可原，固无论人人皆欲战，岂不欲自保其身，自护其地，而于当战之日而竟不战者乎？然战合于人心，事自乎天理。如匪盗打劫村场，谁不与之抗拒？是理所必然，势当如是，是故应战。应不战者，皆以合义为贵，非可苟焉而已也。①

将伯驾的译文逐行比对英语原文，当可发现前者首段第一、二句大致

---

① 详见《海国图志》第八十三卷《夷情备采三·滑达尔各国律例》第二百九十二条首段及第二段前半部分。《魏源全集》第七册，魏源全集编辑委员会编，第 1979 页。

分别对应英文首句及第二段，但删节了注释版第二句，且增译"盖打仗者，有公私之分"部分文本。至于汉语第二段严格意义上都不能算纯粹的翻译，更像是对源语后续数段文字（主要涉及下文引录的袁德辉所译第二百九十二条部分原文）的评述。尤其"应不战者，皆以合义为贵，非可苟焉而已也"在英文本内只字未提，反映的完全是译者自己的观点，似有劝说林则徐以和为贵，同欧美各国订立通商条约之意，与其所撰倡议书一脉相承。

（二）袁德辉生平与《法律本性正理所载》

有关袁德辉生平事迹的中文史料可谓凤毛麟角，但《中国丛报》（Chinese Repository）上登载着仿佛与之相关的两则信息：

1837 年 7 月有关新加坡海峡的报道[①]

. . . One who was educated in the college at Malacca, has for several years been employed as interpreter as the court of Peking: he has recently visited Canton, and brought with him an order for Morrison's dictionary and other philological works.

1839 年 6 月裨治文等人记述的《镇口销烟》（*Destruction of the opium at Chunhow*）[②]

P. S. The commissioner has in his service four natives, all of whom have made some progress in the English tongue. The first is a young man, educated at Penang an Malacca, and for several years employed by the Chinese government at Peking. The second is an old man, educated at Serampore. The third is a young man who was once at the school at Cornwall, Conn., U. S. A. The fourth is a young lad, educated in China, who is able to read and translate papers on common subjects, with much ease,

---

① *Chinese Repository* Vol. VI. No. 3（July, 1837）ART. VIII. *Straits of Singapore*: *criminal courts and trial by jury*; *secret associates*; *tenure of lands*; *agricultural and horticultural society*, p. 153.

② *Chinese Repository* Vol. VIII. No. 2（June, 1839）ART. I. *Crisis in the opium traffic*; *continuation of the narrative, with official papers, & c.*（*Continued from page 37.*）, No. 50. *Destruction of the opium at Chunhow*（*Chinkow*）, p. 77.

correctness, and facility. ①

再结合袁氏的同学且与之交往匪浅的广州旗昌洋行股东美国人亨德（William C. Hunter）所撰《旧中国杂记》（*Bits of Old China*, 1911）的记述，粗略勾勒其人身份背景如下:

袁德辉，四川人，生于 1800 年左右。19 世纪 20 年代曾先后数载在槟榔屿天主教学校（Roman Catholic School in Penang）及马六甲英华书院（Anglo-Chinses College in Malacca）学习拉丁文和英文，后经广州十三行总商伍秉鉴（伍浩官）推荐出任理藩院通事;30 年代期间至少两次前往广州搜罗外国书籍，并成为林则徐的幕僚兼主要译员，林氏许多译著殆出其手。

综合上述记载，我们可以推测袁德辉曾经系统修读英文，"不是稍学一点，而是熟练地掌握"（Hunter, 1911: 260 – 262），水平应当优于伯驾运用汉语的能力，这对英汉翻译而言显然至关紧要。但看主要由其参与翻译的《澳门新闻纸》、《四洲志》等文笔之流畅，便可见一斑。只是他同样欠缺法律领域的背景，故对理解迥异日常用语的国际法著作也时常力有不逮。

另需注意，袁德辉常年担任清政府的通事，必然在某种程度上认同或至少通晓华夏礼法观念。正如他传译的钦差谕示近似文言文，通篇俱是汉化措辞，且未加注任何标点符号。请看《中国文丛》添附的编者注如何评论:

Note. So far as we know, this is the first document which ever came

---

① 意大利学者马西尼（Federico Masini）著《现代汉语词汇的形成:十九世纪汉语外来词研究》（*The Formation of Modern Chinese Lexicon and its Evolution toward a National Language*: *The Period from* 1840 *to* 1898），记载了林则徐幕僚中的主要译员，正好可以印证《中国丛报》的说法。据黄河清先生的译文所述（1997:21—23），陪同林则徐前往广州的译员除袁德辉外，还有"会同四译馆"的老译员亚孟。亚孟的父亲是中国人，母亲是孟加拉人，笔者曾在印度塞兰布尔（Serampore）的英国教区求学。此外，林则徐又在广州聘用了两位年轻的本地翻译:一位是林阿适，1822 年至 1825 年期间在美国康涅狄格州（Connecticut）康沃尔市（Cornwall）专门招收外国人的学校接受教育，但英文水平不高;另一位是梁进德，马礼逊为其洗礼，裨治文担任其监护人，就读于马礼逊教育会创办的学校，擅长口译，后在澳门为美国商人查尔斯·W.金（Charles W. King）工作。

from the Chinese in the English language. It is evidently the work of the commissioner's senior interpreter, who has for many years been in the employment of the government, at Peking. Its idioms are perfectly Chinese; and, like all the documents in their own language, it is without punctuation. ①

经袁氏润色的伯驾译文，同样"去除了其中所有'晦涩的'西方文法，而代之以直白的汉语论证方式，这样的方式背后是一整套的中国传统价值"（鲁纳，2000：307）。

袁德辉所译第二百九十二条部分原文② （Vattel，1834：291 – 292）：

In treating of the right to security (Book II. Chap. IV.), we have shown that nature gives men a **right** to employ force, when it is necessary for their defence, and for the preservation of their **rights**. This **principle** is generally acknowledged: reason demonstrates it; and nature herself has engraved it on the heart of man. Some fanatics indeed, taking in a literal sense the moderation recommended in the gospel, have adopted the strange fancy of suffering themselves to be massacred or plundered, rather than oppose force to violence. But we need not fear that this error will make any great progress. The generality of mankind will, of themselves, guard against its contagion—happy, if they as well knew how to keep within the just bounds which nature has set to a right that is granted only through necessity! ...

... In the bosom of society, the public authority decides all the disputes of the citizens, represses violence, and checks every attempt to do ourselves justice with our own hands. If a private person intends to prosecute his right against the subject of a foreign power, he may apply to the

---

① *Chinese Repository* Vol. VIII. No. 3 (July, 1839) ART. VII. *Great imperial commissionary's governor's of two Kwang province lieutenant-governor's of Canto earnest proclamation to foreigners again issued*, p. 168.

② 粗体与下划线由本书作者添加。

sovereign of his adversary, or to the magistrates invested with the public authority: and if he is denied justice by them, he must have recourse to his own sovereign, who is obliged to protect him. It would be too dangerous to allow every citizen the liberty of doing himself justice against foreigners; as, in that case, there would not be a single member of the state who might not involve it in war. And how could peace be preserved between nations, if it were in the power of every private individual to disturb it? A **right** of so momentous a nature, —the **right** of judging whether the nation has real **grounds** of complaint, —whether she is authorized to employ force, and justifiable in taking up arms, —whether prudence will admit of such a step, —and whether the welfare of the state requires it, —that **right**, I say, can belong only to the body of the nation, or to the sovereign, her representative. It is doubtless one of those rights, without which there can be no salutary government, and which are therefore called rights of majesty (Book I. § 45).

Thus the sovereign power alone is possessed of authority to make war. But as the different rights which constitute this power, originally resident in the body of the nation, may be separated or limited according to the will of the nation (Book I. § § 31 and 45), it is from the particular constitution of each state, that we are to learn where the power resides, that is authorized to make war in the name of the society at large. The kings of England, whose power is in other respects so limited, have the right of making war and peace. * Those of Sweden have lost it.

袁氏译文: 兵者,是用武以伸吾之道理,有公斗、私斗。公斗系两国所兴之兵,私斗乃二家所怀之怨。以妥当道理而论,凡保护自身及保全自己**道理**,自然可以有用武之**道理**。此等**道理**常在人心中,亦人人所共知。有些迂儒,用经典上义理,如己身已被人杀害,犹曰只好任他杀去而已,总不任杀人之名。此等错意见,终怕行不开。原其故,无非为避害保身,此亦人之常情。然兵亦不是乱用,若知夫天性所赋之理,不得已而用兵,总合夫道理,以仁义之律法而节制之。国中权柄,是决断争辩,镇压伤害,禁止我们私自所欲伸之义理。欲与外国人争论,先投告对头之王,或有大权之官。设或都不伸理,可奔回本国，禀求本国王保护。核其可行则行，可止则止。若概而准之，与外国人理论相对，则国中无一人不连累其中。人人亦可扰乱，何以保全两国和气，此系大危险之事。先要审定虚实，有何怨的**道理**？或是应该兴兵，或是应该不兴兵，或是须要用兵，国中方才太平，悉听国王裁夺。无此法度，何能一国太平？

如此，惟国王有兴兵的权。但各国例制不同，英吉利王有兴兵将和的权，绥领王无有此权。

英吉利王无有巴厘满衙门会议，亦不能动用钱粮，不能兴兵，要巴厘满同心协议始可。①

袁译第二百九十二条前两句及末段与伯驾译文同源，其余部分语篇则大致基于上述所引英文本。诸如"有些迂儒，用经典上义理"、"若知夫天性所赋之理，不得已而用兵，总合夫道理，以仁义之律法而节制之"，此类措辞明显是套用宋学伦常术语替换源语中"gospel"、"nature"等格老秀斯（Hugo Grolius）主义折中学派以基督教为基础演变而成的自然法概念。当然，部分原因也是考虑到古文言汉语的词汇难以充分表述现代西方法治思想，只能求助近在咫尺的传统文化解燃眉之急。鲁纳将其称作"儒家伦理之下的瓦泰尔"——国际惯例化为人际关系；客观法律化为主观情感（2000：308—309），的确所言非虚。

第三节 《万民法》摘译活动影响
权力博弈的实效研究

徐中约教授及很多其他较新近的史学家都认为伯驾与袁德辉的译文对林则徐实施禁烟政策产生了决定性影响（1960：125）：

The translation by Parker and Yuan undoubtedly had a decisive influence on Lin, as he later followed exactly the course of action discussed in them. He proclaimed opium a contraband in 1839 and demanded its de-

---

① 详见《海国图志》第八十三卷《夷情备采三·法律本性正理所载》第二百九十二条。《魏源全集》第七册，魏源全集编辑委员会编，第1981—1982页。

struction; he wrote to Queen Victoria requesting her to order the stoppage of opium traffic. When these measures failed to bring the desired results, he resorted to force, fully confident of both the moral and legal correctness of his action, even in the context of Western international law. One may say that the initial effect of Western international law in China was a strengthening of Lin's determination to take a firm stand against the English.

　　然而，笔者感觉伯驾和袁德辉的措辞颇有出入，这从上节【5.2.1 断章取义】所讨论的书名取向问题便可窥知一二。前文又以所谓第二百九十二条为例，着眼译者生平对各自翻译活动的侵扰展开研究，更是凸显两语篇间的差异与矛盾及其根源。译文传递的信息如此不相和谐，这至少在某种程度上直接导致其对帝国权力博弈的实质影响未必似现代分析者想象得那样深刻。

**　一　译文不谐：禁止商品进口的国际惯例译文自相矛盾、不堪使用**

　　正如前文所述，林则徐早于道光十九年二月初四日（1839 年 3 月 18 日）就已晓谕外商，令其承诺永不夹带鸦片来华。但英国在华商务总监义律（Charles Elliot）对具结要求阳奉阴违，反借领事名义致函两广总督，要求"给领红牌"，企图带离鸦片走私贩，还美其名曰"保驻省本国诸人之命家资"①。

　　随着情势的发展，林则徐当然希望了解不列颠政府的思维方式，以便推进禁烟政策的顺利贯彻实施。收集情报的途径之一即翻译有关禁止商品进口的国际惯例，可实际效果并非尽如人意。

涉及禁止商品进口的国际惯例原文② （Vattel，1834：38）：

　　Every state has consequently a **<u>right</u>** to prohibit the entrance of *foreign*

---

　　①　详见《札广州府广州协传谕义律批驳请给红牌禀（道光十九年二月十一日）》之附录《原禀（道光十九年二月十一日）》。《林则徐全集》第五册，林则徐全集编辑委员会编，第 122 页。

　　②　粗体与下划线由本书作者添加。

merchandises; and the nations that are affected by such prohibition have no right to complain of it, as if they had been refused an office of humanity. Their complaints would be ridiculous, since their only ground of complaint would be, that a profit is refused to them by that nation, who does not choose they should make it at her expense. It is, however, true, that if a nation was very certain that the prohibition of her merchandises was not founded on any reason drawn from the welfare of the state that prohibited them, she would have cause to consider this conduct as a mark of ill-will shown in this instance, and to complain of it on that footing. But it would be very difficult for the excluded nation to judge with certainty that the state had no solid or apparent reason for making such a prohibition.

（**今译**：每个国家都有禁止外国商品进入的**权利**；而受该禁止影响的国家则无权抗议，仿佛她们在出于人性的好意方面遭到拒绝。她们的抗议将是荒谬的，因为她们唯一的抗议理由将是，该国家拒绝她们获取利润，该国家不愿以牺牲自身利益为代价选择让外国获利。然而，如果一个国家非常确信，对其商品的禁止并非建基于任何源自该禁止国福利的理由，在这种情形下，她就将有理由将这一行动视为恶意的标志，并在此基础上就此提出抗议。但要被禁止国去有把握地断定禁止国没有可靠或明显理由以发出禁令，这也是非常困难的。——赖骏楠译[1]）

伯驾译文：尝思各国皆有当禁外国货物之**例**，其外国不得告诉委曲而违此禁，亦不得以仁情推辞。若他告诉委曲，是不过欲利而已，该国必不以他得利而违自己之禁。试思凡国有禁，皆有所谓而然也。[2]

袁氏译文：各国有禁止外国货物，不准进口的**道理**。贸易之人，有违禁货物，格于例禁不能进口，心怀怨恨，何异人类背却本分，最为可笑。若不分别违禁不违禁，以及将本求利，均不准进口，可以含

---

① 详见赖骏楠撰《林则徐与国际法：虚构的与真实的》（载《北京大学研究生学志》2011年第 1 期）。

② 详见《海国图志》第八十三卷《夷情备采三·滑达尔各国律例》。《魏源全集》第七册，魏源全集编辑委员会编，第 1979 页。

怨。即如甲国货物而至乙国，并不见有违碍，而乙国禁之，此谓之不是好意，亦可含怨。已无遗碍，而又无实在明白说出其所以不准之理，立此等例禁，令人难以推测，算是与人隔别，断绝往来也。①

比较伯驾译文和袁译，不难发现他们的差异并非止于术语层面，譬如"right"被分别译成"例"或"道理"等，更重要的是语篇层面的信息传递。特别原文后半截，伯驾或因畏难情绪等，索性将之缩译为"试思凡国有禁，皆有所谓而然也"，尽管未能体现作者的初衷，倒也没有过分违背其本意；而袁德辉的评论式演绎则完全是画蛇添足，直接走向原著阐释举证责任的反面。

若说林则徐摘译国际法旨在为办理禁烟事宜提供可被外国人接受的理据，那么这样矛盾的译文只能使他疑窦丛生、无所适从。尤其袁译中被禁止国"可以含怨"的表述，岂不是令大清朝平添道义上的负担？

有学者认为林则徐在《议复曾望颜条陈封关禁海事宜折（道光二十年三月二十六日）》中称"将现未犯法之各国夷船与英吉利国一同拒绝，是违抗者摒之，恭顺者亦摒之，未免不分良莠，事出无名"②，乃立足袁译"无实在明白说出其所以不准之理，立此等例禁，令人难以推测，算是与人隔别，断绝往来也"，提出区别鸦片走私与正当贸易的外交策略（陆玉芹，2006：14）。

先不论袁德辉如何曲解瓦泰尔论述的国际惯例，深究林氏本意也只是延续"以夷治夷"的既定方针，"使其相间相睽，以彼此之离心，各输忱而内向。若概与之绝，则缺望之后，转易联成一气，勾结图私"③。他还引述《左传》为证："彼则惧而协以谋我，故难间也"。换言之，这不过"驭诸夷"的策略——"驱夷宜刚柔互用，不必视之太重，亦未便视之太轻。与其泾渭不分，转至无所忌惮……而且用诸国以并拒英夷，则有如踏鹿，若因英夷而并绝诸国，则不啻驱鱼"④。

---

① 详见《海国图志》第八十三卷《夷情备采三·法律本性正理所载》。《魏源全集》第七册，魏源全集编辑委员会编，第1981页。

② 详见《议复曾望颜条陈封关禁海事宜折（道光二十年三月二十六日）》。《林则徐全集》第三册，林则徐全集编辑委员会编，第326页。

③ 同上。

④ 同上书，第327页。

本质上，林则徐始终固守朝贡贸易思想，认为"准令诸夷互市，原系推恩外服，普示怀柔"①。要求具结虽旨在向外商主张中国的司法管辖权，但该管辖权的依据并非国际法意义上的主权而是皇权或者说皇恩："知感天朝通市之恩，必遵天朝禁私之令"②。正如赖骏楠博士所言，清廷官员无法想象管辖权之类概念在西方人心目中的神圣地位（2001：95），妄自揣度各国领事推诿拖延，"盖以缴烟系一时之事，尚可借以求生，而具结乃长远之事，适恐自陷于死也"③。

就此而言，袁氏译文同化处理国际惯例所隐含的历史渊源及其原理的表现形式更符合林则徐所代表的清廷官员的普遍意识形态，特别是由他单独译出的第一百七十二条尤为典型。

二 译文归化：外商属地管辖的国际惯例译文难脱朝贡贸易体制

研究者普遍认为林则徐通过行商委托美国传教士翻译《万民法》片段是 1839 年 7 月间事④。另根据伯驾本人的日记和信件，亦可大致断定他于同年 9 月完成这项工作（吉利克，2008：83）。而袁氏的翻译显然在伯驾译文的基础上润色而成，并专门增译了论及外商属地管辖的段落⑤。由此揣测，该部分国际惯例的摘译与办理林维喜案的交涉应当有所关联。

所谓林维喜案，是指道光十九年五月二十七日（1839 年 7 月 7 日）发生的英国水手酗酒棍殴九龙附近尖沙村村民林维喜致死事件。林则徐得报后令新安知县梁星源查办此案，并与两广总督邓廷桢、广东巡抚怡良会衔发布《严禁本地民人与外人非法往来交易告示》，要求英国领事义律"交出凶夷。按成法惯例，杀人偿命"⑥。布告中提及的"成法惯例"无

---

① 详见《议复曾望颜条陈封关禁海事宜折（道光二十年三月二十六日）》。《林则徐全集》第三册，林则徐全集编辑委员会编，第 325 页。

② 详见《批义律拒绝转令商人具结禀（道光十九年二月二十五日）》。《林则徐全集》第五册，林则徐全集编辑委员会编，第 151 页。

③ 详见《驱逐英国趸船烟贩并饬取切结催交命案凶手情形折（道光十九年九月二十八日）》。《林则徐全集》第三册，林则徐全集编辑委员会编，第 213 页。

④ 请参阅本章【5.1.22】所引《一八三九年广州眼科医院第十次报告》（TENTH REPORT of the Ophthalmic Hospital, Canton, being for the year 1839）的片段。

⑤ 即《法律本性正理所载》第一百七十二条。

⑥ 详见《严禁本地民人与外人非法往来交易告示（道光十九年六月二十三日）》。《林则徐全集》第五册，林则徐全集编辑委员会编，第 231 页。

非从前援引《大清律例·名例律》之"化外人有犯"条办理的案件①。然而，义律故意抵制，宣布在停泊中国领海的"威廉姆堡"号（Fort William）船上"设立公案"，并请林则徐委派官员观审②，妄图攫取治外法权，实现其对巴麦尊子爵（Viscount Palmerston）的承诺——尽一切努力抵制根据中国法律逮捕或判决英国臣民的行为：

> ... till I am differently instructed I should hold it to be my duty to resist to the last the seizure and punishment of a British subject by the Chinese law, be his crime what it might; and crimes of the gravest character have lately been of every-day probability. ③

毫无疑问，办理交涉受阻的林则徐要求袁德辉翻译有关外商法律地位的片段，难免怀有刺探"夷人风俗"的意图。

涉及外商属地管辖的国际惯例原文④（Vattel, 1834：172）：

> There are states, such asChina and Japan, into which all foreigners are forbid to penetrate without an express permission; but, in Europe, the access is everywhere free to every person who is not an enemy of the state, except, in some countries, to vagabonds and outcasts.
>
> But evenin those countries which every foreigner may freely enter, the sovereign is supposed to allow him access only upon this tacit condition,

---

① 林则徐所撰《示谕外商速缴鸦片烟土四条稿（道光十九年二月十二日）》提出"恭查大清律例，内载'化外人有犯，并依律拟断'等语。从前办过夷人死罪，如打死人偿命之类，都有成案"；《外人夹带鸦片罪名应议专条片（道光十九年四月初六日）》中亦有"即近年奏办夷案……皆引名例'化外有犯依律拟断'之条"。《林则徐全集》，林则徐全集编辑委员会编，第2413、1269 页。

② 详见《会批澳门厅转禀义律抗不交凶说贴（道光十九年七月初九日）》之附录五《义律请派员观审说帖（道光十九年六月二十六日）》。《林则徐全集》第五册，林则徐全集编辑委员会编，第229 页。

③ 详见 1839 年 1 月 2 日义律致巴麦尊子爵恳请授予其更多职权的信函（No. 138 Captain Elliot to Viscount Palmerston）。摘自 The Sessional Papers（printed by order of the House of Lords or presented by Royal command, in the session 1840）Vol. VIII, pp. 339 – 340。

④ 下划线由本书作者添加。

that he be subject to the laws, —I mean the general laws made to maintain good order, and which have no relation to the title of citizen or of subject of the state. The public safety, the rights of the nation and of the prince, necessarily require this condition; and the foreigner tacitly submits to it, as soon as he enters the country, as he cannot presume that he has access upon any other footing. The sovereignty is the right to command in the whole country; and the laws are not simply confined to regulating the conduct of the citizens towards each other, but also determine what is to be observed by all orders of people throughout the whole extent of the state.

In virtue of this submission, foreigners who commit faults are to be punished according to the laws of the country. The object of punishment is to cause the laws to be respected, and tomaintain order and safety.

（**后两段今译**：但是，即使在那些每个外国人都可以自由进入的国家，主权者仍被期望是在以下默认条件下来允许他（外国人）进入，即他必须服从法律——我意指用于保持良好秩序的一般法律，而与国家的公民或臣民资格无关。公共安全、国家和王室的权利，必然要求这项条件；而外国人只要进入该国，就必须默认服从该条件，因为他不能假定自己是以其他条件进入该国的。主权是一种在整个国家内发布命令的权利；而法律不纯粹限于调整公民相互间的行为，而且也决定在整个国家范围内所有的人应该遵守什么。

由于这一服从，从事不法行为的外国人必须接受其所进入国家的法律的惩处。惩处的目的是敦促人们尊重法律，并保持秩序和安全。——赖骏楠译①）

袁氏译文：中国、日本国无有照会某处之船准进，某处之船不准进，皆禁止外国人，不许进口。在欧罗巴洲中各国，除与有仇敌之数国，此外人人皆可游行，国国可以进口。一经准其进口，就当遵顺其律例。我思律例之设，原为保存身家性命起见，非关遵其例，即子其民之理。国家立法，应须如此。而外国人，一入其地，即该凛然遵顺。国家抚有天下，治理亿兆，而律例亦不止此。自法制一定，普天

---

① 详见赖骏楠撰《林则徐与国际法：虚构的与真实的》（载《北京大学研究生学志》2011年第1期）。

<u>之下莫不遵守</u>。故外国有犯者，即各按各犯事国中律例治罪。其治罪之意，不过令人保全身家性命也。①

切第英文注释本提出属地管辖原则，目的是保持所在国"良好秩序"，理由是尊重所在国属地主权。而经袁德辉同化的译文言辞闪烁，很大程度上将前者改写成"非关遵其例，即子其民之理"、变后者为"国家抚有天下，治理亿兆，而律例亦不止此。自法制一定，普天之下莫不遵守"。这又何异"普天之下莫非王土，率土之滨莫非王臣"的封建正统思想呢？

笔者同意赖骏楠博士的观点，林则徐于道光十九年七月初九日（1839 年 8 月 17 日）《会批澳门厅转禀义律抗不交凶说帖》中指出"查该国向有定例，如赴何国贸易即照何国法度，其例甚为明白"②，引述的并非袁译国际惯例片段，而是《英吉利国王发给该国商船禁约八条》之首款："往别国，遵该国禁例，不可违犯。如违犯亦有罪"③，并据此推断林则徐考虑到林维喜案肇事者系英国水手，方才决定组织翻译有关英吉利如何管理本国商船及水手的法规（赖骏楠，2001：94）。

不过，谕帖中如此引证恐非纯粹因为国际法译文语言较为繁复，更可能是袁氏改写的文本与朝贡贸易体制过分吻合，令我们视而不见、湮没无闻了。实际上，林则徐也强调"在别国尚当依该处法度，况天朝乎？……但犯罪若在伊国地方，自听伊国办理，而在天朝地方，岂得不交官宪审办？且从前内地所办命案夷犯，历历有据，各国无不禀遵，岂义律独可违此例乎？"④ 这虽老调重弹，亦透露出属地管辖的理念。只一味将之上升到"引证各国当时都有引渡刑事罪犯的习惯"层面（张劲草，1982：45），似乎言过其实，难以令人信服。

---

① 详见《海国图志》第八十三卷《夷情备采三·法律本性正理所载》第一百七十二条。《魏源全集》第七册，魏源全集编辑委员会编，第 1981 页。

② 详见《会批澳门厅转禀义律抗不交凶说帖（道光十九年七月初九日）》。《林则徐全集》第五册，林则徐全集编辑委员会编，第 226 页。

③ 详见《英吉利国王发给该国商船禁约八条》。《林则徐全集》第十册，林则徐全集编辑委员会编，第 376 页。

④ 详见《会批澳门厅转禀义律抗不交凶说帖（道光十九年七月初九日）》。《林则徐全集》第五册，林则徐全集编辑委员会编，第 226 页。

三　余论《致英国国王檄谕稿》

很多学者从时间上论证，钦差大臣林则徐奉旨照会不列颠政府极可能是直接促使其组织翻译国际法的最初动因。

鉴于义律串通美、荷等国领事以"人即正法"①　有悖本国法律为由，拖延遵式具结②，还动辄借口"须俟国主批谕"③　敷衍推诿，林则徐着手拟具《致英国国王檄谕稿》，既"希望英女王配合禁烟，就需要换位思考"（韩琴，2008：131），且"为了说服'夷人'，当然必须借助'夷理'——国际法"（赖骏楠，2011：92）。

可惜，这篇被道光皇帝赞为"所议得体周到……即行照录颁发"④　的檄文并非如某些研究者想当然地那样出于袁译《法律本性正理所载》中提到"两国遇到重大问题，'欲与外国人争论，先投告对头之王，或有大权之官'"的考虑⑤，反倒是延续了喋喋不休的仁义道德说教及朝贡体制下夜郎自大的惯性思维："我天朝君临万国，尽有不测神威，然不忍不教而诛，故特明宣定例。该国夷商，欲图长久贸易，必当禀遵宪典，将鸦片永断来源。切勿以身试法，王其诘奸除匿，以保乂尔有邦。益昭恭顺之

---

①　详见《谕洋商责令外商呈缴烟土稿（道光十九年二月初四日行）》、《谕各国商人呈缴烟土稿（道光十九年二月初四日行）》。《林则徐全集》第五册，林则徐全集编辑委员会编，第114—118页。

②　详见《批义律拒绝转令商人具结禀（道光十九年二月二十五日）》之附录《原禀（道光十九年二月二十五日）》、《催取不带鸦片甘结谕帖（道光十九年二月二十三日）》之附录二《美国领事吐哪遵谕以后来船不带鸦片禀（道光十九年三月初三日）》及附录三《荷兰国总管曙吧臣遵谕永远不贩鸦片禀（道光十九年三月初三日）》。同上书，第150—151、153页。

③　详见《会札刘丞转谕义律饬令货船空趸分别进埔开行（道光十九年四月十七日）》之附录二《义律复船只进埔须俟国主批谕禀（道光十九年四月）》、《会札佛山同知刘丞传谕义律酌赏茶叶分给缴烟各外商（道光十九年四月十四日）》之附录《义律复不敢私领赏还茶叶禀（道光十九年四月二十日）》。同上书，第203、204页。

④　详见《著钦差大臣林则徐等即将颁发英国国王檄谕照录发出事上谕（七月十九日上谕档）》。《鸦片战争档案史料Ⅰ》，中国第一历史档案馆编，第661—662页。

⑤　陆玉芹即持国际法译文促使林则徐撰写致英吉利国王檄文的观点（2006：14）；而韩琴令人信服地驳斥了这种值得商榷的看法：清廷对袁译的理解更可能是换位思考——"英国鸦片走私贩'欲与中国人争论'，先投告道光帝或钦差大臣林则徐，'设或都不伸理，可奔回本国禀求本国王保护'，请求对中国发动战争，英女王'核其行则行，可止则止'"（2008：132—133）。

忧，共享太平之福。"① 无怪当时澳门刊发的《广州周报》(Canton Press)
评论说"此信之知识，可谓微小"②。伯驾也认为它"充斥着很多废话和
带有侮辱性质的语言"（吉利克，2008：84），即便婉拒林则徐通过伍秉
鉴提出的翻译请求亦算事出有因。

　　特别值得一提的是，林则徐不仅指示袁德辉将《谕英国国王檄》译
成英文，还委托袁氏就读马六甲英华书院期间的同窗好友亨德回译汉
语，以核实其准确性（张馨保，1989：132）。道光十九年十一月十一日
(1939 年 12 月 16 日) 又在天后宫接见遭遇海难的英国海员③，顺便请随
船的喜尔医生帮忙修改译文。遗憾的是未能查阅到该英文版谕稿，否则交
叉对比必定十分有趣。

　　无论怎样，辗转至道光十九年十二月十四日 (1840 年 1 月 18 日)，
方才觅得已经具结的英国"担麻士葛"号船主弯喇④愿将谕稿译文带往伦
敦，却终难逃不列颠外交部断然拒绝的命运。适时，林则徐早已遵道光皇
帝圣谕，"即将英吉利国贸易停止，所有该国船只尽行驱逐出口，不必取
具甘结。其殴毙华民凶犯，亦不值令其交出"⑤，战事如箭在弦、一触
即发。

　　语境的时代局限与译者的自身缺陷共同决定了《万民法》片段的摘
译既不可能向林则徐提供任何关于国际惯例的有效信息，更无法成为其说
服外国政府支持禁烟方略的充分理据。

　　随着鸦片战争局势恶化，道光皇帝竟将林则徐"照部议革职"⑥，继

　　① 详见《钦差大臣林则徐等奏呈拟具致英国国王檄谕底稿折（六月二十四日）》所附《致
英国国王檄谕稿（六月二十四日）》。《鸦片战争档案史料Ⅰ》，中国第一历史档案馆编，第
646 页。

　　② 详见《澳门十二月十四日新闻纸即中国十一月初九日》。《林则徐全集》第十册，林则
徐全集编辑委员会编，第 214 页。该报道译自当时英国人办的《广州周报》(Canton Press)。

　　③ 详见林则徐日记（道光十九年十一月十一日）。《林则徐全集》第九册，林则徐全集编
辑委员会编，第 416 页。

　　④ 详见《拟颁发檄谕英国国王稿（道光十九年六月二十四日）》之附录《英船主弯喇收领
照会文书字据（道光十九年十二月十四日）》。《林则徐全集》第五册，林则徐全集编辑委员会
编，第 224 页。

　　⑤ 详见《为英船胆敢首先开炮接仗著即停止对英贸易等事上谕（十一月初八日上谕档）》。
《鸦片战争档案史料Ⅰ》，中国第一历史档案馆编，第 742 页。

　　⑥ 详见《著将林则徐邓廷桢均照部议革职事上谕（道光二十年九月初八日剿捕档）》。《鸦
片战争档案史料Ⅱ》，中国第一历史档案馆编，第 438 页。

而"风闻有英吉利国王给林则徐文书之事"①，便令钦差大臣大学士署两广总督琦善彻查"通夷"情弊，实是匪夷所思。历史意义深远的宏伟创举转眼亦少人问津，除被编入《海国图志》外，甚至未能对后世的法律翻译活动及中文国际法语言与逻辑的形成产生任何重要影响②。

_____

① 详见《著钦差大臣琦善抵粤后将广东确情及风闻英王有给林则徐文书事查奏上谕（道光二十年九月十七日剿捕档）》。《鸦片战争档案史料Ⅱ》，中国第一历史档案馆编，第471页。

② 徐中约教授曾经指出："With the removal of Lin from his post in 1840 and the cessation of hostilities in 1842, interest in international law subsided"（Hsü, 1960: 125）；鲁纳博士也认为这至少部分是因为"第一次鸦片战争后的中国政治形势不再适宜译介国际法。瓦泰尔著作的翻译在《海国图志》（1847年）出版后的数十年间没有引起太多注意"（2000: 309）。

第 六 章

洋务运动上篇:和平外交

——京师同文馆与《万国公法》兼及《公法便览》

第一节　洋务运动时期和平外交的
社会文化背景概览

一　不平等条约体系的构建

第一次鸦片战争（1840 年 6 月—1842 年 8 月）的失利无情地粉碎了清廷天朝上国的美梦，被迫于道光二十二年七月二十四日（1842 年 8 月 29 日）签订屈辱的《中英南京条约》（*Treaty of Nanking*）及随后的《议定广州、福州、厦门、宁波、上海五港通商章程》（*General Regulations，under Which the British Trade is to be Conducted at the Five Ports of Canton，Amoy，Fuchow，Ningbo，and Shanghai*）与《五口通商附黏善后条款》（或称《虎门条约》）（*Supplementary Treaty of Hoomun Chai*）①等；旋即又在道光二十四年因美、法两国使团的胁迫，分别缔结《望厦条约》（*Treaty of Wang-Hea*）②和《黄埔条约》（*Treaty of Whampoa*）③。

度其之意，无非是抚夷派既想避免新的冲突，又渴望观列强争利，延续"以夷制夷"的传统政策。可正如徐中约教授敏锐地指出："在这些条约中，有三项规定对中国的危害最大——核定关税、治外法权和最惠国待遇。中国人同意这些条款部分是出于权宜之计，部分是由于不懂国际法和国家主权概念"（2002：187）。蒋廷黻先生也认为："不平等条约的根源一部分由于我们的无知，一部分由于我们的法制未达到近代文明的水准"

---

① 上述两份和约于道光二十三年八月十五日（1843 年 10 月 8 日）在虎门签订。

② 本和约于道光二十四年五月十八日（1844 年 7 月 13 日）在望厦村签订。

③ 本和约于道光二十四年九月十三日（1844 年 10 月 23 日）在黄埔签订。

(2004: 42)。

接踵而来的第二次鸦片战争（1856 年 10 月—1860 年 10 月）仍以颟顸昏聩的清政府惨败告终，更多不平等条约（unequal treaty）相继出炉：

1. 咸丰八年四月十六日（1858 年 5 月 28 日），签订《中俄瑷珲条约》（*Treaty of Aigun*）；

2. 咸丰八年（1858 年），分别与俄、美、英、法等国签订《天津条约》（*Treaty of Tientsin*）；

3. 咸丰十年（1860 年），分别与英、法、俄等国签订《北京条约》（*Convention of Peking*）。

上述条约罗织成枷锁重重的殖民体系，欧美各国既得以租借甚或直接攫取大量领土，还勒索种种经济特权及贸易利益。

二 合作政策与外交现代化

两次鸦片战争结束后，中国与西方列强间出现了持续数十载相对稳定的和平时期。但不平等条约各款具体规定的逐项落实，使得已沦为半殖民地（semi-colonial status）的清王朝面临"数千年未有之变局"、"数千年未有之强敌"[①]。

增开商埠，倾销工业制品，令丧失关税保护的民族手工业遭遇空前挤压，濒临破产；深入传教，强购腹地田宅，致使不明就里的官吏华民与洋人间摩擦日增，教案频发。更不必说内河自由航运、外交使节驻京等，这些特权虽说是不同条约分别议定的，然而依据"片面最惠国待遇"，各国援例享受，利益均沾。"从此中国与西洋的关系更要密切了。这种关系固可以为祸，亦可以为福，看我们振作与否。奕䜣与文祥绝不转头回看，留恋那已去不复回的闭关时代。他们大着胆向前进，到国际生活中去找新出路"（蒋廷黻，2004: 56）。

与此同时，西方人为确保其在华条约权利，转而扶持清王朝镇压太平天国起义，力图维护中央政府的独立、稳定与繁荣。借用英国公使卜鲁斯

---

① 详见《筹议海防折（同治十三年十一月初二日）》。《李鸿章全集》，李鸿章全集编辑工作委员会编，第 1063 页。

(Frederick William Adolphus Bruce, 1814 – 1867) 的话说:"地方上的行动及谈判充其量只是权宜之计;英国的利益取决于中央政府的存在,因为中央政府的管辖权在全国都受到认可,故而能够肩负起对外事务的责任。"①(Wright, 1957: 26 – 27)。为此,他与美国公使蒲安臣(Anson Burlingame, 1820 – 1870)提出所谓"合作政策"(Cooperative Policy),主张"以正常的外交措施替代武力"②(同上, 21—22):

> (1) cooperation among Western powers, (2) cooperation with Chinese officials, (3) recognition of China's legitimate interests, and (4) just enforcement of treaty stipulations.

不干涉及有限合作(nonintervention and moderate cooperation)得到了驻华外国使节的积极响应。因其界限仍以欧美列强的利益为出发点和归宿,于此前提下发生的任何中外关系终究无法摆脱殖民掠夺的总体特征。但不可否认的是,西方各国毕竟在某种程度上放弃了坚船利炮。这种行为方式的转变赋予晚清政府相对宽松的生存环境,并推动清廷最终决定暂时搁置朝贡体制,译介且有选择地接纳国际法原则,逐步迈向世界大家庭(the family of nations)。

第二节 和平外交对京师同文馆选译公法的影响

作为美国派驻丹麦和普鲁士的首任大使,亨利·惠顿(Henry Wheaton, 1785 – 1848)享有"十九世纪最有影响力的法学家之一"的盛誉,先后成为法兰西学会(Institut de France)通讯会员及普鲁士科学院(Prussian

---

① 英语原文:"Bruce had analyzed the relation between central and provincial government in China and had concluded that local action and local negotiation were at best temporary expedients; that British interests were dependent on the existence of a central government whose jurisdiction would be accepted throughout China, and which could therefore assume responsibility for foreign affairs. Local action would undercut the central authority."

② 英语原文:"You will perceive that we are making an effort to substitute fair diplomatic action in China for force."

Academy of Sciences）院士。他最杰出的名著《国际法原理》（*Elements of International Law with a Sketch of the History of the Subject*）自 1836 年问世以来，译介、再版、重印接踵而至①。

同治三年末（1865 年初），京师同文馆总教习美国新教传教士丁韪良（William Alexander Parsons Martin，1827 - 1916）在总理各国事务衙门的资助下将威廉·比奇·劳伦斯（William Beach Lawrence）编辑的英文注释版（1855）②译入四卷本《万国公法》③刊行于世。这是晚清第一部全面系统介绍国际法的译著，对亚洲各国接受现代外交理念发挥了不可磨灭的重要作用。

寒暑易节十三载，至光绪三年（1877 年），丁氏复率同文馆优秀学员汪观藻、凤仪、左秉隆、德明等译出耶鲁大学知名教授吴尔玺（Theodore D. Woolsey）的著作《国际法导论》（*Introduction to the Study of the International Law*，1864）④，并刊印发行六卷本《公法便览》⑤。较之《万国公法》，其影响力虽相去甚远，却亦可给研究者些许启迪。

一　赞助人及译者

（一）赞助人：总理各国事务衙门（亦称"洋务内阁"）

咸丰十年十二月初一日（1961 年 1 月 11 日），接办抚夷局⑥的恭亲王

----

①　惠顿的《国际法原理》最初于 1836 年在英国伦敦（2 卷本）和美国费城（1 卷本）同时出版；1846 年经修订后于费城再版（通称为第 3 版）。紧接着，法文版先后在法国巴黎、德国莱比锡发行（1848 年和 1852 年）。惠顿去世后，劳伦斯（William Beach Lawrence）又在波士顿发行了经其编辑的两个注释本（1855 年和 1863 年）。1866 年，由达纳（Richard Henry Dana, Jr.）编辑的第 8 版也在波士顿发行（张用心，2005：76）。

②　多数研究者认同《万国公法》的翻译蓝本就是 1855 年在波士顿发行的《国际法原理》第 6 版。对此，张用心和傅德元两位学者各自基于原始资料，从段落、标题及文章编排等各方面进行了详尽考证（张用心，2005：77；傅德元，2008：48—49）。因此，本书所引《国际法原理》原文，除非特别说明，均出自 1855 年第六版。

③　同治三年岁在甲子孟冬月（1864 年 11 月）镌，京都崇实馆存板。本书所引《万国公法》译文，除非特别说明，均出自京都崇实馆版。

④　本书所引《国际法导论》原文，除非特别说明，均出自 1864 年第二版。

⑤　光绪三年岁在丁丑（1877 年）同文馆聚珍版。本书所引《公法便览》译文，除非特别说明，均出自同文馆聚珍版。

⑥　即第二次鸦片战争期间，中国遣使与英法媾和，官方文书称抚务，又称抚局。今外交部尚藏有抚局档案。

奕䜣、大学士桂良和户部左侍郎文祥感觉改良措施已在所难免，"中国应在外交上接纳西方以获得一段时期的和平，并于这期间在西方帮助下加强军事力量"（徐中约，2002：266），故"为通筹夷务全局，酌拟章程六条"，首款即"京师请设立总理各国事务衙门，以专责成也"①。

考虑到惠亲王、总理行营王大臣、御前大臣、军机大臣等"公同详阅，悉心酌覆"，认为"筹议各条，按切时势，均是实在情形"，咸丰十年十二月初十日（1961年1月20日）上谕"著礼部颁给钦命总理各国通商事务关防"。②后经钦差大臣奕䜣等奏准又"节去通商二字以免外人饶舌"③。

总理衙门（Tsungli Yamen）成立伊始，设想仿军机处的临时性办事机构："以王大臣领之，军机大臣承书谕旨……俟军务肃清，外国事务较简，即行裁撤，仍归军机处办理，以符旧制"④。

然而实际上，"总理衙门之事，固不独繁于六部，而实兼综乎六部矣"⑤，非但接管从前礼部和理藩院及两广总督办理的洋务，还辖制南、北洋通商大臣，统揽一切涉外财政、军事、教育、交通、矿务等诸多职权，故亦称"总署"。直至光绪二十七年（1901年）正式更名外务部，仍班列首位。

换言之，总理衙门虽按军机处组织、沿袭六部体制，办理的却是新式外交事务，即以传统封建专制的管理形式来应对近代资本主义的工作内容。这不仅反映在其职能与特征的过渡性上，而且历任总署大臣多为科举正途出身，从"思想意识和知识结构方面讲，显然是中国传统的封建的

---

① 详见《钦差大臣奕䜣等奏通筹洋务全局酌议章程六条折（咸丰十年十二月初一日）》。《中国近代史资料丛刊·第二次鸦片战争》第五册，中国史学会主编，第340—341页。

② 详见《咸丰十年庚申十二月戊辰惠亲王等奏十二月初三日恭亲王奕䜣等奏统筹全局酌拟章程条款请旨遵行一折》及已上上谕。《续修四库全书·史部·纪事本末类·筹办夷务始末》咸丰卷七二，（清）文庆、贾桢、宝鋆等纂辑，《续修四库全书》编纂委员会编，第1—2页。

③ 详见《钦差大臣奕䜣等奏总理各国通商事务关防请节去通商二字以免外人饶舌片（咸丰十年十二月十三日）》。《中国近代史资料丛刊·第二次鸦片战争》第五册，中国史学会主编，第358页。

④ 详见《钦差大臣奕䜣等奏通筹洋务全局酌议章程六条折（咸丰十年十二月初一日）》。同上书，第341—342页。

⑤ 详见《刑部郎中沈瑞琳折（光绪二十四年七月二十八日）》。《戊戌变法档案史料》，沈云龙主编，佚名辑，第179—180页。

东西占着绝对优势"（吴福环，1995：57）。

无论如何，既专管外洋事宜，首先亟须翻译人才。早在受命留守京师为"钦差便宜行事全权大臣督办和局"①期间，奕訢已认识到"与外国交涉事件，必先识其性情，今语言不通，文字难辨，一切隔膜，安望其能妥协？"②

再者，欲对欧美列国保持友好关系虽是清廷借法自强争取时机的权宜之计，接轨西方外交惯例却势在必行。奕訢等上折称"中国语言文字外国人无不留心学习。其中之尤为狡黠者，更于中国书籍潜心探索。往往辩论事件，援据中国典制律例相难。臣等每欲借彼国事例以破其说，无如外国条例具系洋字，苦不能识"③，信为实情。

正是于此背景下，清代最早培养译员的洋务学堂和从事翻译的出版机构——京师同文馆应运而生。

（二）京师同文馆

据考证，隋唐时期即设四方馆，为明翰林院四夷馆之先驱；满清入主中原，将其更名会同四译馆，至乾隆年间改隶礼部（庄泽宣、陈学恂，1947：151—153），唯朝贡外交的大一统政策始终沿袭。

同治元年七月二十五日（1862年8月20日），总理各国事务奕訢等呈折称："臣等伏思欲悉各国情形，必谙其语言文字方不受人欺蒙。各国皆以重资聘请中国人讲解文艺；而中国迄无熟习外国语言文字之人，恐无以悉其底蕴。广州、上海既无咨送来京之人，不得不于外国延访。旋据英国威妥玛言及，该国包尔腾兼通汉文，堪充此席。因于五月十五日先令挑定之学生十人来馆试行教习，仍另请汉人徐树琳教习汉文，即以此学为同文馆。"④

---

① 详见《内阁明发撤去载垣穆荫钦差大臣改授奕訢为钦差便宜行事全权大臣上谕（咸丰十年八月初七日）》。《中国近代史资料丛刊·第二次鸦片战争》第五册，中国史学会主编，第113页。

② 详见《钦差大臣奕訢等奏通筹洋务全局酌议章程六条折（咸丰十年十二月初一日）》。同上书，第345页。

③ 详见《续修四库全书·史部·纪事本末类·筹办夷务始末》同治卷二七，（清）文庆、贾桢、宝鋆等纂辑，《续修四库全书》编纂委员会编，第25页。

④ 详见《奏请创设京师同文馆疏》。《中国近代出版史料初编》，张静庐辑注，第3页。

其创设早期全在回应《中英天津条约》第五十款规定:

> 嗣后英国文书俱用英字书写,暂时仍以汉文配送,俟中国选派学生学习英文,英语熟习即不用配送汉文。自今以后,凡有文词辩论之处,总以英文作为正义。①

另有《中法天津条约》第三款亦载类似表述。形势逼迫清廷培养精干的语言专家,方能摆脱洋人翻译及广东通事的掣肘,外国亦常称为"翻译学院"或"外语学院"(徐中约,2002:269)。

最初定稿的《同文馆学习外国语言文字章程六条》,仿俄罗斯文馆旧例②,并未囊括西学技艺的内容。至同治五年十一月初五日(1866年12月11日),奕䜣等奏请添设天文、算学馆③,却遭遇以理学宗师内阁大学士倭仁为代表的传统卫道派坚决反对,他们崇信程朱思想,认为"立国之道,尚礼仪不尚权谋;根本之图,在人心不在技艺。今求之一艺之末,而又奉夷人为师"④,唯恐"未收实效,先失人心"⑤。结果仅有七十二名"衰颓无能的人,为着总理衙门对同文馆学生发给的优饩而不顾他们的名誉"应考(刘广京,1982:100)。

尽管夹杂着宫廷权术阴谋的中西文化碰撞充满崎岖坎坷,可西学东渐毕竟是愈行愈近。同文馆总教习丁韪良采取系列措施,改善师资并编排了中国教育史上首部分年制教学计划⑥。其中,最引人瞩目的就是除洋文而及算格诸学外,还包括《万国公法》在内。

---

① 对照英文版条约: "All official communications addressed by the Diplomatic and Consular Agents of Her Majesty the Queen to the Chinese authorities shall, henceforth, be written in English. They will for the present be accompanied by a Chinese version, but, it is understood that, in the event of there being any difference of meaning between the English and Chinese text, the English Government will hold the sense as expressed in the English text to be the correct sense."

② 详见《同治元年七月二十五日总理各国事务奕䜣等折》所附章程。《中国近代史资料丛刊·洋务运动》第二册,中国史学会主编,第8—11页。

③ 详见《同治五年十一月初五日总理各国事务奕䜣等折》。同上书,第22—23页。

④ 详见《同治六年二月十五日大学士倭仁折》。同上书,第30页。

⑤ 详见《同治六年三月初八日大学士倭仁折》。同上书,第35页。

⑥ 详见《同文馆题名录》之课程表。同上书,第84—86页。

（三）洋人译者：美国传教士丁韪良

据王维俭教授考证（1987 年），并查《同文馆题名录》等史料记载，同时参照丁韪良半自传性质的《花甲记忆》（*A Cycle of Cathay or China, South and North with Personal Reminiscences*, 1896），得其生平概况。

美国人丁韪良出生牧师家庭，先后就读新阿尔巴尼神学院及印第安纳州立大学，除宗教和法律外，还广泛涉猎算术、物理、化学、天文与机械等自然科学知识，毕业时荣获博士学位。

1850 年，受美国长老会（American Presbyterian Church）派遣携妻来华。最初十余年在宁波传教，学习汉语官话及当地方言，并研读四书五经等中国经典。1863 年，举家迁居北京，开辟新的布道据点。

1865 年，经美国驻华公使蒲安臣和英国使馆参赞威妥玛（Thomas Francis Wade, 1818 - 1895）介绍，受聘京师同文馆为英文教习；1867 年，改授《万国公法》和《富国策》；1869 年，由海关总税务司赫德（Robert Hart, 1835 - 1911）推荐，升任同文馆总教习。

综上所述，与摘译《滑达尔各国律例》的先辈伯驾相比，丁韪良至少具有三项迥异处，必然深刻影响国际法翻译活动，特别是主要由他独自完成的《万国公法》及其率学员协作完成的《公法便览》等。

1. 熟识官话

丁韪良研读汉语绝非浅尝辄止。他在宁波传教期间，为能尽快与当地人交流，从学习方言着手，甚至自创基于欧洲语言的拼音；然后逐步探索被其称作"表意系统"的文言文，数年间便开始用官话写作，并完成了有关基督教义的论著《天道溯源》，许多华人知识分子竟因之皈依上帝（丁韪良，2004：27—31）。担任美华书馆经理期间，他还编纂中文教科书如《常字双千》（*The Analytical Reader: A Short Method for Learning to Read and Write Chinese*, 1863）等（孙玉祥，2003：55）。由此可见，丁韪良熟识文言官话，汉语功底颇深。

2. 了解儒学

值得注意的是，丁韪良修习文言文的同时，还诵读中国传统的四书五经。他能够了解儒学经典的某些义理，并将之与《旧约》的摩西五书和《新约》的四福音书对应起来，认为这些古书的道德教诲质朴纯正，"除了希伯来人之外，世界上没有一个民族曾经从古人那儿继承过这么珍贵的遗产"（丁韪良，2004：32）。当然，这也表明丁韪良对华夏文明的认识仍流于肤浅，既将儒家学派视为宗教①，还总以基督为尺度，进行批判性的衡量，因而感觉儒教作为"道德体系……缺乏神的权威"（王美秀，1995：48）。尽管如此，他毕竟已意识到儒学义理塑造清朝文士思想观念的巨大能量。

3. 精通法律

法律是丁韪良就读大学期间的主攻专业之一，造诣匪浅。其个人译著亦偏向该领域，故被梁启超誉为"公法专家"②，"中国旧译，惟同文馆本，多法家言，丁韪良盖治此学也"③。正是凭借《万国公法》的盛名，他于1867年辞去英文教习职务，由同文馆委以传授国际法及政治经济学的重任，这当然也是"考虑到此项职位对这个国家的重要人物的影响"（王维俭，1987：69）。他甚至还专门研究并撰写了题为《中国古世公法论略》（*International Law in Ancient China*）的学术论文，虽然开篇即片面强调清政府签订国际条约、与西方互设使领馆的积极作用：

> The recent treaties, by which China has been brought into closer relations with the nations of the West, and especially the establishment of intercourse by means of permanent embassies, have led Chinese statesmen to turn their attention to the subject of international law. (Martin, 1894: 111)

却也洞若观火地指出中国古代因缺乏平等独立的邻邦，故而不可能产生近似欧洲的国际法（同上，113—114）：

> During this long period, it was no more possible that an international code should spring up in China than it would have been for such a thing to

---

① 丁韪良所著《汉学菁华》（*Lore of Cathay*）第三卷第十一章名为"三教"或中国的三大宗教，便将儒家学派称为"儒教"（2010：109）。他收集在 *Hanlin Papers* 中的一篇论文"Stages of Religious Thought in China"也有"These are known as the three religions, —Confucian, Taoist, and Buddhist"之类表述（Martin, 1894：259）。

② 详见梁启超先生所撰《读西学书法》。《西学书目表四卷附读西学书法一卷》，光绪丙申（1896年）冬十月质学会用时务报馆本重校付刊。

③ 详见《论译书》。《梁启超全集》第一册第一卷"变法通议"，张品兴等主编，第47页。

appear in Europe, had the Roman empire remained undivided until the present day. The requisite conditions were wanting. Where they exist, a code based upon usage, and more or less developed, comes into being by the necessities of the human mind.

These conditions are: —

1st—The existence of a group of independent States, so situated as to require or favor the maintenance of friendly intercourse;

2nd—That those States should be so related as to conduct their intercourse on a basis of equality.

二 选译惠顿的因缘

追溯选译惠顿的因缘,向存两说:诱迫说——欧美帝国主义软硬兼施,诱迫清廷遵循西式游戏规则,接受不平等条约;自发说——总理衙门官员借法图强,自发引进西方外交惯例,尝试维护本国权益。笔者以为此二者各有偏颇。

(一) 丁韪良:国家利益至高无上

有研究者认定具备法律知识背景的丁氏暂任美国驻大清国特命全权公使 (Envoy Extraordinary and Minister Plentipotentiary to the Qing Empire) 列卫廉 (William Bradford Reed) 和华若翰 (John Elliott Ward) 的翻译期间,因参与拟定《中美天津条约》及北京换约事宜,洞悉清廷办理外交磋商错漏百出的弊端在于缺乏制度保障,皇帝的随心所欲反易致理屈词穷,故决心译介国际法 (Hsü, 1960:126;孙玉祥, 2003:56)。持此观点的欧美专家、中国台湾学者绝非少数,但他们大多讳言丁韪良亦曾公开叫嚣,教导这样不循惯例的国家,"最佳良药就是授之以荆棘"[①] (1864:4)。

另外,丁氏本人在 1863 年 10 月 1 日致长老会传教士娄理华 (Walter Lowrie, 1819 - 1847) 的私函中强调从事这项工作并未得到任何指示,只求将基督文明最优秀的成果输入华夏:

> ... a work which might bring this atheistic government to the recognition of God and his Eternal Justice; and perhaps impart to them something

---

[①] 英语原文:"... the best remedy is to teach it with thorns."

of the Spirit of Christianity. （Boggs，1948：34）

他坚信自己的所作所为与传教士的身份职责是相称的：

> ... not unsuitable for a missionary who feels in duty bound to seek the welfare of the country he has chosen for the seat of his labors. ①

可细察其译文的儒化程度，虽不无汉官斧凿的痕迹，仍难免令读者怀疑该说仅为托词罢了。

实际上，丁韪良曾借时过境迁后纽约首版的英文著作《花甲记忆》委婉地承认"本来打算翻译瓦岱尔（Vattel②）的作品，但华若翰先生建议我采用惠顿氏的"（2004：150）。这从某个侧面暗示最终选定惠顿"同样权威，且更现代一些"的国际法著作，至少部分出自国家利益的考虑：华若翰作为美国使节，其意见代表政府观点；而惠顿亦是美国法学家兼外交官。由此也就不难解释为什么蒲安臣通过上海领事西华德（George Seward）知道相关情况后立即写信鼓励他继续翻译并承诺向清政府推荐其作品。

《万国公法》卷前的英文题词是献给蒲安臣的；译者序与中文凡例首款的措辞③相仿佛，同样只字不提美国官方政策，仅强调该书观点全面公正、风行欧洲：

> For the choice of my author I offer no apology. My mind at first inclined to Vattel；but on reflection，it appeared to me，that the work of that excellent and lucid writer might as a practical guide be somewhat out of date；and that to introduce it to the Chinese would not be unlike teaching them the Ptolemaic system of the heavens. Mr. Wheaton's book，besides the

---

① 详见《万国公法》译者序，第1—2页。

② 今译瓦泰尔，即本章第一节讨论的瑞士国际法专家。

③ 详见《万国公法·凡例》首款："是书原本出美国惠顿氏选缮。惠顿氏奉命驻扎普鲁京都多年，间尝遍历欧罗巴诸国。既已深谙古今书籍，更复广有见闻，且持论颇以不偏著名。故各国每有公论，多引其书以释疑端。奉使外出者无不携贮囊箧，时备参考。至派少年学翻译等职，亦每以是书课之。"

advantage of bringing the science down to a very recent day, is generally recognized as a full and impartial digest, and as such has found its way into all the Cabinets of Europe. ①

　　紧接着又盛赞清帝国海关总税务司英国人赫德能够克服民族偏见②，欣赏"一部美国文本的美国版本"③，岂非欲盖弥彰？否则何必在光绪三年（1877年）刊印的《公法便览》自序中重申"惠氏之书虽出于美国，而余译之无所嫌疑者，盖以行世既久，早经各国奉为典则也"，顺势还就"兹率馆生复译新书，不惮讥评而仍取诸敌国之作"的决定进行辩护，理由却如出一辙："问世已十有五载，至今声名颇著，法家视之为权衡准则……其所论公而且直，既不徇本国之私，亦不惮斥本国之谬"④。

　　（二）总理衙门：两害相权取其轻

　　正如前文所述，总理衙门办理对外交涉过程中深觉熟习西方国际惯例的重要性，故而才有同治二年（1863年）夏，文祥借口与法国发生摩擦，请求蒲安臣译介权威著作之事（Hsü，1960：126；张用心，2005：79）。笔者以为清廷的初衷不外乎两点：一方面，美国于历次鸦片战争中均扮演调停人的温和角色，非似英法等徒恃武力；另一方面，美国公使还兼任列

────────────

　　① 详见《万国公法》译者序，第3页。

　　② 据赫德本人的日记所载，早在1863年7月至8月，他就应总理衙门官员董恂、薛焕、恒祺、崇纶等请求，摘译了惠顿国际法的第三部分，包括通使权和缔约权，汇集成"二十四款"（Bruner，Fairbank & Smith，1986：295 - 306）；1864年8月见丁韪良来访并展示其所译惠顿的首页，他又承诺向清政府争取出版经费，且负责具体执行总署拨付银两印刷《万国公法》的公文（Smith，Fairbank & Bruner，1991：182 - 187）。详见《赫德日记（1854—1863）：步入中国清廷仕途》（*Entering China's Service：Robert Hart's Journals*，1854 - 1863）（14，15，23 & 26 JULY and 3，6 &17 AUGUST of 1863）和《赫德日记（1863—1866）：赫德与中国早期现代化》（*Robert Hart and China's Early Modernization：His Journals*，1863 - 1866）（17，20 & 25 AUGUST of 1864）。

　　③ 详见《万国公法》译者序，第3页。

　　④ 详见《公法便览》自序（译洋文），该书凡例中更有四款专论译介吴氏国际法著作之因缘："一、惠氏之万国公法行世已久，兹译吴氏公法便览以补旧书之不足。二书皆出美国而征引各国之论颇广，使阅者不啻便览各国之书。倘本馆异日能将各国原书陆续译出以资参考，则更觉详备。一、吴君尔玺美之名士也，年近八旬，曾于雅礼学院总理学政，迨以老乞休而致力于公法，爰著此书，以课子弟云。一、此书之旨简而赅，其所征引博而正。不但学院子弟读之进益，即大国执政亦每玩索而有得焉。不独见重美国，即他国亦屡经刊刻而广行之。一、余于丁卯年请假回国，曾在雅礼学院得识吴君。观其教法，心甚美之。复读是书，窃思吴君已用之于本国以课其子弟，曷不可携之于中国而课诸馆生。兹既以洋文课读，复今译以汉文，俾得公诸同好。"

强驻北京外交使团团长，具有相对公信度。

当时，蒲安臣推荐的就是惠顿的《国际法原理》，随后了解到丁韪良的翻译活动，便在该年九月正式将其引见文祥等总署大臣。同治三年七月二十九日（1864 年 8 月 30 日），奕䜣称"于各国彼此互相非毁之际，乘间探访，知有《万国律例》一书。然欲径向索取并托翻译，又恐秘而不宣。适美国公使蒲安臣来言，各国有将《大清律例》翻出洋字一书，并言外国有通行律例，近日经文士丁韪良译出汉文，可以观览"，即指此事。但自愿献书的动机颇可疑，"窥其意一则夸耀外国亦有政令；一则该文士欲效从前利玛窦等在中国立名"。

事实上，这份在法律交流史上意义深远的奏折①更隐晦地揭示了清政府进退维谷的心态"就好像特洛伊人对待希腊人的礼物一般"（丁韪良，2004：160）：既欲辩论事件之时，"借彼国事例以破其说"；也"防其以书尝试，要求照行"，反致欲罢不能。

虽有丁韪良再三解释："《大清律例》现经外国翻译，中国并未强外国以必行，岂有外国之书转强中国以必行之礼"，终难令颇具戒心的洋务官员完全释怀。好在译文初稿"第字句拉杂，非面为讲解，不能明晰。正可借此如其所请"，派出总理衙门章京陈钦、李常华、方睿师、毛鸿图等四员，"与之悉心商酌删润，但易其字，不改其意"。

这无疑远较现代的出版审查更为严苛，足可确保译入文化的主导意识形态少受外来因素的侵凌。所谓"易字不改意"全是伪饰，否则何来"借此"之说？且嗣后丁氏主持同文馆译介公法类书籍，均需总署王大臣批阅方可付梓，遂成惯例。

（三）余论

综合前述分析可见，《万国公法》的传译并非全然是清政府内改良派官员尝试和平交涉的自发设想，亦颇受美国使馆乘势扩张自身对华影响力的意图干扰。牵涉至历史转折变局中的各色人等尽管同床异梦，联袂促成此事亦算是殊途同归、水到渠成了。

事实上，若国际法果真反映的是普适性诉求，那么当时的中国人和西方人"谁也不清楚这本书到底对谁更有利"（刘禾，2000：76）。无怪乎

---

① 详见《续修四库全书·史部·纪事本末类·筹办夷务始末》同治卷二七，（清）文庆、贾桢、宝鋆等纂辑，《续修四库全书》编纂委员会编，第 25—26 页。

办理三口通商大臣（亦称"北洋大臣"）崇厚"对于该书稿跟中国建立新的外交关系的需求之间的契合印象十分深刻"（丁韪良，2004：150）；英国公使卜鲁斯却认为此书"可以让中国人看看西方国家也有'道理'可讲。他们也是按照道理行事的，武力并非他们的唯一法则"（同上，159）。

第三节　权力博弈对馆译公法策略定位 及内容增删的影响

无论如何，总理衙门作为近代外交机构雏形的出现，标志着严密封闭的清朝官僚体制完整性出现裂痕（叶翔凤，1994：79）。难怪清议者"日夜恨其不早裁撤，以为一日衙门尚存，即一日国光不复"（孟森，1990：9）。而西方人的回应则截然相反，奕䜣接见英国驻京参赞威妥玛时微露其意，"该公使闻之，甚为欣悦"①。

迥异制度间的博弈绝难简述成单纯的全盘西化，其间必定充满传统卫道派的竭力抵御、洋务改良派的审慎戒备，中外文化双向冲突与妥协亦此起彼伏。譬如同文馆添设天文、算学馆之争便是典型事例，但无论保守抑或激进，清政府上层人士多视西学为"微末技艺"，却是不言自明。

《万国公法》之所以令清廷官员感兴趣，无非"论会盟战法诸事，其于启衅之间，彼此控制箝束，尤各有法"；且"颇有制伏领事官之法，未始不有裨益"②。类似文字极深刻地折射了当时普遍存在的实用主义现象：即便以总理衙门为代表的洋务派关注的也只是西方外交的具"法"，完全不探究字里行间隐含的哲学渊源与平等思想。

毋庸置疑，此指导方针也潜移默化地塑造着最终刊行的国际法译文的表现方式；同样给予译著巨大影响的还有丁韪良本人深受时代局限的知识框架与意识形态。

---

① 详见《钦差大臣奕䜣等奏英使来京意在撤兵并向其微露设立总理衙门事片（咸丰十年十二月初一日）》。《中国近代史资料丛刊·第二次鸦片战争》第五册，中国史学会主编，第346页。

② 详见《续修四库全书·史部·纪事本末类·筹办夷务始末》同治卷二七，（清）文庆、贾桢、宝鋆等纂辑，《续修四库全书》编纂委员会编，第26页。

一　翻译策略定位的时代性：信、达、雅，孰轻孰重？

《万国公法》译者序有云：

> 在文体的选择方面，我的目标是清楚而非优美，尽管在需要充分考虑准确的时候总是牺牲清楚和优美。所以，由于过分忠于原文，对本地读者似乎有所妨碍；但这个缺点得到了充分的弥补，因为翻译者没有抛弃原文自行其是。[①]

中国传统翻译理论素有信、达、雅之说，西方学者亦提出所谓的三原则。以此观之，丁韪良本人更为看重的似乎是"准确"（信），即内容方面的信息传递；其次才是"清楚"（达）和"优美"（雅），或者说表现形式。

然而，徐中约教授比照原著后得出的结论却是该作品的准确性有所欠缺，甚至超出了严格意义上的现代翻译范畴：

> ... Although the accuracy of Martin's translation leaves much to be desired, he is still to be commended for a splendid performance, if one takes into account the unusual difficulties confronting a pioneer intercultural disseminator. Judging by present standards, however, his work cannot strictly be considered a translation, but rather a paraphrastic interpretation of Wheaton...
>
> The edited text of the translation is in good, semi-classical style, which posed no problem for the Chinese literati... (Hsü, 1960: 129)

且不论《万国公法》的文体风格是否会给中国知识分子造成阅读障碍，只问缘何译者本人与后世评论者的观点会如此南辕北辙？笔者以为这应从华洋合译的历程及时代变迁两个维度分别进行考察。

（一）合译历程

据丁韪良本人回忆，自 1862 年返回大清国后即开始翻译《万国公法》，并认为"这部作品可以对我自己的事业，以及中英这两个帝国产生

---

① 详见《万国公法》译者序，第 3 页。

一定程度的影响"（2004：150），此亦该书凡例第四款所谓"视其理足义备，思于中外不无裨益"。但其工作不只是个人独立完成的，参与者尚有"江宁何师孟、通州李大文、大兴张炜、定海曹景荣"①。换言之，当时华人已涉足译文的表述，而呈送总理衙门批阅的书稿依然"字句拉杂"。这足可证明译者深受原著句法及逻辑结构的影响，自以为"过分忠于原文，对本地读者似乎有所妨碍"完全合情合理，故恳请"王大臣派员校正底稿"②。实际上，任何尊重原文的现代译者都曾或多或少地产生过类似疑惑。

相比之下，后世学者阅览的《万国公法》业经奕䜣所遣四位总署章京与丁氏"悉心商酌删润"方才刊印。这些官员均为饱学之士，甚或出自翰林院，由其斧削而成半文言风格的流畅译本又岂能久扰华人知识分子？

（二）时代变迁

更堪忧虑的是，起源欧洲的近代国际法知识体系具有专门性的显著特征，欲在华夏尊奉朝贡思想的传统建构内寻觅兼容相似理念的空间实非朝夕之事。何况"那时英语和汉语之间假设的对等关系尚未建立起来"（刘禾，2000：77），从理念到体系的制度对接无不煞费若心。正因如此，西法东渐始于华洋合译。《万国公法》作为首部完整译介的国际法著作，先后参与的华人多达八位，既有虔诚的基督徒③，也有翰林学士。

当然，新术语的构造在所难免，虽令时人备感晦涩，但随岁月流逝，西学文本汹涌而入，甚至汉语白话文亦受欧化影响，所涉词汇的含义于今日早已不证自明。刘禾先生由此认为"不同语言遭遇后产生可译性和可理解性问题，往往超越当下的历史语境，经过相当长的时间才在后人的语言中达到一定的明晰性"（同上），这无疑是合乎逻辑的推论。

二　内容增删：冲击东方传统文明；垄断西方殖民话语

《万国公法》译者序有云：

---

① 详见《万国公法·凡例》第四款。
② 同上。
③ 即追随丁韪良的基督教徒江宁何师孟、通州李大文、大兴张炜、定海曹景荣。

我认为删去某些冗长的讨论（例如有关惠顿担任驻普鲁士官廷公使时的住宅的豁免权）以及各式各样不重要的细节（例如有关莱茵河、圣劳伦斯河和密西西比河航行的规定）是合适的。有时候，为了避免不必要的细节，我作了一点压缩；而在另外一些地方，为了说清楚，我又作了某种程度的扩写。[①]

（一）丁氏之增

正如张用心先生所言，丁韪良的译文偶有增添原著未见的词句，但并不存在所谓的"扩写"（2005：82）。当然，那绝非意味着译者就无所作为。

实际上，初刻《万国公法》（京都崇实馆版）中紧随凡例之后的并非正文，而是两页短篇说明，描述世界主要国家分布状况，同时配发东、西半球简图各一幅。这都是惠顿的国际法原著所未有的。

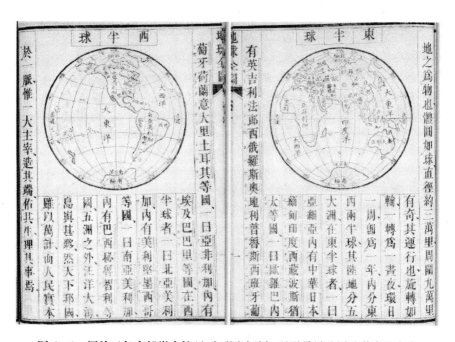

图6—1　同治三年京都崇实馆版《万国公法》所附世界地图及其介绍文字

---

① 详见《万国公法》译者序，第3页。被删节部分主要包括《国际法原理》（1855年第六版）第二卷第IV章第17、18、19三节（第255—270页），及其序言和附录（第626—669页）。

联想十三年后丁氏主持翻译的《公法便览》（同文馆聚珍版），亦在正文前添附此图及说明。不言而喻，其目的自是开宗明义地向闭目塞听的清廷官员宣告中国在当时最科学的世界地图上所处位置。正如其凡例有云："阅是书者，应于地球各国图记先略为熟悉，所以附地球图说一页，系借《万国公法》原板刷印。然欲求其详，莫如考查《瀛寰志略》、《地球全志》等书，而后泰西各国往来事宜方能洞悉。"①

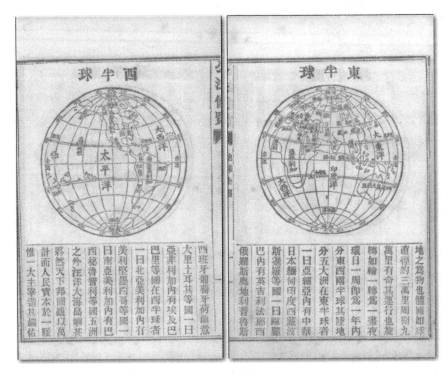

图6—2　光绪三年同文馆聚珍版《公法便览》
所附世界地图及其介绍文字

这样的制图学表象给予传统知识分子的直接视觉冲击胜于千言万语：历代以华夏为核心的"大一统"秩序、"居内制外"的优越性和层次关系已无法适应西方列强纷至沓来的新形势需求。全球意识日渐明朗，国际交往惯例的重要性相应凸显。难怪张斯桂作序直言"统观地球上版图，大

———————————

①　详见《公法便览·凡例》第十款。

小不下数十国,其犹有存焉者,则恃其先王之命,载在盟府,世世守之,长享勿替,有渝此盟,神明殛之,即此《万国律例》一书耳"①;总署大臣董恂也大声疾呼"今九州外之国林立矣,不有法以维之,其何以国?此丁韪良教师《万国公法》之所由译也"②。

尽管魏源编纂的《海国图志》中同样载有类似插图,但对真正办理涉外事宜的官员而言,较之官费刊印且"通商口岸各给一部"③ 的《万国公法》,两者的影响力相去不啻千里。

(二)丁氏之删

据《万国公法·凡例》所言,"译者惟精义是求,未敢旁参己意,原书所有条例无不尽录,但引证繁冗之处,少有删减者。"

实际上,丁氏译文的删节幅度相当可观。《国际法原理》(1855 年第六版)正文部分即有 625 页,总计大约 25 万英文单词;《万国公法》却只八万余汉字,即便考虑到文言文较简洁,也不成比例(张用心,2005:82)。

尽管中文本未译部分内容大都乃"引证繁冗之处",其选择性仍值得研究者思量,特别是原著第二卷第 IV 章第 17、18、19 三节"有关莱茵河、圣劳伦斯河和密西西比河航行的规定"尤引人注目。

自咸丰八年(1858 年)签订《中英天津条约》以来,西方列强凭借"片面最惠国待遇",相继取得内河长江的自由航行权④,结果却是弊端丛

---

① 详见《万国公法》张斯桂序。

② 详见《万国公法》董恂序。

③ 详见《续修四库全书·史部·纪事本末类·筹办夷务始末》同治卷二七,(清)文庆、贾桢、宝鋆等纂辑,《续修四库全书》编纂委员会编,第 26 页。

④ 请读者参阅《中英天津条约》中文本第十款规定:"长江一带各口,英商船只俱可通商。惟现在江上下游均有贼匪,除镇江一年后立口通商外,其余俟地方平靖,大英钦差大臣与大清特派之大学士尚书会议,准将自汉口溯流至海各地,选择不逾三口,准为英船出进货物通商之区。"附英文本如下:"British merchant ships shall have authority to trade upon the Great River [Yangtze]. The Upper and Lower Valley of the River being, however, disturbed by outlaws, no Port shall be for the present opened to trade, with the exception of Chinkiang, which shall be opened in a year from the date of the signing of this Treaty. So soon as Peace shall have been restored, British Vessels shall also be admitted to trade at such Ports as far as Hankow, not exceeding three in number, as the British Minister, after consultation with the Chinese Secretary of State, may determine shall be Ports of Entry and Discharge. "详见《中外旧约章大全(第一分卷)》上册,海关总署《中外旧约章大全》编纂委员会编,第 299 页。

生。故早在 1861 年，总理衙门就曾邀请署理海关总税务司赫德北上，商讨长江流域开放贸易后的关税待遇及如何解决由此引发的遍插"外国旗帜"掩护内河走私问题（魏尔特，1993：265—297）。恭亲王奕䜣等官员坚持内河贸易应由清廷自行管理，因而抵制欧美国家单方面制定无限制全线开放长江沿岸的章程草案。

《公法便览》自序常言："公法得因史案以明，而史案转籍公法以彰。"① 鉴于惠顿撰写的上述章节正为引证河道通航惯例的具体适用性，对诠释相关国际公约的规定至关紧要，此长篇宏论却被无端删译，莫非是不欲授之以柄？

另外，丁韪良的译本还删节了原著作者的自序②及附录。前者对正文的阅读理解具有无法替代的价值；后者则深化了部分争议主题的探讨。译者弃若敝屣，或是希望晚清官员只知其然，而不知其所以然？毕竟，西方人对国际法输入中国的态度也莫衷一是。③

第四节　权力博弈对馆译公法术语
定名的影响（一）

王健博士在《沟通两个世界的法律意义》中将丁韪良翻译西方政法类概念的原则概括如下（2001：49）：

（1）以汉字音译外国的国名、地名和人名；

（2）存在中外对称事物的情况下，以中国的名目指称外国名目；

（3）音、意并立；

（4）另造新词，意译概念。

---

① 详见《公法便览》自序。

② 包括《国际法原理》（1855 年第六版）保留的"第 1 版广告"（Advertisement to the First Edition）、"第 3 版序言"（Preface to the Third Edition）和 1848 年法文版序言。

③ 譬如法国使馆临时代办哥士奇（Cecile Kleczkowski）就对蒲安臣说："这个家伙是谁？竟然想让中国人对我们欧洲的国际法了如指掌？杀了他！——掐死他；他会给我们找来无数麻烦的！"（丁韪良，2004：159）

一　音译专有名词原则

音译专有名词原则早在新教传教士编写《外国史略》（马礼逊①，1807）、《万国地理全图集》（郭实腊②，1838）等中文书刊时便已确立，并由魏源广泛征引至《海国图志》，且多数情况下仅限国名、地名和人名的习惯沿袭至今。只不过晚清社会的汉字注音法，远未形成统一标准，同名异译所在皆是。正如丁氏及其合译者所言，"天下邦国既众，以华文而译诸国名者，其用字、配音率多不同，致一国而有数名，易于舛错"③。因此，同文馆译介公法，"所用国名以及人名、地名，则本条约与《瀛寰志略》，以期划一"④。

（一）姓氏名号

需要特别指出的是，当时译外国姓名不用全称，"虎哥/葛罗丢"（Hugo Grotius）、"霍毕寺"（Thomas Hobbes）、"布番多"（Samuel Pufendorf）、"俄拉费"（Christian Wolff）、"发得耳"（Vattel）等皆无例外。再者，《万国公法》对于三个或三个以上汉字构成的洋名，重复提及时多仿华人习惯简称"某氏"，譬如"布氏"、"俄氏"、"发氏"等；《公法便览》更直呼西洋人为"某氏"，然后才以双行小字注其姓名。试看该书首章"论公法本原"第十一节部分文字：

> 葛氏（名葛罗丢，字虎哥，荷兰人也，实为公法之祖。）曰：人性自具天理，故遇事即能辨其善恶，而知其为天所禁与否。葛氏谓公法即本于是，而以为之准。

似乎合译者总将欧美姓氏误作全称，反视其名为字号。无论怎样，公

---

① 马礼逊（Robert Morrison，1782 – 1834），苏格兰人，新教传教士。1807 年受伦敦传道会（London Missionary Society）派遣前往中国广州，在英属东印度公司任职 25 年。他曾将《圣经》译成中文，并编著《华英字典》（A Dictionary of the Chinese Language）。《外国史略》是否为马礼逊所著及其初版年代，尚有争议，仍需考证。

② 郭实腊（Karl Friedrich August Gützlaff，1803 – 1851），普鲁士人，新教传教士。1829 年受伦敦传道会（London Missionary Society）邀请前往新加坡学习汉语和中国文化，曾任香港殖民政府的高级官员。

③ 详见《公法便览·凡例》第十九款。《星轺指掌·凡例》中亦有相同说明。

④ 同上。

法书籍顺应目的语读者之归化意图确凿无疑。

（二）洲名与国名

尽管《万国公法》及《公法便览》卷首的世界地图依然标注着各大洲及西方主要国家拗口的全名，但今人耳熟能详的简称已在正文中悄然通行：

表6—1　　丁氏公法译著中五大洲及主要西方国家的全称与简称对照表

英语原文	译名全称	译名简称①
England	英吉利	英国
France	法朗西（今译：法兰西）	法国
Russia	俄罗斯	俄国
America	美利坚	美国
Prussia	普鲁士	普国*
Austria	奥地利	奥国*
Portugal	葡萄牙	葡国*
Asia	亚细亚	亚洲
Europe	欧罗巴	欧洲
Africa	亚非利加（亦作：阿非利加）	非洲
North America	北亚美利加	北美洲
South America	南亚美利加	南美洲

先是晚清时期政治、经济交往最频繁的英、法、俄、美、普、奥等列强常被略名为某国，既图指称方便，也不无尊重之意。普鲁士统一德意志民族后更名德国；奥地利则因两次世界大战威势顿减，与东亚联系亦日渐疏远，未能如英、法、俄、美等四强至今称国。

相比之下，洲名变称的渐进过程更能直击问题的核心：《万国公法》还亦步亦趋地套用全名，及至《公法便览》已是唯见简称了。

《万国公法》原文②：

It may be remarked, in confirmation of this view, that the more re-

---

① 晚清公法译著中提及普鲁士、奥地利和葡萄牙三国，以全名居多，偶有用简称的。

② 原文摘录自《国际法原理》第一卷"国际法的定义、渊源和主体（DEFININTION, SOURCES, AND SUBJECTS OF INTERNATIONAL LAW）"第Ⅰ章"定义和渊源（DEFINITION AND SOURCES）"§10"赫夫特学说（System of Heffter）"，第14页。粗体由本书作者添加。

cent intercourse between the Christian nations of **Europe** and **America** and the Mohammedan and Pagan nations of **Asia** and **Africa** indicates a disposition, on the part of the latter, to renounce their peculiar international usages and adopt those of Christendom.

《万国公法》译文①：

赛氏此说，是也。亦可以迩来之事证之。盖**欧罗巴**、**亚美利加**诸**国**，奉耶稣之教者，与**亚细亚**、**阿非利加**之回回等国，交际往来，彼虽教化迥异，亦屡弃自己之例，而从吾西方之公法。

《公法便览》原文②：

All history is full of examples of such recognitions. Holland and Switzerland, long after their independence was acknowledged in the diplomacy of most **European** states, were formally admitted into the brotherhood of nations at the era of the peace of Westphalia. The United States, the Spanish states of **South America**, the two French empires, the kingdom of Greece, all arose from revolutions, and have been acknowledged to possess the full functions of states.

《公法便览》译文③：

考诸往事，历有明证。如荷兰、瑞士，本皆附庸，叛而自立。初认为自主之国虽众，迨威司发里和约之时，始与**欧洲**诸国并列。他若**美国**及**美洲**中日［疑为"西"字］国属部，法君那波仑先后两朝，及希腊国，皆起于叛逆，后皆列为全权自立之国。

---

① 译文摘录自《万国公法》第一卷"释公法之义，明其本源，题其大旨"第二章"释义明源"第十节"海氏大旨"。粗体由本书作者添加。

② 原文摘录自《国际法导论》第 I 卷"国家的核心权力及和平时期的权利与义务（THE ESSENTIAL POWERS OF STATES, AND THEIR RIGHTS AND OBLIGATIONS ESPECIALLY IN A STATE OF PEACE）"第 I 章"独立主权国家的权利——与之相应的不干涉义务及国际惯例主张或承认的例外情况（RIGHTS OF STATES AS INDEPENDENT SOVEREIGNTIES. —CORRESPONDING OBLIGATION OF NON-INTERFERENCE AND EXCEPTIONS TO IT CLAIMED OR ADMITTED IN THE PRACTICE OF NATIONS）"§40，第 55 页。粗体由本书作者添加。

③ 译文摘录自《公法便览》卷一"论邦国平时之权利与应尽之责守"第一章"论邦国自主之权不得互相干预"第五节。粗体由本书作者添加。请读者注意，"美洲中日国属部"疑为"美洲中西（班牙）国属部"之误。

尚记前节述及林则徐令幕僚袁德辉等摘译穆瑞（Hugh Murray）的《地理大全》（*Encyclopedia of Geography*），即名之为《四洲志》。正如齐思和老先生所言："书实记五大洲事，称四洲者，犹沿中国由佛书中所得之旧称"（1954：506）。故所谓"洲"，亦华夏文明所固有。

再比照上述两段译文，足以说明 19 世纪后半叶的中国已然不可逆转地融入世界大家庭，日益密切的邦交关系最终迫使清朝统治者接受"九州外之国林立"① 的现实。而简称的普遍使用必将提升世人对国际形势的熟识程度，并方便其进一步探究与理解。

二　比附说明原则

对于近现代政法制度、机构、职衔方面的概念，中国译者起初亦偏执音译词，泰半是欠缺游历以致难解内涵，只能因陋就简；而西洋传教士却多择意译词，即遵循比附说明原则——以中国的近似名目指称外国名目。

（一）音译、意译，孰优孰劣？

在这方面，《海国图志》表现得尤为突出。魏源广泛收集世界各国地理信息，摘录的资料既有"前两广总督林尚书所译西夷之《四洲志》"②；也包括"近日夷图、夷言"③，譬如《外国史略》（马礼逊，1807）、《万国地理全图集》（郭实腊，1838）、《新释地理备考》（玛吉士④，1845）等中文书刊。

其中，《弥利坚即美里哥国总记》⑤ 与《弥利坚国即育奈土迭国总记》⑥ 两篇文章相互比照最能说明问题。它们描述的虽都是美利坚国家概况，但前者辑入美部会传教士裨治文所撰《美理哥合省国志略》（1838）

---

① 详见《万国公法》董恂序。

② 详见《海国图志》原叙。《魏源全集》第四册，魏源全集编辑委员会编，第 1 页。

③ 同上。其后所列中文书刊见《海国图志》后叙。同上书，第 7—8 页。

④ 玛吉士（José Martinho Marques, 1810 – 1867），出生于中国澳门的葡萄牙籍汉学家。该书又名《外国地理备考》，最初刊行于道光二十五年（1845 年），现存道光二十七年（1847 年）收入"海山仙馆丛书"的版本。

⑤ 此为六十卷篇名，后百卷本更名《弥利坚即美里哥国总记上》。详见《海国图志》卷五十九《弥利坚即美里哥国总记上》。《魏源全集》第六册，魏源全集编辑委员会编，第 1601—1622 页。

⑥ 此为六十卷篇名，后百卷本更名《弥利坚国总记中》。详见《海国图志》卷六十《弥利坚国总记中》。同上书，第 1623—1638 页。

全文，而后者以《四洲志·育奈士迭国》为主要内容。请看表 6—2 所列机构、职衔的译名：

表 6—2　　《美里哥国总记》与《育奈士迭国总记》中部分机构、职衔译名对照表

英文	《弥利坚国即育奈士迭国总记》（林则徐审定）华人译名	《弥利坚即美里哥国总记》（裨治文撰写）洋人译名	今译
President	勃列西领	统领	总统
Vice President	副勃列西领	副统领	副总统
Congress	衮额里士衙门	公堂	国会
Senate	西业	议事阁	参议院
House of Representatives	里勃里先好司　好司二字，犹衙门也。	选议处	众议院
Supreme Court	苏勃林（衙门）	京察院	最高法院
Circuit Court	萨吉（衙门）	巡按察院	巡回法院
District Court	底士特力（衙门）	分巡察院	地方法院

尽管裨治文借用中国类似名目传译西方政法概念，其措辞必然稍欠准确，可较之不知所谓的音译词还是略胜一筹。译名单列时如此，植入文本后的语篇效果更是大相径庭。

《弥利坚即美里哥国总记》片段：
都城内有一**统领**为主，一**副领**为佐，**正、副统领**亦由各人选择。每省择二人至都城合为**议事阁**，又选几人合为**选议处**。**统领**每年收各省饷项，除支贮库不得滥用外，每年定例享禄二万五千元。[①]

《弥利坚国即育奈士迭国总记》片段：
至公举之例，先由各部落人民公举，曰**依力多**，经各部落官府详定，送**衮额里士**衙门，核定人数，与**西业**之**西那多**、**里勃里先特底甫**官额相若，各自保举一人，暗书弥封，存贮公所，俟齐发阅，以推荐最多者为人选。如有官举无民举，有民举无官举，彼此争执，即由**里**

---

① 详见《海国图志》卷五十九《弥利坚即美里哥国总记上》。《魏源全集》第六册，魏源全集编辑委员会编，第 1611 页。

勃里先特底甫于众人所举中，拣选推荐最多者三人，仍由各**依力多**就三择一，膺斯重任。①

前述引录的片段均在介绍美国总统及国会的相关情况：一篇文字生套晚清社会容易接受的意译词粗略勾画西式民主政治；另一篇却满纸汉字注音，读之佶屈聱牙，且云山雾罩，难解其意。孰优孰劣，高下立判。

实际上，对 19 世纪闭目塞听的保守华人而言，裂美国疆域为诸"部落"，以"督抚"、"知府"、"知县"比拟各级地方"首领"，以"六部"比拟中央政府组织形式，这似乎也是扼要阐明异国制度的绝妙良策。正所谓虽不中，亦不远矣。

立一国之首曰**统领**，其权如国王；立各部之首曰**首领**，其权如**中国督抚**；一部中复分中部落若干，如**知府**；再分小部落若干，如**知县**。其国都内立六政府，如**六部尚书**，惟无**工部**，而有**驿部**。②

另外，有关英国地理状况的两篇文章也表现出相似特征，出自《四洲志》的《英吉利国总记》③ 迥别于《英吉利国广述上》④，无非后者部分由新加坡人记述，部分节选自《外国史略》。

表 6—3　　《英吉利国总记》与《英吉利国广述上》中部分职衔译名对照表

英文	《英吉利国总记》 （林则徐审定） 华人译名	《英吉利国广述上》 （新加坡人撰写） 洋人译名	今译
First Lord of the Treasury	法士律阿付厘特利沙利	管国帑大臣	首相
Lord Chancellor	律(古)（占）色拉	审办大臣	大法官
Lord Privy Seal	律布来(阿付)西尔	持玺大臣	掌玺大臣
President of the Council	不列士顿阿付冈色尔	议士协办大臣	枢密院大臣

---

① 详见《海国图志》卷六十《弥利坚国总记中》。《魏源全集》第六册，魏源全集编辑委员会编，第 1625 页。

② 详见《海国图志》卷五十九《弥利坚即美里哥国总记上》。同上书，第 1613 页。

③ 详见《海国图志》卷五十《英吉利国总记》。同上书，第 1357 页。

④ 详见《海国图志》卷五十一《英吉利国广述上》。同上书，第 1383 页。

续表

英文	《英吉利国总记》 （林则徐审定） 华人译名	《英吉利国广述上》 （新加坡人撰写） 洋人译名	今译
Secretary of State for the Home Department	色吉力达厘（阿付） 士迭火厘火伦厘拔盟	内国务宰相	内政大臣
Secretary of State for Colonies and War	色吉力达厘阿付士迭 火哥罗尼士奄窝	外国务宰相 （Secretary of State for Colonies）	殖民地事务大臣
		兵部大臣 （Secretary of State for War）	陆军大臣
First Lord of the Admiralty	法士律阿付押弥拉尔底	水师部大臣	海军大臣
President of the Board of Control/ Secretary of State forIndia	布力士顿阿付离墨 阿付观特罗尔	管印度国务尚书	监督大臣/印度 事务大臣
Chancellor of the Exchequer	占色拉阿付厘士支厥	户部大臣	财政大臣

　　不独《海国图志》如此，梁廷枏的《海国四说》（1846 年）、徐继畲的《瀛寰志略》（1848 年）对政法类概念的处理方式亦雷同。特别是《海国四说》之《合省国说》，同样以裨治文所撰《美理哥合省国志略》为蓝本，照搬了其中比附说明的术语。比较而言，华人译介的资料充斥着怪异冗长的音译词，既无法达意，也难记忆或转述。可堪忧者，唯欧美传教士处心积虑地探究华夏典章制度，可笑夜郎自大的晚清官员直至第二次鸦片战争前夕依然尸位素餐。

　　（二）公法译著中的比附说明

　　鉴于意译政法概念的优越性，丁译公法著作秉承比附说明传统，乃顺理成章之事。在此，笔者仅以《万国公法》论诸国平时往来的第三卷为例。

表6—4 《万国公法·论诸国平时往来之权》首章中部分政法概念的
新旧译名对照表

英文	丁译	今译
ambassador	钦差	大使
public minister	国使/使臣	使节
chief executive magistrate	首领	政府首脑/行政首长
the minister of foreign affairs/council charged with the foreign affairs of the nation	部臣	外交部长
passport	牌票	护照
the letter of credence	玺书	国书
complimentary discourse	称颂	赞美语
an entire exemption from the local jurisdiction, both civil and criminal	不得拿问	民事、刑事司法管辖豁免权

表6—4 所列译名涉及的术语虽只是冰山一角，却也表明比附的概念
范畴并不局限具体的机构、职衔，亦涵盖更为抽象的制度层面。这令译文
读之别具风味，与现代汉语的措辞迥然有异。

原文①：

At this **audience** the **letter of credence** is delivered, and the **minister** pronounces a **complimentary discourse**, to which the **sovereign replies**. In Republican States, the **foreign minister** is received in a similar manner, by the **chief executive magistrate** or **council**, **charged with the foreign affairs of the nation**.

译文②：

其**延见**时，**国使**献**玺书**于君，**善言称颂**，**君**亦当**善言慰答**。在民
主之国，**国使**谒见**首领**亦然，或**部臣**延接亦可。

---

① 原文摘录自《国际法原理》第三卷"和平时期国家享有的国际权利（INTERNATIONAL
RIGHTS OF STATES IN THEIR PACIFIC RELATIONS）"第 I 章"外交特权（RIGHTS OF LEGA-
TION）"§12"国家元首或政府首脑的接见（Audience of the sovereign, or chief magistrate）"，
p. 287。粗体由本书作者添加。

② 译文摘录自《万国公法》第三卷"论诸国平时往来之权"第一章"论通使之权"第十
二节"延见之规"，并根据何勤华点校本加注标点。粗体由本书作者添加。

此款引文固然典型，却远非绝无仅有。再看该卷第二章对政府缔约权的论述，请仔细揣摩以下数例：

（1）互立盟书

原文①：

... in the first case, either **verbally** or **in writing**. It may be expressed by an instrument **signed** by the **plenipotentiaries**, or in the form of letters or notes exchanged between them.

译文②：

明言者，或**口宣盟词**，或**文载盟府**，或两国**全权大臣盖关防**于公函、或两国互行告示及互换照会，俱可。

（2）擅相与盟

原文③：

The municipal constitution of every particular State determines in whom resides the authority to ratify treaties **negotiated and concluded** with foreign powers, so as to render them obligatory upon the nation. In absolute **monarchies**, it is the prerogative of **the sovereign** himself to confirm the act of his **plenipotentiary** by his final **sanction**.

译文④：

约盟既**商定画押**，谁执准许之权，使必遵守，均听各国**律法**所

---

①　原文摘录自《国际法原理》第三卷"和平时期国家享有的国际权利（INTERNATIONAL RIGHTS OF STATES IN THEIR PACIFIC RELATIONS）"第 II 章"磋商并缔结条约的权力（RIGHTS OF NEGOTIATION AND TREATIES）"§2"条约形式（Form of treaty）"，pp. 317 – 318。粗体由本书作者添加。

②　译文摘录自《万国公法》第三卷"论诸国平时往来之权"第一章"论商议立约之权"第二节"盟约式款"，并根据何勤华点校本加注标点。粗体由本书作者添加。

③　原文摘录自《国际法原理》第三卷"和平时期国家享有的国际权利（INTERNATIONAL RIGHTS OF STATES IN THEIR PACIFIC RELATIONS）"第 II 章"磋商并缔结条约的权力（RIGHTS OF NEGOTIATION AND TREATIES）"§6"取决于政府组织法的缔约权（The treaty-making power dependent on the municipal constitution）"，pp. 317 – 318。粗体由本书作者添加。

④　译文摘录自《万国公法》第三卷"论诸国平时往来之权"第一章"论商议立约之权"第六节"谁执定约之权"，并根据何勤华点校本加注标点。粗体由本书作者添加。

定。若**君权**之无所限制者，则**钦差**所行之事，或准或废，必俟**君命**而定。

（3）会盟合兵

原文①：

Treaties of alliance may be either defensive or offensive.

译文②：

立约合兵，名为**会盟**，盖有两种：一则相护以抵御，一则相助以攻伐。

（4）周郑交质

原文③：

The execution of a treaty is sometimes secured by **hostages given** by one party to the other.

译文④：

古时两国立约，往往**交质**以坚其信。

无独有偶，光绪三年刊行的《公法便览》与《万国公法》一脉相承，且论述战争时期国际惯例的口吻与平时往来之权亦相仿佛。

原文⑤：

War may be defined to be an interruption of a state of peace for the

---

① 原文摘录自《国际法原理》第三卷"和平时期国家享有的国际权利（INTERNATIONAL RIGHTS OF STATES IN THEIR PACIFIC RELATIONS）"第 II 章"磋商并缔结条约的权力（RIGHTS OF NEGOTIATION AND TREATIES）"§13"同盟条约（Treaties of alliance）"，pp. 345 - 346。粗体由本书作者添加。

② 译文摘录自《万国公法》第三卷"论诸国平时往来之权"第一章"论商议立约之权"第十三节"合兵之盟"，并根据何勤华点校本加注标点。粗体由本书作者添加。

③ 原文摘录自《国际法原理》第三卷"和平时期国家享有的国际权利（INTERNATIONAL RIGHTS OF STATES IN THEIR PACIFIC RELATIONS）"第 II 章"磋商并缔结条约的权力（RIGHTS OF NEGOTIATION AND TREATIES）"§16"派遣人质作为履行条约的保证（Hostages for the execution of treaties）"，pp. 345 - 346。粗体由本书作者添加。

④ 译文摘录自《万国公法》第 3 卷"论诸国平时往来之权"第 1 章"论商议立约之权"第 16 节"交质以坚信"，并根据何勤华点校本加注标点。粗体由本书作者添加。

⑤ 原文摘录自《国际法导论》第 II 卷"战争时期的国际法与惯例（INTERNATIONAL LAW AND USAGE IN A STATE OF WAR）"第 I 章第 I 节"战争（Of War）"§111，p. 188。

purpose of attempting to procure good or prevent evil by force; and a just war is an attempt to obtain justice or prevent injustice by force, or in other words, to bring back an injuring party to a right state of mind and conduct by the infliction of deserved evil. A just war again, is one that is waged in the last sort, or when self-defense calls for it. We have no right to redress our wrongs in a way expensive and violent, when other methods would be successful.

译文[①]:

暂时失和而用兵,无论侵扰他邦以趋利或力行抵御以避害,皆战也。此国有不法之举,彼国以所应得之罪征之,使不复蹈前愆,义战也。义战者,不得已而为之,或和则大义不伸,或和则本国不保,夫然后义战兴焉。苟犹有术以处之,而劳民伤财以求伸于天下,则断乎不可。

值得肯定的是,丁韪良及其合译者竭力挖掘文言汉语符号系统的现有资源,试图凭此构建与英文术语相对应的虚拟关系,这在中西方文化不期而遇的初级阶段显得尤为可贵。但回眸历史,我们必然会反思:奠定封建专制政体的传统话语体系,果能兼容近现代资产阶级民主理念?归化的译介策略虽可消融中国士大夫"防夷"的戒心,却也极大地妨碍了普通华人洞悉西方国际法的精神实质。恍惚之间,似乎岁月重新穿越到了春秋战国群雄争霸的时代,而非欧美列强殖民东亚的 19 世纪中叶。

难怪晚清士人读西书常浮想联翩,即便梁启超先生也讥讽丁韪良的《中国古世公法论略》:"以西人谭中国古事,大方见之,鲜不为笑",并误以为"中国当封建之世,诸国并立,公法学之昌明不亚于彼之希腊。若博雅君子哀而补成之,可得巨帙也。西政之合于中国古世者多矣,又宁独公法耶。"[②]"春秋大义"与"万国公法"对垒,终成"公法中源"说的根源大约在于此。

---

①　译文摘录自《公法便览》卷三"论交战之例"第一章"论各国自护讨罪等权"第二节。

②　详见梁启超先生所撰《读西学法》。《西学书目表四卷附读西学法一卷》,光绪丙申(1896 年)冬十月质学会用时务报馆本重校付刊。

第五节　权力博弈对馆译公法术语
定名的影响（二）

一　音意并立原则

应当指出，音意并立的处理方式并非丁韪良的原创。实际上，《四洲志》中已有将"First Lord of the Treasury"译作"法士律阿付厘特利沙利（管库官）"、"Lord Privy Seal"译作"律布来阿付西尔（管印官）"的先例（请参阅本章【6.4.21】）。

但意译近现代政法概念的逐渐常态化，决定了公法类著作中音意并立的个案数量极有限。最引人注目的莫过惠顿原文"President"的译介，《万国公法》释其义为"首领乃美国之语，所称'伯理玺天德'者是也"[①]。

究其缘由，实因"伯理玺天德"乃晚清时代美利坚国家元首的正式汉语译称，初载《中美望厦条约》，随后又被《中美天津条约》所承袭，故稍具权威性，是时流传已广。身为美国传教士的丁韪良当然有责任阐明此条约用语的真正内涵。

《中美望厦条约》（TREATY OF WANG-HEA，1844）[②]
英文版：

THE UNITED STATES OF AMERICAN AND THE TA-TSING EMPIRE

desiring to establish firm, lasting, and sincere friendship between the two nations, have resolved to fix, in a manner clear and positive, by means of a Treaty or general convention of peace, amity, and commerce, the rules which shall in future be mutually observed in the intercourse of their respective countries; for which most desirable object the **President** of the United States has conferred full powers on their Commissioner, CALEB CUSHING, Envoy Extraordinary and Minister Plenipotentiary of the United

---

① 摘录自《万国公法》第一卷"释公法之义，明其本源，题其大旨"第二章"论邦国自治、自主之权"第二十四节"美国系众邦合一"。

② 详见《中外旧约章大全（第一分卷）》上册，海关总署《中外旧约章大全》编纂委员会编，第118页。

States to China, and the August Sovereign of the Ta-Tsing Empire, on his Minister and Commissioner Extraordinary, KIYENG, of the Imperial House, a Vice Guardian of the Heir Apparent, Governor-General of the Two Kwangs, and Superintendent-General of the Trade and Foreign Intercourse of the Five Ports:

And the said Commissioners, after having exchanged their said full powers and duly considered the premises, have agreed to the following Articles: —

汉语版：

兹中华

大清国亚美理驾洲

大合众国欲坚定两国诚实永远友睦之条约及太平和好贸易之章程以为两国日后遵守成规是

以

大清

大皇帝特派

钦差大臣太子少保两广总督部堂总理五口通商善后事宜办理外国事务宗室耆

大合众国

大伯理玺天德特派

钦差全权大臣驻中华顾盛　各将所奉便宜行事之

上谕及钦奉全权之

敕谕公同较阅照验俱属善当因将议明各条款胪列

《中美天津条约》（TREATY OF TIENTSIN, 1858）①

英文版：

THE UNITE STATES of AMERICA and the TA-TSING Empire, desiring to

---

① 详见《中外旧约章大全（第一分卷）》上册，海关总署《中外旧约章大全》编纂委员会编，第279页。

establish firm, lasting, and sincere friendship between the two nations, have resolved to fix, in a manner clear and positive, by means of a Treaty or general convention of peace, amity, and commerce, the rules which shall in future be mutually observed in the intercourse of their respective countries; for which most desirable object the President of the United States and the August Sovereign of the Ta-Tsing Empire have named their Plenipotentiaries, to wit; the President of the United States of America, WILLIAM B. REED, Envoy Extraordinary and Minister Plenipotentiary to China; and His Majesty the Emperor of China, KWEI-LIANG, a member of the Privy Council and Superintendent of the Board of Punishments, and HWASHANA, **President** of the Board of Civil Office, and Major General of the Bordered Blue Banner Division of the Chinese Bannermen, both of them being Imperial Commissioners and Plenipotentiaries; and the said Ministers, in virtue of the respective full powers they have received from their Governments, have agreed upon the following Articles: —

汉语版:

兹中华

大清国亚美理驾洲

大合众国欲坚定两国诚实永远友睦之条约及太

平和好贸易之章程以为两国日后遵守成规是

以

大清

大皇帝特派

钦差大臣太子少保两广总督部堂总理五口通商

善后事宜办理外国事务宗室耆

大合众国

大伯理玺天德特派

钦差全权大臣驻中华顾盛　各将所奉便宜行事之

上谕及钦奉全权之

敕谕公同较阅照验俱属善当因将议明各条款胪列

　　熊月之先生认为该词不仅读音酷似，择字亦巧妙，令人不由自主地产生"掌理玉玺、享有天德"的联想，恰与天子之意暗合（1999：60）。也许这正是该汉字注音能于 19 世纪后半叶始终保持正式条约用语地位的根源所在。

二　另造新词原则

　　如果说比附原则利用的仍是现有中文资源，那么另造新词将被迫触探汉语系统的边缘张力。

　　丁韪良宣称"公法既别为一科，则应有专用之字样"①，诚如其所言。但他考虑到译入文化传统的保守性，却又自觉唯有既无法草率回避又不能轻易借助汉语固有词汇来表达的外来概念方才选择造词，即所谓"其文义或有疑难之处，余偶加注释以发明之"②。然而，正是这些中外合译者绞尽脑汁创制的全新术语如"公法"、"权利"等，对近代中国的法律变革产生巨大影响。

　　这些新创术语，有的初时广为流传却行之不远；有的乍见扎眼然终将通行于世，缘何如此？笔者以为，中文符号系统的包容性只是问题的一个方面，更重要的是所涉目标符号的文化底蕴与外来法律理念内涵之间的契合度及译入社会的发展趋势。毕竟，语言具有相对稳定性，"在整个变化中，总是旧有材料的保持占优势；对过去不忠实只是相对的。所以，变化的原则是建立在连续性原则的基础上的"（索绪尔，1980：112）。

　　（一）行之不远：典型者如"（万国）公法"（International Law）

　　1. "International Law" 的名称演变

　　民国学者刘达人和袁国钦在《国际法发达史》（1937）中概览了"国际法"（International Law）名称演变的曲折过程。

　　近现代国际法学奠基之初，格劳秀斯等研究者仍沿用拉丁语 *Jus gentium*（万民法）。直至 1650 年，牛津大学教授苏世（Richard Zouche，1590 – 1660）通过《万国法的解释和一些有关的问题》（"Juris et judicii fecialis sive Juris inter gentes et quaestionum de eodem explicatio"）正式提出 *Jus intergentes*（万国法），此即"Law of Nations"。该词风行欧美百余

---

　　① 详见《公法便览·凡例》第九款。
　　② 详见《公法便览·凡例》第二十一款。

年，方才遭遇英国著名法律改革家边沁（Jeremy Bentham，1748－1832）的质疑。他撰写的《道德及立法原理绪论》（*An Introduction to the Principles of Morals and Legislation*）明确批评"Law of Nations"平凡无意义，且易误作国内法，故主张以新颖却不失表现力的"International Law"取而代之（1789：viii）：

> Principles of legislation in matters betwixt nation and nation, or, to use a new though not inexpressive appellation, in matters of *international law*.

自此，"International Law"开始逐渐被西方社会普遍接受，成为表述国际法的通用术语。

2. "万国公法"译名变迁

惠顿乃19世纪法学家，其名著《国际法原理》（*Elements of International Law*）显然顺应了时代潮流。可丁韪良新造"万国公法"，充作中文对称术语，背后潜伏的深层原因值得探究。

据译者所言，"是书所录条例名为《万国公法》，盖系诸国通行者，非一国所得私也。又以其与各国律例相似，故亦名为《万国律例》云。"①

实际上，《万国律例》极可能是该著作的最初译名，因而出现于同治三年七月二十九日（1864年8月30日）恭亲王奕䜣酌请给银刊印此书的奏折内②。但也正因"律例"二字，引发总署官员疑虑：国际法是否具有绝对的强制性？须知丁氏所谓"各国律例"，绝非伯驾译《滑达尔各国律例》，而是指世界各国自行制定实施的国内法。国内法的约束力自不待言，若说国际法与之"相似"，岂能不令晚清政府忧心此乃请君入瓮之计？也许更名《万国公法》，正为消除中国统治阶层的忐忑难安。

3. 丁译改写别具深意

当然，丁译"公法"之称，未必不存私心。《公法便览·凡例》或者是其真实意思的最好注脚：

---

① 详见《万国公法·凡例》第二款。

② 详见《续修四库全书·史部·纪事本末类·筹办夷务始末》同治卷二七，（清）文庆、贾桢、宝鋆等纂辑，《续修四库全书》编纂委员会编，第25—26页。

一、公法者，邦国所恃以交际者也。谓之法者，各国在所必遵。谓之公者，非一国所得而私焉。①

一、其制非由一国亦非由一世，乃各国之人历代往来习以为常；各国大宪审断交涉公案而他国援以为例；名士论定是非、阐明义理而后世悦服，三者相参，公法始成。②

既"在所必遵"，难免"强中国以必行"③。"习以为常"（即习惯）、"援以为例"（即成例）、"名士论定是非、阐明义理"（即学说）三者说是"诸国通行"，其实不外乎欧美世界的交往规则。联想《万国公法》正文内所谓"各国相待所当守天然之义法"④ 等强调普遍性价值的自然主义理念，莫非仍欲以先入为主之强势，驱使清廷官员轻信国际法准则神圣不可违？

4."公法"译名本有歧义

《国际法原理》开卷首章第十节引赫夫特（Heffter）的论述，分"公法"为内外两支：

According to this writer, the *jus gentium* consists of two distinct branches:

1. Human rights in general, and those private relations which Sovereign States recognize in respect to individuals not subject to their authority.

2. The direct relations existing between those States themselves.

"In the modern world, this latter branch has exclusively received the denomination of law of nations, *Völkerrecht*, *Droit des Gens*, *Jus Gentium*. It may more properly be called **external public law**, to distinguish it from the **internal public law** of a particular State. The first part of the ancient *jus gentium* has become confounded with the municipal law of each particular nation, without at the same time losing its original and es-

---

① 详见《公法便览·凡例》第一款。
② 详见《公法便览·凡例》第二款。
③ 详见《续修四库全书·史部·纪事本末类·筹办夷务始末》同治卷二七，（清）文庆、贾桢、宝鋆等纂辑，《续修四库全书》编纂委员会编，第26页。
④ 详见《万国公法》第一卷第一章第一款。

sential character. This part of the science concerns, exclusively, certain rights of men in general, and those private relations which are considered as being under the protection of nations. It has been usually treated of under the denomination of *private international law.*"①

上述引文表明所谓"内公法",实际上就是"国际私法"。而丁氏比照"公法",将之简化成"私权之法":

今时所谓公法者,专指交际之道,可称之曰"外公法",以别于各国自治内法也。夫此公法之二派,其一则与各国之律法相合,而尤不混,盖专指世人自然之权,及人人相待之当然,并各国所保护人民之私权也。故论者称之为"私权之法"。②

这显然与英美法理学中传统的"公法"(public law)和"私法"(private law)二元对立概念相矛盾。实际上,惠顿正为避免混淆,才提出与其称"内公法"、"外公法",不若改作"宪法"及"国际法"更为恰当:

Internal sovereignty is that which is inherent in the people of any people of any State, or vested in its ruler, by its municipal constitution or fundamental laws. **This is the object of what has been called <u>internal public law</u>**, *droit public interne*, **but which may more properly be termed <u>constitutional law</u>**.

External sovereignty consists in the independence of one political society, in respect to all other political societies. It is by the exercise of this branch of sovereignty that the international relations of one political society are maintained, in peace and in war, with all other political societies. **The law by which it is regulated has, therefore, been called external pub-**

① 摘录自《国际法原理》第一卷"国际法的定义、渊源和主体(DEFININTION, SOURCES, AND SUBJECTS OF INTERNATIONAL LAW)"第Ⅰ章"定义和渊源(DEFINITION AND SOURCES)"§10"赫夫特学说(System of Heffter)",p.14。粗体及下划线由本书作者添加。
② 摘录自《万国公法》第一卷"释公法之义,明其本源,题其大旨"第二章"释义明源"第十节"海氏大旨",并根据何勤华点校本加注标点。

lic law，*droit public externe*，**but may more properly be termed inter-**
national law．①

5. 高开低走，行之不远

丁韪良选择"公"字，取其"共同"之意②。所谓"万国公法"，即
世界各国共同遵守的律法。洋务运动时期，晚清政府感兴趣的只是如何办
理对外交涉事宜，并无制度层面近代化的整体规划。或者说，译介公法著
作的同时，并未设想真正意义上的私法体系，也就不存在所谓的概念冲
突。然而，甲午战争惨败，最终揭开宪政革命的序幕。"国际法"一词从
日本传入后，不久即取"公法"而代之，很大程度上也是适应国内社会
法制建设的需要。

（二）通行于世：典型者如"权利"

目前业经考证的文献资料表明，近代法律术语"权利"最早出现于
《万国公法》，且使用频率颇高，称得上屡见不鲜。然而，直至十余年后
译者仍需借助《公法便览·凡例》特别释义并阐明其构造缘由：

> 公法既别为一科，则应有专用之字样，故原文内偶有汉文所难达
> 之意，因之用字往往似觉勉强。即如一权字，书内不独指有司所操之
> 权，亦指凡人理所应得之分，有时增一利字，如谓庶人本有之权利云
> 云，此等字句初见多不入目，屡见方知为不得已而用之也。③

当见首创之艰辛，可终能在固步自封的晚清社会获得接受并日渐流
行，这又是因何所致？

1. 文言汉语中的"权利"

推本溯源，"权利"在文言汉语中虽罕见，然古已用之。以《荀子》
为例，《劝学》篇即云："是故**权利**不能倾也，群众不能移也，天下不能

---

①　摘录自《国际法原理》第一卷"国际法的定义、渊源和主体（DEFININTION，SOURCES，
AND SUBJECTS OF INTERNATIONAL LAW）"第 II 章"民族和主权国家（NATIONS AND SOVER-
EIGN STATES）"第 5 节"赫夫特学说（System of Heffter）"，p. 29。粗体及下划线由本书作者
添加。

②　详见《辞源》。广东、广西、湖南、河南辞源修订组及商务印书馆编辑部编，第 311 页。

③　详见《公法便览·凡例》第九款。

荡也。生乎由是，死乎由是，夫是之谓德操"；《君道》篇又说："故校之以礼，而观其能安敬也；与之举措迁移，而观其能应变也；与之安燕，而观其能无流慆也；接之以声色、**权利**、忿怒、患险，而观其能无离守也"。①《史记·魏其武安侯列传》也有"家累数千万，食客日数十百人。陂池田园，宗族宾客为**权利**，横于颍川"② 等句。

依据《辞源》的解释，"权利"无非并置"权势及货利"③。但查考先秦典籍，亦见"权利"作动宾短语，譬如《商君书·算地》曰："夫民之情，朴则生劳而易力，穷则生知而**权利**。易力则轻死而乐用，**权利**则畏罚而易苦"④，此处所谓"权利"就是权衡利弊。正如李贵连教授所言，这皆可视作古意，与丁译"权利"，无论内涵抑或外延都大异其趣（1998：117）。

2. 追溯"权"、"利"二字本源

古汉语中的"权利"固不足为凭，考察近代"权利"术语构造的合理性仍须追索"权"、"利"二字的本源。

所谓"权"，初指秤⑤或秤锤⑥，亦谓称量⑦。但春秋战国时已常用于表示权力。权力者，"权势和威力"也⑧。《庄子·天运》谓："亲**权**者，不能与人柄"⑨；《战国策·齐一》谓："田忌亡齐而之楚，邹忌代之相齐，恐田忌欲以楚**权**复于齐"⑩，两者皆有此意。

---

① 详见《荀子集解》。（清）王先谦撰，沈啸寰、王星贤点校，第19、241 页。粗体由本书作者添加。

② 详见《史记》卷一百七。"二十五史"卷一，二十五史编委会，第273 页。粗体由本书作者添加。

③ 详见《辞源》。广东、广西、湖南、河南辞源修订组及商务印书馆编辑部编，第1649 页。

④ 详见《商君书锥指》卷二。蒋礼鸿撰，第44 页。粗体由本书作者添加。

⑤ 譬如《论语·尧曰》说："权，称也。"详见《十三经注疏·论语注疏》解经卷第二十。（魏）何晏注，（宋）邢昺疏，朱汉民整理，张岂之审定，第266 页。

⑥ 譬如《广雅·释器》说："锤，谓之权。"详见《广雅疏证》。（三国魏）张揖撰，（清）王念孙疏证，第254 页。

⑦ 譬如《孟子·梁惠王章句上》说："权，然后知轻重。"详见《十三经注疏·孟子注疏》解经卷第一下。（汉）赵岐注，（宋）孙奭疏，廖名春、刘佑平整理，钱逊审定，第21 页。

⑧ 详见《辞源》。广东、广西、湖南、河南辞源修订组及商务印书馆编辑部编，第1648—1649 页。

⑨ 详见《庄子集解》卷四。（清）王先谦撰，第127 页。粗体由本书作者添加。

⑩ 详见《战国策》卷八。（西汉）刘向集录，第322 页。粗体由本书作者添加。

至于"利"，则自古蕴含"利益，功用"之意①。《商君书·算地》曾详述法家的名利观：

> 夫治国者能尽地力而致民死者，名与**利**交至。民之性，饥而求食，劳而求佚，苦则索乐，辱则求荣，此民之情也。民之求**利**，失礼之法；求名，失性之常……故曰："名**利**之所凑，则民道之"……故民生则计利，死则虑名，名**利**之所出，不可不审也。**利**出于地，则民尽力；名出于战，则民致死。入使民尽力，则草不荒；出使民致死，则胜敌。胜故而草不荒，富强之功可坐而致也。②

3. "权"与"Right"之辨异

综上所述，古汉语中的"权"指权力、权柄时，更近似英文"Authority/Power"，尤其是"Governmental power or jurisdiction"。而广义的"Right"虽涵盖"由宪法、制定法或判例法所保障的或由于习惯而被主张的一种权力、特权、豁免权"（薛波，2003：1200），或者说"A power, privilege, or immunity secured to a person by law"（Garner，2004：1347），但不独指"有司所操之权"，亦指"凡人理所应得之分"，即"Something that is due to a person by just claim, legal guarantee, or moral principle"（同上），甚至更偏重后者。

那么具体而言，何谓"分"？李贵连教授引证《荀子·礼论》，提出"人生而有欲，欲而不得，则不能无求；求而无度量分界，则不能不争；争而乱，乱则穷。先王恶其乱也，故制礼义以**分**之，以养人之欲，给人之求"③ 中的"分"与凡人的"欲"、"求"相衔接，明显包含近代的"权利"意蕴（1998：118）。但严格来说，荀卿所谓"分之"，至多只是分配"欲求"的权利而已。当然，"分"亦可作"职分，名分"④ 解，而"名分"也泛指"财物的所属关系"⑤。《商君书·定分》说："一兔走，百人

① 详见《辞源》。广东、广西、湖南、河南辞源修订组及商务印书馆编辑部编，第348页。
② 详见《商君书锥指》卷二。蒋礼鸿撰，第45—46页。粗体由本书作者添加。
③ 详见《荀子集解》卷十三。（清）王先谦撰，沈啸寰、王星贤点校，第346页。粗体由本书作者添加。
④ 详见《辞源》。广东、广西、湖南、河南辞源修订组及商务印书馆编辑部编，第339页。
⑤ 同上书，第481页。

逐之，非以兔为可分以为百，由**名分**之未定也。夫卖者满市而盗不敢取，由**名分**已定也"①，即有此意。

4. 添"利"构词的合理性

尽管丁氏所谓"应得"只是在抽象意义上指出"权利"的正义或道德正当性，然而考虑到19世纪功利主义法学派提出的利益说当时正风靡欧美，丁氏受其影响"增一利字"，岂不是水到渠成？

正如《**牛津法律大辞典**》(*The Oxford Companion to Law*) 针对"Right"概念变迁作出的深刻揭示 (Walker, 1980: 1070):

> In a legal context it is a legal concept denoting an **advantage** or **benefit** conferred on a person by rules of a particular legal system. In Greek philosophy and Roman law, a right seems to have been identified with what was right and just. Later, a right was sometimes deduced from the fundamental datum of free will or sometimes seen as essentially based on legal relationships between persons, determined by a rule of law and sanctioned and protected by the legal order, or sometimes as an interest recognized and protected by a rule of legal justice. ②

5. 先抑后扬，通行于世

换言之，法律术语"权利"之所以能在重刑轻民、义务本位的晚清时代历经曲折而通行于世，是因为其构成词素承继文言汉语的深厚渊源，不仅未脱离母体文化底蕴；更暗合英文"Right"所包含的功利主义法哲思想，顺应了国际政法理念的发展趋势。事实上，随着中国近现代社会制度的渐次形成，民事"权利"概念直指个体现实"利益"的密切联系也日益受到学界关注。

三 余论

综上所述，丁氏及合译者更倾向于归化翻译策略，尤其是比附说明式的阐释。体现在文化上的显著特征就是尽可能套用传统中国的伦理术语来

---

① 详见《商君书锥指》卷五。蒋礼鸿撰，第145页。粗体由本书作者添加。

② 粗体由本书作者添加。

表述异质的现代西方法律概念（俞江，2008：10）。丁韪良本人也说："余督率馆生翻译此书，既将洋文为之讲解于前，复将译稿详加校阅于后"①，期以中文表达方式适应国人的阅读习惯。其实，这也是19世纪特定环境制约下，华洋译者寻求沟通东西文化之公度性的尝试。有关这个问题，笔者将在下章第六节进一步探讨。

---

① 详见《公法便览·凡例》第二十款。

第七章

洋务运动下篇:借法自强

——沪局翻译馆与《各国交涉公法论》及《各国交涉便法论》

第一节　借法自强对沪局翻译馆选书的影响

费利摩罗巴德从男爵（Rt. Hon Sir Robert Phillimore, 1st Baronet, 1810－1885）是 19 世纪英国最具影响力的宗教及国际法学家之一，自 1858 年受封御用大律师（Queen's Counsel）称号，先后被任命为高等海事法院大法官（the advocate general of the High Court of Admiralty）及坎特伯雷大主教法院（the Arches Court covering the Province of Canterbury）法官，并在 1867 年宣誓加入英国枢密院司法委员会（the Judicial Committee of the Privy Council）。

其鸿篇巨制《国际法评注》（*Commentaries on International Law*）首两册于 1854 年问世，1857 年和 1861 年又相继出版了第三、四册，其中末册（*Private International Law or Comity*）专攻国际私法。

光绪二十年（1894 年），江南机器制造总局翻译馆首席译员英国基督徒傅兰雅（John Fryer, 1839－1928）以该书为蓝本①口述的《各国交涉

① 费利摩罗巴德的《国际法评注》第一、二、三册初版于美国费城；第四册则于 1861 年在英国伦敦发行。1871 年，该书前两册又在英国伦敦再版，作者为此特撰第二版序言（Preface to the Second Edition）。察《各国交涉公法论》初集所附续序中有云："此书初集在一千八百五十四年第一次刊印，其二集在一千八百五十七年刊印，三年之间增益各国交涉之事。兹将三集续序附于原序之后，又自一千八百五十七年至一千八百七十年所有最要之事复行增入。"除个别词句错漏外，其与英文首册第二版序言中的以下文字可谓如出一辙："The first edition of this volume, which was published in 1854, has been for some time out of print. The third volume, which closed the Commentaries on Public International Law, was published in 1857 (a). In the preface to that volume a

公法论》初集、二集和三集及《各国交涉便法论》①刊布发行，卷帙浩繁稳居晚清公法译著首位。

一　赞助人及译者

（一）赞助人：江南机器制造总局（亦简称"沪局"）

两次鸦片战争相继丧师辱国，惊醒了清廷部分具体办理攘外安内诸般事宜的封疆大吏。以外省督抚为中坚的洋务派官员逐渐意识到改弦更张的迫切性——"既不能拒之使不来，即当穷其所独往"②。

是故北京换约方成，两江总督曾国藩便于咸丰十年十一月初八日（1860年12月19日）《复陈洋人助剿及采米运津折》内颇具洞鉴地指出："此次款议虽成，中国岂可一日忘备？……无论目前资夷力以助剿济运得纾一时之忧。将来师夷智以造码制船，尤可期永远之利。"③越年七月十八日（1861年8月23日）又上书疾呼购买外洋船炮并进行试造"为今日救时之第一要务"。④

久在曾幕襄办营务的李鸿章受其影响，同治元年（1862年）率淮军入沪后升任江苏巡抚，"随时购买外洋枪炮，设局铸造开花炮弹"⑤，常思发展新式军事工业；同治三年（1864年）向总署转呈丁日昌密禀，得恭亲王奕䜣首肯"广购机器"、"精求洋匠"等举措；同治四年（1865年）收买上海虹口能修造轮船及枪炮的美商旗记机器铁厂，旋即"改为江南制造总局，正名辨物，以绝洋人觊觎"⑥，且将旧有丁日昌及韩殿甲主持的

---

summary of the historical events which in the interval of these three years（1854 to 1857）had affected International Law was given. I propose to place that summary in the present preface, adding to it a brief notice of historical events of the like character which have happened during the second interval of thirteen years（1857 – 1870）."（Phillimore, 1871：v）这足以证明《各国交涉公法论》最初两集以1871年在英国伦敦发行的《国际法评注》为蓝本。因此本书所引《国际法评注》原文，除非特别说明，首两册均出自1871年第二版，而后两册出自初版。

① 光绪二十年（1894年）江南制造局翻译馆聚珍版。
② 详见《机器局（一）》。《海防档》丙，台北中央研究院近代史研究所编，第5页。
③ 详见《覆陈洋人助剿及采米运津折（十一月初八日）》。《曾文正公全集·奏稿》卷十二，（清）李翰章编纂，（清）李鸿章校勘，第755页。
④ 详见《覆陈购买外洋船炮折（七月十八日）》。同上书，第804页。
⑤ 详见《置办外国铁厂机器折（同治四年八月初一日）》。《李鸿章全集·奏稿》卷九，李鸿章全集编辑工作委员会编，第422页。
⑥ 同上书，第424页。

两所洋炮局并入该厂。

沪局乃晚清洋务派创建的首座也是规模最大、预算最高的近代军工企业。李鸿章会同曾国藩奏报开办情形时就已认定"机器制造一事为今日御侮之资，自强之本"，"当尽其心力所能及者而为之，日省月试不决效于旦夕，增高继长尤为望于方来，庶几取外人之长技以成中国之长技，不致见绌于相形，斯可有备而无患"①。

正因如此，江南制造局迥异先前仓促组建的安庆内军械所，创设伊始即聘请欧美工程师负责机械生产，"查原厂所用之洋匠计留八人，其匠目一名科而，技艺甚属精到，所有轮船、枪炮、机器俱能如法制造"②；且倡导本国技术工人精习西艺，"拟于华匠中留心物色，督令操习，如有技艺与洋人等者，即给以洋人工食；再能精通，则拔为匠目，以示鼓励"③。

由于长期大量聘用外籍雇员参与基础建设并主持日常生产，克服语言沟通障碍成为当务之急。所以，同治六年（1867年）江南制造局迁址高昌庙镇，随即附设翻译馆，旋又移广方言馆到局，旨在引进西学，培养语言和科技人才。

（二）广方言馆（原名"上海同文馆"）与翻译馆

江南机器制造总局尚酝酿未定，时任江苏巡抚的李鸿章已在同治二年二月初十日（1863年3月28日）奏请"仿照同文馆之例，于上海添设外国语言文字学馆"④。同治六年（1867年）更名"广方言馆"；同治九年（1870年）并归沪局。

上海同文馆成立初衷，实为通商督抚衙门及海关监督培养承办洋务的翻译官，取代"难保无偏袒捏架情弊"的外国翻译及鱼龙混杂的本地通事。然而，折内另有数语足可表明李鸿章志不止于此："彼西人所擅长者，推算之学，格物之理，制器尚象之法，无不专精务实。渤有成书，经译者十才一二，必能尽阅其未译之书，方可探赜索隐，由粗浅而入精微。

──────────

① 详见《置办外国铁厂机器折（同治四年八月初一日）》。《李鸿章全集·奏稿》卷九，李鸿章全集编辑工作委员会编，第425—426页。

② 详见《同治四年，李鸿章会同曾国藩奏开办情形》。《中国近代史资料丛刊·洋务运动》第四册，中国史学会主编，第76页。

③ 同上。

④ 详见《同治二年二月初十日江苏巡抚奏》。《中国近代史资料丛刊·洋务运动》第二册，中国史学会主编，第140页。

我中华智巧聪明,岂出西人之下?果有精熟西文者转相传习,一切轮船火器等技巧,当可由渐通晓,于中国自强之道似有裨助。"① 换言之,翻译科技书籍,仿制轮船火器,才是洋务官员孜孜以求的宏伟目标。

因此,江南制造局迁址上海城南后,隔年(1868 年)即由徐寿②、华衡芳③提议另立学馆以习翻译,"盖翻译一事,系制造之根本"④。此馆与偏重政法类书籍的京师同文馆截然不同,在傅兰雅主持下渐成晚清最大的科学译书传播机构,广泛涉足算学测量、汽机、化学、地理、地学、天文行船、博物学、医学、工艺、水陆兵法、年代表新闻纸、造船、国史等各色领域⑤。交涉公法不过其中一门,且深受科技翻译传统的影响。

(三)洋人译者:英国基督徒傅兰雅

据顾长声先生对来华新教传教士的评传(1985),结合王扬宗教授所著《傅兰雅与近代中国的科学启蒙》(2000)及加州大学伯克利分校中国研究中心戴吉礼博士(Dr. Ferdinand Dagenais)主编的《傅兰雅档案》(*The John Fryer Papers*,2010),得其生平概况。

英国人傅兰雅出生于肯特郡(Kent)海斯(Hythe)镇的贫苦家庭,父亲是狂热的宗教信徒、没有神职的巡回布道者。中学毕业即考取政府一等奖学金,随后就读伦敦附近的海伯里教育学院(Highbury College)。

1860 年,受英国圣公会(Church of England)聘请前往香港圣保罗书院(St. Paul College)任校长;1863 年,转派至北京执教同文馆。1865年,应邀南下经营新筹办的上海英华学堂。在此期间,他努力学习中文,并表现出相当的语言天赋。

1868 年 5 月 31 日,经徐寿推荐并得曾国藩同意,正式入江南制造局专司翻译。直至 1896 年因接受加州大学东方语言文献教授聘书而辞馆,

①　详见《同治二年二月初十日江苏巡抚奏》。《中国近代史资料丛刊·洋务运动》第二册,中国史学会主编,第 140—141 页。

②　徐寿(1818—1884 年),字雪邨,号生元,江苏金匮(今无锡)北乡人。中国近代化学的启蒙者,曾与傅兰雅等合作翻译出版科技著作 13 部。

③　华衡芳(1833—1902 年),字畹香,号若汀,江苏金匮(今无锡)南延乡荡口人。中国近代数学家及机械工程专家,曾与傅兰雅等合作翻译出版科技著作 12 部。

④　详见《同治七年九月初二日调任直隶总督曾国藩折》。《中国近代史资料丛刊·洋务运动》第四册,中国史学会主编,第 18 页。

⑤　详见傅兰雅所撰《江南制造总局翻译西书事略》。《中国近代出版史料初编》,张静庐辑注,第 24—25 页。

前后共计二十八年，口述译著何止百部，终成鼎鼎大名，向往西方科技的晚清华人无不慕其名而思见其人。

综上所述，傅兰雅的生平经历较之伯驾、丁韪良等美国传教士各有异同不等，于其国际法翻译活动难免有所影响。

1. 擅长汉语

清末著名学者夏曾佑言："近日在中国能通华语之西人无逾傅先生"①，这绝非过誉。早在乘船驶向香港途中，傅兰雅便开始学习汉语。辗转华夏各地执教期间，很快掌握了粤语、北京话和上海方言。正因为此，圣公会传教士包尔腾（John Shaw Burdon）竭力向总理衙门推荐其接替京师同文馆英语教习的职位。执教英华学堂期间，其出众的中文写作能力更是蜚声上海滩，故被字林洋行聘为《上海新报》②的兼职编辑。

尽管傅兰雅的中文水平较其先辈伯驾更胜一筹，但没有资料表明他亦曾仿效丁韪良研读儒家传统经典。也许是因为傅氏本非职业传教士，自身的学历背景亦难使其认识到沟通文化差异的重要性。这对他的科技翻译事业当然构成不了太大威胁，但在译介公法著作过程中或多或少会产生可接受性的问题。

2. 普通教育

与伯驾或丁韪良相比，傅兰雅的受教育水平并不耀眼。他毕业的海伯里学院只是所培训见习教师的学校，掌握的亦无非英国大学本科程度的一般数理化知识。故应聘沪局译员不过两月，很快发觉自身学养有所欠缺。他在给叔父的信中写道："我现在已获得了一个新的翻译职务，为中国政府翻译科学书籍……我立即开始学习和翻译三个专题，上午学习和翻译关于煤和煤采掘的具体知识。下午钻研化学。而在晚上则研习声学"（Benett，1967：23）。这种现学即译的模式应当不只限于科技领域，对其而言更为陌生、更具专业性的法学著作必定也是如此炮制的。

3. 欲作传教士而不得

傅兰雅的另一特异处在于他并非正统的传教士。尽管其始终是虔诚的

---

① 详见《夏曾佑一百通之七》。《汪康年师友书札》，上海图书馆编，第1319页。

② 《上海新报》是上海最早的中文报纸，主要内容摘译自字林洋行出版的，也是当时最具影响力的英文报刊《字林西报》（North China Daily News）和《北华捷报》（North-China Herald）。

基督徒，但从未入神学院进修；又因坚持与据说品行有亏的未婚妻安娜·罗拉斯顿（Anna Rolestion）结为夫妇，终被圣公会拒绝接纳。可能正为这样，他的思想意识发生了微妙变化："名义上我是英国国教的一员，但在中国期间，我的宗教视野扩展了，所以我倾向于很自由的思想……"①勉强来到上海执教英华学堂的傅氏，试图避免过分灌输学生宗教理念，又引发圣公会控制下的校董强烈不满。

传教、办学皆遇阻力的傅兰雅，急于摆脱自己及家人的穷困窘境，只能另觅晋身之阶，兼职《上海新报》编辑。他密切关注清朝社会动向，配发新闻评论，不仅积累了翻译和写作经验，还在爱好科技的华人圈内声名鹊起。

他在致亲友的信函中嘲弄汉语蹩脚的传教士，同时认为写作、办报比教书更能传播西方思想与科技，中国人不喜欢西方的基督说教，可需要西方的科学技术（王扬宗，2000：27）：

> 在那些外国人为中华帝国谋求福祉所从事的慈善事业中，把科学著作翻译成中文无疑是其中最有效的工作之一。已经出版的译著正在文士中逐渐传开来。究其缘由，简而言之就是因为它们适应了这个国家最迫切需要的一个方面。②

毋庸置疑，傅兰雅从未翻译过任何宗教典籍，并坚持倾向科学的宗教观："无论何国何教，其教中有与格致之理相反者，则其教必名不正。来中国传教之西人，如能兼行格致之务，则受益不更无穷乎？"③

二　选择费利摩罗巴德的因缘

目前对傅兰雅的研究多注重其自然科学领域的贡献，对其社会科学方面的译介活动常点到即止。此种现状与梁启超先生称"局译《各国交涉

---

① 详见戴吉礼博士（Dr. Ferdinand Dagenais）所编 *Calendar of the Correspondence, Publications, and Miscellaneous Papers of John Fryer* (1839–1928) *with Selected Experts.* Center for Chinese Studies, University of California, Berkeley, 1996.

② 来源傅兰雅保留的1867年5月的英文剪报。

③ 详见傅兰雅所撰《狄考文在格致书院讲解电学》（载《格致汇编》第二年卷五）。

公法论》分三集，为书十六本，视馆译为优"① 的评语完全不相适应。何况尚有原书第四册的中文本《各国交涉便法论》，乃我国第一部国际私法译著，岂可置之不论？

首先值得我们探讨的就是"西人治公法有声于时者，无虑数十百家"②，为什么选译费利摩罗巴德的著作？

（一）傅兰雅：送妻回国，受邀译书

傅兰雅应聘江南制造局，自陈"惟冀中国能广兴格致至中西一辙耳"③，翻书合约亦写明"除译西国格致制器等书之外，局中不可另有他事以分译书之心"（王扬宗，2000：30）。

毫无疑问，译介西学特重选材。起初，徐寿、华衡芳等属意《泰西大类编书》（即《大英百科全书》），但傅氏以为内容欠详，且没有收录最新科技成果，同时受制清廷官员的目光短浅，此事终究未成。他曾在《江南制造总局翻译西书事略》中解释道：

> 至于所译各书若何分类，若何选择，试略言之。初译书时，本欲作大类编书，而英国所已有者虽印八次，然内有数卷太略，且近古所有新理新法多未列入，故必察更大更新者始可翻译。后经中国大宪谕下，欲馆内特译紧用之书，故作类编之意渐废，而所译者多零件新书，不以西国门类分列。平常选书法，为西人与华士择其合己所紧用者，不论其书与他书配否，故有数书如植物学、动物学、名人传等尚未译出。另有他书虽不甚关格致，然于水陆兵勇武备等事有关，故较他书先为讲求。④

该文撰于 1880 年，对翻译馆选书所论甚详，却无只字片语提及邦交政法，这的确也与傅氏关注的格致之学相去较远。那又何以突然在 1878 年译出《各国交涉公法论》与《各国交涉便法论》？

---

① 详见梁启超先生所撰《读西学书法》。《西学书目表四卷附读西学书法一卷》，光绪丙申（1896 年）冬十月质学会用时务报馆本重校付刊。所谓"馆译"，是指同文馆译书；所谓"局译"，是指江南制造局译书。

② 同上。

③ 详见傅兰雅所撰《江南制造总局翻译西书事略》。《中国近代出版史料初编》，张静庐辑注，第 9 页。

④ 同上书，第 17 页。

事虽偶然，倒也并非无因。是年夏天，傅兰雅请假陪其夫人回国治病，按照合约①本应六个月内返回上海。与此同时，曾在沪局翻译馆任职的李凤苞②正率晚清第一批海军留学生赴欧，并由驻英公使郭嵩焘保举署理出使德国钦差大臣。初任公使的李凤苞急于了解各国交涉惯例，故邀请本就相熟的傅兰雅到中国驻德使馆译介公法③。

傅兰雅的求学经历及其所译书籍均表明除英文外，他并不十分精通其他欧洲语言④，对法律所知亦有限，拣择交涉类著作的范畴必定捉襟见肘。而《国际法评注》乃当时英语文献中最知名的两部国际法作品之一；另一部即惠顿的《国际法原理》，早已由丁韪良译入《万国公法》。且费利摩罗巴德的专著分册出版，随时补充最新资料，内容更为翔实，理所当然地成为首选。

（二）江南制造局：外敦和好，内要自强

洋务运动发展至光绪年间，开明的官僚士绅已然发现"西法兼博大潜奥之理"⑤，只"苦于语言文字不同"⑥，故而"将欲因端竟委，穷流溯源，舍翻书读书无其策"⑦。

尽管如此，制造为先、实用至上始终被奉作借法自强的既定方针。李鸿章曾奏报沪局"陆续访购西书数十种，厚聘西士，选派局员，相与口述笔译。最要为算学、化学、汽机、火药、炮法等编，固属关系制造；即

---

① 详见《机器制造总局聘请傅兰雅先生翻书合约》（王扬宗，2000：30）。

② 李凤苞（1834—1887），字丹崖，江苏崇明人。清末外交家。

③ 详见《使德日记》光绪四年十月初六日载："适西士傅兰雅亦到，谓妻病稍愈，业与筠帅订定，新正伴送回华，愿先随往德国，将飞尔摩耳公法论译全。"后十一日又载："是日始令庆常、傅兰雅二人译述公法论。"《使德日记及其他二种》，王云五主编，第3、6页。另据《伦敦与巴黎日记》光绪四年九月初六日载："李丹崖见［疑脱'赠'字］傅兰雅所译英人费利摩所著《万国交涉公法论》十三卷，凡分四集，初、二、三集各四卷，四集一卷则尚未译也，三集亦余二卷未译成"（郭嵩焘，1984：746）。凭此推断，我们可以大致确定傅兰雅译《各国交涉公法论》正是受李凤苞所托。且前三集主要是在伦敦完成的，否则仍在船政留学生监督任上逗留英国的李凤苞不太可能随身携有尚未刊印的书稿；唯有残余部分方由李凤苞邀至中国驻德使署译毕。

④ 傅兰雅懂法语，曾兼任上海格致书院的法文教习，却从未译过法文版书籍。实际上，希望译者在两种非母语文字之间进行转换，也是相当苛刻的要求。

⑤ 详见《光绪元年十月十九日直隶总督李鸿章等奏折》。《中国近代史资料丛刊·洋务运动》第四册，中国史学会主编，第30页。

⑥ 同上。

⑦ 同上。

如行船、防海、练军、采煤、开矿之类，亦皆有裨实用"。①

实际上，光绪六年（1880 年）前，沪局刊行的译述从未涉及公法领域。即便延展至翻译馆的完整存续期间，真正意义的国际法理论著作亦不过三部②：《公法总论》、《各国交涉公法论》与《各国交涉便法论》（王扬宗，1995：6），且皆初刻于光绪二十年（1894 年）前后③。若说巧合，似乎牵强。笔者以为事出必有因。

《公法总论》译自英国法学家罗伯村（Edmund Roberson, 1845 - 1911）所撰《国际法》（*International Law*），原载《大英百科全书》（*Encyclopedia Britannica*）第九版。这只是简明读本，姑且不论。但《各国交涉公法论》和《各国交涉便法论》的书稿早在光绪四年（1878 年）已于中国驻德使署译就，时隔十六年方才付样。个中缘由，值得玩味。

据《续修四库全书总目提要》的编者所言："此本虽详，然译名歧出，卷帙割裂，殊无裨于寻觅，翻译十载，未能付刊，殆亦自嫌译文之陋软。"④ 这可能是原因之一，然而绝非全部，甚至算不得关键。细考江南制造局的主要奠基人李鸿章的态度，也许能略窥其奥。

同治元年（1862 年），李鸿章初入上海即提出"外敦和好，内要自强"⑤，明确主和为其外交理念，期待通过妥协换取加速国内建设的长期稳定的生存环境。然而，洋务革新初见成效，沾沾自喜的官员便以为中兴

---

① 详见《光绪元年十月十九日直隶总督李鸿章等奏折》。《中国近代史资料丛刊·洋务运动》第四册，中国史学会主编。

② 另说还有光绪二十七年（1901 年）的《邦交公法新论》，傅兰雅与程瞻洛合译自荷兰佛楷孙（J. H. Ferguson）的英文版《国际法手册》（*Manual of International Law*, 1884）（顾长声，1985：262），但并未收录在《江南制造局记》（光绪三十一年九月编印）或《江南制造局译书提要》（宣统元年七月印）。据王扬宗先生考证，此书虽译于沪局，却是上海格致书院刊行的（1995：16）。至于金楷理口译、蔡锡龄笔述的《公使指南》，译自《外交与条约指南》（*Guide Diplomatique and Treaties from* Chas. V. De Maertens），根本未曾刊印发行（同上，17）。

③ 王扬宗先生曾撰文考证《各国交涉公法论》初刊于 1895 年（1995：6），而据《续修四库全书总目提要》记载，应为光绪二十年（1894 年）。负责复核该书的吴县钱国祥有《各国交涉公法论校勘记》署"光绪甲午孟秋之月吴县钱国祥识于江南制造局之翻译馆"，又附《中西纪年》注"光绪二十一年乙未六月初八日丁丑一千八百九十五年七月二十九日礼拜一校印竣"。无论如何，我们可以确定译著的刊印总在甲午战争期间。

④ 详见《各国交涉公法论十六卷（江南制造局本）》。《续编四库全书总目提要·史部政书类》，中国科学院图书馆整理，第 2—742 页。

⑤ 详见《上曾相（同治元年五月初二日）》。《李鸿章全集·朋僚函稿》卷一，李鸿章全集编辑工作委员会编，第 3039 页。

有望，略生懈怠之心，军纪渐弛，武备日荒。

转眼已是甲午年，中日两国就朝鲜问题发生冲突，久任直隶总督兼北洋大臣的李鸿章犹寄希望于列强干预，幻想"以夷制夷"；更迷信国际法的效力，坚持"两国交涉全论理之曲直，非恃强所能了事"①，"日虽竭力预备战守，我不先与开仗，彼谅不动手，此万国公例，谁先开战，即谁理诎"②。

在此时势动荡之际，沪局紧锣密鼓地校正、复核并刊印仅有的公法译著，难免心存为和议张本的意思。及至战败订立《马关条约》后，翻译馆几乎再没推出过任何其他国际法书籍，这亦可算是颇具说服力的旁证。

第二节 权力博弈对局译公法卷帙割裂的影响

《各国交涉公法论》乃《续修四库全书总目提要》收录的仅有的公法译著，"原名《国际法注解》，亦名著也，翻译较后，译文较详"③。尽管如此，编者也不无遗憾地提出"于原书卷帙颇有分合，原书卷九，译本分为卷九、卷十、卷十一、卷十二，共四卷；原书卷十分为卷十三、卷十四，共两卷；原书卷十一、卷十二改为卷十五、卷十六。原书各章亦按卷厘定次第。"④

上述评论直指译著第三集，该集目录结尾处对此附有详细说明：

原编目录⑤

卷九凡十一章，今分为卷九、卷十、卷十一、卷十二，共四卷。其卷十之第一章，原编卷九之第六章也；卷十一之第一章，原编卷九之第九章也；卷十二之第一章、第二章，原编卷九之第十章、第十一章也。

① 详见《寄朝鲜成欢交叶提督（光绪二十年六月初六日午刻）》。《李鸿章全集·电稿》卷十六，李鸿章全集编辑工作委员会编，第5992页。
② 详见《复叶提督（光绪二十年六月十八日巳刻）》。《李鸿章全集·电稿》卷十六，李鸿章全集编辑工作委员会编，第6013页。
③ 详见《各国交涉公法论十六卷（江南制造局本）》。《续编四库全书总目提要·史部政书类》，中国科学院图书馆整理，第2—742页。
④ 同上。
⑤ 详见光绪二十二年（1896年）小仓山房石印本富强斋丛书正全集之《各国交涉公法论三集·目录》。本书所引《各国交涉公法论》译文，除非特别说明，均出自该版；而《各国交涉便法论》译文出自光绪二十七年（1901年）小仓山房石印本富强斋丛书续全集。

卷十凡六章，今分第一章、第二章为卷十三，其第三章以下为卷十四。

卷十一凡四章今改为卷十五。

卷十二凡九章今改为卷十六。

毋庸置疑，是集的确重新划分了卷帙，但能否算得有碍阅读呢？为更直观地说明问题，笔者在此列表比照该书原文与译文的卷次章节及相应页码张数。

表7—1　《各国交涉公法论三集》原、译文卷次章节及相应页码、张数对照表

原文卷次	原文章节①	原文页码	译文卷次	译文章节②	译文张数
Part IX	International Right of Action	1—9	卷九 凡五章	论各国交涉事内可起衅端	17（连同序言及目录共20）
	Reprisals	10—35		论取质之理	
	Embargo	36—66		论暂行扣留抵押	
	War	67—74		论交战	
	War—Declaration of, unnecessary	75—102		论交战不必报明之理	
	How War affects the Relations of all States	103—136	卷十 凡三章	论交战改变各国之相关	20
	War—Who may make	137—145		论谁可任交战之事	
	War—Intercourse between Enemies during	146—200		论交战时彼此交涉之事	
	War—Effect of, upon Neutrals	201—237	卷十一 凡一章	论局外之国及局外应守之事	14
	Neutral—Rights and Duties of	238—297	卷十二 凡二章	论局外之国分所当得当为之事又论敌国人之产业	16
	Colonial and Coasting Trade. Rule of 1756	298—314		论战时英国海滨及各属地之通商贸易又论一千七百五十六年所设之章程	

① 详见《国际法评注》第三册目录，第 xi - xv 页。

② 详见《各国交涉公法论三集·目录》。

续表

原文卷次	原文章节	原文页码	译文卷次	译文章节	译文张数
Part X	Contraband	315—381	卷十三 凡二章	论私货	20
	Blockade	382—416		论封口	
	Right of Visit and Search	417—448	卷十四 凡四章	论交战国查验船之利权	19
	Right of Capture—Duty of Captor	449—485		论挐获之利权并挐获者之本分	
	I. Non-commissioned Captors II. Joint Capture III. Captures by Tenders	486—501		论无国家准挐凭据而挐船又数船合挐一船又转运副船去挐一船	
	Postliminium—Recapture—Ransom	501—532		论善后之利权挐回与赎回之事	
Part XI	General Character and Duty of tribunals of prize	533—541	卷十五 凡四章	论审理缉获敌船之公堂应办事宜	19
	Constitution of Prize Tribunals in different States	542—550		论各国设立审问挐获敌国船案公堂之法	
	Principles and Practice of Prize Tribunals.—General Outline	551—559		论审问挐获敌国船案衙门所凭之理法纲领	
	Principles and Practice of Prize Tribunals	560—637		论审问堂办理船案条目	
Part XII	Of the Manner of ending War and the re-establishing of Peace	638—659	卷十六 凡九章	论停战议和之法	4（连同附《校勘记》及《中西纪年》共20）
	How Treaties entered into before the War are affected when the War is concluded and Peace restored	660—679		论未战以前之条约于议和后应如何办理	
	Where, how, and under what Limitations the doctrine of Postliminium may be applied to States and the Subjects of States on the Return of Peace	680—684		论两国停战议和所有民国往来事宜当遵何法何限并于何处归复旧制以示限制	

续表

原文卷次	原文章节	原文页码	译文卷次	译文章节	译文张数
Part XII	The Theory of International Law as to the Power of the Conqueror, and of the Sovereign de facto, over Incorporeal things	685—699	卷十六凡九章	论交涉公法料理得胜而为主者与当时为主者管理无形无体之物之理	14（连同附《校勘记》及《中西纪年》共20）
	International Practice as to the Power of the Conqueror and the Sovereign de facto, over Incorporeal Thing	700—707		论征收地方之主及实位君主之权力于不随身之物件	
	Case of the Debts and Domains of Hesse-Cassel confiscated or alienated by Napoleon I	708—719		论黑辛咯色耳邦被人所欠之债及地方被拿破仑没入充公一案	
	Postliminium—Decisions in English Courts of Justice	720—727		论生擒之人回本国后得回从前一切之利权并英国律宪所断定之案	
	Doctrine of Postliminium as to Private Rights and Property which have been, during the War, under the Dominion of the Enemy, and not confiscated by the State	728 to End		论利权私业被敌所取未经没入一经收复其情形与未失之前相同	
				论已经失和之办法并总结之说	

纵览表7—1，我们不难注意到以下两个问题：

（1）原文分卷著述，虽未注明卷标，却各自章节数目迥然有异。不仅本册如此，前两册亦无例外，仅论国际私法的第四册没再细化。可见该书固繁，但卷帙是否划分及如何划分自有其内在标准。

（2）译文重新分配原第九、十两卷后，第三集中唯有卷十一、十二张数相对较少，这也是权宜之举。若将两卷合并，书页明显较他卷偏多，更有失平衡。莫非煞费苦心的调整，全是为了刊印美观？

另据驻英公使郭嵩焘所撰《伦敦与巴黎日记》，光绪四年九月初六日载："李丹崖见［疑脱"赠"字］傅兰雅所译英人费利摩所著《万国交涉公法论》十三卷，凡分四集，初、二、三集各四卷，四集一卷则尚未译也，三集亦余二卷未译成。"（1984：746）

　　凭此可以推断，傅氏口述的译稿并未割裂原著的卷帙。重新划分第三集前两卷，极可能是校勘者的别出心裁。事实上，该书初集和二集的卷数固无增减，然各自所辖章节亦存大幅调整。负责复核的钱国祥本人则明言："是书三集，每集四卷，统编为十二卷，而卷帙之多寡悬殊，太不匀称，略为厘定，以便于装订成编。"①

　　钱国祥，字乙生，号吴下迂叟，江苏吴县人。常年行医，曾撰《身体解》、《药性要略》两书，临时入沪局译馆校稿。《各国交涉公法论》和《各国交涉便法论》也是其复核过的仅有两部作品。由于他本身不具备任何法律知识背景，也没有校勘译著的经验，单凭译稿仿原书未标注分卷名称，就以为仅将章节重组，"次第悉仍"，便无伤大雅。殊不知这样割裂主题的编排方式，绝非仅仅"无裨于寻觅"②，实已对目标读者群的整体理解构成巨大障碍③。

　　当然，这也从某个侧面说明江南制造局对公法著作的译介完全是仓促应景之举，缺乏长远充分的规划。

第三节　权力博弈对局译公法术语
歧出的影响（一）

　　《续修四库全书总目提要》苛责《各国交涉公法论》译名歧出④，但笔者以为傅兰雅冤矣。实际上，研究晚清西学东渐的现代文献，推崇备至

---

　　① 详见《各国交涉公法论初集·目录》。

　　② 据钱国祥言："惟原书中有引及某卷某章而反致不合者，如原序中所注第十三章第二百五十五款，今改为卷三之第七章；又续序中所云'第四卷第一章论干预别国之事'，今改为第四章等类，未及详细注明，则须查其原编卷帙以寻之。"或者说，该书目录虽已重编，可书中前后参照的索引仍依原本，这自然有碍查询。详见《各国交涉公法论校勘记》。

　　③ 譬如第三集中卷十一与卷十二首章论述的都是战争期间中立国的权利和义务，却被无端割裂。

　　④ 详见《各国交涉公法论十六卷（江南制造局本）》。《续编四库全书总目提要·史部政书类》，中国科学院图书馆整理，第2—742页。

的就是其最重"名目"①。他在光绪六年（1880 年）撰写的《江南制造总局翻译西书事略》② 中专门论及译书之法，无论批驳语言霸权思想，抑或尝试统一汉译术语，均不乏可圈可点之处。

一　批驳语言霸权思想

所谓语言霸权，乃文化帝国主义的重要表征。广而言之，就是本应双向互动的文化交流严重失衡，居于压倒性地位的优势语言企图对输入地区固有文明施加单方面的侵蚀与破坏。典型者如寓华洋人尤其传教士竭力鼓吹西式宗教、科学、民主、自由，乃至思想观念、生活方式，梦想基督征服中国，彻底取代儒家传统。

当然，身为虔诚信徒的英国人傅兰雅无法企及这样的认识高度，但他始终坚持倾向科学的宗教观（孙邦华，1993：67），并极具说服力地驳斥了汉语陈腐论。

19 世纪下半叶，西方人对汉译近代科技文献持反对论者多出于以下两种片面认识：或说文言汉语艰深，"最难为西人所通，即通之亦难将西书之精奥译至中国"③，甚至揣度"华文不能显明泰西近来之格致，非用西文，则甚难传至中国"④；或说英文将取汉语而代之，故"西学虽可勉强译以华文，然不久英语必为万国公言，可以不必译书"⑤。

（一）绝非枉费工力

对于视译书"不过枉费工力"的前者，傅兰雅即以名目为例破其说。尽管晚清社会并无格致之学，更未建立相关术语体系，"然中国语言文字与他国略同，俱为随时逐渐生新，非一旦而忽然俱有。故前时能生新者，则后日亦可生新者，以至无穷"⑥。只字片语虽是他依据常年实

---

①　相关学者的论述请参阅王扬宗先生的专著《傅兰雅与近代中国的科学启蒙》（1985 年）、孙邦华撰《论傅兰雅在西学汉译中的杰出贡献——以西学译名的确立与统一问题为中心》（载《语言学研究》2006 年第 4 期）、王树槐撰《清末翻译名词的统一问题》（载《中央研究院近代史研究所集刊》1969 年第 1 期）等。

②　详见傅兰雅所撰《江南制造总局翻译西书事略》。《中国近代出版史料初编》，张静庐辑注，第 9—26 页。

③　同上书，第 14 页。

④　同上书，第 19 页。

⑤　同上。

⑥　同上书，第 15 页。

践总结出的个体经验，竟能与现代语言学奠基人费尔迪南·德·索绪尔（Ferdinand de Saussure）深思熟虑的符号可变性理论不谋而合。

符号的可变性根植于能指与所指之间联系的任意性原则，该原则决定了符号的稳定性特征仅是相对的，任何与符号相关的因素发生变化，都有可能导致能指和所指关系的转移（索绪尔，1980：111—112）。

《荀子·正名》："名无固宜，约之以命。约定俗成谓之宜，异于约则谓之不宜。"① 此虽自然常态，难抵清末西学术语东传，由渐而至汹涌，时不我待，人为干预在所难免。傅兰雅提出"若所用名目必为华字典内之字义，不可另有解释，则译书事永不能成"②，岂不正欲将"能指"导向新的"所指"？或者更确切地说，为新的"所指"选择"能指"。

他还借自己的祖国说事，"二三百年前，英国多藉希腊与罗马等国文字以作格致与制造内之新名，后则渐除不用，或换以更妥者，而中国亦难免此举。凡自他国借用之名，则不能一时定准，必历年用之始能妥协"③。此番言论又令读者不由自主地联想起前文所引刘禾先生对超越历史语境的可译性及可理解性问题的评述④。厘定译名之难可见一斑，却也并非"不能越之难也"。

（二）必须设此一举

对于视译书"何必设此一举"的后者，傅兰雅更不屑其鄙薄中文的无知妄语，反诘道："有自主之大国，弃其书文而尽用他邦语言文字者耶？"⑤ 且将矛头指向急欲瓜分神州、均沾利益的欧美列强——"若中国为他邦所属，或能勉强行以西文；惟此事乃断不能有者，故不必虑及焉"⑥。挪揄挖苦，溢于言表。

何况直觉告诉他"中国书文流传自古，数千年来未有或替，不特国人视之甚重，即国家亦赖以治国焉"⑦，无意间揭示了表意汉字克服辽阔疆域内重峦叠嶂间方言南腔北调的天然功效。

---

① 详见《荀子集解》卷第十六。（清）王先谦撰，沈啸寰、王星贤点校，第420页。
② 详见《江南制造总局翻译西书事略》。《中国近代出版史料初编》，张静庐辑注，第15页。
③ 同上。
④ 请参阅本书【6.3.1】。
⑤ 详见《江南制造总局翻译西书事略》。《中国近代出版史料初编》，张静庐辑注，第20页。
⑥ 同上。
⑦ 同上。

二 尝试统一汉译术语

嘉庆十二年（1807 年），英国伦敦会（London Missionary Society）传教士马礼逊抵达广州，由此开启清末西学东渐的序幕。

新教基督徒们热衷介绍西洋文化，但无论执教、办报或译书，"名目"皆是无法回避的重要议题。故于道光十四年（1834 年），在广州成立益智会（The Society for the Diffusion of Useful Knowledge in China），其宗旨之一就是要编辑现有科技术语译名，然后加以选择，厘定标准（王树槐，1969：48）。但多数传教士如合信（Benjamin Hobson，1816 - 1873）、玛高温（Daniel Jerome Macgowen，1814 - 1893）、伟烈亚力（Alexander Wylie，1815 - 1887）等依然自行其是，各造新词。难怪有人感慨："译名的不统一，甚至没有译名，实在是中国文化进步的最大障碍。"①

真正在这方面率先做出重要贡献的是沪局翻译馆。主持实际工作的傅兰雅视"译西书第一要事为名目"②，故与其他中西译员仔细商讨，"欲设法以定之"，并大致概括了三项纲领性原则。相关中文本收录于《江南制造总局翻译西书事略》第二章"论译书之法"；而英文版原载《字林西报》，后由他闻名遐迩的长篇演讲《科学名词混乱的状况和统一的方法》（"Scientific Terminology：Present Discrepancies and Means of Securing Uniformity"）详尽引述③。

---

① 详见王光撰《外交名词译名的商榷》（载《东方杂志》1935 年第 32 卷第 13 期）。

② 详见《江南制造总局翻译西书事略》。《中国近代出版史料初编》，张静庐辑注，第 15 页。

③ 傅兰雅所撰《科学名词混乱的状况和统一的方法》中引述的三原则英文版如下："1. *Existing nomenclature*：—Where it is probable a term exists in Chinese，though not to be found in dictionaries：—（a.）To search in the principle native works on the arts and sciences，as well as those by the Jesuit missionaries and recent Protestant missionaries．（b.）To enquire of such Chinese merchants，manufacturers，mechanics，etc.，as would be likely to have the term in current use. 2. *Coining of new terms*. — Where it becomes necessary to invent a new term there is a choice of three methods：—（a.）Make a new character，the sound of which can be easily know from the phonetic portion，or use an existing but uncommon character，giving it a new meaning．（b.）Invent a descriptive term，using as few characters as possible．（c.）Phoneticize the foreign term，using the sounds of the Mandarin dialect，and always endeavoring to employ the same character for the same sound as far as possible，giving preference to characters most used by previous translators or compilers. All such invented terms to be regarded as provisional，and to be discarded if previously existing ones are discovered or better ones can be obtained. 3. *Construction of a general vocabulary of terms and list of proper names*. During the translation of every book it is necessary that a list of all usual terms or proper names employed should be carefully kept. These various lists should be gradually collected and formed into a complete volume for general use as well as with a view to publication. "（1890：536）

尽管这些原则主要针对"格致之学"，但仔细揣摩其精神实质，必能对探索傅氏公法译介活动的研究给予启迪。下文仅以江南制造局刊印的《化学鉴原》（Well's *Principles of Chemistry*）① 为例择要阐明。

（一）查询现名

对于"华文已有之名"，傅兰雅认为应当尽量沿袭。何谓"已有之名"，根据《化学鉴原》的实践，包括"中华古昔已有者"和"昔人所译而合宜者"。如无法在辞典内觅得，则可循以下两种路径解决：

1. "可察中国已有之格致或工艺等书，并前在中国之天主教师及近来耶稣教师诸人所著格致、工艺等书"②；
2. "可访问中国客商或制造或工艺等应知此名目等人"③。

（二）设立新名

若"华文果无此名"，就只能另创新术语，其方式亦有三。

1. 造字

1. 实际造字："以平常字外加偏旁而为新名，仍读其本音，如镁、砷、铈、矽等"④；
2. 虚拟造字："以字典内不常用之字释以新义而为新名，如铂、钾、钴、锌等"⑤。

---

① 详见同治十一年（1872年）江南制造总局版《化学鉴原》卷一第二十九节"华字命名"。该节细述了化学物质的汉译思维："西国质名字多音繁，翻译华文不能尽吐，今惟以一字为原质之名，原质连书即为杂质之名。非特各原质简明，而各杂质亦不过数字，该之仍于字旁加指数以表分剂，名而兼号矣。原质之名，中华古昔已有者仍之，如金、银、铜、铁、锡、汞、硫、磷、炭是也。惟白铅一物，亦名倭铅，乃古无今有，名从双字，不宜用于杂质，故译西音作锌。昔人所译而合宜者亦仍之，如养气、淡气、轻气是也。若书杂质，则原质名号概从单字，故白金亦昔人所译，今改作铂。此外尚有数十品，皆为从古所未知，或虽有其物，而名仍阙如。而西书赅备无遗，译其意义，殊难简括；全译其音，苦于繁冗。今取罗马文之首音译一华字，首音不合则用次音，并加偏旁，以别其类，而读仍本音。"

② 详见《江南制造总局翻译西书事略》第二章"论译书之法"。《中国近代出版史料初编》，张静庐辑注，第16页。

③ 同上。

④ 同上。

⑤ 同上。

仅凭《翻译西书事略》所举数例，便不难窥知此路径主要针对化学元素的译名。早在同治十一年（1872 年）刊行的《化学鉴原》，就已首创完整的元素汉译规则，即 "取罗马文之首音译一华字，首音不合则用次音，并加偏旁，以别其类，而读仍本音"[1]。

上述形声造字法，充分利用象形文字的 "偏旁部首"，不仅符合汉字的整体结构，且延续了汉字的表意传统。

> *New terms ought to accord as far as possible with the general construction of the language.* —The **radicals** form one of the most distinctive features in the Chinese language, and new terms ought not to ignore their extensive importance. [2] （Fryer, 1890: 542）

傅氏对中国文化及语言习惯的尊重尚不止于此，他还擅长从《康熙字典》中撷取非常见字赋予全新含义：

> There are thousands upon thousands of Chinese characters that appear to find no place except in the dictionaries, where they are carefully arranged according to the **radicals**, waiting as it were to be called into active use. Of the eighty thousand or more of characters in *Kanghi*'s dictionary, only about eight thousand are ever used, except on the most extraordinary occasions... Shall we not unearth some of these authorized fossil characters which have only a very vague meaning, and apply them judiciously to practical use?[3] （Ibid. ）

可即便是选择现成的罕用字充作能指，再将之导向新的所指，这种虚拟造字思路遵循的也是相同的命名原理。

---

① 详见《化学鉴原》卷一第二十九节 "华字命名"。

② 粗体由本书作者添加。

③ 同上。

2. 意译："用数字解释其物，即以此解释为新名"①

当然，更多时候西学术语的汉译无法仅靠创设单字解决问题，譬如《化学鉴原》对化合物译名的处理："今唯以一字为原质之名，原质连书即为杂质之名。非特各原质简明，而各杂质亦不过数字，该之仍于字旁加指数以表分剂，名而可兼号矣。"

由此亦可发现，傅兰雅非常强调意译名"字数以少为妙"②，需要保留的唯有区别性特征：

> . . . *new terms should be short and terse*. . . The fewer characters that can be used the better. It is not necessary that a technical term should be complete in itself, and be an exhaustive description or definition. All that is wanted is one or more characters, enough to distinguish the object or action by. The salient feature is what has to be grasped as the basis, and the complete meaning must depend on the definition that is given. The longer the term the more burdensome and awkward it becomes. There is a constant tendency to abbreviation, however. （Ibid. 544）

另鉴于中文缺乏丰富的曲折变化，新术语必须体现相当的灵活性，具备充任多项句法功能的潜势：

> . . . *new terms must be elastic*. —The same terms may perhaps have to do duty as nouns, adjectives, verbs and adverbs, according to their position in a sentence. A technical term may appear very appropriate when standing alone in a vocabulary, but when brought into actual use, may be so inconvenient and inflexible that it has to be discarded. （Ibid. 545）

他还高屋建瓴地指出新术语的构造应当与同类其他术语保持家族相似性，以便凸显相互间的内在联系：

---

① 详见《江南制造总局翻译西书事略》第二章"论译书之法"。《中国近代出版史料初编》，张静庐辑注，第16页。

② 同上。

New terms must bear an analogy with all others of the class they belong to.

—There has to be something done to mark the connection. Hence in fixing a new term we must not regard it as a mere isolated unit, but as one of a class. The whole series or category it forms a part of must be taken into careful consideration, so that the connecting link or relationship may be realized. (Ibid.)

实际上也正因思虑及此，傅兰雅才效仿另造新字的标准，选取罕用字指示化学元素。

3. 音译："用华字写其西名"①

音译是西学汉译过程中永远不可能完全回避的一种方式，但正如《化学鉴原》所述："西国质名字多音繁，翻译华文不能尽吐。"这个问题绝非化学物质所独有。

中文属表意语言，若似英语借用希腊文和拉丁语表述科学术语般大量引入西学概念的音译名，则完全不符合中国人独爱描述法（descriptive method）、次及音意结合（a combination of the descriptive and phonetic method）的天性：

The Chinese seem to have naturally preferred descriptive terms where they were possible. Such carry with them their own terms explanation, lessening the labor of the reader or learner, and, if at all appropriate, becoming at once popular. Next come the combined terms, which are at the same time phonetic and descriptive, and which accord most with the general construction of the language as well as with its ideographic nature. (Ibid. 534)

故在任何可能的情形下，意译才是首选，音译乃不得已而为之。且"以官音为主，而西字各音亦代以常用相同之华字，凡前译书人已用惯者

---

① 详见《江南制造总局翻译西书事略》第二章"论译书之法"。《中国近代出版史料初编》，张静庐辑注，第16页。

则袭之，华人可一见而知为西名"①：

> *New terms ought to be translations, where possible, and not mere transliterations.* （Ibid. 538）
>
> *New terms if positively untranslatable must be transliterated by the most suitable Chinese characters obtainable.* （Ibid.）

4. 补充说明

尤令人钦佩的是傅兰雅从事科技翻译的严谨心态，重申术语的定义必须准确、清晰②；且不以新设译名沾沾自喜，反而补充说明无论造字、意译或音译，"所已设之新名，不过暂为试用，若后能察得中国已有古名，或见所设者不妥，则可更易"③。

（三）作中西名目字汇

洋务运动以来，译者越众、介书越多，名词术语或音译或意译，各凭己见，率性而为。相同概念，迥异译名，"不独读之难、记之艰，实使学者不能顾名思义"④。"然而西人在华初译格致各书时，若留意于名目，互相同意，则用者初时能稳妥，后亦不必大更改。"⑤ 有鉴于此，沪局翻译馆设计了两项行之有效的措施：

> 1. 随时记录、书末附表。"凡译书时所设新名，无论为事物人地等名，皆宜随时录于华英小簿，后刊书时可附书末，以便阅者核察西书或问诸西人"⑥；
> 2. 汇成总书、制成大部。"而各书内所有之名，宜汇成总书，制

---

① 详见《江南制造总局翻译西书事略》第二章"论译书之法"。《中国近代出版史料初编》，张静庐辑注，第16页。

② 英语原文："New terms must be accurately and clearly defined."（Fryer, 1890：544）

③ 详见《江南制造总局翻译西书事略》。《中国近代出版史料初编》，张静庐辑注，第16页。

④ 虞和钦语，转引自谢振声撰《近代化学史上值得纪念的学者——虞和钦》（载《中国科技史料》2004年第25卷第3期）。

⑤ 详见《江南制造总局翻译西书事略》。《中国近代出版史料初编》，张静庐辑注，第15页。

⑥ 同上书，第16页。

成大部，则以后译书者有所核察，可免混名之弊"①。

对于规范术语译名的问题，傅兰雅完全是身体力行，不遗余力。譬如以下所引《化学鉴原》卷一附录的元素汉译表就是他与徐寿合作的成果。

西名	分剂	西号	华名	西名	分剂	西号	华名
Carbon.	六	C	炭	Oxygen.	八	O.	養
Kalium.	三九二	K	鉀	Hydrogen.	一	H.	輕
Natrium.	二三	Na.	鈉	Nitrogen.	一四	N.	淡
Lithium.	六九	Li.	鋰	Chlorine.	三五五	Cl.	綠
Caesium.	一三三	Cs.	鑬	Iodine.	一二七	I.	碘
Rubidium.	八五三	Rb.	鑪	Bromine.	八〇	Br.	溴
Barium.	六八五	Ba.	鋇	Fluorine.	一九	Fl.	弗
Strontium.	四三八	Sr	鎴	Sulphur.	一六	S.	硫
Calcium.	二〇	Ca.	鈣	Selenium.	四〇	Se.	硒
Magnesium.	一二二	Mg.	鎂	Tellurium.	六四	Te.	碲
Aluminum.	一三七	Al.	鋁	Phosphorus.	三二	P.	磷
Glucinum.	六九	G.	鉻	Boron.	一一	B.	硼
Zirconium.	二二四	Zr.	錯	Silicon.	二一三	Si.	矽

图7—1　光绪辛丑冬仲月上海日新社石印《化学鉴原》卷一所附化学元素汉译表

另外，他还先后主持编制并由江南制造局刊行了四种译名表（王扬宗，1991：13—14）：

1.《金石中西名目表》：又名《矿学表》，英文名 *Vocabulary of Mineralogical Terms Occurring in the Manual by J. D. Dana A. M.* 。此书序于1883年3月，系根据玛高温和华衡芳合译的《金石识别》所定译名编辑整理而成，并补充了其中漏译的术语；

① 详见《江南制造总局翻译西书事略》第二章"论译书之法"。《中国近代出版史料初编》，张静庐辑注，第16页。

華名	西號	分劑	西名	華名	西號	分劑	西名
釷	Th.	五九六	Thorium.	鎘	Cd.	五六	Cadmium.
鈇	Y.	三二二	Yttrium.	銦	In.		Indium.
鉺	E.	一二六	Erbium.	鉛	Pb.	一三五	Plombum.
鉽	Tb.		Terbium.	鉈	Tl.	二〇四	Thallium.
鐯	Ce.	四七	Cerium.	錫	Sn.	五九	Stannum.
鑭	La.	三六	Lanthanium.	銅	Cu.	三一八	Cuprum.
鏑	D.	四八	Didymium.	鉍	Bi.	二二	Bismuth.
鐵	Fe.	二八	Ferrum.	鈾	U	六〇	Uranium.
錳	Mn.	二七六	Manganese.	釩	V.	六八六	Vanadium.
鉻	Cr.	二六二	Chromium.	鎢	W.	九二	Wolframium.
鈷	Co.	二九五	Cobalt.	鉭	Ta.	九二	Tantalum.
鎳	Ni.	二九五	Nickel	鈦	Ti.	二五	Titanium.
鋅	Zn.	三二八	Zinc.	鉬	Mo.	四六	Molybdenum

華名	西號	分劑	西名
鈮	Nb.	九八	Niobium.
銻	Sb.	一二二	Stibium.
砷	As.	七五	Arsenic.
汞	Hg.	一〇〇	Mercury.
銀	Ag.	一〇八	Argentum.
金	Au.	一九六七	Aurum.
鉑	Pt.	九八六	Platinum.
鈀	Pd.	五三三	Palladium.
鑪	Ro.	五二二	Rhodium.
釕	Ru.	五二二	Ruthenium.
銤	Os.	九九六	Osmium.
銥	Ir.	九九	Iridium.

上海曹鍾秀繪圖
新陽趙元益校字

2. 《化学材料中西名目表》：简称《化学表》，英文名 *Vocabulary of Names of Chemical Substances*。此书序于 1885 年 1 月，系根据傅兰雅和徐寿合译的《化学鉴原续编》和《补编》所定译名编辑整理而成；

3. 《西药大成药品中西名目表》：简称《西药表》，英文名 *Vocabulary of Names of Meteria Medica，Occurring Chiefly in Royle's "Manual of Meteria Medica and Therapeutics"*。此书序于 1887 年 7 月，系根据傅兰雅和赵元益合译的《西药大成》所定译名编辑整理而成；

4. 《汽机中西名目表》：英文名 *Vocabulary of Terms Relating to the Steam Engine*。此书刊于 1890，其小序云："以《汽机发轫》所定名为主，因《发轫》译于同治十年，为汽机第一书，后更续译《汽机必以》、《汽机新制》等书，名目亦逐渐增多，今拟译《兵船汽机》一书，恐前后名目或有互异，故先将光绪十五年（1889）以前所有成书内已定汽机名目辑成中西名目表"。

傅兰雅不仅自己重视科学名词术语汉译问题，且呼吁所有参与西学东渐的寓华洋人共同关注并寻求译名的统一。1877 年，新教传教士召开首届全国大会，决定成立益智书会（原名 "School and Textbook Series Committee"，后改为 "Educational Association of China"）编写教科书。正是根据傅兰雅的倡议，该会明确规范译名亦为其核心工作，努力将教科书编写与译名规范结合起来。实际上，沪局刊印的中西名目表都是益智书会规划的《译者指南》（*Translator's Vade Mecum*）分册，出版后均曾提交委员会讨论（王扬宗，1991：14）。1890 年，傅兰雅又在第二次全国大会上发表了著名演讲《科学名词混乱的状况和统一的方法》，剖析译名混乱的危害根源，宣扬西学术语的汉译原则，并再次强调协同努力的必要性。

In a word, we want **union**, **unanimity** and **uniformity**. With these, much may be accomplished. Without them, individual effort will accomplish but little... (Fryer, 1890: 535)

（四）余论

综上所述，沪局翻译馆基于长期译介科学书籍积累的实践经验，确立的三项译名规范原则不可谓不严密周到，也必定对傅兰雅及其合作者传译《各国交涉公法论》及《各国交涉便法论》产生潜移默化。

譬如《交涉公法论三集》篇末所录钱国祥撰写的校勘记，鉴于"外国文字既与汉文不同，而各国口音亦相去绝远"①，故表列人名、地名不尽相同的汉字注音；又附中西纪年对照表。这自然是对"作中西名目字汇"倡议的积极响应，也成为晚清国际法翻译史上绝无仅有的创举。

但总体而言，局译公法著作中的译名问题远较科技术语更为突出。何以规范原则更难通行于法律翻译？笔者以为这与当时中西方社会宏观层面的权力博弈密不可分，并将在后续两节详细展开论述。

第四节　权力博弈对局译公法术语歧出的影响（二）
——洋务派的重实用主义思想

正如本章第一节所言，洋务派官员成立江南机器制造总局，秉承的是中体西用思想，希冀借法自强，重振华夏声威。即便翻译馆选书，也都本着实用主义理念，欠缺完善的长远规划。因此才会发生"另有他书虽不甚关格致，然于水陆兵勇武备等事有关，故较他书先为讲求"② 等急功近利现象。傅兰雅本人亦无奈"中国大宪已数次出谕，令特译紧要之书"③，甚至专门提及李鸿章。

在此种意识形态支配下，如何尽可能短时间译出尽可能多的"紧要"西书，成为重中之重，直接关系华洋雇员的功名利禄。故而傅兰雅主张的汉译规范措施未能得到普遍贯彻，导致局刊书籍译者不同，措辞便存差异，且大多没有附表注释，故"常有混名之弊，将来甚难更正"④。对此，他也只能扼腕叹息中国人的迫不及待：

---

① 详见《各国交涉公法论校勘记》。

② 详见傅兰雅所撰《江南制造总局翻译西书事略》。《中国近代出版史料初编》，张静庐辑注，第17页。

③ 同上书，第14页。

④ 同上书，第16页。

But it was too slow and tedious a process to suit the eager demand for Western knowledge, and my native colleagues could not realize its importance. (Fryer, 1890: 537)

"惟望此馆内译书之中西人以此义为要务。用相同之名，则所译之书，益尤大焉。"①

何况《各国交涉公法论》及《各国交涉便法论》的翻译，更囿于环境欠佳及合作不充分，很难日臻尽善尽美，特别是术语译名问题，既未能沿袭先前京师同文馆的公法译著，新造名词又缺乏必要的完备体系。

一 译介环境的远离性与仓促性

首先受到影响的是译介环境。傅兰雅的公法论并非在江南制造局译馆内完成，而是远离东亚的欧洲大陆。现有文献虽无法肯定偏重格致制造的沪局完全未参与其中，但直接发起该项目的乃驻德公使李凤苞，利用的也是傅氏送妻回国治病的偶然机遇。

毋庸讳言，我们很难指望临时受命的傅兰雅及其合译者能在仓促之间，就英、德等国收罗齐全同文馆刊印的公法译著作参考，何况《万国公法》等书发行量本有限。至于咨询重洋阻隔的寓华传教士，自是提也不必提了。

表 7—2 　　　　　　　　馆译和局译典型国际法术语对照表 A②

英文术语	馆译《万国公法》	馆译《公法便览》	局译《各国交涉公法论》	今译
Natural Law/Law of Nature	性法（卷一 §1—3）	理法（§总论—13）	天然律法（卷一 §3—22）	自然法

---

① 详见傅兰雅所撰《江南制造总局翻译西书事略》。《中国近代出版史料初编》，张静庐辑注，第16—17页。

② 脚注所录引文中的粗体由本书作者添加。

续表

英文术语	馆译 《万国公法》	馆译 《公法便览》	局译 《各国交涉公法论》	今译
International Private Law/Private International Law (*jus gentium privatum*)	公法之私条①	通融公法/ 民间公法②	私（立之公）法③	国际私法

---

① 原文：The collection of rules for determining the conflicts between the civil and criminal laws of different States, is called **private international law**, to distinguish it from public international law, which regulates the relations of States. （摘录自《国际法原理》第二卷 "ABSOLUTE INTERNATION-AL RIGHTS OF STATES" 第 II 章 "RIGHTS OF CIVIL AND CRIMINAL LEGISLATION" §1 "Exclusive power of civil legislation", p. 112。）译文：各国之律法如此不合而起争端，别有条款以息之，名曰**公法之私条**。盖公法所以明各国交际之例，而此条所以变通各国律法之不合者，故称之为私条也。（摘录自《万国公法》第二卷 "论诸国自然之权" 第二章 "论制定律法之权" 第一节 "制律专权"。）

② 原文：It is the province of ***private international law*** to decide which of two conflicting laws of different territories is to be applied in the decision of cases; and for this reason this branch is sometimes called the ***conflict of laws***. （摘录自《国际法导论》第 I 卷 "THE ESSENTIAL POWERS OF STATES, AND THEIR RIGHTS AND OBLIGATIONS, ESPECIALLY IN A STATE OF PEACE" 第 III 章 "RIGHTS OF INTERCOURSE. RELATIONS OF FOREIGNERS WITHIN A TERRITORY OF THE STATE" §69, p. 109。）译文：遇此等案件，从何法以拟断，惟公法得而裁夺之。故公法专有一门，谓之律法纷纷，亦谓之**通融公法**，又谓之**民间公法**。（摘录自《公法便览》卷一 "论邦国平时之权利与应尽之责守" 第三章 "论邦国相交之权及款待外国人民之例" 第十一节。）

③ 原文：With regard to the intercourse of individual members of different States, this Comity has been suffered to grow up into what may be termed a ***jus gentium privatum***… （摘录自《国际法评注》第一册第 III 卷第 I 章 "Objects of International Law" §CXLI, p. 182。）译文：如非同国之人有交涉事件，由此便法而渐成为**私立之公法**……（摘录自《各国交涉公法论初集》卷二第八章 "论交涉公法相关之事" 第一百四十一款。）

续表

英文术语	馆译 《万国公法》	馆译 《公法便览》	局译 《各国交涉公法论》	今译
Balance of Power	均势（之法）①	均势（之法）②	权势相平③	均势

---

① 原文：The independence and integrity of the Ottoman Empire have been long regarded as forming essential elements in the European **balance of power**, and, as such, have recently become the objects of conventional stipulations between the Christian States of Europe and that Empire, which may be considered as bring it within the pale of the public law of the former. （摘录自《国际法原理》第一卷"DEFINI-TION, SOURCES, AND SUBJECTS OF INTERNATIONAL LAW"第 I 章"DEFINITION AND SOURCES OF INTERNATIONAL LAW"§10"System of Heffter", p. 21。）译文：欧罗巴诸国常以土耳其之自主、不分裂，与**均势之法**所谓均势之法者，乃使强国均平其势，不恃以相凌，而弱国赖以获安焉，实为太平之要术也大有相关，故与土国互相公议盟约，土因而服欧罗巴之公法也。（摘录自《万国公法》第一卷"释公法之义，明其本源，题其大旨"第一章"释义明源"第十节"海氏大旨"。）

② 原文：Having premised thus much in regard to justifying pretexts for interference, let us look now at the actual cases in which international law gives, or is claimed to give to it a sanction. We shall consider first **the balance of power**. （摘录自《国际法导论》第 I 卷"THE ESSENTIAL POWERS OF STATES, AND THEIR RIGHTS AND OBLIGATIONS, ESPECIALLY IN A STATE OF PEACE."第 I 章"RIGHTS OF STATES AS INDEPENDENT SOVEREIGNITIES. RULE OF NON-INTERFERENCE AND ITS EXCEPTIONS."§43, p. 58。）译文：公法所许可干预者首在**均势之法**。（摘录自《公法便览》卷一"论邦国平时之权利与应尽之责守"第一章"论邦国自主之权不得互相干预"第八节。）

③ 原文：To preserve the **Balance of Power**；that is, to prevent the dangerous aggrandizement of any one State by external acquisition. （摘录自《国际法评注》第一册第 IV 卷第 I 章"intervention"§CCCXCIII, p. 468。）译文：一欲常保各国**权势相平**，不准一国争城夺地，俾日强大，以致无国可以抵御。（摘录自《各国交涉公法论初集》卷四第四章"论干预别国之事"第三百九十三款。）

续表

英文术语	馆译《万国公法》	馆译《公法便览》	局译《各国交涉公法论》	今译
Sovereignty	主权①	（自）主（之）权②	自主（之国）③	主权

---

① 原文：**Sovereignty** is the supreme power by which any State is governed.（摘录自《国际法原理》第一卷"DEFINITION, SOURCES, AND SUBJECTS OF INTERNATIONAL LAW"第 II 章"NATIONS AND SOVEREIGN STATES"§5"Sovereignty defined", p. 29。）译文：治国之上权，谓之**主权**。（摘录自《万国公法》第一卷"释公法之义，明其本源，题其大旨"第二章"论邦国自治、自主之权"第五节"主权分内外"。）

② 原文：It is scarcely necessary to add, that difference of size or of power neither adds to or subtracts from the **sovereignty** of a state, nor affects its rights in any particular.（摘录自《国际法导论》第 I 卷"THE ESSENTIAL POWERS OF STATES, AND THEIR RIGHTS AND OBLIGATIONS, ESPECIALLY IN A STATE OF PEACE."第 I 章"RIGHTS OF STATES AS INDEPENDENT SOVEREIGNITIES. RULE OF NON-INTERFERENCE AND ITS EXCEPTIONS."§37, p. 51。）译文：至国之大小强弱，于自有之权利无所关系，即于**主权**亦不能有所增损也。（摘录自《公法便览》卷一"论邦国平时之权利与应尽之责守"第一章"论邦国自主之权不得互相干预"第二节。）

③ 原文：This Firman can hardly be said to affect the International relations of the Pacha；the principal derogation from the **Sovereignty** of the latter consisting in the reservation to the Sultan of the power as to life and death over the subjects of the Pacha.（摘录自《国际法评注》第一册第 II 卷第 II 章"Different Kinds of States"§XCIX, p. 130。）译文：但虽有土国之律法，而埃及与他国交涉之事，仍与**自主**之国无异也。唯土耳其管理埃及之事，仅有一件最为紧要，凡埃及要处死一人，必先申请土耳其核准，不可擅行。（摘录自《各国交涉公法论初集》卷二第二章"论国有数等之分"第九十九款。）

续表

英文术语	馆译 《万国公法》	馆译 《公法便览》	局译 《各国交涉公法论》	今译
Court/Tribunal	法院①/法堂(罕)②	法院③	审问堂④/律堂⑤	法院/法庭

　　表7—2所列国际法术语尽管数量有限，却构成馆译公法著作中最脍炙人口的精华所在。且不难注意到《万国公法》与《公法便览》的刊行时间虽相去甚远，但因主持其事的同是丁韪良，译介对象也俱为美国法学

---

　　① 原文：If the legislation of the State is positive either way, the **tribunals** must necessarily conform to it. In the event only of the law being silent, the **courts** may judge, in the particular cases, how far to follow the foreign laws, and to apply their provisions.（摘录自《国际法原理》第二卷"ABSOLUTE INTERNATIONAL RIGHTS OF STATES"第Ⅱ章"RIGHTS OF CIVIL AND CRIMINAL LEGISLATION"§2"Conflict of laws", p. 113。）译文：国权既如何定律，则**法院**断案必当遵之。若本地无律可制其事，则**法院**或可斟酌其间，仿照他国之律而行之也。（摘录自《万国公法》第二卷"论诸国自然之权"第二章"论制定律法之权"第二节"变通之法大纲有二"。）

　　② 原文：Distinction between municipal **tribunals** and **courts** of prize.（摘录自《国际法原理》第四卷"INTERNATIONAL RIGHTS OF STATES IN THEIR HOSTILE RELATIONS"第Ⅱ章"RIGHTS OF WAR AS BETWEEN ENEMIES"§16"Responsibility of the captor's government for the acts of its commissioned cruisers and courts", p. 461。）译文：地方**法堂**与战利**法院**有别。（译文摘录自《万国公法》第四卷"论交战条规"第二章"论敌国交战之权"第十六节"照例所捕在国不在民枉理断案自行理直"。）

　　③ 原文：It is worthy of notice that our **courts** have followed English precedents, while our Government, as that of a nation generally neutral, has for the most part learned in its doctrines and treaties towards Continental views.（摘录自《国际法导论》导言"INTRODUTORY CHAPTER"§32, p. 46。）译文：至美国**法院**多援英国成案，而与邻国立约，恒从德法等国宽厚之论。（摘录自《公法便览》总论第三十三节。）

　　④ 原文：As a general rule, no objection to the forms of procedure, or the mode of administering justice in the **Courts** of the country, can found any such demand; the foreigner should have considered these things before he entered into transactions in the country.（摘录自《国际法评注》第二册第Ⅴ卷第Ⅱ章"Right of protecting Citizens in Foreign Countries"§Ⅲ, p. 5。）译文：如彼国**审问堂**之律法不合于此国，然不能议其非，因此国人往彼国时，应早知其国法也。（摘录自《各国交涉公法论二集》卷五第一章"论相等之国有理所当得之事"第三款。）

　　⑤ 原文：A Dane, who had been for many years naturalized by Act of Parliament, and resided in this country, brought an action in the English **Court** against a Danish subject, who had been arrested and held to bail in this country.（摘录自《国际法评注》第三册第Ⅻ卷第Ⅶ章"Postliminium.—Decisions in English Courts of Justice"§DLXXⅥ, p. 720。）译文：有一丹国人，久由英国议政院准入英籍，在英**律堂**控告丹人欠债。（摘录自《各国交涉公法论三集》卷十六第七章"论生擒之人回本国后得回从前之一切利权并英国律堂所断定之案"第五百七十六款。）

家的理论，故译名的传承性显而易见。

譬如"自然法"（Natural Law）一词，《万国公法》译"性法"，与《公法便览》的"理法"貌似有异，实则同名。究其本源，程朱儒学惯以为"性即理也"。严格来说，丁韪良也曾将罕用以指示"国内法"（Internal Law of Nations）的"Natural Law of Nations"称作"理法"①。何况吴尔玺的原著是从道德高度论述国际法渊源，提出了"国际道德"（International Morality）的概念②，将之译入"理法"以示区别，更无可厚非。再者，《公法便览》总论部分第二十七节还特别强调"发式曰，公法分有两种，曰性法，即前所云理法；曰例法。其性法者，系出于自然之理，而世人即秉此天性，有不得不遵守者"③。请注意，此处"自然"即沃尔夫和瓦泰尔所谓"necessary"，取自然而然之意。这与近乎直译的"天然律法"蕴含的哲学思维显现出本质差异。

至于《各国交涉公法论》，初稿在光绪四年（1878 年）完成，距《公法便览》的刊印（光绪三年即 1877 年）间隔如此短促，可译名迥然有别。孰优孰劣，自不能以成败论英雄。人文社科术语的汉译名词，如何能够流传至今，取决多种权力因素的综合影响。笔者在此想要说明的只是，傅兰雅翻译国际法的环境远离汉语文化中心，显然制约了其沿袭现有

---

① 原文：This application of the **natural law**, to regulate the conduct of nations in their intercourse with each other, constitutes what both Wolf and Vattel term the *necessary law of nations*. It is *necessary*, because nations are absolutely bound to observe it. The percepts of the **natural law** are equally binding upon states as upon individuals, since states are composed of men, and since the **natural law** binds all men, in whatever relation they may stand to each other. This is the law which Grotius and his followers call the *internal law of nations*, as it is obligatory upon nations in point of conscience. Others term it the ***natural law of nations***. This law is immutable, as it consists in the application to States of the **natural law**, which is itself immutable, because founded on the nature of things, and especially on the nature of man. （摘录自《国际法原理》第一卷 "DEFINITION, SOURCES, AND SUBJECTS OF INTERNATIONAL LAW" 第 I 章 "DEFINITION AND SOURCES OF INTERNATIONAL LAW" §9 "System of Vattel", pp. 12 - 13。）译文：以**性法**推及诸国交通之事，俄氏与发氏名之为自然之法，其所谓自然者，盖诸国不得不服此理也。**性法**人人必守，各国亦必守。盖众人合成诸国，而人之于人，断无出乎**性法**之范围也。此虎哥与门人，所称"公法有内外"。而在内之公法，诸国之人心，无不知其当服也。称之曰"**理法**"亦有之。盖此法不偏不倚，即以不偏不倚之**性法**，推及国事。（摘录自《万国公法》第一卷"释公法之义，明其本源，题其大旨"第一章"释义明源"第九节"发氏大旨"。）

② 详见《国际法导论》导言 "INTRODUTORY CHAPTER" §3, pp. 18 - 19。

③ 原文：Vattel divides the law of nations into the ***natural*** or *necessary*, so called because nations are absolutely obliged to observe it... （摘录自《国际法导论》导言 "INTRODUTORY CHAPTER" §26, p. 40。）

术语的选择。莫看"公法之私条"和"私立之公法"措辞相仿佛，实际上丁韪良首译《万国公法》时对"国际私法"（International Private Law/Private International Law）的汉译并无定论，只是述其大意而已，《公法便览》的处理方才接近译名；而傅兰雅改弦更张，另取"私立之公法"，直到《各国交涉便法论》将之正式缩略为"私法"。

无可否认，馆译和局译公法术语亦有偶合相通处，表7—3 罗列的概念便是例证。但笔者以为相当部分原因仍可归结为傅兰雅译介公法的场所乃中国驻德使署，对于当时办理交涉的官员已耳熟能详者，自不难觅得先立之惯称。

表7—3　　　　　　　　馆译和局译典型国际法术语对照表 B①

英文术语	馆译《万国公法》	馆译《公法便览》	局译《各国交涉公法论》	今译
International Law	公法	公法	公法	国际法
Ambassador	公使	公使（§总论—25）	公使	大使
Consul	领事	领事	领事	领事
Neutral/Neutrality	局外②	局外③	局外④/中立⑤	中立

① 脚注所录引文中的粗体由本书作者添加。

② 原文：Definition of **neutrality**.（摘录自《国际法原理》第四卷"INTERNATIONAL RIGHTS OF STATES IN THEIR HOSTILE RELATIONS"第 III 章"RIGHTS OF WAR AS TO NEUTRALS"§1 "Definition of neutrality"，p. 480。）译文：解**局外**之意。（摘录自《万国公法》第四卷"论交战条规"第三章"论战时局外之权"第一节"解局外之意"。）

③ 原文：Doctrine of **neutrality** of modern growth. **Neutrals**, who? Gradations of **neutrality**. Permanent **neutrality**. Armed **neutrality**.（摘录自《国际法导论》第 II 卷"INTERNATIONAL LAW AND USAGE IN A STATE OF WAR"第 II 章"OF THE RELATIONS BETWEEN BELLIGERENTS AND NEUTRALS"§155，p. 261。）译文：**局外**权利古人未论 中古亦鲜论之 **局外**者差等有三 国有永守**局外**者 **局外**团防之例。（摘录自《公法便览》卷四"论战国与局外交际之例"第一章"论局外所享有之权利与所任之责守"第一节。）

④ 原文：The relation of **Neutrality** will be found to consist in two principal circumstances：—1. Entire abstinence from any participation in the War. 2. Impartiality of conduct towards both Belligerents. Klüber says, tersely and happily，"A **Neutral** state is neither judge nor party."（摘录自《国际法评注》第三册第 IX 卷第 IX 章"NEUTRALS AND NEUTRALITY"§CXXXVI，p. 201。）译文：**局外**之国与交战之国，其关系有二：一则概不问其战争，二则待交战之国公平无偏。有法师枯虑巴论**局外**之国甚为精当，云**局外**之国非审断者，又非偏袒者。（摘录自《各国交涉公法论三集》卷十一第一章"论局外之国及局外应守之事"第一百三十九款。）

⑤ 原文：7. Belgium, within the limits specified in Arts. 1，2，and 4，shall form an *independent and perpetually* **neutral** State. It shall be bound to observe such **neutrality** towards all other States.（摘录自《国际法评注》第一册第 II 卷第 II 章"DIFFERENT KINDS OF STATES"§LXXXIII，p. 114。）译文：七、比利时国可依第一、第二、第四等款所论之界限以内永远自主为**中立**之国，无论何国亦必待为**中立**之国。（摘录自《各国交涉公法论初集》卷二第二章"论国有数等之分"第八十三款。）

这无非"成也萧何，败也萧何"。然从整体看，地缘的局限性还是严重阻碍了傅兰雅贯彻"凡前译书人已用惯者则袭之"的原则。借用钱国祥的话说，即便"人名、地名，则十人译之而十异"①，也充分说明该书措辞与同文馆先前所译颇有差距。

二　译介合作的非专业性

《各国交涉公法论》的译介合作乃至十余年后的校勘，都缺乏既兼通双语且深研法学或熟悉外交事宜的中西译员。

傅兰雅本人虽中文功底匪浅，然而从未系统学习法律，更兼此前应制造局官员的要求，专注格致领域，没有翻译国际法的实践经验。这与丁韪良的情形恰成鲜明对比。后者不仅在大学期间主修法律，还曾担任美国驻华公使的翻译官并参与拟定《中美天津条约》及北京换约事宜。为能更好地在京师同文馆教授万国公法，他又专程回国入耶鲁大学进修，师从著名法学家吴尔玺。所以，无论国际法知识，或对外交涉背景，丁韪良均远胜傅兰雅不止一筹。

再论汉语笔述者俞世爵，名不见经传，难以揣度他的背景来历，可其有明文记载的译著仅此而已。相比之下，《各国交涉便法论》的合作者汉军旗人庆常（字霭堂），毕竟与联芳共同翻译过《星轺指掌》②。因此，两书共涉的术语便有了某种程度的衔接性，尤为典型的是"权利"译名的逐渐确立。

本书第六章已详细论述过"权利"（Right）术语的来龙去脉，无论"初见多不入目"，但在丁韪良及其学生的共同努力下，馆译公法著作迭出，却能大致保持其名称的统一性。

与之形成鲜明对照的是，《各国交涉公法论》和《各国交涉便法论》的译名歧出③：

---

①　详见《各国交涉公法论校勘记》。

②　此书译自德国学者马顿斯（Charles de Maetens）于 1866 年在莱比锡发行的法文版著作《外交指南》（*Manuel diplomatique*）。联芳、庆常译，丁韪良鉴定校核，光绪二年（1876 年）初刻，同文馆聚珍版。

③　此处所引原文均摘录自《国际法评注》；译文均摘录自《各国交涉公法论》及《各国交涉便法论》。粗体由本书作者添加。

1. （分/理）所当得之事/有所当得者/分所应得者/分所当然之事

原文：Part III. CHAPTER II **Rights** OF INDEPENDENCE AND EQUALITY. (Vol. I, p. 184)

译文：卷二第九章　论国能自主**所当得之事**并相等各国交涉之**有所当得者**（初集）

原文：CXLIV. (Vol. I, p. 184)

Some of the **Rights** of nations appear to flow more directly from the first, and some more directly from the second of those propositions which have been laid down as together constituting the basis of International Law.

译文：第一百四十四款（初集）

凡国之**分所应得者**，有数事从交涉公法之原，而得其原有二理。

原文：CXLVI. (Vol. I, p. 185)

The limitations which the abstract **Rights** of one nation may receive in their practical exercise, from the existence of similar Rights in another nation, will be considered in a chapter on the doctrine of INTERVENTION.

译文：第一百四十六款（初集）

凡一国行其**分所当然之事**，为他国所禁阻，而他国反自行之，此在与闻他国之事一章内论及之。

2. 能/应

原文：CXLV. (Vol. I, p. 184)

The **right** to a Free Choice, Settlement, and Alteration of the Internal Constitution and Government without the intermeddling of any foreign State.

译文：第一百四十五款（初集）

一**能**增改其国政，他国不得与闻。

原文：CXLVII. (Vol. I, p. 185)

The **Right** of a State to afford protection to her lawful subjects wheresoever commorant; and under this head may be considered the question of debts **due** from the Government of a State to the subjects of another

State.

译文：第一百四十七款（初集）

一应保护本国之人任往他国，如两国民人负欠债项，可以理问。

3. 利

原文：Part III. CHARPTER XI. Right to a free Development of National Resources by Commerce. （Vol. I, p. 262）

译文：卷三第五章 论各国可与通商之**利**（初集）

4. 理

原文：Part III. CHAPTER XII. Right of Acquisition. （Vol. I, p. 264）

译文：卷三第六章 论得新地之**理**（初集）

5. 利权

原文：Part X. CHAPTER III. Right of Visit and Search. （Vol. III, p. 417）

译文：卷十四第一章 论交战国查验船之**利权**（三集）

6. 权

原文：CHAP. XXIII. Paternal Rights. （Vol. IV, p. 351）

译文：第二十三章 论父能管子之**权**（《便法论》）

7. 分当得之益处/应得之益处

原文：CHAP. XXVI. Right relating to Property. （Vol. IV, p. 389）

译文：第二十六章 论与产业相关**分当得之益处**（《便法论》）

原文：CHAP. XXIX. DXCV. （Vol. IV, p. 420）

Each person has his own sphere of **rights** limited and circumscribed by the **rights** of others.

译文：第五百九十五款（《便法论》）

凡人各得之**益处**，亦为别人**应得之益处**。

8. 权利

原文：CHAP. XXXIX. DCCLXXIV.（Vol. IV，p. 553）

The decisions of the courts of the United States of North America, contrary to the opinions both of Story and Kent, do not admit this extra-territorial operation of foreign bankruptcy laws; grounding their breach of comity in this respect upon the plea that the admission of the foreign law would in this case prejudice the **right** of their own citizens.

译文：第七百七十四款（《便法论》）

美国所断之案，与士托氏、根得皆相反。盖不以格外之**权利**与外国人也。其言曰：如引外国之律，以保外国之民，于本国民人之**权利**，岂不有碍？

上述杂乱无序的情形足可说明傅兰雅及其笔述者对法律术语"Right"意义的认识尚停滞在萌芽阶段，唯有根据各处行文需要，临时搪塞某个不致过分影响读者理解原著含义的描述性表达方式。故其译文有外延型的"所当得之事/有所当得者/分所应得者/分所当然之事"等；有内涵型的"利/理"；及两者兼顾型的"利权/权/益处"之流，难以逐一而论。但因译者本身欠缺连贯缜密的法律思维，未能提升至另创新词的高度。

直至该书末册，或者更准确地说，自《各国交涉便法论》第三十七章始，该术语的译名方才趋同"权"或"权利"。有学者认为这标志着"当时主要的翻译重镇同文馆和江南制造总局在'权利'一词的翻译和理解上取得了一致，同时也预示着当时国人对'权利'一词普遍的认同"（李贵连、俞江，2002：346）。此说也许不无道理，但其间居功至伟并催化其发生的乃代俞世爵续笔的庆常。

作为京师同文馆最杰出的学生之一，庆常必曾研习万国公法，故其参与翻译的法文版《星轺指掌》在很大程度上保持了包括"权利"在内的馆译核心术语的相对统一。只不过其最为精通的并非英语,看其历任清朝驻巴黎参赞、出使法国钦差大臣等职便知端倪。也许笔述便法论之初,他只能依靠傅兰雅对原著的理解,但随着译介活动的逐步推进,凭借自身的国际法知识及译述经历,终究洞察到该术语的实质,因而再现了译名的回归。

实际上,一词多译的现象不止于此,"Neutral/ Neutrality"(中立)同样典型,时而沿用"局外",时而化身"中立",亦无丝毫脉络可循。反之,多词一译也非偶然,似"Independence"(独立)和"Sovereignty"(主权),大都统作"自主"。

若两相纠缠,译名混淆,则更堪忧虑。譬如"Civil Law"(民法),虽为大陆法系的核心概念之一,但在《各国交涉便法论》中或称"国律"①,或称"民律"②,或称"文律"③;同时"国律"④ 又用于指示通常译成"刑律"的"Criminal Law(刑法)"。真可说是杂乱无章。

就某种程度而言,这类现象可以被理解。毕竟《各国交涉便法论》

---

① 原文:There may be obligations springing from promise or contract which the **civil law** of a country does not enforce, for which it allows no *action* to be brought in its Courts of Municipal Law.(摘录自《国际法评注》第四册第 XXIX 章 "OBLIGATIONS—GENERAL REMARKS UPOR" § DXCVI, p. 421。)**译文**:有合同内生出分当为之事,而**国律**不理会者,不许在审问堂内成案审问。(摘录自《各国交涉便法论》卷五第二十九章"总论分当为之事"第五百九十六款。)——粗体由本书作者添加。

② 原文:The **civil Law**, if the place of Contract be identical with the place of performance of the Contract, appears to be in favour of the English practice.(摘录自《国际法评注》第四册第 XXXVI 章 "CONTRACT—INTERPRETATION—MERCHANT ACCOUNTS" § DCCXV, p. 514。)译文:如造约之地即行律之地,**民律**皆以英律为长。(摘录自《各国交涉便法论》卷五第三十六章"论合同解说与通商之帐"第七百十五款。)——粗体由本书作者添加。

③ 原文:This administration may require, in the case of the foreigner, as of the subject, the application of the **civil** or the **criminal law**.(摘录自《国际法评注》第四册第 XLIV 章 "ADMINISTRATION OF JUSTICE IN THE CASE OF FOREIGNERS" § DCCCLXXX, p. 637。)译文:以外国人当为本地人,而施其**文律**、**刑律**。(摘录自《各国交涉便法论》卷六第四十四章"论办理别国人之案,并钱债人命,各种律法,与不能移动之产业"第八百八十款。)——粗体由本书作者添加。

④ 原文:The peculiar status of ambassadors, their exterritorial privileges and immunities from the **civil** and **criminal law** of the state in which they represent the person of a foreign sovereign, have been fully discussed in a former volume of this work.(摘录自《国际法评注》第四册第 XLIV 章 "ADMINISTRATION OF JUSTICE IN THE CASE OF FOREIGNERS" § DCCCCIII, p. 652。)译文:外国使臣不能以**民律**、**国律**相管辖,因其替代君身也。此理已于上文详明。至于外国君王、政府,亦以待使臣者待之。(摘录自《各国交涉便法论》卷六第四十四章"论办理别国人之案,并钱债人命,各种律法,与不能移动之产业"第九百三款。)——粗体由本书作者添加。

是我国近代史上引进的首部国际私法著作，同时涉及大相径庭的英美法系和大陆法系，海量民事法律概念汹涌澎湃。要求不晓法律的傅兰雅和只对公法有所认识的庆常在有限的时间内筑就完善的术语体系，无疑是异想天开。须知这并非查阅字典式的普通名词替换，这是沟通东西法文化的初始阶段，尚未确立任何可以假想的对等关系。在此情形下，译名的合理化过程实际上亦是法律移植或者说外国法律本土化的进程。不是任何人，甚至不是任何一代人可以胜任的，只有长期不断地积累、修正、融合，方能万丈高楼平地起。

但同样必须承认的是，傅兰雅本人对此项突如其来的译介任务思想准备有限，也欠缺堪与徐寿或华衡芳媲美的、具备专业素养的合作助手，故而未能在法律翻译活动中贯彻科学译名的规范原则，至少没将新设译名随时"录于华英小簿，后刊书时可附书末"。否则，无论其汉译术语恰当与否，总不致如此缺乏协调性。难怪钱国祥感慨："一人译之而前后又异。甚至有一帙之中，数行之内，明系一人一地，而通用假借杂出不伦，亥豕鲁鱼，混淆满纸，博雅君子不欲观之矣。"①

第五节　权力博弈对局译公法术语
歧出的影响（三）
——传教士的西方语言优越观

干扰傅兰雅译介公法著作的另一权力因素是欧美传教士集团对西方文化优越性的深信不疑。后者借助几乎雷同的基本原则，竭力推行着与前者截然相反的实践策略。其中以常年在山东登州文会馆办学的美国长老会传教士狄考文（Calvin Wilson Mateer，1836–1908）最为典型。

一　英文语言霸权

1877 年，狄考文在《中国教科书》（*School Books for China*）中概括了他的术语翻译原则（Mateer，1877：427–432）：

一、术语应该简短，不必要求它从字面上准确反映定义或说明

---

① 详见《各国交涉公法论校勘记》。

含义；

　　二、术语应该能够方便使用，适用于各种场合；

　　三、同类术语应该相互协调一致；

　　四、术语应准确地界定，每拟译一新术语时都要给出其确切含义。

　　这貌似和前文探讨的傅氏规范无甚本质差异，可具体到实用策略方面，狄考文更倾向于音译或简洁的直译，与傅兰雅的意译或描述性解释法完全是南辕北辙：

The question whether, in general, technical terms should be translated, or transferred, has often been raised. It seems clear that in case a brief and expressive term can be found, it is the best, and is generally preferred by Chinese scholars. Rather, however, than use a long, or an awkward term, or one that does not strike the essential idea in the case, it is better to transfer the sound of the term used in the West. (Mateer, 1904：2)

　　传教士们如此那般操纵的终极目标，无非想要持续巩固英文语言霸权地位。对此，傅兰雅的态度是明确而坚决的，他从不掩饰自己对华夏传统文明中有益部分的尊重甚至推崇：

The fact is that in all such trivial points we must be willing to sink our distinctive and conventional Western practices. We must carefully avoid standing in our own light if we want the Chinese to respect our Western learning. Our systems have no more right to universal use than the Chinese. Their ancient and wonderful language, which for some reasons is more suited to become the universal language of the world than any other, must not be tampered or trifled with by those who wish to introduce Western sciences. (Fryer, 1890：543)

二 西方文化殖民

针锋相对的思想言论也明白昭示了西学译名之争的本质，根植于更深层次的殖民主义文化路线。

事实上，傅兰雅在寓华新教传教士成立的益智书会中很有些特立异行。邀请这位已相对脱离教会的基督徒加盟并推举其担任委员，只是借重他丰富的翻译及编辑经验，同时又在江南制造局身居高位①。

另外，发起书会的传教士们包括首任主席丁韪良在内，无不是长期从事教育和西学译介活动，且享有相当知名度，却都主张将科学传播与宗教渗透结合起来。

譬如狄考文就认为，"如果科学不是作为宗教的盟友，它就会成为宗教最危险的敌人"：

> Moreover true science and the arts which proceed from it, will effectually uproot heathen superstition, and if rightly controlled and directed, prepare a highway for the general triumph of Christianity... **Science is either the ally of religion, or the most dangerous enemy.**② (Mateer, 1877: 177)

创建同文书会 (Society for Diffusion of Christian and General Knowledge among the Chinese) 的苏格兰传教士、法学博士韦廉臣 (Rev. Alexander Williamson, LL. D. , 1829 – 1890) 则更危言耸听："科学和上帝分离，将是中国的灾难。"③

> *The action of the Chinese government.* —I look upon the present action of the Chinese government in this respect as simply suicidal. They are establishing schools and colleges in which science, pure and simple in its narrowest acceptation, is taught to the exclusion both of mental and moral

---

① 清政府曾授予傅兰雅三品官衔和勋章。

② 粗体由本书作者添加。

③ 英语原文："Science divorced from God will be the ruin of China."

science. Science alone is allowed in their translations, and they believe that science in this sense will strengthen and advance the nation. (Williamson, 1890: 526)

显然，传教士们不希望自己的事业被本末倒置。或者更确切地说，他们忧心忡忡、耿耿于怀的正是中国人的舍"本"求"末"——只借西方科技强国、不受上帝福音教化，终将"基督征服中国"的宏伟大业化为黄粱美梦。

三　四面楚歌、矫枉过正

能担翻译家盛誉者，自有独特鲜明的风格，既为其长，亦为其短，皆受制于时代背景、个人经历。傅兰雅亦无例外，尊重华夏文明与汉语传统也是一柄锋利的双刃剑。

傅兰雅与徐寿着眼中文特征，通过形声造字，成功给出当时已经发现的 64 种化学元素术语（其中新设译名 49 个，包括 21 个出自《康熙字典》的非常用汉字）。该汉译表流传甚广，被清末学界普遍奉为善本。但在他离华赴美执教加州大学后，实际负责益智书会（Educational Association of China）的狄考文另行发表了《修订化学元素译名表》，提出"主要元素的名称要能表示其特性和来源，而非其发音"（戴吉礼，2010：（Ⅱ）433），还将碘、氮、磷等分别改译成"紫"、"育"、"硫"。可想而知，这些罔顾汉语传统的译名始终未被国人接受。

但很多学者也因此认为傅兰雅过分保守，既在官办机构任职，更兼为其笔述者多是徐寿、华衡芳等饱学之士，本身精于格致之学，又偏好意译，崇尚古词，摒弃洋名，希望方便读者理解，结果时常低估"中国人接受和适应外来新知识的能力"（王扬宗，2000：106）。譬如他不顾狄考文的教学实践经验[1]，近乎固执地反对引进阿拉伯数字：

---

[1]　狄考文对傅兰雅反对使用阿拉伯数字的顽固态度曾作批评，现引英语原文如下："I differ *in toto* from Mr. Fryer in regard to the Arabic numerals and mathematical nomenclature. I consider that the effort to propagate in China a system of mathematical nomenclature, different from that which prevails in the whole civilized world outside of China, is to put a block in the way of progress, and greatly to retard the advancement of modern science in China."（Mateer, 1890: 550）.

What shall we say of those teachers of mathematics who insist on sub-
stituting the Arabic numerals for the Chinese throughout their text books? Is
not any Chinese figure, 三 "three," for instance, every bit as easy to
read, write or print as the Arabic numeral 3? Is there any magic charm in
the Arabic-figures that we must drag them into Chinese books to suit our
hobbies, and to the perplexity or annoyance of the conservative Celestial
mind? (Fryer, 1890: 543)

毫无疑问，欲将西方科学术语全由中文意译是不可能的；情非得已之
时，甚至需要完整引进西方的符号系统或命名体系（王扬宗，2000：
67）。然而，争论发展至如火如荼的情景绝非单纯个人意气（戴吉礼，
2010:（Ⅱ）433）：

> （傅兰雅语）除非我的术语存在根本性的错误或根本无法使用，
> 否则，你们委员会就不应该改变它们。如果我的术语被证明存在错误
> 的、荒谬的或其他不可使用的情况，而别人的完美无缺，我将乐意接
> 受别人的；否则，决不。
> （狄考文语）依照这种言论，我们就只有采用傅兰雅博士的术语
> 体系了。数学、物理、天文学、药学等都存在这种现象，这使我们的
> 工作非常难做，也让我们委员会失去了存在的理由。傅兰雅博士这段
> 话的实质就是过去 20 多年来阻碍术语发展的东西。

这是传教士与非传教士、正统与非正统意识形态间的权力博弈。正如
长期研究傅兰雅的美国专家阿德里安·阿瑟·贝内特（Adrian Arthur Ben-
nett）教授所言，"我们不能忘记这一事实，那些本身就致力于翻译工作
的传教士也是术语委员会的成员。这些传教士们当然希望看到他们的出版
事业在全中国日益发展，但是他们并不希望这些翻译活动被一个世俗之人
所主持"（1967：32—33）。因为，这个充满叛逆精神的"世俗之人"自
始要求区别对待科学书籍与宗教经典，也只有他参与创办的上海格致书院
(the Shanghai Polytechnic Institution) 可以不习基督教义。他认为这"可能
造成中国人同西方人疏远，只有通过共享科学领域的成果，才能找到一个
共同的立场"（顾长声，1985：236—237）。

于此背景下，本可通过正常交流加以调和的任何渠道都相继关闭，唯能助长各方人士自以为是的心态。而傅兰雅矫枉过正的思维在公法译介中强烈地表现为，不准确且偏重归化的意义阐释更易将抽象概念的专业名称消于无形，这即王扬宗教授说的"以对术语的解释代替对术语的翻译"（2000：68）。所谓"解释"，字数必难控制，当然不可能处处一成不变，译名歧出也是意料中事。

第六节　西译中述：字里行间的帝国博弈与妥协

洋务运动时期的华人常视西学为技艺。微末与否姑且不论，即便皮毛，何则为"皮"？何则为"毛"？仅公法而言，自以法理渊源为"皮"；以公约惯例为"毛"。

譬如惠顿原著共分四卷，开卷首章提纲挈领①，名即"国际法的定义和渊源"（Definition and Sources of International Law），论的就是法理，为后续勾勒的邦交准则奠定基础。此部分译述亦是中西方帝国权力博弈的主战场。正所谓"皮之不存，毛将焉附"？

一　自然法思想的脱颖而出

徐中约教授所撰《中国在外交上进入世界大家庭（1858—1880）》（*China's Entrance into the Family of Nations*, *the Diplomatic Phase*, *1858 – 1880*）中曾引证日本国际法学者大平善梧的观点（1960：129）：

> Martin's background as a close associate of the Natural Law School of international law was clearly reflected in his translation, which is more strongly tinged with Natural Law than the original Wheaton, also a product of that school.

---

① 惠顿原著首卷名为"DEFINITION, SOURCES, AND SUBJECTS OF INTERNATIONAL LAW"（国际法的定义、渊源和主体），反观丁译的表述"释公法之义，明其本源，题其大旨"并没涉及"subjects"，使得该卷第二章"论邦国自治、自主之权"的内容安排显得有些突兀，实际上该章原名"NATIONS AND SOVEREIGN STATES"，论述的正是适用国际法的主体。将"subjects"视为"主题、要旨"，这未必就是误译，更可能文言汉语中本无与之近似的词汇储备。

需要指出的是，惠顿实属法学调和主义者（林学忠，2009：63）。他（Wheaton，1866：21 – 22）既视国际法为"不完美的实在法"（imperfect positive law），缺乏确定性及相应的立法、执法、司法机制：

International law may therefore be considered as a positive law, but as an imperfect positive law, both on account of the indeterminateness of its precepts, and because it lacks that solid basis on which rests the positive law of every particular nation, the political power of the State and a judicial authority competent to enforce the law.

同时又憧憬着"立足基督教的文明进步"，推动国际法的全球化：

The progress of civilization, founded on Christianity, has gradually conducted us to observe a law analogous to this in our intercourse with all the nations of the globe, whatever may be their religious faith, and without reciprocity on their part.

相比原著，汉译本片面强调国家交往过程中相互间道德义务的自然法理念却是跃然纸上。《万国公法》首章首节即刻意模糊"性法"（natural law）之于"公法"（international law），其间差异似有若无，相当暧昧。

原文①：
§1 Origin of International Law
There is no legislative or judicial authority, recognized by all nations, which determines the law that regulates the reciprocal relations of States. The origin of this law must be sought in the principles of justice, applicable to those relations. While in every civil society or state there is always **a legislative power** which establishes, by express declaration, the civil law of that State, and **a judicial power**, which interprets that law, and applies it to individual cases, in the great society of nations there is no

──────────────

① 原文摘录自《国际法原理》，粗体及下划线由本书作者添加。

legislative power, and consequently there are no express laws, except those which result from the conventions which States may make with one another. As nations acknowledge no **superior**, as they have not organized **any common paramount authority**, for the purpose of establishing by an express declaration their international law, and as they have not constituted any sort of **Amphictyonic magistracy** to interpret and apply that law, it is impossible that there should be a code of international law illustrated by judicial interpretations.

The inquiry must then be, what are the principles of justice which ought to regulate the mutual relations of nations, that is to say, from what authority is international law derived?

When the question is thus stated, every publicist will decide it according to his own views, and hence the fundamental differences which we remark in their writings.

译文①:

第一节　本于公义

天下无人能定法，令万国必遵；能折狱，使万国必服。然万国尚有公法，以统其事，而断其讼焉。或问此公法，既非由**君**定，则何自而来耶？曰：将诸国交接之事，揆之于情，度之于理，深察公义之大道，便可得其渊源矣。夫各国固有**君**，为己之民，制法断案。万国安有如此统领之**君**，岂有如此通行之法乎？所有通行之法者，皆由公议而设。但万国既无统领之**君**，以明指其往来条例，亦无公举之**有司**，以息其争端，倘求公法，而欲恃一国之君操其权，一国之**有司**释其义，不可得矣。欲知此公法，凭何权而立，惟有究察各国相待所当守天然之义法而已。至于各公师辩论此义法，则各陈其说，故所论不免歧异矣。

原文作者开篇直言"世上并无各国公认的立法或司法机构能制定法律以调整国家之间的相互关系"（There is no legislative or judicial authority, recognized by all nations, which determines the law that regulates the reciprocal

---

① 译文摘录自《万国公法》，粗体及下划线由本书作者添加。

relations of States），因而国际法的起源只可求诸"公平正义的原则"
（principles of justice）。至于何谓"公平正义的原则"，国际法学家（pub-
licist）各持己见。

反观崇实馆译本，先亦云"天下无人能定法"，但笔锋随即转向"万
国尚有公法"，且其渊源无非是"情"、"理"及"公义之大道"。正如林
学忠博士所言，这无疑肯定了国际法的客观存在（2009：65）。特别是
"欲知此公法，凭何权而立，惟有究察各国相待所当守天然之义法而已"
一句，完全抛开原文，妄自断言"天然之义法"具有绝对的道德价值：
公法学家虽"各陈其说"，可辩论的皆为"此义法"。

开宗明义的首节文字即遭篡改，自始操纵着惠顿国际法思想在晚清时
期的演绎。实际上，原书后续第2—10节均为追溯国际法学发展史上各派
名家理论，从"格劳秀斯"（Grotius）、"霍布斯"（Hobbes）、"普芬道
夫"（Puffendorf）、"沃尔夫"（Wolf）、"瓦泰尔"（Vattel）直至"赫夫
特"（Heffter）。这些大师的姓名都直接标注于章节题目内，以区别不同
学派的观点。

然而，译文第二至七节标题并未出现任何人名。若按常理，只能推断
作者（实际上是译者）认同前四位早期国际法学家的古典自然主义倾向，
或是引用他们的观点来印证自己的理论。唯有第九、十两节的名称提及从
自然法主义向实在法主义过渡阶段的二位学者，显是为强调其特异性。

表7—4　《国际法原理》与《万国公法》首章各节名称英汉对照表

1855 年版原著首卷首章各节名称	崇实馆译本首卷首章各节名称	
§ 2. Natural law defined, by Grotius	第二节	出于天性
§ 3. Natural law identical with the law of God, or divine law	第三节	称为天法
§ 4. Law of nations distinguished from natural law, by Grotius	第四节	公法、性法犹有所别
§ 5. Law of nature and law of nations asserted to be identical, by Hobbes and Puffendorf	第五节	理同名异
§ 6. Law of nations derived from reason and usage	第六节	理、例二源
§ 7. System of Wolf	第七节	性理之一派
§ 8. Differences of opinion between Grotius and Wolf on the voluntary law of nations	第八节	二子所论微异
§ 9. System of Vattel	第九节	发氏大旨
§ 10. System of Heffter	第十节	海氏大旨

令人啼笑皆非的是，惠顿本人的学说也延续着自然法过渡至实在法的转向。原著第 11 节"国际法的定义"（Definition of International Law）很好地说明了这一点：

International law, as understand among civilized nations may be defined as consisting of those rules of conduct which reason deduces, as consonant to justice, from the nature of the society existing among independent nations; with such definitions and modifications as may be established by general consent.

为顺应"公法、性法犹有所别"但"理同名异"的思路，译文同样对此进行了改写：

第十一节　公法宗旨
服化之国，所遵**公法**条例，分为两类，以人伦之当然，诸国之自主，揆情度理，与公义相合者，一也；诸国所商定辨明，随时改革，而共许者，二也。

据刘禾先生逻辑缜密的分析，惠顿定义国际法虽然调用了"理性"（reason）和"社会性质"（the nature of the society）等概念，但其核心在于从实在法（positive law）角度理解"普遍同意"（general consent）（Liu，2004：135）：

Note that the emphasis here is not on the moral being or reciprocal obligation so much as on a positive understanding of "general consent."

而《万国公法》所述"条例"显露浓厚的自然法色彩："揆情度理，与公义相合"蕴含的仍是普遍性价值观；以"人伦之当然"比拟"诸国之自主"，即便是各国"共许"亦无非道德意义上"相待所当守天然之义法"，两者皆与前文首尾呼应。

二 缘何如此？众说纷纭

然而，糅合"西洋的自然法思想和东洋的天道思想以至性理思想"（林学忠 2009：63），这是否全然丁氏之功？法学家们对此问题众说纷纭，支持者有之，反对者亦有之，却大多语焉不详。

支持者立论无非是丁韪良身为传教士，宣扬基督教义乃长老会遣其来华的神圣使命，信仰势必驱使他不自觉地强化自然法色彩。正因如此，丁氏所译其他公法类著作若《公法便览》等亦表现出近似倾向。

原文①：

International Law, as we have viewed it, is a system of rules, adopted by the free choice of certain nations for the purpose of governing their intercourse with each other, and not inconsistent with the principles of natural justice.

译文②：

公法者，乃天地自然之理义，邦国交际之规例，二者相合以成之，而听人用舍者也。

本例所引吴尔玺的原著视国际法为实在的规范体系（a system of rules），由"特定国家为管理相互间邦交而自由选择采纳"（adopted by the free choice of certain nations for the purpose of governing their intercourse with each other），只需无悖于"自然公平正义的原则"（principles of natural justice）即可。这与译文首先强调公法"乃天地自然之理义"存有质的差异。

不过，反对者同样指出自然主义特征并非丁译国际法的专利，傅兰雅口述的《各国交涉公法论》原序所议与其如出一辙：

───────────────

① 原文摘录自《国际法导论》结论部分"国际法的缺陷、制裁措施、发展及前景（DEFECTS, SANCTIONS, PROGRESS, AND PROSPECTS OF INTERNATIONAL LAW）"§203"国际法的缺陷（Defects of international law）"，p. 346。

② 译文摘录自《公法便览》卷四"论战国与局外交际之例"第七章"论公法利弊大旨即今日以逆计将来"第一节。

原文①：

The necessity of natural intercourse is laid in the nature of States, as it is of individuals, by God, who willed the State and created the Individual. The intercourse of Nations, therefore, gives rise to International Rights and Duties, and these require an **International Law** for their regulation and their enforcement.

译文②：

人不能独立于世，则有交涉之事。人与人有交涉，国与国有交涉。交涉中有分所当为，与分所应得者，皆有**公法**以定之。<u>**公法**非一人一国所能定，乃天命之理。各国皆以为然，此即**公法**也</u>。

林学忠博士比照上述片段后，认定傅译"特别强调公法的自然法精神及普遍价值，加插了原文没有的'天命之理'"（2009：67）。此结论似有断章取义之嫌。其实，前引英语序言后续尚有以下文字紧随，寓意恰与中译本相仿佛：

That law is not enacted by the will of any common Superior upon earth, but it is enacted by the will of God; and it is expressed in the consent, tacit or declared, of Independent Nations.

由此可见，原著观点本即偏重自然法主义，非关傅氏改写之事。实际上，宗教法官出身的费利摩罗巴德从男爵在论述国际法渊源的过程中，始终贯彻"圣法"（Divine Law）的第一性地位，由公约和惯例构成的"实在法"仅被视为其补充。以下数节足可引为佐证。

原文③：

XXII. Moral persons are governed partly by **Divine law** (*leges divinœ*),

---

① 原文摘录自《国际法评注》第一册"第一版序言（Preface to the First Edition）"，p. xliii。粗体由本书作者添加。

② 译文摘录自《各国交涉公法论初集》原序。粗体及下划线由本书作者添加。

③ 原文摘录自《国际法评注》第一册第 I 卷第 III 章"国际法的渊源（Sources of International Law）"，p. 15。粗体由本书作者添加。

which includes **natural law**—partly, by **positive instituted human law**, which includes written and unwritten law or custom (*jus scriptum*, *non scriptum consuetudo*).

States, it has been said, are reciprocally recognized as moral persons. States are therefore governed, in their mutual relations, partly by **Divine**, and partly by **positive law. Divine Law** is either (1) that which is written by the finger of God on the heart of man, when it is called **Natural Law**; or (2) that which has been miraculously made known to him, when it is called revealed, or Christian law.

XXIII. The Primary Source, then, of International Jurisprudence is **Divine Law**...

译文①：

第二十二款　凡人所奉之律法，半为天所定，即**天然之理**；半为人所定，即国家之律例并行惯之规条，历久以为成法者也。

各国彼此相交与人之好善恶恶同，故各国交涉所凭之法不外乎**天律与人律**。而**天律**则有两种：一为天所赋予人之良心，谓之**天然律法**；二为天所示人以遵守，即教会书中所记之律法也。

第二十三款　公法之第一根原为**天律法**……

尽管笔者并不否认《各国交涉公法论》反映的自然法思想确在很大程度上发端于原书，但译文对"Divine Law/Natural Law"和"Positive Law"这组关键术语的迥异处理更使其脱颖而出，此亦毋庸置疑。

刘禾先生的研究指出丁韪良及其合译者借用了理学概念中的"性"与"公"（Liu，2004：131）：

In the main text, Martin and his Chinese collaborators render "natural law" as *xingfa* and occasionally as *ziran zhi fa*. In contrast, "positive law" is rendered as *gongfa* (the same compound used to render "law of nations" and "public international law") and occasionally *liifa*.

---

① 译文摘录自《各国交涉公法论初集》卷一第三章"论各国交涉公法之原"。粗体由本书作者添加。

　　傅氏团队构造的"天律（法）"、"天然之理"、"天然律法"等新术语同样扎根华夏传统文明。另外，将"Positive Law"别出心裁地译作"人律（法）"，天人相对亦相合，深谙原文"positive instituted human law"的内涵。这也是不错的创意，只可惜未能一以贯之，反而频频归化为意义过分宽泛的"公法"，与"International Law"的译名相混淆，完全模糊了西方法哲学中"自然法"与"实在法"的二元对立。难怪他们在诠释该章第三十一款时还是不由自主地扩张了自然法的范畴，更与第三十二款所述自相矛盾:

　　原文①:

　　XXXI. . . . But it is of great practical importance to mark the subordination of the law derived from the consent of States to the law derived from God.

　　XXXII. . . . **Positive Law**, whether National or International, being only declaratory, may add to, but cannot take from the prohibitions of **Divine Law**. . .

　　译文②:

　　第三十一款……要知各国所服膺之**公法**不外于天所赋人之**公法**也。

　　第三十二款……无论一国之律法或各国之**公法**都不可违悖**天之律法**，但**天律法**所不及之处，须有**人律法**以补之……

　　综上所述，我们不难发现自然法主义价值观似乎是洋务运动时期公法类译著的共通特征，这种普遍性显然非丁韪良或傅兰雅个人所能左右，甚至以他们为代表的庞大欧美传教士集团整体充其量也不过是对西法东渐施加重要影响的权力因素之一。

―――――――――――

　　①　原文摘录自《国际法评注》第一册第 I 卷第 III 章"国际法的渊源（Sources of International Law）"，pp. 25 - 26。粗体由本书作者添加。

　　②　译文摘录自 1894 年富强斋版《各国交涉公法论》卷一第三章"论各国交涉公法之原"。粗体由本书作者添加。

三 西译中述——博弈与妥协

刘禾先生在探讨 19 世纪西方国际法的输入时曾有如下评论，令人闻之茅塞顿开：

> Where Wheaton simply equates Christianity with the universal and refuses to consider reciprocity, Martin, his translator, talks about reciprocal obligations and the communicability of universal laws across cultures and languages. Is Martin trying to manipulate Wheaton's complex arguments to suit his own evangelical purpose? It seems to me that the situation is more complex than the translator's intentional use or misuse of the original text. **For no translator can afford to do away with a certain assumption of linguistic or cultural commensurability between the languages he or she works with.** [1]（Liu, 2004: 135）

其实，不只是丁韪良，也不只是傅兰雅，所有身处晚清社会的中外译者都必将深陷东西方权力博弈的旋涡，并受制于文明碰撞初级阶段的种种掣肘与局限性。

（一）西译中述

首先值得关注的就是当时西译中述的现实窘况，然后这一切就不难阐明了。无论丁韪良还是傅兰雅；亦不辨《万国公法》、《公法便览》抑或《公法总论》、《各国交涉公法论》、《各国交涉便法论》及其他国际法译著，所有这些作品均非由洋人或华士独自完成。

丁氏译《万国公法》之初便有"江宁何师孟、通州李大文、大兴张炜、定海曹景荣"[2] 相随，后经恭亲王奕䜣派出总理衙门章京陈钦、李常华、方睿师、毛鸿图等四员"校正底稿"[3]。至于《公法便览》，严格意义上更未必可视为丁氏译作，而是同文馆学员"汪凤藻、凤仪、左秉隆、

---

① 粗体由本书作者添加。
② 详见《万国公法·凡例》第四款。
③ 同上。

德明"① 等合作完成的，又经贵荣和前馆生桂林仔细"琢磨而润色之"②。尤其汪凤藻出力独多，令丁韪良大加赞赏：

> 兹译以华文而词义尚能明晰者，则汪君芝房（凤藻）之力为多。芝房既具敏才，复精英文。（余）为之讲解一切，易于领悟。其笔亦足以达之，且能恪遵原本，不减不增，使（余）省点窜之劳焉。③

沪局翻译馆西译中述的传统与京师同文馆的华洋合译异曲同工。譬如傅氏口译的《公法总论》便由六合汪振声笔述；《各国交涉公法论》、《各国交涉便法论》则分别借笔太仓俞世爵和汉军旗人庆常，并经吴县钱国祥复核。长期担任首席译员的傅兰雅描述馆内译书方法如下：

> ……必将所欲译者，西人先熟览胸中而书理已明，则与华士同译，乃以西书之义，逐句读成华语，华士以笔述之；若有难言处，则与华士斟酌何法可明；若华士有不明处，则讲明之。译后，华士将初稿改正润色，令合于中国文法。④

西译中述、华洋合译的工作模式并非针对公法类著作所特创，其他诸如科学书籍的译介也多采此法，甚至小说等文学作品亦有如此操作，名噪一时的林纾便是个中典型。究其原因，精通中外双语的人才匮乏乃异质文化体系早期接触不可避免的缺陷。

梁启超先生曾言及此："彼时笔受者，皆馆中新学诸生，未受专门，不能深知其意，故义多暗智。"⑤ 这说的虽是丁译公法著作，傅氏所译也难免粗鄙。仅以号称篇幅首屈一指的《各国交涉公法论》为例，时人评价"译笔沓冗，且重复意殊多"（孙宝瑄，1983：138）。

---

① 详见《公法便览·凡例》第二十二款。
② 同上。
③ 详见《公法便览》自序（译洋文）。
④ 详见傅兰雅所撰《江南制造总局翻译西书事略》。《中国近代出版史料·初编》，张静庐辑注，第18页。
⑤ 详见《论译书》。《梁启超全集》第一册第一卷"变法通议"，张品兴等主编，第47页。

当然，语言技能只是问题的一个方面；另一方面，合译者的文化背景及社会主导意识形态所起作用亦不容小觑。欲沟通长久隔阂的东西方文明，绝无可能一蹴而就，也非任何单方面力量得以畅所欲为。

（二）西洋传教士与欧美列强的意识形态扩张

诚然在 19 世纪中国，以近乎执着的热忱投身西学东渐浪潮的多为欧美传教士。他们宣扬宗教教义的使命感或多或少、或明或暗地折射于各类译著，希望以上帝之名潜移默化国人，从而建构西方基督文明横扫东方儒家学说的优越感。

但殖民扩张时期的国际法著作迥异科学书籍，所述原理准则难载超然的普遍性价值①，更未能于欧美外的国家创立绝对权威。且国籍有别的法学家泰半各陈己见，直接关系到外交政策的贯彻、民族利益的实现。传译何家学说及如何传译，至少不完全是译者可独自操控的。前文对此已有论述，丁韪良和傅兰雅各自倾向本国学者的公法名著，个中缘由当然不言而喻。

那么西方列强针对大清朝的官方主流意识形态究竟是什么？推本溯源，早在两次鸦片战争结束之初，英美政府即倡导合作政策，且日益甚嚣尘上，并逐渐取代炮舰外交，为中西方短暂的和平共处创造了先决条件。欧美国家需要中央集权的政府来确保业已签订的不平等条约得以充分实施。坚船利炮虽可奏功于当时，同化思想方是长久之计策。若能披上仁慈的假面，温情脉脉地将西方社会的外交惯例输入中国，岂不一劳永逸？

但如何才能说服保守的清代统治精英欣然接纳通行欧美的国际法，并将之悄无声息地拓展至所谓未开化的远东地区？毫无疑问，唯有竭力掩饰其局部性特征，转而从自然法的角度强调国家间交往规范的普遍性道德价值。所谓自然法主义，本以基督教为起源演化而成，由西洋传教士充任改写译著的媒介恰是顺理成章。

---

① 正如刘禾先生所言，19 世纪国际法强调的并非人性与道德，而是共同认可、条约义务、势力均衡和国际制裁等："As the Western powers sought to increase their colonial possessions and conquer the world in the nineteenth century, the emphasis shifted more and more toward universal consent, treaties, balance of power, and international tribunals and away from commonly shared humanity or moral vision among the different nations." (Liu, 2004：134)

（三）洋务派官员与晚清政府的意识形态保护

毫无疑问，借法自强对晚清政府中实际办理内忧外患诸般棘手事宜的洋务派官员而言，既是自发也是无奈的选择。引进西洋技艺将不可避免地触及传统卫道士严防"用夷变夏"的敏感神经，如何占据道德高地成为曾国藩、李鸿章、张之洞等所谓"中兴名臣"的朝思暮想。

圣祖皇帝倡导的"西学中源"说固不可恃①，然"中本西末"、"中主西辅"、"中体西用"等器道有别论却是雄辩滔滔②，既可塞保守主义者悠悠众口，同时却也揭示了洋务诸臣的核心意识形态。毕竟，他们亦多科举出身，素以儒学为"万古不易之常经"。

薛福成先生曾于光绪五年（1879 年）作《筹洋刍议》述其精神实质："今诚取西人器数之学，以卫吾尧舜、禹汤、文武、周孔之道，俾西人不敢蔑视中华。吾知尧舜、禹汤、文武、周孔复生，未始不有事乎此，而其道亦必渐被乎八荒，是乃所谓用夏变夷者也……且今日所宜变通之法，何尝不参古圣人之法之精意也。"③

科学技术自是"艺事"，国际法亦无非"器数"。译介公法本为对外交涉计，当然不得背离张之洞所谓"保种必先保教，保教必先保国"④ 的宗旨。故而欧美的交往准则"衡以中国制度，原不尽合"，虽"间有可采之处"⑤，仍需将其嫁接于程朱理学，方能格物致知。

（四）权力博弈与妥协：探求中西文化的公度性

权力博弈终将回归妥协，探求异质文化的公度性，成为团队译介活动成功的关键。须知华洋合译固是欠缺跨语际书写人才的窘迫现状使然，却也为中西方主流意识形态诉求的合理接轨创造了条件。丁韪良和傅兰雅等

---

① 有关圣祖钦定的"西学中源"说，请参阅王扬宗所撰《"西学中源"说和"中体西用"论在晚清的盛衰》（载《故宫博物院刊》2001 年第 5 期）。

② 相关论述请参阅戚其章老先生撰《从"中本西末"到"中体西用"》（载《中国社会科学》1995 年第 1 期）、王哲教授撰《论洋务运动时期"中体西用"文化语境的合理诉求》（载《河南师范大学学报》（哲学社会科学版）2009 年第 3 期）等。

③ 详见薛福成所撰《筹洋刍议》。《中国近代史资料丛刊·戊戌变法》第一册，中国史学会主编，第 160—161 页。

④ 详见《劝学篇·内篇·同心第一》。《张之洞全集》，张之洞全集编撰委员会编，第 9708 页。

⑤ 详见《续修四库全书·史部·纪事本末类·筹办夷务始末》同治卷二七，《续修四库全书》编纂委员会编，第 26 页。

洋译员对中国传统文明有所了解，而华人合译者于西学也不可谓完全无知。两相参酌商议，试图"在语言与知识传统大相径庭的政治话语之间构建初步的虚拟对等关系或可译性"①（Liu，2004：131）。

《万国公法》的英文序言宣称儒家文化可以包容自然法原则：

> To its fundamental principle, the Chinese mind is prepared to yield a ready assent. In their state ritual as well as their canonical books, they acknowledge a supremearbiter of human destiny, to whom kings and princes are responsible for their exercise of delegated power; and in theory, no people are more ready to admit that His law is inscribed on the human heart. The relations of nations, considered as moral persons, and their reciprocal obligations as deduced from this maxim, they are thoroughly able to comprehend. ②

即便如此，中译本所谓"性法"、"天律"，不可简单混同欧美世界的"自然法"（natural law）或"神法"（divine law），其精神实质风马牛不相及：基督教义早已由程朱新儒学（neo-Confucianism）的"天理人性"③或更古老的"天人合一"取而代之。或者说，西方列强推行的国际法，借助某种完全中国式的话语体系得以输入。

譬如前文所引原著屡屡提及的"立法或司法机构"（legislative or judicial authority）、"立法权"（legislative power）、"司法权"（judicial power）等隐含资产阶级三权分立思想的术语，于华人眼中无非"君"命。即便"上帝"（God）也难在中国替"天"行道。

因此，笔者认为晚清社会探求国际法可译的文化公度性，旨在为其虚

---

① 英语原文："... to create a preliminary level of hypothetical equivalence or makeshift translatability between the political discourses of two very different languages and intellectual traditions."

② 详见《万国公法》译者序。

③ 朱子云："孔子所谓'克己复礼'，《中庸》所谓'致中和'、'尊德性'、'道问学'，《大学》所谓'明明德'，《书》曰'人心惟危，道心惟微，惟精惟一，允执厥中'：圣贤千言万语，只是教人明天理、灭人欲。天理明，自不消讲学。人性本明，如宝珠沉溷水中，明不可见；去了溷水，则宝珠依旧自明。"（出自《学六》，详见《朱子语类》卷第十二。（宋）黎靖德编，王星贤点校，第 207 页。）

构通行"万国"的普世价值。至于这些价值观源自儒家学说抑或基督教文明已偏离问题的核心，完全可视目的国家情势需要而定。

只不过借助宋学义理通向绝对道德本原的儒化自然法，虽迁就了中国人的思维方式，但于传统文明的发扬光大并没有实际益处，成就的反而是国际法的全球化进程。正如刘禾先生所言：

> These neologistic compounds borrowed the universality of Neo-Confucian thinking to promote the translatability of international law. In that sense, the interjection of a notion of reciprocity and commensurability into Wheaton's argument by Martin and his collaborators did not help the cause of Confucianism so much as it did the universalist agenda of international law. (Liu, 2004: 135 – 136)

难怪理查德·亨利·达纳（Richard Henry Dana, Jr.）在《国际法原理》第八版的注释中无法掩饰内心得意：

> The most remarkable proof of the advance of Western civilization in the East, is the adoption of this work of Mr. Wheaton, by the Chinese Government, as a text-book for its officials, in International Law, and its translation into that language, in 1864, under imperial auspices. The translation was made by the Rev. W. A. P. Martin, D. D., an American missionary, assisted by a commission of Chinese scholars appointed by Prince Kung, Minister of Foreign Affairs, at the suggestion of Mr. Burlingame, the United States Minister, to whom the translation is dedicated. Already this work has been quoted and relied upon by the Chinese Government, in its diplomatic correspondence with ministers of Western Powers resident at Peking. (1866: 22)

无论如何，晚清公法译介正是不约而同地通过剥离"天理人性"、"天人合一"的传统哲学语境，然后沿袭欧美法理的逻辑程式重新定位，客观上为西法东渐奠定了更具普遍性的基础。

不幸的是，这还直接影响着 19 世纪华人形而上的国际法观。甚至延及维新时期，黄庆澄（1863—1904 年）在《中西普通书目表》① 中总结自己对丁韪良和傅兰雅所作国际法译著的理解依然是："悉本性理而出，读之大足发人智慧，不独有裨交涉也。"

① 光绪戊戌七月算学馆自刻本，第11页。

第 八 章
立宪新政:苟延残喘

第一节　清末变法新政时期的社会意识形态嬗变与"宪法"术语的定型(一)
——戊戌变法与"Constitution"概念的混乱状态

甲午战争烽烟再起,堂堂大清朝被蕞尔岛国日本严重挫败,号称亚洲最盛的北洋舰队稍触即溃,几无还手之力。推行和平外交、意欲借法自强的洋务运动,历经三十余年的沉浮,终于走向幻灭的边缘。

对恭亲王奕䜣、曾国藩、李鸿章等所倡导的体用有别的改良措施,梁启超先生的批评可谓针针见血:"知有兵事而不知有民政,知有外交而不知有内治,知有朝廷而不知有国民,知有洋务而不知有国务,以为吾中国之政教风俗,无一不优于他国,所不及者惟枪耳,炮耳,船耳,机器耳。吾但学此,而洋务之能事毕矣。"[1] 自此,轰轰烈烈的政治改革即将席卷神州大地的舞台。

一　戊戌变法:拟开议院,改良专制政体

宽泛意义上,戊戌变法的序幕启于光绪二十一年四月十七日(1895年5月11日),即《马关条约》烟台换文后第三天,皇帝明发朱谕:"嗣后我君臣上下,惟期坚苦一心,痛除积弊,于练兵筹饷两大端实力研求。"[2] 仁人志士乘势而动,希图仿效日俄等国借重君权推进政治改良,其性质究竟是否可纳入立宪范畴?专家尚且争论不休,自非笔者区区数语可解。

---

[1] 转引自蒋廷黻先生所著《中国近代史》,2004年版,第137—138页。

[2] 详见《宣示和议:诏谕》。《光绪政要》卷二十一,沈桐生辑,第12页。

　　然仅百日维新而言，无论宣布变法的《明定国是诏》①，抑或官吏士民的历次奏议②，均未深涉制宪分权的内容。即便光绪二十四年七月初三日（1898 年 8 月 19 日）康有为代内阁学士兼礼部侍郎阔普通武所撰《变法自强宜仿泰西设议院折》，亦不过"拟请设立上下议院，无事讲求时务，有事集群会议，议妥由总理衙门代奏，外省由督抚代奏。可行者，酌用；不可行者，置之。事虽议于下，而可否之权仍操之自上，庶免泰西君民争权之弊"。③

　　难怪茅海建教授细考故宫博物院珍藏的内务府抄本《杰士上书汇录》等史料后，认定维新变法也只是在伦常礼教的基本框架内追求政治改良（2005：286—299）。

　　无论这样判断是否稍嫌过急，倒恰如其分地展现了当时康、梁等中坚力量对西方代议制的理解依然肤浅模糊。譬如梁启超先生的议院强国论，便停滞于"上通下达"的层面：

　　　　问泰西各国何以强？曰：议院哉！议院哉！问议院之立，其意何在？曰：君权与民权合，则情易通。议法与行法分，则事易就。④

　　同时却又坚持国家风气未开、文学未盛、民智未成，"今日而开议院，取乱之道也"⑤。因而他在追溯变法本原时，"一言以蔽之曰：变法之本在育人才，人才之兴，在开学校，学校之立，在变科举；而一切要其大成，在变官制。"⑥

---

　　① 详见《光绪二十四年四月二十三日内阁奉上谕》。《光绪朝上谕档》第二四册，中国第一历史档案馆编，第 177 页。

　　② 据茅海建教授考证，故宫博物院珍藏的内务府抄本《杰士上书汇录》中存有康有为上书的抄件，表明康有为撰写的《戊戌奏稿》曾经窜改，本无立宪开国会的内容（2005：286）。另有王宪明、张勇及蔡乐苏等学者（2001）指出参与变法的绝非只有所谓维新人士，还包括奕䜣、张之洞、孙家鼐等很多支持洋务的朝廷大员。

　　③ 详见《内阁学士阔普通武折（光绪二十四年七月初三日）》。《近代中国史料丛刊·戊戌变法档案史料》，沈云龙主编，佚名辑，第 172 页。

　　④ 详见《古议院考（1896 年）》。《梁启超全集》第一册第一卷"变法通议"，张品兴等主编，第 61 页。

　　⑤ 同上书，第 62 页。

　　⑥ 详见《论变法不知本原之害（1896 年）》。同上书，第 15 页。

笔者以为晚清知识精英的观念之所以仍较狭隘封闭,很大程度上根植于近代政法知识的输入欠均衡。纵观19世纪,毫不夸张地说,中国人对西方法律的认识仅限国际交涉领域。此外,唯有法国人毕利干所译《法国律例》,可惜质量欠佳,"往往不能达其意,且当有一字一句之颠倒漏略,至与原文相反者"①。更糟糕的是,脱离法理支撑的典章译介活动,不足以令国人窥得西政之堂奥,须知"律法之读尤重在律意,法则有时与地之各不相宜,意则古今中外之所同也"②。

戊戌变法前的"宪法"(Constitution)概念正是在此背景下传入中国的,因而译名歧出,且相关政治制度无任何具体明确的界定或详尽论述,与"民主"、"民权"等俱为空中楼阁。

"Constitution"一词源出拉丁文"*constitutio*",在政法领域多见三种含义(Garner,2004:330 – 331):

1. The fundamental and organic law of a nation or state that establishes the institutions and apparatus of government, defines the scope of governmental sovereign powers, and guarantees individual civil rights and civil liberties.

2. The written instrument embodying this fundamental law, together with any formal amendments.

3. A nation's history of government and institutional development.

薛波主编的《元照英美法词典》将上述解释,无论成文与否、刚性或柔性,概称为"宪法",并另行补充了现代社会已不太常用的译名——"政体"(2003:292—293)。

二 欧美公法著作东渐与"Constitution"概念的混乱状态

(一)鸦片战争之前

饶传平博士在《从设议院到立宪法——晚清"Constitution"汉译与立宪思潮形成考论》(2011年)中考察了鸦片战争之前"宪法"概念的输

① 详见《论译书》。《梁启超全集》第一册第一卷"变法通议",张品兴等主编,第47页。
② 同上。

入。显然，西方传教士编撰的地理文献功不可没。

其中尤引人注目的是，道光十八年（1838 年）裨治文在新加坡出版的《美理哥合省国志略》。该书卷之十四"国政二：制例之设定"称：

> 国无例则不立，例不制则不成……合省国制例有五：一曰**国例**，为二十六省所通行；二曰省例，各省不同，惟各守其省例而已；三曰府例，每府亦不同，惟生于斯者，即守于斯焉；四曰县例，各县自立其规，各民自遵其制；五曰司例，亦由各司自立，惟所属者则恪遵焉。此五例中，又小不能犯大，如司则不得犯县例焉。①

所谓"国例"，饶传平博士认为指的就是美国联邦宪法（2011：29）。此说似可斟酌。"国例"，顾名思义即国家制定的律例。宪法当然构成"国例"，但也不应忘却同样通行各州的其他联邦法律。实际上，作者用以指称"Constitution"的译名乃"国法"：

> 时国泰民安，必须立首领，设**国法**，使邻邦知而不正视，群庶畏而勉恪遵，此要务也。故乾隆五十三年春，有各省袷耆至费拉地费议其事，共推华盛顿为首。议四月毕，及散归，各执所议之条款回省，告于省内之人，再议一年，复至费拉地费再议，然后定。**国法**虽定，尚未有文武员弁，遂议立华盛顿为国首领，文武各员，亦议定焉。②

此段引文出自《美理哥合省国志略》卷之五"开国以后史略"，描述的正是 1787 年费城立宪会议。所称"国法"，当可确定为美国宪法无疑。

尽管用该书点校者刘路生先生的话说，裨治文的著述为魏源的《海国图志》、梁廷枏的《海国四说》、徐继畬的《瀛环志略》等作品中介绍美国概况的章节提供了很多素材，但"国法"一词却没有能够就此流传：

---

① 粗体由本书作者添加。
② 同上。

《海国图志》称其为"章程"①；《海国四说》以"立国规条"泛指各级法律②；《瀛环志略》则根本未曾置喙。

继之而起的汉语译名应推林则徐令其幕僚袁德辉摘译的《法律本性正理所载》第二百九十二条：

> . . . it is from the particular **constitution** of each state. . .（Vattel，1838：292）
>
> ……各国**例制**不同……③

当然，袁译与裨治文无异，也循着归化思路，选用"例"字和译文中反复出现的"例禁"等语并没有本质差别，均脱胎于传统法学术语"律例"，很难引起读者的特别关注。

（二）洋务运动时期

洋务运动时期，"Constitution"概念屡屡现身公法译著中有关国家及其主权的篇章，但译名不统一问题反而愈演愈烈。这难保与晚清政府只关注对外交涉事宜的倾向无关，以致罕有人深究近代泰西内政制度的优越性。

1. 馆译公法著作——"国法"与"政体"

首当其冲的就是同治初年刊行的《万国公法》。丁译"（Municipal④）Constitution"亦多作"国法"，并于该书第二卷"论诸国自然之权"第十二节"各国自主其事"，通过双行小字对此术语进行了注释：

---

① 原文："于是乾隆五十三年春，各省衿耆会议于费治弥亚，共推华盛顿为首，身后公举贤者更代，不世及，不及任，议四月毕。乃散归，各执所议**章程**回告部内之人，再议一年，复至费治弥亚再议，然后定，并公举文武各员。"详见《海国图志》卷五十九《弥利坚即美里哥国总记上》。《魏源全集》第六册，魏源全集编辑委员会编，第1605页。粗体由本书作者添加。

② 详见《海国四说·合省国说卷二》。原文："先前华盛顿随宜权理，相与议定**立国规条**，行于国者，曰国例，行于诸省者曰省例，曰府例，曰州县例，曰司例。"（梁廷枏，1993：72）粗体由本书作者添加。

③ 详见《海国图志》第八十三卷《夷情备采三·法律本性正理所载》第二百九十二条。《魏源全集》第七册，魏源全集编辑委员会编，第1982页。粗体由本书作者添加。

④ "Municipal"在此意为"Of or relating to the internal government of a state or nation（as contrasted with *international*）"（Garner，2004：1042）。

原文①：

Among these is that of establishing, altering, or abolishing its **own municipal constitution** of government.

译文②：

其**国法** _{所谓国法者，即言其国系君主之、系民主之，并君权之有限、无限者，非同寻常之律法也。} 或定或改或废，均属各国主权。

该定义虽不甚完整，却能把握宪法确定政体、非比普通法律的精髓，这应当主要归功于丁氏深厚的法律学识。惜乎神来之笔，不过惊鸿一瞥。

尽管"国法"在《万国公法》内反复出现数十百次，但该译名是否业已形成"较为固定"的用法（鲁纳，2000：307），笔者以为仍值得商榷。

一方面，瓦泰尔原著中的"Constitution"并非总是译入"国法"，其他名词亦颇为显眼，尤其"合盟（之法）"更常用于指称联邦制或邦联制国家的根本大法。

原文③：

The **Constitution** of the United States of America is of a very different nature from that of the Germanic Confederation... It was established, as the **Constitution** expressly declares, by "the people of the United States, in order to form a more perfect union, establish justice, insure domestic tranquility, provide for the common defence, promote the general welfare, and secure the blessings of liberty to them and their posterity." This **con-**

---

① 原文摘录自《国际法原理》第二卷 "ABSOLUTE INTERNATIONAL RIGHTS OF STATES" 第 I 章 "RIGHTS OF SELF-PRESERVATION AND INDEPENDENCE" §12 "Independence of the State in respect to its internal government"，p. 106。粗体由本书作者添加。

② 译文摘录自《万国公法》第二卷"论诸国自然之权"第一章"论其自护自主之权"第十二节"各国自主其内事"。粗体由本书作者添加。

③ 原文摘录自《国际法原理》第一卷 "DEFINITION, SOURCES, AND SUBJECTS OF IN-TERNATIONAL LAW" 第 II 章 "NATIONS AND SOVEREIGN STATES" §24 "United States of America"，pp. 72 - 76。粗体及下划线由本书作者添加。

stitution, and the laws made in pursuance thereof, and treaties made under the authority of the United States, are declared to be the supreme law of the land... But since all those powers, by which the international relations of these States are maintained with foreign States, in peace and in war, are expressly conferred by the **constitution** on the federal government, whilst the exercise of these powers by the several States is expressly prohibited...

译文①:

若美国之合邦,其**合之之法**,与日耳曼迥不相同……其**合盟**有云:"<u>此盟为合邦庶民所立,而其所以立之之故,盖欲相合更密,坚公义,保民安,御外暴,聚众庆,且保自主之福,爰及后世。</u>"此**合盟**与凭盟而制之法,并盟约章程,凭国权而立者,即为国内无上之法……但其平战交际外国之权,既按**合盟**尽让与其所合成之国,而各邦禁用此权。

该文本选自《国际法原理》开篇第 II 章第 24 节。且不论"Constitution"首字母大写表示特指,仅据引号间划线部分内容②即可断定作者讨论的恰是美国宪法。"合盟"等在今人看来更适宜描述行为、事件的译名,极可能受到此前第 23 节所用动词"constituted"的影响③。

另一方面,丁译《万国公法》中的"国法"也不只是对应"Constitution"。紧随其后的第二十五节伊始,便毫无犹疑地将"Federal Pact"纳入范畴。

---

① 译文摘录自《万国公法》第一卷"释公法之义,明其本源,题其大旨"第二章"论邦国自治、自主之权"第二十四节"美国系众邦合一"。粗体及下划线由本书作者添加。

② 所引文字乃美国宪法的序言。

③ <u>原文</u>: Germany, as it has been **constituted** under the name of the Germanic Confederation, presents the example of a system of sovereign States, united by an equal and permanent Confederation. (摘录自《国际法原理》第一卷"DEFINITION, SOURCES, AND SUBJECTS OF INTERNATIONAL LAW"第 II 章"NATIONS AND SOVEREIGN STATES"§23"Germanic Confederation", p. 59。) <u>译文</u>: 日耳曼现为众盟邦,即系自主之国各邦平行,**会盟**永合者也。(摘录自《万国公法》第一卷"释公法之义,明其本源,题其大旨"第二章"论邦国自治、自主之权"第二十三节"日耳曼系众邦会盟"。)——粗体由本书作者添加。

原文①：

The Swiss Confederation, asremodeled by the **federal pact** of 1815, consists of a union between the then twenty-two Cantons of Switzerland. . .

译文②：

瑞士合邦于一千八百十五年间，改其**国法**，有二十二邦相合。

此节着重论述瑞士联邦与德意志、美利坚等国家政权的组织形式有何异同，然而，丁氏并未认真区分"Compact"、"Confederation"和"Constitution"等法律概念的细微差别。

原文③：

The **compact**, by which the sovereign Cantons of Switzerland are thus united, forms a federal body, which, in some respects, resembles the Germanic **Confederation**, whilst in others it more nearly approximates to the American **Constitution**,

译文④：

瑞士之合盟既如此，则其**国法**与日耳曼有所相似，与美国亦有相似。

尽管译者的措辞在很大程度上受制目的社会法律文化发展水平低下、专业术语体系构建缺损的现实窘况，但数节之内一词多译、多词一译，相互纠缠的情形绝非零星个别，必然严重妨碍"宪法"概念在中文语境的固化。不妨再以该书第三卷第Ⅰ章为例，更能直白地说明问题。

────────────────

① 原文摘录自《国际法原理》第一卷"DEFINITION, SOURCES, AND SUBJECTS OF IN-TERNATIONAL LAW"第Ⅱ章"NATIONS AND SOVEREIGN STATES"§25"Swiss Confederation", p. 79。粗体由本书作者添加。

② 译文摘录自《万国公法》第一卷"释公法之义，明其本源，题其大旨"第二章"论邦国自治、自主之权"第二十五节"与前二国异同如何"。粗体由本书作者添加。

③ 原文摘录自《国际法原理》第一卷"DEFINITION, SOURCES, AND SUBJECTS OF IN-TERNATIONAL LAW"第Ⅱ章"NATIONS AND SOVEREIGN STATES"§25"Swiss Confederation", pp. 80 – 81。粗体由本书作者添加。

④ 译文摘录自《万国公法》第一卷"释公法之义，明其本源，题其大旨"第二章"论邦国自治、自主之权"第二十五节"与前二国异同如何"。粗体由本书作者添加。

原文①：

So also of confederated States; their right of sending public ministers to each other, or to foreign States, depends upon the peculiar nature and **constitution** of the union by which they are bound together.

译文②：

合盟之邦互相通使，或遣使至外国，其可否必视其**合盟之法**而定。

上文出自该章第三节，阐释哪些国家有权通使。"Constitution"可说是贯彻了原语篇始终，均被译作"合盟之法"。未曾想笔锋突转，刚进入第四节，即刻又见"国法"。

原文③：

The question, to what department of the government belongs the right of sending and receiving public ministers, also depends upon the municipal **constitution** of the State.

译文④：

遣使、接使，其职属国内何部，仅归其**国法**自定。

更糟糕的是，"国法"一词本身不具有鲜明的标志性，有时还混同"根本法"（Fundamental Law）及其他普通法律（Law），所指外延近似国

---

① 原文摘录自《国际法原理》第三卷"INTERNATIONAL RIGHTS OF STATES IN THEIR PACIFIC RELATIONS"第Ⅰ章"RIGHTS OF LEGATION"§3"Rights of legation, to what States belonging", pp. 274–275。粗体由本书作者添加。

② 译文摘录自《万国公法》第三卷"论诸国平时往来之权"第一章"论通使之权"第三节"何等之国可以通使"。粗体由本书作者添加。

③ 原文摘录自《国际法原理》第三卷"INTERNATIONAL RIGHTS OF STATES IN THEIR PACIFIC RELATIONS"第Ⅰ章"RIGHTS OF LEGATION"§4"How affected by civil war or contest for the sovereignty", p. 275。粗体由本书作者添加。

④ 译文摘录自《万国公法》第三卷"论诸国平时往来之权"第一章"论通使之权"第四节"国乱通使"。

内法①；有时又被泛化为"国之法度"②。

此译名的不确定性，还可察之于丁韪良的另一部国际法著作《公法便览》。该书处理"Constitution"，除偶尔沿用旧称外，时而又有"治法"③另起炉灶。特别是引入了新名词"政式/政体"，专指政权组织方式，此亦宪法规范的主要内容。最为典型者当属开卷首章第三至五节④。

原文：（§38, p. 52）

These relations continue after it has passed through a change of **constitution**, for not withstanding the change the state may still preserve its attributes and functions. No act of its own can annihilate an obligation to another state; and its rights still continue, unless its former **constitution**

---

① 原文：The first is, that "by the **law and constitution** of Great Britain the sovereign alone has the power of declaring war and peace." （摘录自《国际法原理》第四卷 "INTERNATIONAL RIGHTS OF STATES IN THEIR HOSTILE RELATIONS" 第Ⅰ章 "COMMENCE OF WAR, AND ITS IMMEDIATE EFFECTS" §13 "Trading with the enemy, unlawful on the part of subjects of the belligerent State", p. 383。）译文：其一，盖照**国法**，应和、应战皆君自定……（摘录自《万国公法》第四卷 "论交战条规" 第一章 "论战始" 第十三节 "与敌贸易"。）——粗体由本书作者添加。

② 原文：The power of concluding peace, like that of declaring war, depends upon the municipal **constitution** of the State.（摘录自《国际法原理》第四卷 "INTERNATIONAL RIGHTS OF STATES IN THEIR HOSTILE RELATIONS" 第Ⅳ章 "TREATY OF PEACE" §1 "Power of making peace depending on the municipal constitution", p. 607。）译文：宣战之权，谁执其端，必视各**国之法度**，至议和之权亦然。（摘录自《万国公法》第四卷 "论交战条规" 第四章 "论和约章程" 第一节 "谁执和权惟国法所定"。）——粗体由本书作者添加。

③ 原文：There is a weak point in our **Constitution** in this respect, for the responsibility must be borne by the central government, but the evil cannot always be abated.（摘录自《国际法导论》第Ⅰ卷 "THE ESSENTIAL POWERS OF STATES, AND THEIR RIGHTS AND OBLIGATIONS, ESPECIALLY IN A STATE OF PEACE." 第Ⅰ章 "RIGHTS OF STATES AS INDEPENDENT SOVEREIGNITIES. RULE OF NON-INTERFERENCE AND ITS EXCEPTIONS." §37, p. 52。）译文：然即美国**治法**而言，亦有未尽善者，因合成之国虽为任咎，终不能尽除其弊也。（摘录自《公法便览》卷一 "论邦国平时之权利与应尽之责守" 第一章 "论邦国自主之权不得互相干预" 第二节。）——粗体由本书作者添加。

④ 以下原文摘录自《国际法导论》第Ⅰ卷 "THE ESSENTIAL POWERS OF STATES, AND THEIR RIGHTS AND OBLIGATIONS, ESPECIALLY IN A STATE OF PEACE." 第Ⅰ章 "RIGHTS OF STATES AS INDEPENDENT SOVEREIGNITIES. RULE OF NON-INTERFERENCE AND ITS EXCEPTIONS.";译文摘录自《公法便览》卷一 "论邦国平时之权利与应尽之责守" 第一章 "论邦国自主之权不得互相干预"。粗体由本书作者添加。

of government was the condition on which the obligations of other states towards it were founded. . . When at the formation of the Federal **Constitution** the States' debts were assumed. . .

译文：（第三节）

国法有变革，而责守常存，责守所系，虽偏端不得或废也，两国相通之故。若专指保卫当时**政式**^{政式有三：如民政之国与}_{君权有限、无限之国。}则遇有兴亡变革，而权利责守遂有变异……昔美国**会合**之时，各邦债款累计筹偿……

原文：（§39，p. 54）

The law of nations preserves an entire indifference to **constitutions**, so long as they do not prevent fulfillment of obligations. Every state is in its eye legitimate. And in matter of fact the countries which profess to be bound by the Christian or European law of nations, differ exceedingly from one another in their **constitutions**, which contain specimens of absolute and constitutional hereditary monarchy, of confederated democracies, and of an elective ecclesiastical principality.

译文：（第四节）

各国**政体**虽有互异，而应尽之责守苟无阻碍，则公法视同一律，皆予以正名。如欧洲列国悉奉公法，实则**政体**彼此各异：或君权无限，或君权有限，而同为以国传世者；有民主政权者^{民主政权者，}_{是为民政。}；有教会公举理政者^{即教皇}_{之国。}。以公法视之，无分轩轻。

原文：（§40，p. 55）

And if this rule could be overthrown, if a nation or set of nations should act on the plan of withholding their sanction from new nations with certain **constitutions**, such a plan would justify others who thought differently in refusing to regard the former any longer as legitimate states.

译文：（第五节）

盖非此例，邦国之间，或因**律法**有不协，或因**政体**有不同，便可互相不认为国矣，有是理乎？

单看上述译文，貌似该名词术语的使用已相当稳定，实际上它也的确流传至今始终未替。然而，比较原文便不难发现，译者对"Constitution"的理解并没贯彻始终：何时指成文宪法？何时指联盟？何时指政体？常常模糊不清。尤其到第五节，索性一词两译，形式与内容同列。

2. 局译公法著作——"国政（之章程）"

本书第七章已然论及，傅兰雅口述的局译公法著作，至少措辞层面与馆译专业术语欠缺沟通与衔接。这在"Constitution"概念的输入过程中表现得也很充分。

当然，译名不统一问题是多方面原因共同造成的。沪局译员本身法律知识匮乏亦为其严重障碍，以致最初绞尽脑汁尚且只能泛称"律法"、"国书"等①。而原著作者的差异也是导致译名歧出的根源：馆译多为美国法学家，局译多为英国法学家；美国是民主联邦制国家，英国是君主立宪制国家。所以，前者常用"Constitution"，既指宪法，也指政体；后者常用"Constitutional Charter"指宪章，"Constitution"则专指政体②。

原文：(§LXXV, p. 97)

The Swiss Cantons and the States forming the Confederation of the Rhine, to say nothing of other countries, were nominally free and independent when their armies were under French officers, their cabinets under French ministers, and their whole **constitution** entirely subject and subservient to their French ruler and protector Napoleon.

---

① 原文：By the first act of that Congress the Duchy of Warsaw, with the exception of certain districts, was united to the Russian Empire, and was irrevocably bound by its **constitution** to belong to the Emperor of Russia, and his heirs in all perpetuity... In conformity with these stipulations, the Emperor Alexander granted a **constitutional charter** to the Kingdom of Poland, November 15 (27), 1815. This **charter** declared that The Kingdom of Poland was united to Russia by its **constitution**—that the sovereign authority in Poland was to be exercised in conformity therewith—that the coronation of the King of Poland was to take place in the Polish capital, where he was bound to take an oath to observe the **charter**. （摘录自《国际法评注》第一册第 II 卷第 II 章 "DIFFERENT KINDS OF STATES" §LXXIII, pp. 94 - 95。）译文：一千八百三十二年，俄王为波兰国订定新**律法**云：波兰为俄国之一分，其吏治、律法、军政必与俄国相同……发一**国书**于波兰云：波兰联属于俄国，波兰国之王即系俄国王，必在波兰京都行登位之礼，又发誓凡事必照所发之**国书**而行一应公事。（摘录自《各国交涉公法论初集》卷二第二章 "论国有数等之分" 第七十三款。）——粗体由本书作者添加。

② 以下原文摘录自《国际法评注》第一册第 II 卷第 II 章 "DIFFERENT KINDS OF STATES"；译文摘录自《各国交涉公法论初集》卷二第二章 "论国有数等之分"。粗体由本书作者添加。

译文：（七十五款）

如瑞士国及来纳河边之数邦名为自主，而其兵马有法国管理；其公会亦有法国官主政；**国之政**为法国王拿破仑所定。

原文：（§LXXVII，p. 102）

IV. In order to carry into execution without delay the stipulations mentioned in the articles preceding and to ground the political re-organization of the United Ionian States upon that organization which is actually in force the Lord High Commissioner of the protecting Power shall regulate the forms of convocation of a legislative assembly, of which he shall direct the proceedings, in order to draw up a new **Constitutional Charter** for the States, which his Majesty the King of the United Kingdom of Great Britain and Ireland shall be requested to ratify.

译文：（第七十七款）

一千八百十七年五月初二日伊鸟呢牙岛公会所定**国政之章程**内有数款议各国交涉条例开列于下：……

（三）甲午战争之后

有趣的是，1897 年日本文经号出版的《新增英华字典》① 中，"Constitution" 词条将"国法"、"国政"兼容并蓄。对此，笔者以为可否这样理解：一方面，馆译、局译"Constitution"的名称顺应甲午战争后变革内政的新形势，在清末知识精英圈内有了相当程度的传播与影响力；另一方面，这也说明"Constitution"概念无论从其汉译名词，还是从含义及其所涉近代民主制度方面考察，较之严格界定的专业术语尚存距离。

几乎与此同时，曾经赴欧的留学生回国后亦间有论及宪法。较为著名的包括马建忠先生撰写的《法律探源》，提出"国律"的概念，并释其义为"定国之体式"：

律分二门：一以制民与民交涉之事，曰民律；一以制国与国交涉

---

① 原作者罗布存德（Wilhelm Lobscheid），经冯镜如等人增订，由日本文经号出版。实际上，更早问世的《英华字典》亦将"国法"、"国政"并列为"Constitution"的释义（Lobscheid，1866：481）。只是增订本对此未作修改，本身也能说明问题。

之事，曰公律。民律区为三类：一以制户口业产之分，曰户律；一以制商民交易之道，曰商律；一以制商民涉讼之文，曰讼律。公律亦区三类：一以定国之体式，曰**国律**；一以定吏之权制，曰吏律；一以定刑之轻重，曰刑律。终之以公法，所以定国与国交涉之事也。①

另有陈季同在《求是报》上译介《拿布伦律例》，顺便介绍"作为法国立国之本"的"立国律"，名为《法兰西民主国立国律》（饶传平，2011：30）。

饶传平博士认为两位先生既是同窗密友，思想交流必定频繁，见识相近，因此措辞仿佛（同上）。实际上，细微差异还是约略可察的。所谓"国律"，"以定国之体式"，也就是规定国家政权组织方式的法律；而"立国律"，事涉建国或确保国家延续，故曰"立国之本"。前者从其规范内容的特殊性着眼，后者强调其根本性与重要性。陈季同先生的"国律"乃"立国律"的简称，非马建忠之"国律"。

三　余论

狭义的戊戌变法始于光绪二十四年四月二十三日（1898 年 6 月 11 日）颁布"明定国是诏"，至八月初六日（9 月 21 日）慈禧太后发动政变，历时 103 天，史称"百日维新"。

学者们查阅原始史料后得出结论：尽管时人对议院的评述颇多，但在正式上书中言及者甚为罕见，更没能触碰西方代议制的实质，即议会的权限及议员的公举方式（茅海建，2005：286—299）。至于西学中的"自主（自由）"、"平权（平等）"之说，"民主"、"民权"理念自是提也不必提了。无论如何，这与前文所述宪法概念东渐的迟滞状况是完全一致的。在尚未明确立宪君权理念的专制国家，奢谈什么设议院，至多不过封建帝王的"询谋佥同"②。康有为先生奏请"皇上以俄国大彼得之心为心法，以日本明治之政为治谱"，虽"特置制度局于内廷"，却仍"用南书房、

---

　　① 详见《皇朝经世文新编续集》卷四，晋安甘韩眠羊甫辑，析津杨凤藻兰坡校正，第 6 页。粗体由本书作者添加。
　　② 详见《古议院考（1896 年）》。《梁启超全集》第一册第一卷"变法通议"，张品兴等主编，第 61 页。

会典馆之例"，其性质较民选国会可是天壤之别。①

第二节 清末变法新政时期的社会意识形态
嬗变与"宪法"术语的定型(二)
——立宪新政与"Constitution"译名的逐步明晰

综合前节所述，戊戌变法的各项政治改良措施并未触动君主专制国体。或如某些学者所言，"保皇"、"勤王"也许只不过策略选择（余子明，1998：83）。仍需指出的是，梁启超先生"变法之本在育人才"的言论极具远见卓识。西方世界各国历史早已证明近代化乃系统工程，而民主政治的建立标志着社会由低级向高级逐渐演变的最终转型，因此"必须以教育的普及和经济的发展为前提，只有经济和教育的发展达到一定程度，政治体制的改革才可能取得成功"（王邦翠，1999：44）。

若从该处着眼，维新变法亦不可谓完全无效。首先是经济改革，包括设立农工商总局、路矿总局、邮政局、国家银行等机构，提倡商办实业，鼓励私人筑路开矿，加速了民族资本主义经济的萌芽、促进了民族资产阶级集团的壮大。近代民族工业的奠基人张謇正是在此期间投身实业救国的。这还在某种程度上使得清末商部的组建水到渠成。

当然，文化教育方面的措施更引人注目且影响深远，也是我们考察的焦点。早在光绪二十二年（1896 年），刑部左侍郎李端棻就奏请推广学堂及建设新政五端："一、设藏书楼；二、创仪器院；三、开译书局；四、广立报馆；五、选派游历。"②

同年七月，主持官书局的孙家鼐又于《议复开办京师大学堂折》内针砭时弊并重申新式教育的重要性：

> 若云作育人才，储异日国家之大用，则非添筹经费，分科立学不为功。独是中国京师建立学堂，为各国通商以来仅有之创举，苟谨援前此官学义学之例，师徒受授以经义帖括，猎取科名，亦复何裨大

---

① 详见《请大誓臣工，开制度新政局折（正月初八日）》。《康有为变法奏章辑考》，孔祥吉编著，第 133—141 页。

② 详见《奏请推广学校设立译局报馆折》。《中国近代出版史料二编》，张静庐辑注，第 3 页。

局？即如总署同文馆、各省广方言馆之式，斤斤于文字语言，充其量不过得数十翻译人才而止。福建之船政学堂，江南制造局学堂，及南北洋水师武备各学堂，皆囿于一才一艺，即稍有成就，多不明大体，先厌华风，故办理垂数十年，欲求一缓急可恃之才，而竟不可得者，所以教之之道，固有未尽也。此中国旧设之学堂，不能仿照办理也。①

再说译书，时人有感日本小岛能借明治维新一跃而自立强国之林，急欲效法图存。正如山东道监察御史杨深秀的奏疏所言：

> 臣以为言学堂而不言译书，亦无从收变法之效也。同治时大学士曾国藩，先识远见，开制造局，首译西书，而奉行者不通本原，徒译兵学、医学之书，而政治经济之本，乃不得一二。然且泰西文义迥异，译者极难，越月逾岁乃成一种，故开局至今数十年，得书不满百种，以是而言变法，是终不得其法也……日本变法，以尽译泰西精要之书，且其文字与我同，但文法稍有颠倒，学之数月而可大通，人人可为译书之用矣。②

梁启超先生在《大同译书局叙例（1897年）》中也倡导"以东文为主，而辅以西文；以政学为先，而次以艺学"③。故有光绪二十四年（1898年）总理衙门奏请将京师大学堂附设的编译局并归举人梁启超主持之事④。

尽管"戊戌大学"不及为变法培养人才；编译政法书籍开启民智亦尚需时日，所幸维新虽百日夭折，努力却非全然白费，"如通商、惠工、

---

① 详见《议复开办京师大学堂折》。《中国近代史资料丛刊·戊戌变法》第二册，中国史学会主编，第425页。

② 详见《山东道监察御史杨深秀片（光绪二十四年四月十三日）》。《近代中国史料丛刊·戊戌变法档案史料》，沈云龙主编，佚名辑，第446页。

③ 详见《大同译书局叙例（1897年）》。《梁启超全集》第一册第一卷"变法通议"，张品兴等主编，第132页。

④ 详见《奏请京师编译局归并举人梁启超主持片》。《中国近代出版史料二编》，张静庐辑注，第8—9页。

重农、育才，以及修武备、浚利源，实系有关国计民生者，即当切实次第举行"①，唯独顽固派认为"无裨时政而有碍治体者，均毋庸置议"②。

一　清末新政：筹立宪法，维护君主统治

庚子年，八国联军踏破京师火烧圆明园，慈禧太后挟持光绪帝仓皇西狩。随后签订的《辛丑条约》更标志着列强"对中国主权及其岁入的控制达到顶点"（罗兹曼，1992：289）。国势倾颓如此，"甚至使那些最仇外的旧保守派分子也认为急需进行制度上的彻底改革"（同上，290）。

光绪二十六年十二月初十日（1901 年 1 月 29 日），慈禧太后令光绪帝颁发丁未上谕③，宣布变法，实施新政，企图挽救皇朝统治。此谕虽斥责"康逆之谈新法，乃乱法也，非变法也"，但这不过表面文章，只欲为戊戌政变正名而已。诏书的实质在于变更成法："世有万古不易之常经，无一成不变之治法。穷变通久见于大易，损益可知著于论语。盖不易者三纲五常，昭然如日星之照世。而可变者令甲令乙，不妨如琴瑟之改弦。"且笔锋直指洋务运动的弊端，"至近之学西法者，语言文字制造机械而已。此西艺之皮毛而非西政之本源也"。故其深度与广度迅速突破了"中体西用"理论，除君主国体外，似无一不可改。此所谓"法令不更，锢习不破。欲求振作，当议更张"。

霎时，勋戚重臣纷纷上书言事。其中，最著名的当属两江总督刘坤一领衔、湖广总督张之洞主稿的《江楚会奏变法三折》④。即便是顽固绝顶的政务处大臣荣禄等也说："变法一事，关系甚重。请申诚谕示天下以朝

---

① 详见《（十一日）壬辰（二十六日）谕内阁》。《中国近代史资料丛刊·戊戌变法》第二册，中国史学会主编，第 102 页。

② 同上。

③ 出自《光绪二十六年庚子十二月丁未谕内阁》，详见《德宗景皇帝实录》卷四七六。《清实录》第五八册，中华书局影印，第 273—275 页。

④ 《江楚会奏变法三折》由《变通政治人才为先遵旨筹议折（光绪二十七年五月二十七日）》、《遵旨筹议变法谨拟整顿中法十二条折（光绪二十七年六月初四日）》、《遵旨筹议变法谨拟采用西法十一条折（光绪二十七年六月初五日）》、《请专筹巨款举行要政片（光绪二十七年六月初五日）》等三折一片组成，参与策划的包括主张立宪的张謇、沈曾植、汤寿潜等民族资产阶级知名人士。《张之洞全集》第二册卷五十二至卷五十四，苑书义、孙华锋、李秉新主编，第 1393—1452 页。

廷立意坚定,志在必行,并饬政务处随时督催,务使中外同心合力,期于必成。"① 因而光绪二十七年八月二十四日(1901 年 10 月 6 日)圣驾回銮前,慈禧又以皇太后名义下诏:"尔中外臣工,须知国势至此,断非苟且补苴所能挽回厄运。惟有变法自强,为国家安危之命脉,亦即中国民生之转机。予与皇帝为宗庙计、为国民计,舍此更无他策。"②

随后数年间,废科举、兴学堂、倡留洋、广译书等维新变法欲行未竟的文教改革措施居然逐项成为现实,史称"癸卯学制"的《奏定学堂章程》也因此而颁布。特别是"同州同文同种"的日本成功模式引起国人的极大关注。知识精英们怀着无比热忱,掀起了学习效仿东瀛政法制度的高潮。

二 日本宪政文化输入与"Constitution"译名的逐步明晰

(一)近代"宪法"译名初现

据《辞源》考证,"宪"即"法令"③。唐代孔颖达注疏《尚书正义》,将"率作兴事,慎乃宪"理解成"天子率臣下为起治之事,当慎汝法度,敬其职"④;又将"惟天聪明,惟圣时宪"阐释为"言圣王法天以立教"⑤,由此可见其"权威性"、"重要性"的含义。所谓"宪法",就是"国法,根本大法"⑥。《国语·晋语九》曰:"赏善罚奸,国之宪法也。"⑦《管子·七法》也说:"有一体之治,故能出号令,明宪法矣。"⑧两者皆本此宽泛古意。

若要追溯汉语名词"宪法"在近代民主分权意义上的使用,则有学

① 出自《光绪二十七年辛丑八月癸丑谕内阁,钦奉慈禧端佑康颐昭豫庄诚寿恭钦献崇熙皇太后懿旨》,详见《德宗景皇帝实录》卷四八六。《清实录》第五八册,中华书局影印,第430 页。

② 同上。

③ 详见《辞源》。广东、广西、湖南、河南辞源修订组及商务印书馆编辑部编,第1164 页。

④ 出自《尚书·益稷第五》,详见《十三经注疏·尚书正义》卷第五。(汉)孔安国传,(唐)孔颖达疏,廖名春、陈明整理,吕绍纲审定,第130 页。

⑤ 出自《尚书·说命中第十三》,详见《十三经注疏·尚书正义》卷第十。同上书,第250 页。

⑥ 祥见《辞源》。广东、广西、湖南、河南辞源修订组及商务印书馆编辑部编,第1164 页。

⑦ 详见《国语集解》卷第十五。徐元浩撰,王树民、沈长云点校,第444 页。

⑧ 详见《管子校注》卷第二。黎翔凤撰,梁运华整理,第120 页。

者认为曙光初现正于戊戌变法前后（饶传平，2011：31）。先是王韬①所撰《法国志略》述及 1791 年"立一定宪法布行国中"即人权宣言。该书初撰本成于 1871 年，历经近二十年的修补重订，终于 1889—1890 年定稿（舒习龙，2002：40—41）。另有郑观应②的《盛世危言》之自强篇（甲午后续）③，也数次闪现"宪法"字眼：

> 夫立君政治，除俄、土二国外（专制政体，在今日称各国例外之政体，将来亦不得不变。俄早议有宪法，但未行耳），文明诸国无不从同。惟君主与民主之国，宪法微有不同。查日本宪法，系本其国之成法，而参以西法，中国亟宜仿行，以期安攘。或谓恐失君权。不知君主之国，如英德议院，所议之事与君不合者，可置不行。昔英儒矮利斯托路氏云："政府之强大，古则尚立，今则尚德，反是则势涣国衰。"故皆设宪法而开议院。（2002：50）

当然，他们的著作只是稍涉"宪法"译名罢了，对其概念及相关原理制度不仅没有深究，而且似乎理解有所偏差，仍未超越"政通人和"的传统"大同"观念——"拟立宪法，冀当轴者合群图治，以顺人心，虽参用西法，实亦三代之遗规也"（同上），多少囿于"中体西用"、"借法图强"思维的局限。尤需注意，此时的"宪法"不过是"Constitution"诸多汉语译名之一，真正揭示宪政实质精神还有待后来者的努力开拓。

（二）旅日华人的立宪观

戊戌变法失败，维新志士避居日本者不在少数。特别值得一提的是梁

---

① 王韬（1828—1897 年）。原名利宾；道光二十五年（1845 年）改名瀚，字仲薇，号懒今，一号兰卿；清同治元年（1862 年）亡命香港后，易名韬，字仲弢，一字子潜，又字紫诠，号天南遁叟。苏州府长洲县甫里村人。著名的洋务政论家、中国新闻业之父。除《法国志略》外，尚有《普法战纪》、《韬园文录外编》、《韬园尺牍》、《西学原始考》、《弢园文录外编》、《淞滨琐话》、《漫游随录图记》、《淞隐漫录》等四十余种著述。

② 郑观应（1842—1921 年）。本名官应，字正翔，号陶斋，别署罗浮偫鹤山人等。广东香山县（今中山市）三乡镇雍陌村人。中国近代最早具有完整维新思想体系的理论家，揭开民主与科学序幕的启蒙思想家，也是实业家、教育家、文学家、慈善家和热忱的爱国者。

③ 八卷本《盛世危言》初版于 1900 年，其中《自强》篇撰于甲午战败之后，观文中辞句所及，譬如"今朝廷有更新之诏……惜守旧者恶谈西法，维新者不知纲领。而政府志在敷衍，惮于改革，不求中外利病是非，只知安富尊荣，保其禄位"，应当撰于维新变法时期（郑观应，2002：49）。

启超先生君主立宪思想的成熟历程，正可视为此段历史的缩影。

早在 1897 年，梁氏读康有为先生的《日本书目志》后便感慨道："愿我公卿，读政治、宪法、行政学之书，习三条氏之政议，择究以返观，发愤以改政，以保我四万万神明之胄；愿我君后，读明治之维新书。"① 其所撰《大同译书局叙例》中也有："欲变总纲，而宪法之书，靡得而读焉。欲变分目，而章程之书，靡得而读焉"、"译宪法书，以明立国之本。译章程书，以资办事之用"② 等字句。

这充分说明梁启超的宪法观念多源自日文书籍，只是当时但知其名目及其提纲挈领的重要性，尚未能够深入通读，否则亦不会稍言辄止，东渡后更不会有"哀时客既旅日本数月，肆日本之文，读日本之书，畴昔所未见之籍，纷触于目；畴昔所未穷之理，腾跃于脑，如幽室见日，枯腹得酒，沾沾自喜"③ 之叹。

梁先生在日本目睹明治维新之实效，亲历宪政制度之繁荣，因而于1899 年撰写了《各国宪法异同论》，且开篇即言：

> 宪法者英语称为 Constitution，其义盖谓可为国家一切法律根本之大典也。故苟凡属国家之大典，无论其为专制政体（旧译为君主之国）、为立宪政体（旧译为君民共主之国）、为共和政体（旧译为民主之国），似皆可称为宪法。虽然，近日政治家之通称，惟有议院之国所定之国典乃称为宪法，故今之所论述，亦从狭义，惟就立宪政体之各国，取其宪法之异同，而比较之云尔。④

此段简明扼要的评述在我国近代宪政发展史上具有重要意义：它不仅明确了所谓"宪法"，指的就是西方社会的"Constitution"；且该译名古已有之，无非近代惯常用于专称"议院之国所定之国典"。所以，该文立足政体，比较立宪各国行政、立法、司法之分权。

---

① 详见《读〈日本书目志〉书后（1897 年）》。《梁启超全集》第一册第一卷"变法通议"，张品兴等主编，第 129 页。

② 详见《大同译书局叙例（1897 年）》。同上书，第 132 页。

③ 祥见《论学日本文之益（1899 年）》。《梁启超全集》第一册第二卷"瓜分危言"，张品兴等主编，第 324 页。

④ 详见《各国宪法异同论（1899 年）》。同上书，第 318 页。

1900 年，梁先生又发表《立宪法议》①，重申宪法乃"立万世不易之宪典。而一国之人，无论为君主为官吏为人民皆共守之者也。为国家一切法度之根源，此后无论出何令，更何法，百变而不许离其宗者也。西语原字为 THE CONSTITUTION，译意犹言元气也，盖谓宪法者一国之元气也。"

他认为立宪政体的精髓在于确定权限，"故各国宪法，皆首言君主统治之大权，及皇位继袭之典例，明君之权限也；次言政府及地方政治之职分，明官之权限也；次言议会职分及人民自由之事件，明民之权限也"，并由此强调"苟无民权，则虽有至良极美之宪法，亦不过一纸空文，毫无补济"、"宪法与民权，二者不可相离，此实不易之理，而万国所经验而得之也"。

从此，"宪法"术语不仅有其名，更有其实，且为 20 世纪最初十年日本政法文化的输入浪潮做好了铺垫。难怪他要说"今日中国欲为自强第一策，当以译书为第一义矣。吾师南海先生，早睊睊忧之，大收日本之书，作书目以待天下之译者。"②

（三）汉译日本宪法著作

据《中国译日本书综合目录》统计，1896—1911 年翻译的社会科学著作多达 366 部，包括法律图书 98 部、政治图书 96 部［谭汝谦，1981：(47)］。这些政法书籍多在某种程度上与宪政联系紧密。

但严格意义上的日本宪法学译著最早出版于光绪二十七年（1901 年），此后十年内有案可查的约四十部（不同学者的统计略有出入，其中个别仅是译本不同）。

表 8—1　　　　　　清末（1901—1911 年）译日本宪法学书目③

书名	作者	译者	出版年代	出版机构
日本帝国宪法义解	伊藤博文	沈纮	光绪二十七年	上海金粟斋

---

①　详见《立宪法议（1900 年）》。《梁启超全集》第一册第一卷"变法通议"，张品兴等主编，第 405—408 页。

②　详见《读〈日本书目志〉书后（1897 年）》。同上书，第 128 页。

③　数据来源于俞江博士所撰《清末法学书目备考（1901—1911）》（2005 年），该文的考证相对较为完备。

书名	作者	译者	出版年代	出版机构
日本皇室典范义解	伊藤博文	沈纮	光绪二十七年	上海金粟斋
国法学	岩崎昌、中村孝	章宗祥	光绪二十七年	东京译书汇编社
英国宪法论	天野为之、石原健三	周逵	光绪二十八年	上海广智书局
宪法要义	高田早苗	稽镜	光绪二十八年	上海文明书局
万国宪法比较	辰巳小三郎	戢翼翚	光绪二十八年	商务印书馆
国宪泛论	小野梓	陈鹏	光绪二十九年	上海广智书局
宪政论	菊池学而	林棨	光绪二十九年	商务印书馆
英国宪法史	松平康国	麦孟华	光绪二十九年	上海广智书局
日本帝国宪法论	田中次郎	范迪吉等	光绪二十九年	上海会文学社
国法学	岩崎昌、中村孝	范迪吉等	光绪二十九年	上海会文学社
宪法要义	高田早苗	戢翼翚	光绪二十九年	上海作新社
日本宪法全书	田中次郎	范迪吉、李思慎	光绪三十一年	上海群益社
国法学	笕克彦	陈武	光绪三十一年	湖北法政编辑社
比较国法学	末冈精一	商务印书馆编译所	光绪三十二年	商务印书馆
宪法新书	添田寿一	杨兆鹏	光绪三十二年	不详
万国比较日本宪法义解	伊藤博文	丁德威	光绪三十二年	日本春樱馆
宪法	清水澄	卢弼、黄炳言	光绪三十二年	东京政治经济社
日本宪法一览表	矢川庄治	法政普及社	光绪三十二年	东京神田活版所
日本议会法	工藤重义	施尔常	光绪三十二年	北京第一书局
日本宪法法理图解	羽田智证	中国法政研究会	光绪三十三年	中国书林
日本宪法说明书	穗积八束	不详	光绪三十三年	政治官报局
宪法	穗积八束	河北宪政研究社	光绪三十三年	东京共成舍
宪法	笕克彦	戴忠骏	光绪三十三年	湖北编辑社
宪法要论	末村光惠	李维翰	光绪三十三年	上海普及书局
国宪泛论	笕克彦	李家祥	光绪三十三年	东京
宪法讲义	美浓部达吉	王运嘉、刘蕃	光绪三十三年	宪学社
国法学	笕克彦	陈时夏	光绪三十三年	商务印书馆
比较宪法	美浓部达吉	张孝慈等	光绪三十三年	东京秀光社
国法学	笕克彦	熊范舆	光绪三十三年	丙午社

续表

书名	作者	译者	出版年代	出版机构
宪法	清水澄	陈登山、朱德权	光绪三十四年	湖北地方自治研究社
日本宪法疏证	日本政府	载泽等	光绪三十四年	政治官书局
汉译日本议会法规	日本政府	商务印书馆编译所	光绪三十四年	商务印书馆
宪法泛论	清水澄	陈登山	光绪三十四年	湖北地方自治研究社
宪法论纲	法曹阁	陈文中	宣统元年	日本
宪法研究书	富冈康郎	吴兴让	宣统二年	商务印书馆

表8—1开列所谓"黄金十年"的汉译东文宪政书籍虽不至善完备,却已囊括当时最负盛名的日本宪法学者,素称明治维新之父的伊藤博文亦是其中翘楚。

仅凭书名也可确定,正是日本政法著作的海量涌入,最终固化了"宪法"作为"Constitution"译名的用法。同样毋庸置疑的是,这些译著由浅入深逐步阐明现代宪政制度的原理与精神实质,对清末立宪思想的发展起到巨大的推动作用。

三 余论

正是在此民智渐开、物议沸腾的背景下,清政府于光绪二十八年二月(1902年3月)颁诏:"中国律例,自汉唐以来,代有增改。我朝《大清律例》一书,折中至当,备极精详。惟是为治之道,尤贵因时制宜,今昔情势不同,非参酌适中,不能推行尽善。况近来地利日兴,商务日广,如矿律、路律、商律等类,皆应妥议专条"①,并根据袁世凯、刘坤一、张之洞等官员的举荐,派沈家本、伍廷芳主持修律馆,"将一切现行律例,按照交涉情形,参酌各国法律,悉心考订,妥为拟议,务期中外通行,有裨治理"②。从此,修订律法正式提上议事日程,"预备立宪"也将

---

① 出自《光绪二十八年壬寅二月癸巳谕军机大臣等》,详见《德宗景皇帝实录》卷四九五。《清实录》第五八册,中华书局影印,第536—537页。

② 出自《光绪二十八年壬寅夏四月丙申谕内阁》,详见《德宗景皇帝实录》卷四九八。同上书,第577页。

次第展开，为捍卫千年帝制做最后的困兽犹斗。

第三节　宪政运动蓬勃发展对选译
《英国国会史》的影响

随着"Constitution"汉译名的日益固化，分权理念亦渐入民心。20世纪最初十年，向往西方近代改革的开明知识分子前赴后继，掀起了波澜壮阔的宪政运动。这期间既包括戊戌变法后流亡日本的维新改良志士倡议君主立宪，更有孙文先生等人领导同盟会奔走呼号的民主政治革命。

社会科学院研究员雷颐曾撰文《1905：三种力量角力中国》①（2007），极具洞见地细述了他们与晚清政府间错综复杂的妥协与斗争。对比悬殊的逐鹿形态正是在光绪三十一年悄然发生质变，而《英国国会史》恰于此时编译出版，难免受到新旧意识形态冲突的深刻影响。

一　改良与革命

毋庸置疑，清末资产阶级各派人士，无论投身温和改良抑或激烈革命，均主张实施宪政，只是就何种手段、采何种政体的问题，所持观点大相径庭。

初时，革命派亦对封建王朝抱有幻想。先驱如孙中山也曾于光绪二十年（1894年）上书直隶总督兼北洋大臣李鸿章，极言"人能尽其才，地能尽其利，物能尽其用，货能畅其流"的改革措施。惜哉话不投机，失望之余方在香港成立兴中会，誓将"驱除鞑虏，恢复中国，创立合众政府"，随即密谋广州起义，却因事泄被迫流亡。

孙先生趁势遍游欧美列强，探索西方政法理论，酝酿民主、民权、民生思想，并于光绪三十一年（1905年）在日本东京创建全国性资产阶级政党——同盟会，密切联络海内外仁人，矢志不渝地颠覆封建帝制。虽星星之火，终成晚清统治的心腹大患。

相比而言，立宪派孜孜以求者，无非皇朝体制框架内的渐进式改良。其所作所为仅限策动王公贵族、封疆大吏自发变法，翘首静待君民共治的和平过渡。

---

① 该文收录在雷颐著《历史的裂缝：近代中国与幽暗人生》（2007年）。

二 日俄战争

几乎与此同时爆发的日俄战争（Russo-Japanese War）犹胜烈火烹油，确实助推了立宪民权思潮迅速席卷全国。

光绪二十九年十二月二十三日（1904 年 2 月 8 日）至三十一年五月初四日（1905 年 6 月 6 日），日俄为争夺满洲及朝鲜地区的殖民垄断利益，竟借满清龙兴之地划界交战，而势穷力蹙的清政府只能屈辱地宣布"局外中立"。

国运衰微以致生灵涂炭，当然令人备感痛心疾首。可改良派更注重的是此战结局关系"亚洲之荣落、黄白种之兴亡、专制立宪之强弱"①。"盖专制、立宪，中国之一大问题也。若俄胜日败，则我政府之意，必以为中国所以贫弱者，非宪政之不立，乃专制之未工"②。

所幸日胜俄败遂其所愿。这也是近代以来东亚黄色人种首次战胜西方白人，故被立宪议者广泛视作"非军队之竞争，乃政治之竞争"（雷颐，2007：78），并果断宣称"专制国与立宪国战，立宪国无不胜，专制国无不败"③ 实属客观真理，企盼借此说服保守的清政府改弦更张。

适逢秉承丁未上谕实施各项新政，逡巡畏缩难解内忧外患纷至沓来。有鉴于此，朝野皆以为"非立宪不足以振民心，非立宪不足以强国家"（张朋园，2007：5），已势在必行。

三 仿行宪政与选译《英国国会史》

现有文献资料表明，"国会"术语可能初现于丁韪良主持翻译的《星轺指掌》与《公法便览》。两书凡例部分对此均有述及④：

> 一、各国政式不一，有君位世传而君权无限者，有君位世传而君权有限者，二者皆谓君主之国。复有庶民公举国主，而其在位限有年数者，是谓民政之国。

---

① 详见《论立宪为万事根本》（载《南方报》1905 年 8 月 23 日）。
② 详见《论中国所受俄国之影响》（载《中外日报》1904 年 4 月 4 日）。
③ 详见《日俄战后中国所受之影响若何》（载《大公报》1905 年 4 月 13 日）。
④ 粗体由本书作者添加。

一、凡君权有限之国与民政之国，皆公举大臣，会议国政，是谓**国会**。君位虽尊，而权执往往操之于国会也。

一、凡君权无限之国，莫不设有议政院，其大臣皆由国君简派。而君权有限之国及民政之国所设**国会**，亦以议政院称之。

一、君权有限之国及民政之国，率由**国会**公议以制法，国君秉权而行法，复有专设法司以执法，而审讯不法之事者，此谓之法院或法堂。

清末宪法译著虽层出不穷，然专注国会者屈指可数。据李祝环、田涛教授所撰《清末翻译外国法学书籍评述》（2000 年）及俞江博士的《清末法学（1901—1911）书目备考》（2005 年）记载，除却光绪三十四年后刊行的《十六国议院典例》①和《德国议院章程》②，唯《英国国会史》尤引人注目。笔者以为，其选译缘由与筹备立宪的历史跨越密不可分。

（一）尊英仿日

光绪三十一年（1905 年），直隶总督袁世凯、湖广总督张之洞、两江总督周馥联名奏请"变革政体"，寄望君主立宪，缓和渐成燎原之势的反清动乱。被迫表示认可的慈禧太后亦妄图借机扑灭革命党、使朝基永固，故遣五大臣"分赴东西洋各国考求一切政治，以期择善而从"③，并设馆参酌各国政法"与中国治体相宜者"④，纂书呈送御览。

众所周知，"东西宪法宗于英国"⑤。选择《英国国会史》，正可"通英国历史、明国会发达"⑥，对"宪政之如何成立，如何变更，如何审慎，靡不周密完备，反复引申"（张謇，1994：105），故"此编宜译而版之"⑦。若问该书为何从日文本转介而非原版直译，则完全是顺应甲午以来东学兴盛的时代潮流，满拟效仿同文同种的邻邦行宪强国之捷径。

---

① 蔡文森转译自日本元老院所编《欧美各国议院典例要略》。

② 原著由德国人芬福根等撰写。

③ 详见《光绪三十一年六月十四日内阁奉上谕》。《光绪朝上谕档》第三一册，中国第一历史档案馆编，第 90 页。

④ 详见《设立考察政治馆参酌各国政法纂订成书呈进谕（光绪三十一年十月二十九日）》。《清末筹备立宪档案史料》上册，故宫博物院明清档案部编，第 43 页。

⑤ 详见《英国国会史·序》，序 2。

⑥ 详见《英国国会史·点校者序》，"点校者序"第 3 页。

⑦ 详见《英国国会史·序》，序 2。

（二）议开国会

无论如何，谕旨所示种种假象颇令时人鼓舞，积极开展国会请愿运动。诚然，晚清社会处民族危殆的边缘，"立宪"吸引民众的根本在救亡图存（雷颐，2007：78）。不过，恰似《英国国会史》汉译序文所言："国会者，宪法之基础；无国会，则日日哗然说宪法，亦将无以征其实行。"①

尽管中文译员的姓名现已湮没难考，仍能查知编辑出版该书的是翰墨林编译印书局。局如其名，乃翰林院修撰张謇所设②。由此也可推断，当时具有官商背景的近代资产阶级对宪政事宜已倍加关注。

值得钦佩的是，参与刊行者深知强国非一部宪法空文所能了事，更未惑于"立宪之制，我国今日朝野之士，所乐闻之"的盛况，反而清醒地指出"立宪以前之往迹，立宪以后之前途，其亦不能不熟思而审虑矣"③。遑论译著以史为鉴，借古讽今，将无国会难行宪政的道理娓娓述来，确有远见卓识。

（三）余论

清廷行宪只求掩人耳目，绝无还政的真心诚意。光绪三十二年七月十三日（1906年9月1日）颁旨"仿行宪政，大权统于朝廷，庶政公诸舆论，以立国家万年有道之基"④。有现代学者评论这"不仅奠定了清末制宪的基本格调，而且奠定了近现代中国宪政史的基本格调，即对于臣民或公民自由权利的漠视与束缚，君权或中央权力的刻意维护与巩固"（陶钟灵，2007：143）。但迁延至光绪三十三年（1907年），终究还是宣布筹设资政院及各省咨议局，近代国会分权的实质功能固付之阙如，却也为辛亥革命彻底破除君主专制政体奠定了民众基础。这虽非译书之全功，亦不无微劳。

---

① 详见《英国国会史·序》，序1。

② 详见《英国国会史·点校者序》，点校者序3。江苏通州（今南通市）翰墨林编译印书局是清末状元张謇于光绪二十八年（1902年）集资创办的近代出版机构，也是东南立宪派翻译刊印宪政书籍的重要阵地。

③ 详见《英国国会史·序》，序2。

④ 详见《宣示预备立宪先行厘定官制谕》。《清末筹备立宪档案史料》上册，故宫博物院明清档案部编，第44页。

四　《英国国会史》简介

《英国国会史》① 原著名为《国会简史》 (*A Short History of Parliament*)②，由英国法学家比几斯渴脱男爵 (Britiffe Constable Skottowe，Baron) 撰于 1886 年。光绪三十一年 (1905 年)，江苏翰墨林编译印书局刊行了该书汉语版，且在其后补录《近代英国政党组织沿革》并附年表两篇。

何勤华教授主编的中国近代法学译丛将《英国国会史》 (2003 年) 收录在内，其点校者刘守刚先生认定此书乃依据镰田节堂的日文本转译而成，然此说似乎尚可斟酌。

汉译序言有云："英国国会史，总二十三章，为英人比几斯渴脱所纂录，其纪近代英国政党组织沿革，别为一卷，则英人义特瓦普利脱所补著，译之者日人镰田节堂也。"③ 该句陈述的信息颇具歧义——日人所译究竟只是"别为一卷"的"补著"还是囊括全书在内？"译之"入中文抑或日语？

笔者以为，镰田节堂所作仅限《近代英国政党组织沿革》的汉译，但看《英国国会史补》卷首特意另行标注译者姓名④，当可证明其不同于该书主体部分。

另查 19 世纪末 20 世纪初，日本国译西方宪政著作中确有《英国国会史》(1899 年)，但译者是杰出的政法学者、早稻田大学 (Waseda University) 的奠基人之一高田早苗 (Takata Sanae)。⑤

请特别注意，该日文版除《国会简史》外，同样包含原著所未有的《近代英国政党组织沿革》及《英国历代诸王及重要事件年表》和《哈老

---

① 光绪三十一年 (1905 年) 翰墨林编译印书局编译版。本书所引《英国国会史》译文，除非特别说明，均出自中国政法大学出版社以该版为底本的刘守刚点校本 (2003 年)。

② 本书所引《国会简史》原文，除非特别说明，均出自 1886 年初版。

③ 详见《英国国会史·序》，序 1。

④ 详见《英国国会史补》，第 265 页。

⑤ 请读者查阅 Google 图书《英国国会史》(B. C. Skottowe 著，高田早苗译，东京专门学校出版部出版)。[2013/8/14]（http://books.google.co.jp/books? ei = DHwLUrOmIMnZigfLhoGwBA&hl = zh-CN&id = TReRDVqhye8C&dq = % E8% 8B% B1% E5% 9B% BD% E5% 9B% BD% E4% BC% 9A% E5% 8F% B2 + % E9% AB% 98% E7% 94% B0% E6% 97% A9% E8% 8B% 97&q = % E6% 94% BF% E5% 85% 9A#search_ anchor）。

巴尔王朝首相年表》。鉴于中、日译本在书名、补录、附件等方面的高度相似性，我们有理由认为高田早苗的译文即便不是翰墨林版的蓝本，至少也是编译者的重要参考文献。

无论如何，《英国国会史》在清季筹备立宪伊始由华人独自编译，较之此前洋务运动期间的《佐治刍言》（1885 年）① 及民国肇基近二十年后的《英宪精义》（1930 年）②，表现出迥然有异的鲜明特色。

《佐治刍言》由傅兰雅口译、应祖锡笔述英国人约翰·希尔·伯顿（John Hill Burton，1809 – 1881）所撰钱伯斯教育丛书（*Chambers' Educational Course*）之《政治经济学》（*Political Economy*，1852）③；《英宪精义》（1935 年）则由雷沛鸿先生研译英国法学教授戴雪（A. V. Darcy）所撰《英吉利宪法的初步研究》（第八版）（*Introduction to the Study of the Law of the Constitution*（8th *Edition*），1915)④。或因意识形态局限，前者颇有偷梁换柱之嫌而后者不乏添砖加瓦之举。

本章后续数节将对上述三种译文进行比较，期望能够更有说服力地揭示社会场域在翻译活动中发挥的直接作用，即但凡历史进程中影响深远的译作，均是顺应时代要求的改写。

第四节　改头换面——《英国国会史》

自西法东渐伊始，华洋译者为适应晚清时期国内外意识形态冲突及权力博弈的需要，任意改写原著内容的做派行之已久，前文探讨的《各国律例》、《万国公法》、《公法便览》、《各国交涉公法论》及《各国交涉便法论》等均无例外。当然，《英国国会史》亦是如此，且与其前后问世的《佐治刍言》和《英宪精义》相比，别具特色。

《国会简史》初撰时距英伦立宪已垂两世纪，各项政治制度与传统定型久矣，非但宪政意识深入人心，还成为世界各国争相效法的典范。据其

---

① 本书所引《佐治刍言》译文，除非特别说明，均出自光绪十一年（1885 年）江南制造总局刊本，并参照上海书店出版社以该版为底本的叶斌点校本（2002 年）。

② 本书所引《英宪精义》译文，除非特别说明，均出自民国二十四年（1935 年）商务印书馆初版。

③ 本书所引《政治经济学》原文，除非特别说明，均出自 1852 年初版。

④ 本书所引《英吉利宪法的初步研究》原文，除非特别说明，均出自 1915 年第八版。

序言所述，作者著书目的不在立说，而是希望为学习宪法者编写一部生动活泼的教材：

> The object with which it was written was the hope of imparting a certain amount of life to the dry bones which are strewn in the way of the constitutional student, and of combining instruction with a certain amount of amusement. [1]

对此，汉译者了然于胸，原作自序中文版足可佐证："窃谓从来学我国宪法者，多苦干燥无味，故余著此书，欲加以有趣味之事迹，使学者不倦。"[2]

而翰墨林译本刊行在光绪末年，席卷神州大地的立宪之议方兴未艾。草创期间众说纷纭，如何筹划尚待摸索。译介者借古讽今的意图昭然若揭，唯愿爱国志士能从中汲取教训，领悟宪政的真谛：

> 吾今有一言，请为读者正告焉：观第二章之所纪，则知建设一事之前，必有种种之困难也；观第六、第七章之所纪，则知反动力有甚于原动力也；观第十二、第十三章之所纪，则知立宪之流弊，亦易趋于专制政体也……观第十七章之所纪，则知政党之意见，先必发宣于；论辩也；其他如内阁制度之设立，国会之改革，皆可以借镜而审变者。……爱国忧时之彦，幸观览焉。[3]

为将颇具兴味的教科书改写成更严谨周致的政法著作，译文的表述至少在两个重要方面有意无意地操纵了底本：削教材课本的学究气质、删无关宏旨的细节修辞。

一 削教材课本的学究气质

原著《国会简史》具备教科书的显性特征。首章破题之际，比氏

---

[1] 原文摘录自《国会简史》之 "Preface to *A Short History of Parliament*"，p. III。

[2] 译文摘录自《英国国会史自序》。

[3] 详见《英国国会史·序》，序 2。

谈及研习英国国会发展史的重要价值，毫不犹豫地使用了"study"、"student"等有着明确导向的字眼，开宗明义地将目标读者锁定为学生。

原文①：

It possesses therefore a curious interest, not merely for those who desire to study the most important and most interesting branch of the history of their country, but also for the intelligent historical student of every age and race.

反观译文，貌合神离。不仅类似措辞消失殆尽，且论述角度与原文大异其趣，单纯强调自身的普遍阅读意义，无形中将潜在读者群拓展为任何有志于宪政的"爱国忧时之彦"。

译文②：

故欲通英国历史之要目，且得其趣味者，无出此书之右矣。

尽管有时编译本放弃的几乎是整句，但更多情况下，仅部分结构被选择性削改，特别是包含"explain"、"account for"等学究气息浓重的枝节文字。精简后保留下来的紧凑语篇以更确定无疑的口吻陈述相关史实，毋庸纠结其背面可能匿藏的偶然或必然因素。

原文③：

The first difficulty which confronts us is to account satisfactorily for the preference obviously given to Westminster, from the time of Edward I. , as the meeting-place of Parliament, and still more to explain the cause of its gradual restriction to Westminster alone.

---

① 原文摘录自《国会简史》第一章"FORMATION OF PARLIAMENT"第一节"*Folk-moots and Witena-gemots*"，p. 2。

② 译文摘录自《英国国会史》第一章"国会设立"第一节"庶民会议及贤人会议"，第1页。

③ 原文摘录自《国会简史》第二章"THE FORMATION OF PARLIAMENTARY GOVERNMENT"第二节"*Internal Details*"，p. 18。下划线由本书作者添加。

译文①：

国会开设之地，自义特瓦一世之时，多设于威斯脱明士塔，后遂定于此地。

另外，表现信息发送者与接收者超文本互动的话语标记亦被译者悉数剔除。譬如原作结束段落的汉译，若套用"看官"之类称呼，则难免白话演义之嫌。

原文②：

Reader, my task is ended.

译文③：

余所著之国会史，于是乎终。

二　删无关宏旨的细节修辞

原著作者为扭转宪法教材枯燥乏味的传统印象，将关键史实与海量趣闻有机结合起来，并尝试着在字里行间灌注勃勃生机，典型特征即普遍使用多样性、多元化的修辞结构，尤其是通过隐喻和设问，渲染语篇的故事性与文学色彩。

反观译文，删改幅度的确蔚为可观，但这正是其"出彩之处"——"内容详略得到，史实裁剪合理"④。排除相当部分原可直译的冗长细节与

---

① 译文摘录自《英国国会史》第二章"国会政治之设立"第二节"国会内部事情"，第14页。

② 原文摘录自《国会简史》第二十三章"PARLIAMENTARY DEVELOPMENT"第三节"*The House of Commons*"，p. 336。下划线由本书作者添加。

③ 译文摘录自《英国国会史》第二十三章"国会政治之设立"第三节"庶民院"，第264页。

④ 详见《英国国会史·点校者序》，"点校者序"第2页。尽管未明言其所指究竟是译文还是原文，但刘守刚点校本《英国国会史》中多处脚注表明再版时未能对照英文版。譬如该书第十九章"国会改革"第二节"改革讨论"针对"而威灵吞候，则痛反对之"一句提供了以下注释："原文如此，今作'侯'。另，据上下文，似为'公'更准确"（2002：220）。其实，原著明确无误地写道："The Duke of Wellington spoke strongly against the measure"（Skottowe，1886：265）。若有底本在手，称为"公"，根本不必根据上下文推断。故笔者大胆推测刘先生的评语针对的是译文。

过度修辞后，非但事实陈述直入主题，语气亦更为庄重，极大地方便了对英国历史所知有限的读者，贴近国会制度发展的坎坷及其反映的精神实质。

（一）冗长细节

原文①：

Simon de Montfort, the second son of the Simon de Montfort <u>renowned in the Albigensian Crusade, was by accident of birth a foreigner</u>, though descended in the female line from English nobles. The elder Simon had inherited from his mother certain claims to the English earldom of Leicester, <u>which by special arrangement</u> were transmitted to his second son. During his early career the younger Simon <u>gave little promise of fulfilling the part of patriot and statesman which he subsequently assumed.</u>

译文②：

西门特蒙脱福尔脱，其母为英国贵族。初西门之兄受英国来斯塔伯之领有权于其母，后让之西门。西门少时，初不见其才学过人。

值得注意的是，冗长细节的摒弃不止正文比比皆是，早在序言部分就已付诸实践，譬如有关国会腐败的早期证据就未见于汉译本③，以免授人口实。

---

① 原文摘录自《国会简史》第一章 "FORMATION OF PARLIAMENT" 第二节 "*Simon de Montfort*"，p. 6。下划线由本书作者添加。

② 译文摘录自《英国国会史》第一章 "国会设立" 第二节 "西门特蒙脱福尔脱"，第5页。

③ 原文摘录自《国会简史》之 "Preface to *A Short History of Parliament*"，pp. III - IV。序言中包含以下段落：I am indebted to the kindness of Sir George Sitwell for a very early illustration of parliamentary corruption—an isolated evidence but sufficiently pregnant of meaning. Extract from the will of Nicholas Stathum, Esq., of Morley, co. Derby, dated 15, July, 1472. and proved on the fifth of August in the same year in the prerogative court Canterbury. "Item, I received 10s. of... Bemont a worshipful Squier of the West Country by the hands of Page in the last Parleament. I did nothing there... and if I did, it is against my conscience for so moche as I was one of the Parleament and should be indifferent in every matter of the Parleament, I will he have it ageyne."

（二）过度修辞

1. 比喻

原文①：

Deprived of their leaders they were helpless; nor was it till they learned to follow the lead of the king that they emerged again from <u>the pathless slough in which they were plunged</u>.

译文②：

盖庶民院者，既失贵族之指导，则不能为一事也。其后庶民院得再恢复元气者，亦由国王之指导使然耳。

2. 设问

原文③：

What was Parliament itself like? is a question which must often have occurred to our readers.

需要说明的是，适当保留修辞的情形亦非绝无仅有，毕竟在叙事过程中运用描述性语言在所难免，这与纯理论著作差距颇为明显。

原文④：

. . . and added another quarter of a century to <u>the long sleep</u> of Parliament.

---

① 原文摘录自《国会简史》第三章 "PERSONAL GOVERNMENT" 第一节 *"The New Monarchy"*，p. 25。下划线由本书作者添加。

② 译文摘录自《英国国会史》第三章 "国王亲政" 第一节 "新兴君主政体"，第21页。

③ 原文摘录自《国会简史》第十四章 "INNER LIFE OF PARLIAMENT IN THE EIGHTEEN CENTURY"，p. 189。

④ 原文摘录自《国会简史》第三章 "PERSONAL GOVERNMENT" 第一节 *"The New Monarchy"*，p. 25。下划线由本书作者添加。

译文①:

是以二十五年间，国会<u>全结长夜之梦，如陷死境</u>。

三 余论

上述案例只是冰山一角，然译介者的操纵意图已浮出水面，操纵效果更是有目共睹。原著作为充斥奇闻异事的生动教材，和缓地流淌着某种探究学问的互动语气；而经编译的汉语文本抛却了冗长细节与过度修辞，论述口吻自信、沉稳且严谨，毋庸置疑的精炼语言紧扣主题，更易为急于探索救亡图存之捷径的爱国人士留下深刻烙印。这岂非正是在百家争鸣中力求独树一帜所期望的？

尽管如此，《英国国会史》的改写主要停留于文体层面，比较洋务时期"偷梁换柱"或民国时期"添砖加瓦"的西法译著，充其量也只能算是"改头换面"而已。

第五节 偷梁换柱——《佐治刍言》

鉴于本章关注宪法领域，仅以《佐治刍言》作参照并不为过，此乃洋务运动期间唯一系统探讨国政的译著。显而易见的是，该书并未介绍原作最后的四章五十八节，包括"商业震荡"（Commercial Convulsions）、"论积累和消费"（Accumulation and Expenditure）、"论意外保险"（Insurance Against Calamities）、"论税收"（Taxes）等，这至少部分原因是考虑到在封建王朝体制内探讨这些资本主义成熟期的议题为时尚早，无异于天方夜谭。

该书2002年再版时，点校者叶斌先生评说译文"每一节的内容，大多没有按照底本逐字逐句翻译，而是根据中文习惯，调整了原文语序，叙述大体意思。"② 笔者以为此言差矣。改写译文绝非只为迁就"中文习惯"，叙述的"大体意思"较原本亦相去甚远。譬如译者未将大清国置身"半文明国家"（a country partly civilised）的行列，以免触怒目的文化社

---

① 译文摘录自《英国国会史》第三章"国王亲政"第一节"新兴君主政体"，第21页。下划线由本书作者添加。

② 详见《佐治刍言·点校说明》，第2页。

会精英阶层，这就是典型案例：

原文①：

In all savage nations it is customary to leave such objects to be tram-
pled on and cast aside by their stronger brethren; in some, they are at
once put to death; even in a country partly civilised, like China, this is a
common practice.

译文②：

乃野人不明此理，遇有此种婴儿，生出时即抛弃荒僻之处，听其
饿死，或用水淹死，或用别法死之，此诚野人中之恶习也。间有文教
之处如中国等，亦不免此陋。

特别是原书探讨政府组织方式的章节③涉足宪法、国会等诸多领域，
而译作在信仰自由、言论自由、开启明智、改良与革命等问题上变更颇
多，屡屡掺入己见。

1. 信仰自由

原文④：

The emperor of Russia is the most powerful despot in the world, and
his people reverence him more as a god than a man; yet they have peculiar
customs and superstitions with which he could not meddle with safety, and
more than one of his predecessors fell a victim to his plans for the improvement of the Russian people.

译文⑤：

然亦有偏信教门，于国政不无龃龉者，俄王不敢认真办理。尝有

---

① 原文摘录自《政治经济学》之 "ORIGINE OF GOVERNMENT" 第 66 节，p. 21。
② 译文摘录自《佐治刍言》第九章 "论国政之根源" 第六十六节，第 33 页。
③ 即《政治经济学》之 "DIFFERENT KINDS OF GOVERNMENT"，随后四例中的下划线均
由本书作者添加。
④ 原文摘录自《政治经济学》之 "DIFFERENT KINDS OF GOVERNMENT" 第 73 节，
p. 24。
⑤ 译文摘录自《佐治刍言》第十章 "论国政分类" 第七十三节，第 37 页。

数国，其国王欲更变风俗，百姓不服，反受其害。

2. 言论自由

原文①：

It admits of great personal liberty, with liberty of public discussion, because it knows that this freedom of action and speech will not be abused—that, in all circumstances, the law will be respected. It is impossible to conceive a state of things more rational than this—a firm but temperate government, a people knowing their rights and duties, but abstaining from violence, and rectifying abuses only through means authorized by the constitution.

译文②：

故除国政内应行禁止外，百姓之事大半听其自主，即国政亦准民间公议，登诸新闻纸上，以备采择。盖政事虽经国家极力斟酌，究不能无百密一疏之虑，故一令之出，可任民间议论，其中果有不恰舆情之处，亦不妨重加损益，务归至当。若能如是，则百姓向服愈深，国家亦无事刑驱势迫之劳矣。

3. 开启民智

原文③：

We find that in American, education has taken the form of a political necessity. It might be considered equally so in some European countries, with a view to governmental changes which must sooner or later take place.

---

① 原文摘录自《政治经济学》之 "DIFFERENT KINDS OF GOVERNMENT" 第 77 节，p. 25。

② 译文摘录自《佐治刍言》第十章 "论国政分类" 第七十七节，第 38 页。

③ 原文摘录自《政治经济学》之 "DIFFERENT KINDS OF GOVERNMENT" 第 79 节，p. 26。

译文①：

惟美国深知此事紧要，故国中各处设立学塾，令民女，皆照产业亩数，一律书捐。现在欧洲之国，虽未改为民主，然各国所立公学堂亦已不少。<u>近来又有数国设立章程，勒令民间子弟入学读书，每年内以肄业若干日，为最少之限，若年终不满其数则罚其父兄。</u>

4. 支持改良，反对革命

原文②：

It is therefore well for a people, when they can effect needful reforms and improvements in their government, without resorting to violent or extreme measures.

译文③：

可见各国有国政不妥之处，即欲更改，亦须与国家婉转商办，万不可猝然作乱，至鼎革后祸乱迭出。<u>盖革除弊政本非易事，必须渐渐更张，方为妥善。</u>

信仰自由关系宗教传播，言论自由关系新闻出版，开启民智关系兴办学校，此三项事业都是寓华洋人推进文化殖民的朝思暮想，故依据目标社会意识形态的现实状况量体裁衣，改写译文势在必行。

译著时而泛化，譬如例（1）谈信仰自由，将俄王遭遇铺排成数国教训；时而具化，譬如例（2）谈言论自由，专指新闻纸沟通朝野之功效；时而偷换内容，譬如例（3）刻意疏远近代教育与民主政治的密切联系，取而代之的是兴办学校的方法途径。换言之，译文将其介绍的西方政治措施蒙上普世性的面纱，总是强调有利清廷巩固统治的因素，尽量回避削弱王朝专制权力的可能性，这就不难理解为什么例（4）译文一味倾向改良，对暴力革命嗤之以鼻。

---

① 译文摘录自《佐治刍言》第十章"论国政分类"第七十九节，第39—40页。
② 原文摘录自《政治经济学》之"DIFFERENT KINDS OF GOVERNMENT"第81节，p. 27。
③ 译文摘录自《佐治刍言》第十章"论国政分类"第八十一节，第41页。

梁启超《读西学书法》云："《佐治刍言》言立国之理及人所当为之事，凡国与国相处、人与人相处之道悉备焉，皆用几何公论探本穷源，论政治最通之书。"① 可见这类当时仍甚为罕见的西学译著对知识界产生的深远影响，以致清季立宪派多鄙薄革命党之破坏性，未曾想他们正因无路进言，逼不得已方才揭竿而起，其所作所为与原著之论并行不悖——"不诉诸暴力或其他极端措施便能实施亟需的政治改良"（they can effect needful reforms and improvements in their government, without resorting to violent or extreme measures），当然是民族幸事；如若不然，流血牺牲亦在所难免。

毋庸置疑，这种动辄"偷梁换柱"的东渐方式，顶戴西文原著的权威光环，悄无声息地灌输着译者本人沟通社会多元异质因素的思维逻辑，通过操纵目标读者对西方政法制度的理解与领悟，深入干预晚清精英群体的意识形态发展，并由此扭曲权力博弈的进程。

第六节 添砖加瓦——《英宪精义》

《英宪精义》初版于民国二十四年（1935 年），雷沛鸿先生（字宾南，1888—1967）在其序言中专门论述了自己的翻译观及其实践方式，这恰是剖析该书如何削改原著《英吉利宪法的初步研究》最完美的框架，故全文引录如下：

> 著书是一件难事；译书亦是一件难事。著作的困难，尽人皆知，我无庸赘论。至于译述的困难，依译者所有经验说来，不但是在于明澈地索解原书所有词旨，与忠实地传达原书所有文义，而且在于能体会著者的思想行动，与能表现著者的整个人格。根据这种理想，在未执笔作汉译之前，译者已下了许多工夫，务求有所以领略英宪的性质，复求有所以会悟著者的研究方法和精神。而在汉译之际，译者不但于译本每章之首加入全章纲要，每章之末加入解义若干条，而且于译本首册，冠以导言，又于译本末册，缀以著者传略。然而在此际仍

---

① 详见《西学书目表四卷附读西学书法一卷》，光绪丙申（1896 年）冬十月质学会用时务报馆本重校付刊。

有鳃鳃过虑者一事，即是：诚恐有志未逮，力不从心，译本遂不免有许多错误处，亦有许多漏处。于是，提正工夫不能不求之大雅君子。①

显然，亲身体验已明白无误地告知雷先生，译述之难不囿于源语文本，更在文本外的多元异质因素，须据以揣度"著者的思想行动"；也正为展现其领悟"著者的整个人格"，特意添附原书所未见的诸项要件——卷首导言、卷尾传略、章前纲要、章末解义。

一 卷首导言和卷尾传略
——对英宪褒中带贬、对戴雪推崇备至

雷沛鸿先生将译作"冠以导言"，这是很有意思的改写行为。清季民初时期东渐的西方政法类书籍，或编撰译者序言乃至凡例数款，却罕见系统引领读者阅览的阐释性文字，更非学术译著的普遍惯例，况且英文版原本随附导言及全书纲领（Outline of Subject）。

（一）原著导言：补充宪学新发展

起初原著并无导言，而是自"宪法观"（View of Constitution）着手，通过诠释英宪名称及其内涵，勘定宪法学的研究范畴，并以此为提纲挈领之开篇。直至第八版（1915 年），考虑到"修改太过频繁，不但原有文学的意味不免损失过半，而且原有专著的研究精神不免摧残至极"，故决意"保留原书第七版本有面目，惟于书首冠以导言一篇"。

实际上，戴雪撰写导言的宗旨在比较研究，"即以运行于 1884 年之宪法比较现存 1914 年之宪法，而加以研究。由这番工夫，30 年来所有法律与公意的错综变化庶几可以综合观察"。②

---

① 详见《英宪精义·译者序》，第 9—10 页。

② 以上所引三处译文均出自《英宪精义·导言》，第 1 页。附录《英吉利宪法的初步研究》原文如下："Recurring alterations destroy the original tone and spirit of any treatise which has the least claim to belong to the literature of England. The present edition, therefore, of the *Law of the Constitution* is in substance a reprint of the seventh edition; it is however accompanied by this new Introduction whereof the aim is to compare our constitution as it stood and worked in 1884 with the constitution as it now stands in 1914. It is thus possible to take a general view of the development of the constitution during a period filled with many changes both of law and of opinion." (Darcy, 1915: xxxv – xxxvi)

正因如此,作者首先述及正文致力诠释的三项原则,包括(A)巴力门主权(the Sovereignty of Parliament)、(B)法律主治(the Rule of Law)、(C)宪法与宪典(the Law and the Conventions of the Constitution),然后才将目光转向"新宪思想"(New Constitutional Ideas)。

(二)译者导言:关注英宪特征与研究方法

综上所述,原作已充分考虑到论著的专业性与时代变迁,并为读者提供必要的背景知识。与之相比,译者另行撰写导言又有何特殊性呢?

雷先生曾留学欧美,引用哈佛大学门禄教授(Prof. W. B. Munro)的名言:"自由政制的治术是盎格鲁诺尔曼种族对于世界文明的最大贡献"①,强调英宪的重要历史地位顺理成章。

译者导言的前半部分着眼社会学角度,概述英宪的四大特征——"第一样是软性;第二样是守旧精神;第三样是继续性;第四样是名实相违性。"② 其中,特别值得注意的是"名实相违性",借安生(W. R. Anson)的话说:"因此之故,英宪在实际上只是一种畸形发展的制度……所以古制遗俗早成陈迹而不合时宜者,往往仍保留于现代。其结果是:在英宪中不但理论与事实不能时时一致;而且法律与典训不免左右参差。"③ 这与戴雪认为"世界各国亦多采巴力门政治(即代议政制),但惟有英国的巴力门政治运行自如、充满活力"④ 的观点颇有出入。

类似负面评价在前清倡议君主立宪之际闻所未闻,正体现了历经辛亥革命、复辟帝制、军阀割据、北伐战争等风云突变后方才确立共和制度的社会时代特征。

译者导言的后半部分则是对原著研究方法的描写,推崇戴雪立说"自成一家言",旨在弥补历史、法律、政治等诸派研究之不足。

这与卷尾所附著者略传的记述遥相呼应。或者说,记述著者生平事迹正为说明戴雪何以能循科学途径阐释"英吉利法律中最复杂的一部分治理,使之成为有系统的研究,而且能发挥其所有义蕴,与解证之以实例及

---

① 详见《英宪精义·译者导言》,第11页。
② 同上书,第23页。
③ 同上。
④ 详见《英宪精义·中文再版序文》,第6页。该序文由中央财经大学法学院戚渊教授撰写,载于中国法制出版社2001年版。

成案"①，"以为中国读者明白了解原书著者的思想行动之一助"②。

二 章前纲要

雷先生在序言中自谓"每章之首加入全章纲要"，此事颇为蹊跷。查民国二十四年商务印书馆初版，及2001年中国法制出版社中文再版，除技术性处理外，内容一般无异，并未见其所说各章"纲要"。只是译本的部分章节附有类似简介的文字，譬如首章的宗旨③：

> 自法律视察点立论，英国政治制度所有主要特性就是巴力门的主权。因此之故，郑重提示与反复申明此一要旨实为吾书之开宗明义。

第一节 宗旨

> 于是在本章中，我的审问所及约为三事：其一，我要解明何为巴力门主权，并要昭示此项主权的存在是一件法律的事实，久经英吉利法律明明承认。其二，我要证实世间所盛传的法律制限之加于巴力门者无一有真际的存在于英国。其三，我要解答在讨论题义时所遇之疑问，即以辨明巴力门在不列颠宪法之下，实是一所绝对之主权立法机关。

其余章节也将此称为"意旨"（譬如第二、三、十、十二章首节）或"引论"（譬如第四、八、九、十三、十四章首节），但无论"意旨"还是"引论"，绝非译者别出心裁，而皆本其渊源。

请读者详察原著开篇④：

> The sovereignty of Parliament is（from a legal point of view）the dominant characteristic of our political institutions.
> My aim in this chapter is, in the first place, to explain the nature of

---

① 详见《英宪精义·戴雪先生略传》，第713页。

② 详见《英宪精义·译者序》，第9页。

③ 译文摘录自《英宪精义》第一篇"巴力门的主权"第一章"巴力门主权的性质"，第133页。

④ 原文摘录自《英格兰宪法的初步研究》第 I 部分 "The Sovereignty of Parliament" 第 I 章 "The Nature of Parliamentary Sovereignty"，p. 3。

Parliamentary sovereignty and to show that is existence its a legal fact, fully recognized by the law of England; in the next place, to prove that none of the alleged legal limitations on the sovereignty of Parliament have any existence; and, lastly, to state and meet certain speculative difficulties which hinder the ready admission of the doctrine that Parliament is, under the British constitution, an absolutely sovereign legislature.

上述两段文字位于该章首节"NATURE OF PARLIAMENTARY SOVE-REIGNTY"前,且附注侧标题"Aim of Chapter",显然作者旨在概述章节大意。将之比照笔者所引译作,应当说内容几乎是没有差别的。完全出自雷先生手笔的也许仅"因此之故,郑重提示与反复申明此一要旨实为吾书之开宗明义"。

但也不能就这样认定译者完全无所作为,其改写更多表现在将原著大部分篇章的类似文字单列成节,明确地引导目标读者解析中文本。尤需注意的是,另有篇幅较短的数章原本未分节,而译作绝非东施效颦。这至少在一定程度上,降低了论述的艰难深奥。

三 章末解义

雷先生的作品常被推崇为"研译"①,原因之一即在各章末尾罗列原著注释外,另行增添数目不等的解义。

表8—2　　　　　雷译《英宪精义》各章解义条目数列表

导言	解义 10 条
全书纲要	解义 6 条
第一章	解义 24 条
第二章	解义 6 条
第三章	解义 4 条
第四章	解义 11 条
第五章	解义 12 条
第六章	解义 14 条

---

① 详见《英宪精义·中文再版序文》,第12页。

续表

第七章	解义 2 条
第八章	解义 2 条
第九章	解义 1 条
第十章	解义 6 条
第十一章	解义 1 条
第十二章	解义 10 条
第十三章	解义 4 条
第十四章	解义 9 条
第十五章	解义 4 条

就类型而言，雷氏的解义似可作以下区分：

（一）提示背景的解义

Ⅰ　杰出人物

按，布雅克名（Edmund），生于 1729 年，死于 1797 年，为十八世纪中最伟大的英吉利政治思想家。他的全集第一次出现于 1827 年，第二次加入信札一门，都成八册，出版时为 1852 年。①

Ⅱ　经典名著

按，法律与公意互为因果，其间所有错综变化，戴雪先生尝就英格兰的实际经验，著成专论，题曰："法律与公意在十九世纪中之英格兰所有关系。"该书在同类研究中允称杰作。②

Ⅲ　历史事件

按，南堤法令（Edit de Notes）为法国君主亨利四世（Henri Ⅳ）所颁布，时在 1598 年，此法令的主旨是要给予新教徒以信仰自由。

---

① 摘录自《英宪精义·导言》解 6，第 98 页。
② 摘录自《英宪精义·导言》解 3，第 97 页。

迫至 1685 年路易十四世将该法令撤回。他的用意是要顺从法国大多
数人民（即旧教教徒）的宗教感情，而思有所以压服占国民少数的
新教教徒。故戴雪有此等议论。①

　　毫无疑问，背景知识的介绍构成了译者解义的主体内容，这符合原著
针对的英伦学术界远较译文读者更熟悉欧洲社会历史文化的现实状况。但
雷先生在运用补偿策略的同时，亦融合了自己的阐述性评论，因而戚渊教
授称这些解义"集译者的丰富知识、超常智慧与科学精神于一体，实为
同类汉译著作所罕见"②。前文所引数条已见端倪，下例则更能说明问题：

　　　　按，七年巴力门法案的成立原因有两端：其一防止雅各党人恢复
詹姆士第三的王位运动；其二继续民党（the Whigs）所持实施民权
政策。参考格林所著《英国人民历史》，第 8 卷，第四章，汉奴弗
王室。

（二）点拨读者的解义

I　如何理解本书已经详述的特定问题

　　　　按，1911 年巴力门法案，在英吉利宪法史上占据重要位置，学
者须就历史方面考察其前因后果，方能领会个中所有重大意义，方能
欣赏著者在本篇导言中及在附录书后中所有语重心长之论旨，参考
（1）Gilbert Slater The Making of Modern England；（2）Lowell，《英格
兰的政治》，第二十二章。③

II　如何理解本书未及详述的特定问题

　　　　按，裁判官所造的法律构成英美法系的重要成分，故戴雪有如此
郑重提示。徒以此旨非题义所包含，著者遂不于此地详论，只得列举

---

① 摘录自《英宪精义》第一章（解 21），第 180 页。
② 详见《英宪精义·中文再版序文》，第 14 页。
③ 摘录自《英宪精义·导言》解 4，第 97 页。

两书于注 2，以供读者参考。惟该两书俱系英文本，译者恐有不便之感，请介绍下书：

> 滂恩著，雷沛鸿译，（以后引用或简称雷译），《法学肄言》（商务印书馆版）第 70 至 71 页，及第 2 页。①

如果说融合了译者评述的背景知识仍属潜移默化，点拨读者认知关键议题的解义，则可算是直接干预译文的理解，尤其还趁势反复数度推荐另一部雷译名著《法学肄言》（商务印书馆版）。尽管当时可供研习的汉译英美法律作品选择余地相对有限，却也因此方才极大地增强了译者对译文及读者的操控。

（三）译文表述的解义

解义内最有意思的还是译者对中文表述的说明，主要涉及关键法学术语及复杂法律条文。

Ⅰ 关键术语

> （1）按，巴力门一名，原来自 parler la ment 数字，汉译"说出心事"，在寻常会话中概指贵族院及众民院。故云。②
>
> 拉丁语
>
> （2）按，自然法律在英语为 law of nature，来自拉丁语 jus naturale，素无一定界说。但依法家的普通解释，他是一种规则，审判员自理性中抽绎得来；他有时可参合适用以判断人的行为究竟合法与否。参考雷译《法学肄言》第 26 页。③

法学术语的解义始于标注英语或拉丁语原文，这在译本正文中亦是屡见不鲜，譬如导言部分首次提及"巴力门"（Parliament）、"非直道"（injustice）、"官治"（bureaucracy）、"官府化"（officialized）、"司法化"（judicialized）、"国家的役吏"（functionaries）等新造词汇总是英汉文并举。仅关键性的普通法术语，方有解义注录译者的诠释。

---

① 摘录自《英宪精义》第一章（解 2），第 176 页。
② 摘录自《英宪精义》第一章（解 1），第 176 页。
③ 摘录自《英宪精义》第一章（解 16），第 179 页。

Ⅱ　复杂条文

（3）按，下文为巴力门法案之一节条文；全节在原文中计有 293 字，并以一节为一语句。就文法论，他是一句极冗长的复叠句。若用**直译**法译成汉语，这一条文的法理决不可通。因此之故，译者特将原文分析，然后**译意**；译文务求词意显达，并不失法理的本义。①

（4）按，殖民地法律效力法案为本书所称引者共有第二、第三、第四、及第五节；其中以第四节的文义最为复杂，又最难索解。译者初时原欲将其条文**直译**，以至易稿凡四次，仍不能当意。其后卒以直译所得的字句不但不能使文义明晰，而且转滋混淆，故改作**意译**。译完，复取两种译稿互勘，自知在词意间彼此大有出入；但一以原文与两者比对，则见后者实较前者能达意。于是最后乃决定采用后者。译事之难，于此可见一斑。②

正如以上两例所示，法律条文的解义始终在直译和意译间徘徊，雷先生的矛盾心态很值得玩味：信与达，孰轻孰重？若考虑中欧符号体系的巨大差异，非但逐字翻译无从谈起，即便短语、句法结构也难亦步亦趋地保留。故而纵览全书，目光所及无非阐释性翻译的痕迹。

原文③：

The principle of Parliamentary sovereignty means neither more nor less than this, namely, that Parliament thus defined has, under the English constitution, the right to make or unmake any law whatever, and, further, that no person or body is recognized by the law of England as having a right to override or set aside the legislation of Parliament.

---

① 摘录自《英宪精义》第一章（解 7），第 177 页。粗体由本书作者添加。
② 摘录自《英宪精义》第二章（解 2），第 224—225 页。粗体由本书作者添加。
③ 原文摘录自《英格兰宪法的初步研究》第 I 部分 "The Sovereignty of Parliament" 第 I 章 "The Nature of Parliamentary Sovereignty" 之 "NATURE OF PARLIAMENTARY SOVEREIGNTY"，pp. 3 - 4。下划线由本书作者添加。

译文①：

巴力门的本义既得，巴力门主权究为何物自可不烦言而索解：即
是，具有上方界说的巴力门在英宪之下，可以造法，亦可以毁法；而
且四境之内，无一人复无一团体能得到英格兰的法律之承认，使其有
权利以撤回或弃置巴力门的立法。是为巴力门主权的原理所有真谛，
不能增多亦不能减少。

译者根据自己对原文的理解重组语篇，这在《英宪精义》中可谓比比皆是，却从未觉有提供解义的必要。可见令其难以排遣的唯独法条。譬如解义例（3）所指长达"293 字，并以一节为一语句"的王位继承法条文。

原文②：

That if any person or persons shall maliciously, advisedly, and di-
rectly by writing or printing maintain and affirm that our sovereign lady the
Queen that now is, is not the lawful and rightful Queen of these realms, or
that the pretended Prince of Wales, who now styles himself King of Great
Britain, or King of England, by the name of James the Third, or King of
Scotland, by the name of James the Eighth, hath any right or title to the
Crown of these realms, or that any person or persons hath or have any right
or title to the same, otherwise than according to an Act of Parliament made
in England in the first year of the reign of their late Majesties King William
and Queen Mary, of ever blessed and glorious memory, intituled, An Act
declaring the rights and liberties of the subject, and settling the succession
of the Crown; and one other Act made in England in the twelfth year of the
reign of his said late Majesty King William the Third, intituled, An Act
for the further limitation of the Crown, and better securing the rights and
liberties of the subject; and the Acts lately made in England and Scotland

────────────────────

① 译文摘录自《英宪精义》第一篇"巴力门的主权"第一章"巴力门主权的性质"第二节"何为巴力门主权"，第 134 页。下划线由本书作者添加。

② 原文摘录自《英格兰宪法的初步研究》第 I 部分"The Sovereignty of Parliament"第 I 章"The Nature of Parliamentary Sovereignty"之"NATURE OF PARLIAMENTARY SOVEREIGNTY"，p. 6。下划线由本书作者添加。

mutually for the union of the two kingdoms; or the Kings or Queens of this realm, with and by the authority of Parliament, are not able to make laws and statutes of sufficient force and validity to limit and bind the Crown, and the descent, limitation, inheritance, and government thereof; every such person or persons shall be guilty of high treason, and being thereof lawfully convicted, shall be adjudged traitors, and shall suffer pains of death, and all losses and forfeitures as in cases of high treason.

译文①：

任何人，或任何团体中之若干个人，敢有包藏祸心，主使的，或直接的，用文字或印刷品作下列各项之煽惑，均犯叛逆大罪。此项罪名一经法院依法定谳，即处死刑，并受籍没财产与褫夺权利，一如他种叛逆大罪所受刑罚。煽惑项目条例如下：

（1）主张及断定我们的现代君后（Our sovereignty lady the Queen that now is）不应依法继承大业；

（2）主张及断定方今流亡在外面自命本已为大不列颠之伪王，或自号为英格兰之王而袭用詹姆士第三之名号，或自为苏格兰之王而袭用詹姆士第八之名号的伪王嗣，应有权利以统治全国；

（3）不遵历次巴力门的法案所规定，有如下列各案：

（a）当前王威廉与前后美莉（Queen Mary）初来英国即王位之第一年，巴力门曾在英国建立一法案，并正名为'宣布人民权利与自由及确定君主继统法案'；

（b）当前王威廉第三在位之第十二年，巴力门复在英国建立一法案，并定名为'再决限制君权及推广人民权利与自由法案'；

（c）又当最近期间，巴力门屡次为英格兰及苏格兰两国合一而设立之各项法案；

而且反敢主张及断定他人或其他几个人实应有权利以嗣续王位；

（4）主张及断定君王们与君后们，虽得巴力门的助力与有巴力门的威权，却不能制定法律而发生效力以约束君主及他的王嗣所有制限问题，嗣续问题，及统治问题。

---

① 译文摘录自《英宪精义》第一篇"巴力门的主权"第一章"巴力门主权的性质"第二节"何为巴力门主权"，第137—138页。下划线由本书作者添加。

尾　声

纵观本书所论，法律翻译裹胁权力博弈，社会场域操纵改写策略。譬如西译中述《佐治刍言》之际，洋务运动方兴未艾，统治危机隐含未露，思想囚笼依然铜墙铁壁。唯有偷梁换柱，得以略抒欧美政法要务，却仍难免披挂专制皇朝所谓仁德善政的外衣。

邹振环先生在《影响中国近代社会的一百种译作》中称该书"出版即受当时学者的高度重视"，且举梁启超、章太炎、黄庆澄等先贤为例（1996：92—93）。然此观点似可斟酌。光绪丙申（1896年），梁启超首先在《西学书目表》中称其为"言政治最佳之书"①；随后章太炎的《变法箴言》由光绪丁酉七月（1897年8月）出版的《经世报》第一册"本馆论说"栏目发表②；而黄庆澄撰写《中西普通书目表》已是光绪戊戌年（1898年）③。换言之，与其说促使国人猛醒的是刊行已逾十数载的《佐治刍言》，不如说是甲午海战加速中体西用论彻底破产，民族危亡逼迫知识精英们另觅蹊径。否则，章太炎亦不会将其与《管子》同列，紧接着情不自禁地提及"马关之盟"④。

实际上，《佐治刍言》所体现的比附译书法是柄双刃剑：既令国人方便理解并接受西方近代文明；又令国人痴迷封建体制内的改良主义倾向。轰轰烈烈的公车上书、百日维新便是明证。

可叹庚子事变如影随至，终使风雨飘摇的清政府痛定思痛，重修内政

---

① 详见《西学书目表四卷附读西学书法一卷》，光绪丙申（1896年）冬十月质学会用时务报馆本重校付刊。

② 详见《经世报》第一册卷十二（光绪丁酉七月上）。

③ 光绪戊戌（1898年）七月算学馆自刻本。

④ 章炳麟先生在《变法箴言》伊始自言："孙灏与章炳麟见于分江之滨，炳麟方读管子及佐治刍言，魂精泄横，熟然似非人。孙灏曰：自马关之盟，士气振动，至于今三年，与民变革宜得一二成就。"

如箭在弦。《英国国会史》正是在此背景下应运问世。于英国人而言，该书不过是颇具趣味的科普读物；而于国人，这无疑代表着当时最惊世骇俗的改革范式。更何况以史为鉴、援引故事恰合华夏政治传统。编译者减其庞杂的细枝末节，以言简意赅的方式凸显要旨主干，不亦宜乎？

及至民国，君主立宪已成往事，民主共和深入人心。宪政不单是理想，更早已付诸实践。曾经留学国外的雷沛鸿先生怀揣前所未有的严谨态度，秉持批判的目光，以学者身份研译《英宪精义》，旨在取其精华，弃其糟粕，可谓深谙科学移植并本土化异域法律的精髓。这也是中西文化交流近百年后水到渠成之举。自此，西法东渐终究辗转完成了从削足适履到择善而趋的华丽转身，抖擞精神继续浴火重生的荆棘新途。

附 录 一

HISTORIC ROYAL SPEECHES AND WRITINGS

GEORGE III (r. 1760 – 1820)

Letter on the loss of America written in the 1780s (precise year unknown).

America is lost! Must we fall beneath the blow? Or have we resources that may repair the mischief? What are those resources? Should they be sought in distant Regions held by precarious Tenure, or shall we seek them at home in the exertions of a new policy?

The situation of the Kingdom is novel, the policy that is to govern it must be novel likewise, or neither adapted to the real evils of the present moment, or the dreaded ones of the future.

For a Century past the Colonial Scheme has been the system that has guided the Administration of the British Government. It was thoroughly known that from every Country there always exists an active emigration of unsettled, discontented, or unfortunate People, who failing in their endeavours to live at home, hope to succeed better where there is more employment suitable to their poverty. The establishment of Colonies in America might probably increase the number of this class, but did not create it; in times anterior to that great speculation, Poland contained near 10,000 Scotch Pedlars; within the last thirty years not above 100, occasioned by America offering a more advantageous asylum for them.

A people spread over an immense tract of fertile land, industrious because free, and rich because industrious, presently became a market for the Manufactures and Commerce of the Mother Country. An importance was soon generated, which from its origin to the late conflict was mischievous to Britain, because it created an expense of blood and treasure worth more at this instant, if it could be at our command, than all we ever received from America. The wars of 1744, of 1756, and 1775, were all entered into from the encouragements given to the speculations of settling the wilds of North America.

It is to be hoped that by degrees it will be admitted that the Northern Colonies, that is those North of Tobacco, were in reality our very successful rivals in two Articles, the carrying freight trade, and the Newfoundland fishery. While the Sugar Colonies added above three millions a year to the wealth of Britain, the Rice Colonies near a million, and the Tobacco ones almost as much; those more to the north, so far from adding anything to our wealth as Colonies, were trading, fishing, farming Countries, that rivalled us in many branches of our industry, and had actually deprived us of no inconsiderable share of the wealth we reaped by means of the others. This compartative view of our former territories in America is not stated with any idea of lessening the consequence of a future friendship and connection with them; on the contrary it is to be hoped we shall reap more advantages from their trade as friends than ever we could derive from them as Colonies; for there is reason to suppose we actually gained more by them while in actual rebellion, and the common open connection cut off, than when they were in obedience to the Crown; the Newfoundland fishery taken into the Account, there is little doubt of it.

The East and West Indies are conceived to be the great commercial supports of the Empire; as to the Newfoundland fishery time must tell us what share we shall reserve of it. But there is one observation which is applicable to all three; they depend on very distant territorial possessions, which we have little or no hopes of retaining from their internal strength, we can keep them only by means of a superior Navy. If our marine force sinks, or if in consequence of wars, debts, and taxes, we should in future find ourselves so debilitated as to be involved in a new War, without the means of carrying it on with vigour, in these cases, all distant possessions must fall, let them be as valuable as their warmest panegyrists contend. It evidently appears from this slight review of our most important dependencies, that on them we are not to exert that new policy which alone can be the preservation of the British power and consequence. The more important they are already, the less are they fit instruments in that work. No man can be hardy enough to deny that they are insecure; to add therefore to their value by exertions of policy which shall have the effect of directing any stream of capital, industry, or population into those channels, would be to add to a disproportion already an evil. The more we are convinced of the vast importance of those territories, the more we must feel the insecurity of our power; our view therefore ought not to be to increase but preserve them.

附 录 二

HISTORIC ROYAL SPEECHES AND WRITINGS

VICTORIA （r. 1837 – 1901）

Queen Victoria maintained a detailed diary, her famous Journal, which is contained in 111 large manuscript volumes. These volumes constitute about a third of the original, as her diaries were edited after her death by her youngest daughter Princess Beatrice, at Queen Victoria's request. The extracts below cover some of the more momentous events of Queen Victoria's reign, from her accession in 1832 to her Diamond Jubilee in 1897.

On William IV's death, and her accession aged 18 years: Tuesday, 20 June 1837 at Kensington Palace.

I was awoke at 6 o'clock by Mamma, who told me that the Archbishop of Canterbury and Lord Conyngham were here, and wished to see me. I got out of bed and went into my sitting-room (only in my dressing-gown), and alone, and saw them. Lord Conyngham (the Lord Chamberlain) then acquainted me that my poor Uncle, the King, was no more, and had expired at 12 minutes past 2 this morning, and consequently that I am Queen. Lord Conyngham knelt down and kissed my hand, at the same time delivering to me the official announcement of the poor King's demise. The Archbishop then told me that the Queen was desirous that he should come and tell me the details of the last moments of my poor, good Uncle; he said that he had directed his mind to religion, and had died in a perfectly happy, quiet state of mind, and was quite prepared for his death. He added that the King's sufferings at the last were not very great but that there was a good deal of uneasiness. Lord Conyngham, whom I charged to express my feelings of condolence and sorrow to the poor Queen, returned directly to Windsor. I then went to my room and dressed.

Since it has pleased Providence to place me in this station, I shall do my utmost to fulfil my duty towards my country; I am very young and perhaps in many, though not in all things, inexperienced, but I am sure, that very few have more real good will and more real desire to do what is fit and right than I have...

At 9 came Lord Melbourne, whom I saw in my room, and of COURSE *quite* ALONE as I shall *always* do all my Ministers. He kissed my hand and I then acquainted him that it had long been my intention to retain him and the rest of the present Ministry at the head of affairs, and that it could not be in better hands than his... He then read to me the Declaration which I was to read to the Council, which he wrote himself and which is a very fine one. I then talked with him some little longer time after which he left me... I like him very much and feel confidence in him. He is a very straightforward, honest, clever and good man. I then wrote a letter to the Queen...

At about half past 11 I went downstairs and held a Council in the red saloon. I went in of course quite alone, and remained seated the whole time. My two Uncles, the Dukes of Cumberland(who now succeeded William IV as King of Hanover) and Sussex, and Lord Melbourne conducted me. The declaration, the various forms, the swearing in of the Privy Councillors of which there were a great number present, and the reception of some of the Lords of Council, previous to the Council in an adjacent room(likewise alone) I subjoin here. I was not at all nervous and had the satisfaction of hearing that people were satisfied with what I had done and how I had done it.

Receiving after this, Audiences of Lord Melbourne, Lord John Russell, Lord Albemarle(Master of the Horse), and the Archbishop of Canterbury, all in my room and alone. Saw Stockmar (friend and counsellor to Queen Victoria and Prince Albert). Saw Clark, whom I named my Physician... Saw Ernest Hohenlohe who brought me a kind and very feeling letter from the poor Queen. I feel very much for her, and really feel that the poor good King was always so kind personally to me, that I should be ungrateful were I not to recollect it and feel grieved at his death. The poor Queen is wonderfully composed now, I hear.

Wrote my journal. Took my dinner upstairs alone. Went downstairs. Saw Stockmar. At about 20 minutes to 9 came Lord Melbourne and remained till near 10. I had a very important and very *comfortable* conversation with him... Went down and said good-night to Mamma etc.

Coronation : Thursday ,28 June **1838**

I was awoke at four o'clock by the guns in the Park, and could not get much sleep afterwards on account of the noise of the people, bands, etc. Got up at 7 feeling strong and well; the Park presented a curious spectacle; crowds of people up to Constitution Hill, soldiers, bands, etc. I dressed, having taken a little break-fast before I dressed, and a little after. At half past 9 I went into the next room dressed exactly in my House of Lords costume... At 10 I got into the State Coach with the Duchess of Sutherland and Lord Albemarle, and we began our Progress.

It was a fine day, and the crowds of people exceeded what I have ever seen; many as there were the day I went to the City, it was nothing—nothing to the multitudes, the millions of my loyal subjects who were assembled in*every spot*to witness the Procession. Their good humour and excessive loyalty was beyond eve-rything, and I really cannot say*how* proud I feel to be the Queen of*such a Na-tion*. I was alarmed at times for fear that the people would be crushed and squeezed on account of the tremendous rush and pressure.

I reached the Abbey (Westminster) amid deafening cheers at a little after half past 11; I first went into a robing-room quite close to the entrance, where I found my eight Train-bearers—all dressed alike and beautifully, in white satin and silver tissue, with wreaths of silver corn-ears in front, and a small one of pink roses round the plait behind, and pink roses in the trimming of the dresses. After putting on my Mantle, and the young ladies having properly got hold of it, and Lord Conyngham holding the end of it, I left the robing-room and the Procession began. The sight was splendid; the bank of Peeresses quite beautiful, all in their robes, and the Peers on the other side. My young Train-bearers were always near me, and helped me whenever I wanted anything. The Bishop of Durham stood on one side near me.

At the beginning of the Anthem. . . I retired to St Edward's Chapel, a small dark place immediately behind the Altar, with my Ladies and Train-bearers; took off my crimson robe and kirtle and put on the Supertunica of Cloth of Gold, also in the shape of a kirtle, which was put over a singular sort of little gown of linen trimmed with lace; I also took off my circlet of diamonds, and then proceeded bare-headed into the Abbey; I was then seated upon St Edward's chair where the Dalmatic robe was clasped round me by the Lord Great Chamberlain. Then followed all the various things; and last (of those things) the Crown being placed on my head; —which was, I must own, a most beautiful impressive moment; *all* the Peers and Peeresses put on their Coronets at the same instant. . . The shouts, which were very great, the drums, the trumpets, the firing of the guns, all at the same instant, rendered the spectacle most imposing.

The Enthronization and the Homage of, first all the Bishops, then my Uncles, and lastly of all the Peers, in their respective order, was very fine. The Duke of Norfolk (holding for me the Sceptre with a Cross) with Lord Melbourne, stood close to me on my right, and the Duke of Richmond with the other Sceptre on my left. All my Train-bearers standing behind the Throne. Poor old Lord Rolle, who is 82 and dreadfully infirm, in attempting to ascend the steps, fell and rolled quite down, but was not the least hurt; when he attempted to reascend them I got up and advanced to the end of the steps, in order to prevent another fall. . . When Lord Melbourne's turn to do Homage came, there was loud cheering; they also cheered Lord Grey and the Duke of Wellington; it's a pretty ceremony; they first all touch the Crown, and then kiss my hand. When my good Lord Melbourne knelt down and kissed my hand, he pressed my hand and I grasped his with all my heart, at which he looked up with his eyes filled with tears and seemed much touched, as he was, I observed, throughout the whole ceremony.

After the Homage was concluded I left the Throne, took off my Crown and received the Sacrament; I then put on my Crown again, and re-ascended the Throne, leaning on Lord Melbourne's arm; at the commencement of the Anthem I descended from the Throne, and went into St Edward's Chapel. . . where I took off the Dalmatic robe, Supertunica, and put on the Purple Velvet Kirtle and Mantle, and proceeded again to the Throne, which I ascended leaning on Lord

Melbourne's hand... I then again descended from the Throne, and repaired with all the Peers bearing the Regalia, my Ladies and Trainbearers, to St Edward's Chapel, as it is called; but which, as Lord Melbourne said, was more *unlike* a Chapel than anything he had ever seen; for, what was *called* an *Altar* was covered with sandwiches, bottles of wine etc. The Archbishop came in and *ought* to have delivered the Orb to me, but I had already got it. There we waited for some minutes... the Procession being formed, I replaced my Crown (which I had taken off for a few minutes), took the Orb in my left hand and the Sceptre in my right, and thus *loaded* proceeded through the Abbey, which resounded with cheers, to the first Robing-room... And here we waited for at least an hour, with *all* my ladies and Train-bearers; the Princesses went away about half an hour before I did; the Archbishop had put the ring on the wrong finger, and the consequence was that I had the greatest difficulty to take it off again,—which I at last did with great pain. At about half past 4 I re-entered my carriage, the Crown on my head and Sceptre and Orb in my hand, and we proceeded the same way as we came—the crowds if possible having increased. The enthusiasm, affection and loyalty was really touching, and I shall ever remember this day as the proudest of my life. I came home at a little after 6,—really *not* feeling tired.

At 8 we dined. My kind Lord Melbourne was much affected in speaking of the whole ceremony. He asked kindly if I was tired; said the Sword he carried (the first, the Sword of State) was excessively heavy. I said that the Crown hurt me a good deal. He was much amused at Uncle Ernest's being astonished at our still having the Litany; we agreed that the whole thing was a very fine sight. He thought the robes, and particularly the Dalmatic, "looked remarkably well"... The Archbishop's and the Dean's Copes (which were remarkably handsome) were from James I's time; the very same that were worn at his Coronation, Lord Melbourne told me.

After dinner, before we sat down, we... spoke of the numbers of Peers at the Coronation, which Lord Melbourne said was unprecedented. I observed that there were very few Viscounts; he said "there are very few Viscounts"; that they were an odd sort of title, and not really English; that they came from Vice—Comités; that Dukes and Barons were the only *real* English titles; that Marquises were likewise not English; and that they made people Marquises when they did not wish to make them Dukes. . . I then sat on the sofa for a little while. . . Mamma. . . remained to see the Illuminations, and only came in later. . . I said to Lord Melbourne when I first sat down, I felt a little tired on my feet. . . Spoke of the weight of the robes etc. . and he turned round to me and said *so* kindly, "And you did it beautifully, —every part of it, with so much taste; it's a thing that you can't give a person advice upon; it must be left to a person. " To hear this from this kind impartial friend, gave me great and real pleasure. . . Spoke of my intending to go to bed; he said, "You may depend upon it, you are more tired than you think you are. " I said I had slept badly the night before; he said that was my mind, and that nothing kept people more awake than any consciousness of a great event going to take place and being agitated. . . Stayed in the drawing-room till 20 minutes past 11, but remained till 12 o'clock on Mamma's balcony looking at the fireworks in Green Park, which were quite beautiful.

Great Exhibition: 1 *May* **1851**

This day is one of the greatest and most glorious days of our lives, with which, to my pride and joy the name of my dearly beloved Albert is forever associated! It is a day which makes my heart swell with thankfulness. . . The Park presented a wonderful spectacle, crowds streaming though it—carriages and troops passing, quite like the Coronation Day, and for me, the same anxiety. The day was bright, and all bustle and excitement. At half past 11, the whole procession in 9 state carriages was set in motion. Vicky and Bertie(her two eldest children, the Princess Royal and the Prince of Wales) were in our carriage. Vicky was dressed in lace over white satin, with a small wreath of pink wild roses, in her hair, and looked very nice. Bertie was in full Highland dress. The Green Park and Hyde Park were one mass of densely crowded human beings, in the highest good humour and most enthusiastic. I never saw Hyde Park look as it did, being filled with crowds as far as the eye could reach. A little rain fell, just as we started; but before we neared the Crystal Palace, the sun shone and gleamed upon the gigantic edifice, upon which the flags of every nation were flying.

We drove up Rotten Row and got out of our carriages at the entrance on that side. The glimpse through the iron gates of the Transept, the moving palms and flowers, the myriads of people filling the galleries and seats around, together with the flourish of trumpets, as we entered the building, gave a sensation I shall never forget, and I felt much moved... In a few seconds we proceeded, Albert leading me having Vicky at his hand, and Bertie holding mine. The sight as we came to the centre where the steps and chair (on which I did not sit) was placed, facing the beautiful crystal fountain was magic and impressive. The tremendous cheering, the joy expressed in every face, the vastness of the building, with all its decorations and exhibits, the sound of the organ (with 200 instruments and 600 voices, which seemed nothing), and my beloved Husband the creator of this great "Peace Festival", uniting the industry and arts of all nations of the earth, all this, was indeed moving, and a day to live forever. God bless my dearest Albert, and my dear Country which has shown itself so great today... The Nave was full of people, which had not been intended and deafening cheers and waving of handkerchiefs, continued the whole time of our long walk from one end of the building, to the other. Every face was bright, and smiling, and many even had tears in their eyes... One could of course see nothing, but what was high up in the Nave, and nothing in the Courts. The organs were but little heard, but the Military Band, at one end, had a very fine effect...

We returned to our place and Albert told Lord Breadalbane to declare the Exhibition opened, which he did in a loud voice saying "Her Majesty commands me to declare the Exhibition opened", when there was a flourish of trumpets, followed by immense cheering. Everyone was astounded and delighted. The return was equally satisfactory—the crowd most enthusiastic and perfect order kept. We reached the Palace at 20 minutes past 1 and went out on the balcony, being loudly cheered. That we felt happy and thankful,—I need not say—proud of all that had passed and of my beloved one's success. Dearest Albert's name is for ever immortalised and the absurd reports of dangers of every kind and sort, set about by a set of people,—the 'soi-disant' fashionables and the most violent protectionists—are silenced. It is therefore doubly satisfactory that all should have gone off so well, and without the slightest accident or mishap.

Crimean War, ending of the Siege of Sebastopol: 10 September 1855, at Balmoral

Albert said they should go at once and light the bonfire... In a few minutes, Albert and all the gentlemen, in every species of attire, sallied forth, followed by all the servants, and gradually by all the population of the village-keepers, gillies, workmen—up to the top of the cairn. We waited, and saw them light it; accompanied by general cheering. The bonfire blazed forth brilliantly, and we could see the numerous figures surrounding it—some dancing, all shouting... About three-quarters of an hour after, Albert came down, and said the scene had been wild and exciting beyond anything. The people had been drinking healths in whisky and were in great ecstasy. The whole house seemed in a wonderful state of excitement. The boys were with difficulty awakened, and when at last this was the case, they begged leave to go up to the top of the cairn.

We remained till a quarter to twelve; and, just as I was undressing, all the people came down under the windows, the pipes playing, the people singing, firing off guns, and cheering—first for me, then for Albert, the Emperor of the French, and the "downfall of Sebastopol".

Letter to Miss Florence Nightingale: January 1856

You are, I know, well aware of the high sense I entertain of the Christian devotion which you have displayed during this great and bloody war, and I need hardly repeat to you how warm my admiration is for your services, which are fully equal to those of my dear and brave soldiers, whose sufferings you have had the privilege of alleviating in so merciful a manner. I am, however, anxious of marking my feelings in a manner which I trust will be agreeable to you, and therefore send you with this letter a brooch [a badge bearing St. George's Cross in red enamel and the royal cypher surmounted by a crown in diamonds; the inscription 'Blessed are the Merciful' encircled the badge which also bore the word 'Crimea'], the form and emblems of which commemorate your great and blessed work, and which, I hope, you will wear as a mark of the high approbation of your Sovereign!

It will be a very great satisfaction to me, when you return at last to these shores, to make the acquaintance of one who has set so bright an example to our sex.

*The death of Queen Victoria's beloved husband, Prince Albert, who died from typhoid on **14 December 1861** at Windsor Castle, at the age of **42**. On **20 December**, Queen Victoria wrote to her uncle King Leopold of Belgium:*

...to be cut off in the prime of life—to see our pure happy, quiet domestic life, which alone enabled me to bear my much disliked position, cut off at forty-two—when I had hoped with such instinctive certainty that God never would part us, and would let us grow old together...—is too awful, too cruel!

Letter to the recently widowed Earl Canning, Osborne, 10 January 1862

Lord Canning little thought when he wrote his kind and touching letter of the 22nd November, that it would only reach the Queen when she was smitten and bowed down to the earth by an event similar to the one which he describes... To lose one's partner in life is, as Lord Canning knows, like losing half of one's body and soul, torn forcibly away—and dear Lady Canning was such a dear, worthy, devoted wife! But to the Queen—to a poor helpless woman-it is not that only-it is the stay, support and comfort which is lost! To the Queen it is like death in life! Great and small—nothing was done without his loving advice and help-and she feels alone in the wide world, with many helpless children... to look to her—and the whole nation to look to her—now when she can barely struggle with her wretched existence! Her misery—her utter despair—she cannot describe! Her only support—the only ray of comfort she gets for a moment, is in the firm conviction and certainty of his nearness, his undying love, and of their eternal reunion!

May God comfort and support Lord Canning, and may he think in his sorrow of his widowed and broken-hearted Sovereign...

Golden Jubilee: 21 June 1887, at Buckingham Palace

This very eventful day has come and is passed. It will be very difficult to describe it, but all went off admirably. This day, fifty years ago, I had to go with a full Sovereign's escort to St James's Palace, to appear at my proclamation, which was very painful to me, and is no longer to take place.

The morning was beautiful and bright with a fresh air. Troops began passing early with bands playing, and one heard constant cheering... The scene outside was most animated, and reminded me of the opening of the Great Exhibition, which also took place on a very fine day. Received many beautiful nosegays and presents... Then dressed, wearing a dress and bonnet trimmed with white point d'Alençon, diamond ornaments in my bonnet, and pearls around my neck, with all my orders.

At half-past eleven we left the Palace, I driving in a handsomely gilt landau drawn by six of the Creams, with dear Vicky (her eldest daughter) and Alex (her daughter-in-law, the Princess of Wales), who sat on the back seat. Just in front of my carriage rode the 12 Indian officers, and in front of them my 3 sons, 5 sons-in-law, 9 grandsons and grandsons-in-law. Then came the carriages containing my 3 other daughters... All the other Royalties went in a separate procession. George Cambridge rode the whole way next to my carriage, and the Master of the Horse, Equerries, etc. , behind it with of course a Sovereign's escort. It was a really magnificent sight...

At the door (of Westminster Abbey) I was received by the clergy, with the Archbishop of Canterbury and Dean at their head, in the copes of rich velvet and gold, which had been worn at the Coronation... The crowds from the Palace gates up to the Abbey were enormous, and there was such an extraordinary outburst of enthusiasm as I had hardly ever seen in London before; all the people seemed to be in such good humour. The old Chelsea Pensioners were in a stand near the Arch. The decorations along Piccadilly were quite beautiful, and there were most touching inscriptions. Seats and platforms were arranged up to the tops of the houses, and such waving of hands... Many schools out, and many well-known faces were seen.

When all was ready, the procession was formed... *God Save the Queen* was played... as I walked slowly up the Nave and Choir, which looked beautiful, all filled with people. The Royalties of highest rank were seated within the altar rails. The House of Commons was below us to the left, and I recognised several persons amongst them, but did not see Mr Gladstone, thought he was there. The Ambassadors and the Household were to the right.

I sat *alone* (oh! without my beloved husband, for whom this would have been such a proud day!) where I sat forty-nine years ago and received the homage of the Princes and Peers, but in the old Coronation Chair of Edward III, with the old stone brought from Scotland, on which the old Kings of Scotland used to be crowned. My robes were beautifully draped on the chair. The service was very well done and arranged. The *Te Deum*, by my darling Albert, sounded beautiful... When the service was concluded, each of my sons, sons-in-law, grandsons (including little Alfred), and grandsons-in-law, stepped forward, bowed, and in succession kissed my hand, I kissing each; and the same with the daughters, daughters-in-law, grand-daughters, and the granddaughter-in-law. They curtsied as they came up and I embraced them warmly. It was a very moving moment, and tears were in some of their eyes.

The procession then reformed, and we went out as we came in, resting a moment in the waiting-room, whilst the Princes were all getting on their horses. The whole ceremony, particularly the outside procession and progress, took twenty minutes longer than was expected... There were many stoppages, which is almost unavoidable in long processions... The heat of the sun was very great, but there was a good deal of wind, which was a great relief... We only got back at a quarter to three. Went at once to my room to take off my bonnet and put on my cap. Gave Jubilee brooches to all my daughters... and pins to all my sons...

Only at four did we sit down to luncheon, to which all came. The King of Saxony led me in, and the King of Denmark with Marie of Belgium sat on my other side. After luncheon, I stood on the small balcony of the Blue Room, which looks out on the garden, and saw the Bluejackets march past. After this we went into the small Ball-room, where the present given me by all my children was placed. It is a very handsome piece of plate. The Queen of Hawaii gave me a present of very rare feathers, but very strangely arranged as a wreath about my monogram, also in feathers on a black ground, framed.

I felt quite exhausted by this time and ready to faint, so I got into my rolling chair and was rolled back to my room. Here I lay down on the sofa and rested, doing nothing but opening telegrams, coming from every part of the country, so that they could no longer be acknowledged, and this will have to be done through the papers.

Dinner was again in the Supper-room. I wore a dress with rose, thistle, and shamrock embroidered in silver on it, and my large diamonds. The King of Denmark led me in, and I sat between him and Leopold of Belgium. The King of Denmark, who is so kind and amiable, gave out my health at dessert saying, "I beg to propose the health of Her Majesty—God bless her". And after *God Save the Queen* had been played, Bertie (the Prince of Wales) proposed the healths of the Sovereigns and Royal guests now assembled here, doing so in my name... The pipers walked round the table. We went into the Ballroom, where I spoke to the Indian Princes and received all the Corps Diplomatique, Foreign Envoys and suites, the latter being each presented by their Princes. I was half dead with fatigue, and after sitting down a moment with Marie of Belgium, slipped away and was rolled back to my room, and to the Chinese room to try and see something of the very general illuminations, but could not see much. The noise of the crowd, which began yesterday, went on till late. Felt truly grateful that all had passed off so admirably, and this never-to-be-forgotten day will always leave the most gratifying and heartstirring memories behind.

Golden Jubilee:22 June 1887, at Windsor Castle

Very fine and hazy. Breakfasted in the Chinese room (at Buckingham Palace), but such a change from yesterday. No crowd or noise. The illuminations last night are said to have been splendid. Thousands thronged the streets, but there was no disorder. They shouted and sang till quite late, and passed the Palace singing *God Save the Queen* and *Rule Britannia*. Went into the garden for a little while, and on coming home rested. Quantities of telegrams still continued coming in...

Again a big luncheon in the Dining-room... Gave Jubilee medals to the Kings and most of the Princes. I then went with Beatrice (her youngest daughter), preceded by the Lord Chamberlain, to the Ball-room, where were assembled all my Household, and a great number of those who had served me from the beginning of my reign. Lord Mt Edgcumbe, as Lord Steward, presented their gift, a magnificent piece of plate, splendidly worked and executed, representing music and painting. I went round and spoke to as many as I could... (The Queen then received a jewelled pendant from the Prince of Wales's Household, a portrait of himself from the Prime Minister, a watercolour from the other royal Households.)

This over, I went though the Blue Drawing Room and Bow Room, full of ladies, to the White Drawing-room, equally full. This was a Deputation from the "Women of England", who brought me the signatures of the millions who have subscribed to a gift, contained in a splendid gold coffer... and Lady Londonderry presented me with that of another very fine coffer, containing the signatures of the Women of Ireland... From her I passed into the Picture Gallery, where were assembled all the people who came with other presents, which extended down the whole length of the Gallery. Was really touched and gratified.

Rested on the sofa for some time, and took a cup of tea before leaving Buckingham Palace at half-past five. Bertie and Alex could not leave London on account of looking after the guests. Had an escort and an Indian escort. Enormous and enthusiastic crowds on Constitution Hill and in Hyde Park... We drove right on to the grass in the middle of the park, where 30,000 poor children with their schoolmasters and mistresses, were assembled. Tents had been pitched for them to dine in, and all sorts of amusements had been provided for them. Each received an earthenware pot with my portrait on it... We stopped in the middle... and a little girl gave me a beautiful bouquet, on the ribbons of which were embroidered: "God bless our Queen, not Queen alone, but Mother, Queen and Friend"... The children sang *God Save the Queen* somewhat out of tune, and then we drove on to Paddington station. The train stopped at Slough, and we got out there... Different ladies and gentlemen were presented and bouquets were given. Then drove off with an escort to Windsor. All along the road there were decorations and crowds of people. Before coming to Eton, there was a beautiful triumphal arch, made to look exactly like part of the old College, and boys dressed like old Templars stood on the top of it, playing a regular fanfare. The whole effect was beautiful, lit up by the sun of a bright summer's evening. . . The town was one mass of flags and decorations. We went under the Castle walls up the hill, slowly, amidst great cheering, and stopped at the bottom of Castle Hill, where there was a stand crowded with people and every window and balcony were full of people, Chinese lanterns and preparations for illuminations making a very pretty effect. Those of the family who had not come with me were in the front row of the stand. . . An Address was read, to which I read an Answer. . . After this my statue was unveiled. . . Amidst cheering, the ringing of bells, and bands playing, we drove up to the Castle. This completed the pretty and gratifying welcome to good old Windsor.

We had a large family dinner. . . Just as we were beginning dessert, we heard that the torchlight procession of Eton boys was coming into the Quadrangle, and off we hurried, as fast as we could, to the Corridor, from whence we could see it beautifully. They performed all sorts of figures, the band playing marches etc, and they sang an Eton Boat song, a Jubilee song specially composed for the occasion. . . They did it so well and it had a most charming effect. The Head Master came up, and I thanked him, and sent for the Captain of the school. They cheered tremendously. Then we all went down to the Quadrangle, and I said, in as loud a voice as I could, "I thank you very much", which elicited more cheering, after which they all marched past and out at the gate. The Round Tower was illuminated with electric light, and so were parts of the Castle. The town was also illuminated, but I was too tired to go and see it, and went to my room.

These two days will ever remain indelibly impressed in my mind, with great gratitude to that all-merciful Providence, Who has protected me so long, and to my devoted and loyal people. But how painfully do I miss the dear ones I have lost!

Diamond Jubilee : 21 June 1897, at Buckingham Palace

The 10th anniversary of the celebration of my fifty years Jubilee. Breakfasted with my three daughters at the Cottage at Frogmore (Windsor Park). A fine warm morning.

At quarter to twelve we drove to the station to start for London. The town was very prettily decorated, and there were great crowds, who cheered very much. At Paddington I was received by Lord Cork and other Directors of GWR (Great Western Railway). Drove, going at a fast pace to the Paddington Vestry platform, where an address was presented by the Vicar of Paddington. Then we proceeded at a slow trot, with a Sovereign's escort of the 1st Life Guards. Passed through dense crowds, who gave me a most enthusiastic reception. It was like a triumphal entry. We passed down Cambridge Terrace, under a lovely arch, bearing the motto, "Our hearts thy Throne". The streets were beautifully decorated, also the balconies of the houses with flowers, flags, and draperies of every hue... The streets, the windows, the roofs of the houses, were one mass of beaming faces, and the cheers never ceased. On entering the park, through the Marble Arch, the crowd was even greater, carriages were drawn up amongst the people on foot, even on the pretty little lodges well-dressed people were perched. Hyde Park Corner and Constitution Hill were densely crowded. All vied with one another to give me a heartfelt, loyal and affectionate welcome. I was deeply touched and gratified. The day had become very fine and very hot.

Reaching the Palace shortly after 1, and Vicky [her eldest daughter] at once brought me her three daughters... [Queen Victoria is then given a diamond pendant with sapphires, a 'very handsome' book cover and a 'beautiful diamond brooch' as Jubilee presents by her family]... Then I was taken round in my wheeled chair to the Bow Room, where all my family awaited me... Seated in my chair, as I cannot stand long, I received all the foreign Princes in succession, beginning with Archduke Franz Ferdinand [whose assassination in 1914 at Sarajevo marked the beginning of the First World War]... after which Lord Salisbury presented all the special Ambassadors and Envoys... I got back to my room a little before four, quite exhausted. Telegrams kept pouring in. It was quite impossible even to open them... Had tea in the garden ...

Dressed for dinner. I wore a dress of which the whole front was embroidered in gold, which had been specially worked in India, diamonds in my cap, and a diamond necklace, etc. The dinner was in the Supper-room at little tables of twelve each. All the family, foreign royalties, special Ambassadors and Envoys

were invited. I sat between the Archduke Franz Ferdinand and the Prince of Na-
ples. After dinner went into Ball-room, where my private band played and the
following were presented to me: the Colonial Premiers with their wives, the Special Envoys, the three Indian Princes, and all the officers of the two Indian
escorts, who, as usual, held out their swords to be touched by me, and the different foreign suites. The Ball-room was very full and dreadfully hot, and the light
very inefficient. It was only a little after eleven, when I got back to my room,
feeling very tired. There was a deal of noise in the streets, and we were told that
many were sleeping out in the parks.

22 June 1897, at Buckingham Palace

A never-to-be-forgotten day... The night had been very hot, and I was
rather restless. There was such a noise going on the whole time, but it did not
keep me from getting some sleep. Dull early and close. Breakfasted... in the
Chinese luncheon room. The head of the procession, including the Colonial
troops, had unfortunately already passed the Palace before I got to breakfast, but
there were still a great many, chiefly British, passing. I watched them for a little
while.

At quarter-past eleven, the others being seated in their carriages long before, and having preceded me a short distance, I started from the State entrance
in an open State landau, drawn by eight creams, dear Alix (Princess of Wales),
looking very pretty in lilac... sitting opposite me. I felt a good deal agitated, and
had been so all these days, for fear anything might be forgotten or go wrong...
My escort was formed from the 2nd Life Guards and officers of the native Indian
regiments, these latter riding immediately in front of my carriage. Guard of Honour of Bluejackets, the Guards and the 2nd West Surrey Regiment (Queen's)
were mounted in the Quadrangle and outside the Palace.

Before leaving I touched an electric button, by which I started a message
which was telegraphed throughout the whole Empire. It was the following: "From
my heart I thank my beloved people, May God bless them!" At this time the sun
burst out...

We went up Constitution Hill and Piccadilly, and there were seats right along the former, where my own servants and personal attendants, and members of the other Royal Households, the Chelsea Pensioners, and the children of the Duke of York's and Greenwich schools had seats. St James's Street was beautifully decorated with festoons of flowers across the road and many loyal inscriptions. Trafalgar Square was very striking, and outside the National Gallery stands were erected for the House of Lords. The denseness of the crowds was immense, but the order maintained wonderful. The streets in the Strand are now quite wide. . . Here the Lord Mayor received me and presented the sword, which I touched. He then immediately mounted his horse in his robes, and galloped past bare-headed, carrying the sword, preceding my carriage, accompanied by his Sheriffs. As we neared St Paul's the procession was often stopped, and the crowds broke out into singing *God Save the Queen*. In one house were assembled the survivors of the Charge of Balaclava [a Crimean War campaign].

In front of the Cathedral the scene was most impressive. All the Colonial troops, on foot, were drawn up round the Square. My carriage, surrounded by all the Royal Princes, was drawn up close to the steps, where the Clergy were assembled, the Bishops in rich copes, with their croziers, the Archbishop of Canterbury and the Bishop of London each holding a very fine one. A *Te Deum* was sung; the Lord's Prayer, most beautifully chanted, a special Jubilee prayer, and the benediction concluded the short service, preceded by the singing of the *old* 100*th*, in which everyone joined. *God Save the Queen* was also sung. I then spoke to the Archbishop and the Bishop of London. As I drove off, the former gave out, "Three cheers for the Queen".

I stopped in front of the Mansion House, where the Lady Mayoress presented me with a beautiful silver basket full of orchids. Here I took leave of the Lord Mayor. Both he and the Lady Mayoress were quite*émus.* We proceeded over London Bridge, where no spectators were allowed, only troops, and then along the Borough Road, where there is a very poor population, but just as enthusiastic and orderly as elsewhere. The decorations there were very pretty, consisting chiefly of festoons of flowers on either side of the street. Crossed the river again over Westminster Bridge, past the Houses of Parliament, through Whitehall, Parliament Street, which has been much enlarged, through the Horse Guards and down the

Mall. The heat during the last hour was very great, and poor Lord Howe, who was riding as Gold Stick, fainted and had a bad fall, but was not seriously hurt.

Got home at a quarter to two. All the carriages that had preceded mine were drawn up in the courtyard as I drove in. Had a quiet luncheon with Vicky, Beatrice [her youngest daughter], and her three children. Troops continually passing by. Then rested and later had tea in the garden...

There was a large dinner in the supper-room, the same as yesterday. Bertie [the Prince of Wales], who sat at my table, gave out the health of the Empress Frederick [the Queen's eldest daughter] and my distinguished guests. I walked into the Ball-room afterwards, and sat down in front of the dais. Felt very tired, but tried to speak to most of the Princes and Princesses; the suites also came in, but no one else. I wore a black and silver dress with my Jubilee necklace and the beautiful brooch given me by my Household. In the morning I wore a dress of black silk, trimmed with panels of grey satin veiled with black net and steel embroideries, and some black lace, my lovely diamond chain, given me by my younger children, round my neck. My bonnet was trimmed with creamy white flowers, and white aigrette and some black lace. I left the Ball-room at eleven. There were illuminations, which we did not see, but could hear a great deal of cheering and singing. Gave souvenirs to my children and grandchildren.

Final published extracts:

4 January 1901 at Osborne House, Isle of Wight

From not having been well, I see so badly, which is very tiresome.

12 January 1901 at Osborne House, Isle of Wight

Had a good night and could take some breakfast better. Took an hour's drive at half-past two... It was very foggy, but the air was pleasant.

The Queen died at half past six in the evening on 22 January 1901 at Osborne House, surrounded by her children and grandchildren.

附 录 三

HISTORIC ROYAL SPEECHES AND WRITINGS

ELIZABETH I （r. 1558 – 1603）

A message to her army at Tilbury on the eve of the Spanish Armada, 1588

My loving people, we have been persuaded by some that are careful of our safety, to take heed how we commit ourselves to armed multitudes for fear of treachery; but, I do assure you, I do not desire to live to distrust my faithful and loving people.

Let tyrants fear; I have always so behaved myself, that under God I have placed my chiefest strength and safeguard in the loyal hearts and good will of my subjects; and, therefore, I am come amongst you as you see at this time, not for my recreation and disport, but being resolved, in the midst and heat of the battle, to live or die amongst you all—to lay down for my God, and for my kingdoms, and for my people, myhonour and my blood even in the dust. I know I have the body of a weak, feeble woman; but I have the heart and stomach of a king—and of a King of England too, and think foul scorn that Parma or Spain, or any prince of Europe, should dare to invade the borders of my realm; to which, rather than anydishonour should grow by me, I myself will take up arms—I myself will be your general, judge, andrewarder of every one of your virtues in the field.

I know already, for your forwardness, you have deserved rewards and crowns, and, we do assure you, on the word of a prince, they shall be duly paid you. For the meantime, my Lieutenant General Leicester shall be in my stead, than whom never prince commanded a more noble or worthy subject; not doubting but by your obedience to my General, by your concord in the camp, and your valour in the field, we shall shortly have a famous victory over these enemies of my God, of my kingdom and of my people.

参考文献

一 学术著作与论文

1. 埃德加·博登海默：《法理学：法律哲学与法律方法》，邓正来译，中国政法大学出版社 1999 年版。

2. 理查德·波斯纳：《法理学问题》，苏力译，中国政法大学出版社 2002 年版。

3. 曹全来：《国际化与本土化：中国近代法律体系的形成》，北京大学出版社 2005 年版。

4. 程朝阳：《法律权力运动的语言面相——〈法律、语言与权力〉导读（代译序）》，约翰·M.康利、威廉·M.欧巴尔：《法律、语言与权力》，程朝阳译，法律出版社 2007 年版。

5. 陈顾远：《中国法制史概要》，商务印书馆 2011 年版。

6. 陈炯：《法律语言学概论》，陕西人民教育出版社 1998 年版。

7. 崔军民：《萌芽期的现代法律新词研究》，中国社会科学出版社 2011 年版。

8. 戴学稷：《林则徐译编西方书报述要》，《闽都文化研究》2006 年第 1 期，第 137—145 页。

9. 埃尔默·都南、查尔斯·福斯特：《法律文书起草之道》，法律出版社 2006 年版。

10. 傅德元：《丁韪良〈万国公法〉翻译蓝本及意图新探》，《安徽史学》2008 年第 1 期，第 45—53 页。

11. 高鸿钧、贺卫方：《"比较法学丛书"总序》，H.W.埃尔曼：《比较法律文化》，贺卫方、高鸿钧译，清华大学出版社 2002 年版。

12. 顾长声：《从马礼逊到司徒雷登——来华新教传教士评传》，上海人民出版社 1985 年版。

13. 鲁伯特·海埃：《法律英语》，李玉木译，武汉大学出版社 2007 年版。

14. 韩琴：《论林则徐摘译国际法的选择性》，《福建师范大学学报》（哲学社会科学版）2008 年第 4 期，第 127—135 页。

15. 贺力平：《鸦片贸易与白银外流关系之再检讨——兼论国内货币供给与对外贸易关系的历史演变》，《社会科学战线》2007 年第 1 期，第 63—80 页。

16. 何伟亚：《怀柔远人：马嘎尔尼使华的中英礼仪冲突》，邓常春译，社会科学文献出版社 2002 年版。

17. 黄一农：《印象与真相——清朝中英两国的觐礼之争》，《中央研究院历史语言研究所集刊》2007 年第 78 期，第 35—105 页。

18. 蒋廷黻：《中国近代史》，上海古籍出版社 2004 年版。

19. 吉利克：《伯驾与中国的开放》，董少新译，广西师范大学出版社 2008 年版。

20. 瞿同祖：《中国法律与中国社会》，商务印书馆 2010 年版。

21. 科斯坦佐、马戈特：《法律文书写作之道》，王明晰、刘波译，法律出版社 2006 年版。

22. 赖骏楠：《林则徐与国际法：虚构的与真实的》，《北京大学研究生学志》2011 年第 1 期，第 86—100 页。

23. 雷荣广、姚乐野：《清代文书纲要》，四川大学出版社 1990 年版。

24. 雷颐：《历史的裂缝：近代中国与幽暗人生》，广西师范大学出版社 2007 年版。

25. 廖美珍：《国外法律语言研究综述》，《当代语言学》2004 年第 1 期，第 66—76 页。

26. 李健雪：《承诺类言语行为假设空间的建构及特点》，《山东外语教学》2006 年第 4 期，第 27—32 页。

27. 李克兴、张新红：《法律文本与法律翻译》，中国对外翻译出版公司 2006 年版。

28. 李连贵：《话说“权利”》，《北大法律评论》1998 年第 1 期，第 115—129 页。

29. 李连贵、俞江：《简论中国近代法学的翻译与移植——以我国第一部国际私法译著为例》，北京大学法学院编：《价值共识与法律合意》，法律出版社 2002 年版，第 334—366 页。

30. 林学忠：《从万国公法到公法外交：晚清国际法的传人、诠释与应用》，上海古籍出版社 2009 年版。

31. 刘达人、袁国钦著,胡娟勘校:《国际法发达史》,中国方正出版社 2007 年版。

32. 刘广京:《一八六七年同文馆的争议——洋务运动专题研究之一》,《复旦大学学报》(社会科学版)1982 年第 5 期,第 97—101 页。

33. 刘国涛、范海玉:《法律文书学》,重庆大学出版社 2005 年版。

34. 刘禾:《普遍性的历史建构——〈万国公法〉与十九世纪国际法的流通》,陈燕谷译,李陀、陈燕谷主编:《视界》(第 1 辑),河北教育出版社 2000 年版,第 64—84 页。

35. 刘红婴:《法律语言学》(第二版),北京大学出版社 2007 年版。

36. 刘蔚铭:《语言证据范畴下的法律语言学研究》,《广东外语外贸大学学报》2009 年第 1 期,第 68—72 页。

37. 李振宇:《法律语言学新说》,中国检察出版社 2006 年版。

38. 李振宇:《中国法律语言学研究的思考》,王洁、苏金智、约瑟夫 - G. 图里主编:《法律·语言·语言的多样性(第九届国际法律与语言学术研讨会论文集)》,法律出版社 2006 年版,第 182—193 页。

39. 鲁纳:《万民法在中国:国际法的最初汉译,兼及〈海国图志〉的编纂》,王笑红译,《中外法学》2000 年第 3 期,第 300—310 页。

40. 陆文慧主编:《法律翻译——从实践出发》,法律出版社 2004 年版。

41. 陆玉芹:《林则徐与〈滑达尔各国律例〉》,《盐城师范学院学报》(人文社会科学版)2006 年第 3 期,第 11—15 页。

42. 罗兹曼、吉尔伯特:《国家社会科学基金"比较现代化"课题组译》,《中国的现代化》,江苏人民出版社 2010 年版。

43. 茅海建:《戊戌变法史事考》,三联书店 2005 年版。

44. 马楚坚:《中国古代的邮驿》,商务印书馆国际有限公司 1997 年版。

45. 马莉:《法律语言翻译的文化制约》,法律出版社 2009 年版。

46. 马士:《中国海关史研究中心组译》,《东印度公司对话贸易编年史》,中山大学出版社 1991 年版。

47. 马西尼:《现代汉语词汇的形成:十九世纪汉语外来词研究》,黄河清译,汉语大词典出版社 1997 年版。

48. 肯尼思·摩根主编:《牛津英国通史》,王觉非等译,商务印书馆 1993 年版。

49. 潘庆云:《中国法律语言鉴衡》,汉语大词典出版社 2004 年版。

50. 钱大群：《唐律疏议新注》，南京大学出版社 2007 年版。

51. 戚其章：《从"中本西末"到"中体西用"》，《中国社会科学》1995 年第 1 期，第 186—198 页。

52. 饶传平：《从设议院到立宪法——晚清"Constitution"汉译与立宪思潮形成考论》，《现代法学》2011 年第 5 期，第 24—36 页。

53. 沈家本：《历代刑法考》，商务印书馆 2011 年版。

54. 沈宗灵主编：《法理学》，北京大学出版社 2001 年版。

55. 舒习龙：《王韬〈法国志略〉史学思想析论》，《安徽大学学报》（哲学社会科学版）2002 年第 4 期，第 40—45 页。

56. 孙家红：《大清律例》百年研究综述［A/OL］．［2012/4/29］（http: //blog. sina. com. cn/s/blog_ 4b862b3e01009ymb. html）。

57. 孙邦华：《论傅兰雅在西学汉译中的杰出贡献——以西学译名的确立与统一问题为中心》，《语言学研究》2006 年第 4 期，第 133—139 页。

58. 孙玉祥：《丁韪良与〈万国公法〉》，《新闻出版交流》2003 年第 2 期，第 55—56 页。

59. 索绪尔：《普通语言学教程》，高名凯译，商务印书馆 1999 年版。

60. 陶博：《法律英语：中英双语法律文书制作》，复旦大学出版社 2004 年版。

61. 陶钟灵：《清末预备立宪的法文化视角解读》，《贵州社会科学》2007 年第 12 期，第 140—144 页。

62. 谭汝谦主编：《中国译日本书综合目录》，香港中文大学出版社 1981 年版。

63. 滕超、孔飞燕：《英汉法律互译：理论与实践》，浙江大学出版社 2008 年版。

64. 田涛、李祝环：《接触与碰撞——16 世纪以来西方人眼中的中国法律》，北京大学出版社 2007 年版。

65. 田涛、李祝环：《清末翻译外国法学书籍评述》，曾宪义主编：《百年回眸：法律史研究在中国（第二卷/当代大陆卷下）》，中国人民大学出版社 2009 年版，第 67—89 页。

66. 田涛、郑秦点校：《大清律例》，法律出版社 1999 年版。

67. 王邦翠：《戊戌变法与中国近代化》，《安徽史学》1999 年第 4 期，第

43—47 页。

68. 王光：《外交名词译名的商榷》，《东方杂志》1935 年第 13 期，第 175—181 页。

69. 王建：《沟通两个世界的法律意义——晚清西方法的输入与法律新词初探》，中国政法大学出版社 2001 年版。

70. 王利明：《民法疑难案例研究》，中国法制出版社 2002 年版。

71. 王美秀：《丁韪良的中国宗教观》，《北京大学学报》（哲学社会科学版）1995 年第 2 期，第 48—53 页。

72. 王树槐：《清末翻译名词的统一问题》，《中央研究院近代史研究所集刊》1969 年第 1 期，第 47—82 页。

73. 王维俭：《订正若干中外辞书中"丁韪良"词目涉及的史实》，《中山大学学报》1987 年第 2 期，第 68—76 页。

74. 王维俭：《林则徐翻译西方国际法著作考略》，《中山大学学报》1985 年第 1 期，第 58—67 页。

75. 汪熙：《约翰公司：英国东印度公司》，上海人民出版社 2007 年版。

76. 王宪明、张勇、蔡乐苏：《戊戌变法史述论稿》，清华大学出版社 2001 年版。

77. 王扬宗：《"西学中源"说和"中体西用"论在晚清的盛衰》，《故宫博物院刊》2001 年第 5 期。

78. 王扬宗：《傅兰雅与近代中国的科学启蒙》，科学出版社 2000 年版。

79. 王扬宗：《江南制造局翻译书目新考》，《中国科技史料》1995 年第 2 期，第 3—18 页。

80. 王扬宗：《清末益智书会统一科技术语工作述评》，《中国科技史料》1991 年第 2 期，第 9—19 页。

81. 王哲：《论洋务运动时期"中体西用"文化语境的合理诉求》，《河南师范大学学报》（哲学社会科学版）2009 年第 3 期。

82. 威罗贝：《外人在华特权和利益》，王绍坊译，生活·读书·新知三联书店 1957 年版。

83. 魏尔特：《赫德与中国海关》，陈彩才等译，厦门大学出版社 1993 年版。

84. 吴福环：《清季总理衙门研究》，新疆大学出版社 1995 年版。

85. 谢振声：《近代化学史上值得纪念的学者——虞和钦》，《中国科技史料》2004 年第 3 期，第 209—215 页。

86. 熊月之：《晚清几个政治词汇的翻译与使用》，《史林》1999 年第 1
   期，第 57—62 页。

87. 徐中约、郭少棠译：《中国近代史》，香港中文大学出版社 2002 年版。

88. 严元浩：《法律翻译的历史使命》，陆文慧主编：《法律翻译——从实
   践出发》，法律出版社 2004 年版，第 1—9 页。

89. 叶翔凤：《中国晚清外交机构近代化的起步——对"总理衙门"的历
   史考察》，《山西大学学报》（哲学社会科学版）1994 年第 3 期，第
   75—80 页。

90. 杨鸿烈：《中国法律思想史》，上海书店 1984 年版。

91. 俞江：《近代中国的法律与学术》，北京大学出版社 2008 年版。

92. 俞江：《清末法学书目备考（1901—1911）》，何勤华主编：《法律文
   化史研究》（第二卷），商务印书馆 2005 年版，第 450—481 页。

93. 余子明：《维新精英反传统主义取向——兼及戊戌变法民主革命内
   涵》，《史学月刊》1998 年第 6 期，第 83—88 页。

94. 张晋藩：《中国法律的传统与近代转型》，法律出版社 2005 年版。

95. 张晋藩：《中国法律史论》，法律出版社 1982 年版。

96. 张朋园：《立宪派与辛亥革命》，吉林出版集团有限责任公司 2007
   年版。

97. 张馨保、徐梅芬等译：《林钦差与鸦片战争》，福建人民出版社 1989
   年版。

98. 张用心：《〈万国公法〉的几个问题》，《北京大学学报》（哲学社会科
   学版）2005 年第 5 期，第 76—84 页。

99. 邹振环：《影响中国近代社会的一百种译作》，中国对外翻译出版公司
   1996 年版。

100. 庄泽宣、陈学恂：《从四方馆到同文馆》，《岭南学报》1947 年第 1
    期，第 151—154 页。

101. Alcaraz, Enrique & Hughes, Brian. *Legal Translation Explained*. Shang-
    hai: Shanghai Foreign Language Education Press, 2008.

102. Alexander L., 1987 "Striking Back at the Empire: A Brief Survey of Prob-
    lems in Dworkin's Theory of Law". *Law and Philosophy*, (6): 419 –424.

103. Archer, Dawn. *Questions and Answers in the English Courtroom* 1640 –

1760: *A Sociopragmatic Analysis* [M] . Amsterdam/Philadelphia: John Benjamins Publishing Company, 2005.

104. Aristotle. Kennedy, George A. (tr.) *On Rhetoric: A Theory of Civic Discourse (Second Edition)* [M] . New York: Oxford University Press, 2007.

105. Atkinson, John Maxwell. *Order in Court: the Organisation of Verbal Interaction in Judicial Settings* [M] . Unley: Humanities Press, 1979.

106. Austin, John L. *How to Do Things with Words* [M] . Oxford: Cla-rendon Press, 1962.

107. Baker, Mona. (ed.) *Routledge Encyclopedia of Translation Studies* [C] . Shanghai: Shanghai Foreign Language Education Press, 2004.

108. Bassnett, Susan & Lefever, Andre. *Constructing Cultures: Essays on Literary Translation* [M] . Shanghai: Shanghai Foreign Language Education Press, 2001.

109. Bennett, Adrian Arthur. *John Fryer: The Introduction of Western Science and Technology into Nineteenth-Century China* [M] . Cambridge: Harvard University Press, 1967.

110. Bennett, W. Lance & Feldman, Martha S. *Reconstructing Reality in the Courtroom* [M] . London: Tavistock Publications Ltd. , 1981.

111. Bentham, Jeremy. *An Introduction to the Principles of Morals and Le-gislation* [M] . Oxford: Clarendon Press, 1789.

112. Bhatia*t el.* (eds.) *Legal Discourse across Cultures and Systems* [C] . Hong Kong: Hong Kong University Press, 2008.

113. Bix, Brian H. Can Theories of Meaning and Reference Solve the Problem of Legal Determinacy [J] . *Ratio Juris.* 2003 (16): 281 –295.

114. Bix, Brian. Cautions and Caveats for the Application of Wittgenstein to Legal Theory [A] . Campbell, Joseph Keim, O'Rourke, Michael & Shier, David. (eds.) *Law and Social Justice* [C] . Cambridge: MIT Press, 2005: 217 –229.

115. Bix, Brian H. *Law, Language, and Legal Determinacy* [M] . Oxford: Clarendon Press, 1993.

116. Boggs, Mary Edna. *William Alexander Parsons Martin, Missionary to Chi-*

na 1850 – 1916 [D]. Chicago: Presbyterian College of Education, 1949.

117. Bourdieu, Pierre. Johnson, Randal. (ed.) *The Field of Cultural Production: Essays on Art and Literature* [M]. New York: Columbia University Press, 1993.

118. Bourdieu, Pierre. Nice, Richard. (tr.) *The Logic of Practice* [M]. Stanford: Stanford University Press, 1990.

119. Brennan, Mark & Brennan, Roslin E. *Strange Language: Child Victims Under Cross Examination* (3rd *Edition*) [M]. Wagga Wagga: Riverina Literacy Centre, 1988.

120. Brennan, Mark. The Discourse of Denial: Cross-examining Child-Victim Witnesses [J]. *Pragmatics*, 1994 (23): 71 – 91.

121. Brown, Cornelia E. Riding the Waves of Fortune: Translating Legislation of theSuccessor Soviet Republics [A]. Morris, Marshall. (ed.) *Translation and the Law* (*American Translators Association Scholarly Monograph Series Volume VIII*) [C]. Amsterdam/Philadelphia: John Benjamins Publishing Company, 1995: 67 – 83.

122. Bussmann, Hadumod. Trauth, Gregory P. & Kazzazi, Kerstin (trans. & eds.). *Routledge Dictionary of Language and Linguistics* [C]. Beijing: Foreign Language Teaching and Research Press, 2000.

123. Butt, Peter & Castle, Richard. *Modern Legal Drafting: A Guide to Using Clearer Language* [M]. Cambridge/New York: Cambridge University Press, 2001.

124. Cao, Deborah. *Translating Law* [M]. Shanghai: Shanghai Foreign Language Education Press, 2008.

125. Chang Hsi-t'ung (张锡彤). The Earliest Phase on the Introduction of Western Political Science into China (1820 – 1852) [J]. *Yenching Journal of Asian Studies* (《燕京学报》), 5.1: 13 (July 1950).

126. Chesterman, Andrew. *Memes of Translation: The Spread of Ideas in Translation Theory* [M]. Shanghai: Shanghai Foreign Language Education Press, 2012.

127. Christie, Goerge C. Vagueness and Legal Language [J]. *Minnesota Law*

Review，1964（48）：885 – 911.

128. Chroma，Marta. Translating Terminology in Arbitration Discourse ［A］．Bhatia*at el.* （eds.） *Legal Discourse across Cultures and Systems* ［C］．Hong Kong：Hong Kong University Press，2008：309 – 327.

129. Chu，Tung-Tsu. *Law and Society in Traditional China* ［M］．商务印书馆，2010.

130. Cohen，Morris L. & Olson，Kent C. *Legal Research* ［M］．Beijing：Legal Press，2004.

131. Conley，John M. & O'Barr，William M. *Just Words：Law，Language and Power（Second Edition）* ［M］．Chicago：The University of Chicago Press，2005.

132. Conley，John M. & O'Barr，William M. *Rules Versus Relationships：The Ethnography of Legal Discourse* ［M］．Chicago：The University of Chicago Press，1990.

133. Cotterill，Janet. （ed.） *Language in the Legal Process* ［C］．Ba-singstoke/New York：Palgrave Macmillan Ltd，2002.

134. Cotterill，Janet. （ed.） *The Language of Sexual Crime* ［C］．Ba-singstoke/New York：Palgrave Macmillan Ltd，2007.

135. Coulthard，Malcolm & Johnson，Alison. *An Introduction to Forensic Linguistics：Language in Evidence* ［M］．London/New York：Routledge，2007.

136. Coulthard，Malcolm & Johnson，Alison. （eds.） *The Routledge Handbook of Forensic Linguistics* ［C］．London/New York：Routledge，2010.

137. Crystal，David. *The English Language* ［M］．London：Penguin，1988.

138. Davis，John Francis. *The Chinese：A General Description of the Empire of China and its Inhabitants* ［M］．London：Charles Knight，1836.

139. Doczekalska，Agnieszka. Drafting or Translation-Production of Multilingual Legal Texts ［A］．Olsen，Frances *at el.* （eds.） *Translation Issues in Language and Law* ［C］．Basingstoke/New York：Palgrave Macmillan，2009：116 – 135.

140. Dworkin，Ronald. *Law's Empire* ［M］．Cambridge：Harvard University Press，1986.

141. Dworsky, Alan L. *The Little Book on Legal Writing* [M]. Beijing: Beijing University Press, 2006.

142. Eades, Diana. *Sociolinguistics and the Legal Process* [M]. Bristol/Buffalo/Toronto: Multilingual Matters, 2010.

143. Edwards, Linda Holdeman. *Legal Writing—Process, Analysis, and Organization* [M]. Beijing: Citic Publishing House, 2003.

145. Ehrlich, Susan Lynn. *Representing Rape: Language and Sexual Consent* [M]. London/New York: Routledge, 2001.

146. Endicott, Timothy A. Herbert Hart and the Semantic Sting [A]. Coleman, Jules. (ed.) *Hart's Postscript: Essays on the Postscript to the Concept of Law* [C]. New York: Oxford University Press, 2001: 39 – 58.

147. Endicott, Timothy A. *Vagueness in Law* [M]. New York: Oxford University Press, 2000.

148. Even-Zohar, Itamar. Polysystem Studies [J]. *Poetics Today*, 1990 (11).

149. Even-Zohar, Itamar. *Papers in Culture Research* [M]. Tel Aviv: Unit of Culture Research, Tel Aviv University, 2010.

150. Flanagan, Brian. Revisiting the Contribution of Literal Meaning to Legal Meaning [J]. *Oxford Journal of Legal Studies*, 2010 (30): 255 – 271.

151. Foucault, Michel. Gordon, Colin, Marshall, Leo, Mepham, John & Soper, Kate. (tr.) *Power/Knowledge: Selected Interviews and Other Writings* 1972 – 1977 [M]. New York: Pantheon Books, 1980.

152. Friedman, Lawrence M. Law and Its Language [J]. *The George Washington Law Review*, 1964 (33): 563 – 579.

153. Garner, Bryan A. *Legal Writing in Plain English: A Text with Exer-cises* [M]. Chicago: The University of Chicago Press, 2001.

154. Garner, Bryan A. *The Elements of Legal style* [M]. Beijing: Intellectual Property Press, 2005.

155. Gibbons, John & Turell, M. Teresa. (eds.) *Dimensions of Forensic Linguistics* [C]. Amsterdam/Philadelphia: John Benjamins Publishing Company, 2008.

156. Glendon, Mary A., Gordon, Michael W. & Carozza, Paolo G. *Compar-

ative Legal Traditions [M] . Beijing: Legal Press, 2004.

157. Gotti, Maurizio. Cultural Constraints on Arbitration Discourse [A] . Bhatia *at el.* (eds.) *Legal Discourse across Cultures and Systems* [C] . Hong Kong: Hong Kong University Press, 2008: 221 – 252.

158. Gotti, Maurizio. Globalizing Trends in Legal Discourse [A] . Olsen, Frances *at el.*, (eds.) *Translation Issues in Language and Law* [C] . Ba-singstoke/New York: Palgrave Macmillan, 2009: 55 – 75.

159. Grice, Herbert Paul. *Studies in the Way of Words* [M] . Cambridge: Harvard University Press, 1989.

160. Haggard, Thomas R. *Legal Drafting* [M] . Beijing: Law Press, 2004.

161. Haigh, Rupert. *Legal English (Second Edition)* [M] . London/New York: Routledge-Cavendish, 2009.

162. Hart, H. L. A. Positivism and the Separation of Law and Morals [J] . *Harvard Law Review*, 1958 (71): 593 – 629.

163. Hart, H. L. A. *The Concept of Law* [M] . Oxford: Clarendon Press, 1961.

164. Hermans, Theo. *Translation in Systems: Descriptive and System-orient-ed Approaches Explained* [M] . Shanghai: Shanghai Foreign Language Education Press, 2004.

165. Heutger, Viola. Law and Language in the European Union [J] . *Global Jurist Topics*, 2003 (3) . http://www. bepress. com/gj.

166. Holmes, James Stratton. *Translated! Papers on Literary and Translation Studies* [M] . Beijing: Foreign Language Teaching and Research Press, 2007.

167. Hsü, Immanuel C. Y. (徐中约) . *China's Entrance into the Family of Nations: The Diplomatic Phase* 1858 – 1880 [M] . Cambridge: Harvard University Press, 1960.

168. Hunter, William C. *Bits of Old China* [M] . Shanghai, Hongkong, Singapore & Yokohama: Kelly and Walsh, 1911.

169. House, Juliane. *A model for Translation Quality Assessment (2nd edition)* [M] . Tübingen: Narr, 1981.

170. Jeffrey, Francis. Ta Tsing Leu Lee; Being the Fundamental Laws, and a

Selection from the Supplementary Statutes, of the Penal Code of China [J].
Edinburgh Review, 1810 (16: 32): 476 - 499.

171. Katz, Daniel Martin *et al.* Legal N-Grams? A Simple Approach to Track the "Evolution" of Legal Language [A]. *Jurix: The 24th International Conference on Legal Knowledge and Information Systems (Vienna 2011)* [C].

172. Kimble, Joseph. Answering the Critics of Plain Language [J]. *The Scribes Journal of Leg al Writing*, 1994/1995: 51 - 85.

173. Kischel, Uwe. *Legal Cultures-Legal Languages* [A]. Olsen, Frances *at el.* (eds.) *Translation Issues in Language and Law* [C]. Basingstoke/ New York: Palgrave Macmillan, 2009: 7 - 17.

174. Kunz, Keneva. Where the Devil Meets his Grandmother: Iceland and European Community Legislation [A]. Morris, Marshall. (ed.) *Translation and the Law (American Translators Association Scholarly Monograph Series Volume VIII)* [C]. Amsterdam/Philadelphia: John Benjamins Publishing Company, 1995: 85 - 92.

175. Lambert, José. The Status and Position of Legal Translation: a Chapter in the Discursive Construction of Societies [A]. Olsen, Frances *at el.* (eds.) *Translation Issues in Language and Law* [C]. Basingstoke/New York: Palgrave Macmillan, 2009.

176. Lefevere, Andre. *Translation, Rewriting and the Manipulation of Literary Fame* [M]. Shanghai: Shanghai Foreign Language Education Press, 2004.

177. Levi, Judith N. & Walker, Anne Graffam. (eds.) *Language in the Judicial Process* [C]. New York: Plenum Press, 1990.

178. Levy, Jirí. Translation as a Decision Process [A]. Venuti, Lawrence. (ed.) *The Translation Studies Reader* [C]. London/New York: Routledge, 2000: 148 - 159.

179. Lindemann, Erika. *A Rhetoric for Writing Teachers* [M]. London: Oxford University Press, 1982.

180. Liu, Lydia H. (刘禾). *The Clash of Empires: The Invention China in Modern World Making* [M]. Cambridge: Harvard University Press,

2004.

181. Lyons, David. [ed.] *Moral Aspects of Legal Theory: Essays on Law, Justice, and Political Responsibility* [C] . Cambridge/New York/Oakleigh: Cambridge University Press, 1993.

182. Lyons, David. Open Texture and the Possibility of Legal Interpretation [A] . *The Boston University School of Law Working Paper Series*, No. 99 – 9. (This paper can be downloaded without charge at: The Boston University School of Law Working Paper Series Index: http://www.bu.edu/law/faculty/papers or The Social Science Research Network Electronic Paper Collection: http://papers.ssrn.com/paper.taf? abstract_ id = 212328.)

183. Marmor, Andrei. *Interpretation and Legal Theory (Second Edition)* [M] . Oxford and Portland, Oregon: Hart Publishing Company, 2005.

184. Mateer, Calvin Wilson. Discussion [C] . *Records of the General Conference of the Protestant Missionaries of China Held at Shanghai, May 7 – 20, 1890* [C] . Shanghai: American Presbyterian Mission Press, 1890: 549 – 550.

185. Mateer, Calvin Wilson. Preface [A] . *Technical Terms English and Chinese Prepared by The Committee of the Education Association of China* [C] . Shanghai: American Presbyterian Mission Press, 1904: 1 – 8.

186. Mateer, Calvin Wilson. School Books for China [A] . *The Chinese Recorder (Vol. 8)* [C] . Shanghai: American Presbyterian Mission Press, 1877: 427 – 432.

187. Mateer, Calvin Wilson. The Relation of Protestant Missions to Education [A] . *Records of the General Conference of the Protestant Missionaries of China Held at Shanghai*, May 10 – 24, 1877 [C] . Shanghai: American Presbyterian Mission Press, 1877: 171 – 180.

188. Mattila, Heikki E. S. Goddard, Christopher. (tr.) *Comparative Legal Linguistics* [M] . Aldershot/Burlington: Ashgate Publishing Limited, 2006.

189. Mey, Jacob L. *Pragmatics: An Introduction* [M] . Beijing: Foreign Language Teaching and Research Press, 2001.

190. McFarlane, John. Modes of Translation [J]. *The Durham University Journal*, 1953 (45): 77 – 93.

191. McMenamin, Gerald R. *Forensic Linguistics: Advances in Forensic Stylistics* [M]. Boca Raton/London/New York/Washington, D. C.: CRC Press LLC, 2002.

192. Mellinkoff, David. *The Language of the Law* [M]. Boston/Toronto: Little, Brown and Company, 1963.

193. Moore, Michael. A Natural Law Theory of Interpretation [J]. *Southern California Law Review*, 1985 (58): 277 – 400.

194. Morris, Marshall. (ed.) *Translation and the Law* (*American Translators Association Scholarly Monograph Series Volume VIII*) [C]. Amsterdam/Philadelphia: John Benjamins Publishing Company, 1995.

195. Morse, Hosea Ballou. *The International Relations of the Chinese Empire: The Period of Conflict* 1834 – 1860 [M]. Shanghai, Hongkong, Singapore & Yokohama: Kelly and Walsh, Limited, 1910.

196. Murray, Hugh. *The Encyclopedia of Geography* [M]. Philadelphia: Lea and Blanchard, 1842.

197. Neumann, Richard K. *Legal Reasoning and Legal Writing* [M]. Beijing: Citic Publishing House, 2003.

198. Nord, Christiane. *Text Analysis in Translation-Theory, Methodology, and Didactic Application of a Model for Translation-Oriented Text Analysis* (Second Edition) [M]. Beijing: Foreign Language Teaching and Research Press, 2006.

199. Nord, Christiane. *Translating as a Purposeful Activity* [M]. Shanghai: Shanghai Foreign Language Education Press, 2001.

200. O'Barr, William. *Linguistic Evidence: Language, Power, and Strategy in the Courtroom* [M]. Salt Lake City: Academic Press, 1982.

201. Olsson, John. *Forensic Linguistics: An Introduction to Language, Crime and the Law* [M]. London: Continuum International Publishing Group, 2004.

202. Patterson, Dennis. *Law & Truth* [M]. New York: Oxford University Press, 1996.

203. Peters, Pam. *The Cambridge Guide to English Usage* [M]. Cambridge/ New York: Cambridge University Press, 2004.

204. Popkin, William D. Law and Linguistics: Is There Common Ground? [J]. *Washington University Law Quarterly*, 1995 (73): 1043 – 1045.

205. Putman, William H. *Legal Analysis and Writing (Third Edition)* [M]. Clifton Park: Delmar, Cengage Learning, 2009.

206. Putman, William H. *Legal Research, Analysis and Writing (Second Edition)* [M]. Clifton Park: Delmar, Cengage Learning, 2010.

207. Reiss, Kathabina. Rhodes, Erroll F. (tr.) *Translation Criticism* [M]. Shanghai: Shanghai Foreign Language Education Press, 2004.

208. Rorty, Richard. *Consequences of Pragmatism (Essays: 1972 – 1980)* [M]. Minneapolis: University of Minnesota Press, 1982.

209. Sarcevic, Susan. *New Approach to Legal Translation* [M]. Cambridge: Kluwer Law International, 1997.

210. Sarcevic, Susan. Translation in International Arbitration [A]. Bhatia *at el.* (eds.) *Legal Discourse across Cultures and Systems.* Hong Kong: Hong Kong University Press, 2008: 291 – 307.

211. Schiess, Wayne. When Your Boss Wants It the Old Way [J]. *The Scribes Journal of Legal Writing*, 2008/2009: 163 – 167.

212. Searle, John R. *Expression and Meaning: Studies in the Theory of Speech Acts* [M]. Beijing: Foreign Language Teaching and Research Press, 2001.

213. Smith, Adam. *An Inquiry into the Nature and Causes of the Wealth of Nations* [M]. New York: P. F. Collier & Son, 1909.

214. Snell-Hornby, Mary. *Translation Studies: An Integrated Approach* [M]. Shanghai: Shanghai Foreign Language Education Press, 2001.

215. Solan, Lawrence M. Statutory Interpretation in the EU: the Augustinian Approach [A]. Olsen, Frances *at el.* (eds.) *Translation Issues in Language and Law.* Basingstoke/New York: Palgrave Macmillan, 2009: 35 – 54.

216. Stanojević, Maja. Legal English—Changing Perspective [J]. *Linguistics and Literature*, 2011 (1): 65 – 75.

217. Steiner, George. *After Babel: Aspects of Language and Translation* [M].
Shanghai: Shanghai Foreign Language Education Press, 2001.

218. Stygall, Gail. *Trail Language: Differential Discourse Processing and Discursive Formation* [M]. Amsterdam/Philadelphia: John Benjamins Publishing Company, 1994.

219. Tiersma, Peter M. *Legal English* [M]. Chicago: The University of Chicago Press, 1999.

220. Tiersma, Peter M. A History of the Languages of Law [A]. Solan, Lawrence M. & Tiersma, Peter M. (eds.) *The Oxford Handbook of Language and Law* [C]. New York: Oxford University Press, 2012: 13 – 26.

221. Toury, Gideon. *Descriptive Translation Studies and Beyond* [M]. Shanghai: Shanghai Foreign Language Education Press, 2001.

222. Verschueren, Jef. *Understanding pragmatics* [M]. Beijing: Foreign Language Teaching and Research Press, 2000.

223. White, James Boyd. *Justice as Translation: An Essay in Cultural and Legal Criticism* [M]. Chicago/London: The University of Chicago Press, 1990.

224. Wierzbicka, Anna. Different cultures, Different languages, Different speech acts [J]. *Journal of Pragmatics*, 1985 (9): 145 – 178.

225. Williamson, Alexander. What Books Are Still Needed? [A]. *Rec-ords of the General Conference of the Protestant Missionaries of China Held at Shanghai, May 7 – 20, 1890* [C]. Shanghai: American Presbyterian Mission Press, 1890: 519 – 531.

226. Willoughby, Westel Woodbury. *Foreign Rights and Interests in China* [M]. Baltimore: The Johns Hopkins University Press, 1920.

227. Witczak-Plisiecka, Iwona. A Note on the Linguistic (In) determinacy in the Legal Context [J]. *Lodz Papers in Pragmatics*, 2009 (5.2): 201 – 226.

228. Wittgenstein, Ludwig. Anscombe, G. E. M., Hacker, P. M. S. & Schulte, Joachim (tr.) *Philosophical Investigations (Revised 4th Edition)* [M]. Chichester: Blackwell Publishing Ltd., 2009.

229. Wright, Mary C. *The Last Stand of Chinese Conservatism*：*The T'ung-chih Restoration*, 1862 – 1874 ［M］. Stanford：Stanford University Press, 1957.

230. Zachariah, Chafee. *The Disorderly Conduct of Words* ［A］. 41 Colum. L. Rev. 381, 382（1941）.

二 辞典
（一）清季辞典

1. Marrison, Robert. *A Dictionary of the Chinese Language* in Three Parts ［C］.

（1）Part I：*Chinese and English*, *Arranged According to the Radicals* ［C］. Macao：The Honorable East India Company's Press, 1815.

（2）Part II：*Chinese and English Arranged Alphabetically* ［C］. Macao：The Honorable East India Company's Press, 1819.

（3）Part III：*English and Chinese* ［C］. Macao：The Honorable East India Company's Press, 1822.

2. Lobscheid, Wilhelm. *English and Chinese Dictionary* ［C］. Hong Kong：The "Daily Press" Office, 1866.

3. Medhurst, Walter Henry. 1843. *Chinese and English Dictionary* ［C］. Batavia：Parapattan,（Vol. 1）1842/（Vol. 2）.

4. Medhurst, Walter Henry. 1848. *English and Chinese Dictioanry* ［C］. Shanghae：Mission Press,（Vol. 1）1847/（Vol. 2）.

（二）现代辞典

1. 夏征农主编：《辞海》，上海辞书出版社 1999 年版。

2. 薛波：《元照英美法词典》，法律出版社 2003 年版。

3. 广东、广西、湖南、河南辞源修订组及商务印书馆编辑部：《辞源》，商务印书馆 1980 年版。

4. Flexner, Stuart Berg. *Random House Compact Unabridged Dictionary*（Special Second Edition）［Z］. New York：Random House, 1996.

5. Garner, Bryan A. *A Dictionary of Modern Legal Usage*（Second Edition）［Z］. Beijing：Law Press, 2003.

6. Garner, Bryan A. *Black's Law Dictionary*（8th Edition） ［Z］. St. Paul：

West，a Thomson business，2004.

7. Walker，David M. *The Oxford Companion to Law* ［Z］.Oxford：Cla-rendon Press，1980.

三　名人史料

（一）外国历史名人文献

1. 马戛尔尼（Macartney，George）

马戛尔尼著，刘半农译，林延清解读：《1793 乾隆英使觐见记》，天津人民出版社 2006 年版。

2. 斯当东（Staunton，George Leonard）

（1）斯当东著，叶笃义译：《英使谒见乾隆纪实》，商务印书馆 1963 年版。

（2）Staunton，George Leonard. *An Authentic Account of and Embassy from the King of Great Britain to the Emperor of China* ［M］.London：Pall-Mall，1797.

3. 小斯当东（Staunton，George Thomas）

（1）Staunton，George Thomas，"*Miscellaneous Notices Relating to China and our Commercial Intercourse with that Country*"，London：John Murray，1822.

（2）Staunton，George Thomas.（tr.）*Narrative of the Chinese Embassy to the Khan of the Tourgouth Tartars* ［M］.London：John Murray，1821.

4. 伯驾（Parker，Peter）

（1）Parker，Peter. "Tenth Report of the Ophthalmic Hospital，Canton，being for the year 1839" ［A］.*The Chinese Repository*，*Vol. VIII* ［C］.

（2）Stevens，George B. & Markwick，W. Fisher. *The life*，*Letters*，*and Journals of the Rev. & Hon*，*Peter Parker*，*M. D.*，*Missionary*，*Physician*，*and Diplomatist*，*the Father of Medical Missions and Founder of the Ophthalmic Hospital in Canton* ［C］.Boston，1896.

5. 丁韪良（Martin，William Alexander Parsons）

（1）丁韪良著，沈弘、恽文捷、郝田虎译：《花甲记忆———一位美国传教士眼中的晚清帝国》，广西师范大学出版社 2004 年版。

（2）丁韪良著，沈弘等译：《汉学菁华：中国人的精神世界及其影响力》，世界图书出版公司 2010 年版。

（3）丁韪良著，沈弘译：《中国觉醒：国家地理、历史与炮火硝烟中的变革》，世界图书出版社 2010 年版。

（4）Martin, W. A. P. *A Cycle of Cathay or China, South and North with Personal Reminiscences* ［M］. New York：Fleming H. Revell Company, 1896.

（5）Martin, W. A. P. *Hanlin Papers：Essays on the History, Philosophy, and Religion of the Chinese（Second Series）*［M］. Shanghai：Kelly & Walsh, 1894.

（6）Martion, W. A. P. *The Analytical Reader：A Short Method for Learning to Read and Write Chinses*［C］. Shanghai：Presbyterian Mission Press, 1863.

6. 傅兰雅（Fryer, John）

（1）戴吉礼编. 弘侠译. 傅兰雅档案［C］. 广西师范大学，2010.

（2）傅兰雅著. 江南制造总局翻译西书事略［A］. 张静庐辑注. 中国近代出版史料初编［C］. 上海书店出版社，2003.

（3）Dagenais, Ferdinand.（ed.）*Calendar of the Correspondence, Publications, and Miscellaneous Papers of John Fryer（1839—1928）with Selected Excerpts*［C］. Berkeley：Center for Chinese Studies, University of California, 1996.

（4）Fryer, John. Scientific Terminology：Present Discrepancies and Means of Securing Uniformity［A］. *Records of the General Conference of the Protestant Missionaries of China Held at Shanghai, May 7 – 20, 1890*［C］. Shanghai：American Presbyterian Mission Press, 1890：531 – 548.

7. 赫德（Hart, Robert）

（1）凯瑟琳·F. 布鲁纳、约翰·K. 费正清 & 理查德德·J. 司马富编. 傅曾仁等译. 赫德日记（1854—1863）：步入中国清廷仕途［C］. 中国海关出版社，2003.

（2）凯瑟琳·F. 布鲁纳、约翰·K. 费正清 & 理查德德·J. 司马富编. 陈绛译. 赫德日记（1863—1866）：赫德与中国早期现代化［C］. 中国海关出版社，2005.

（3）Brunner, Katherine F., Fairbank, John K. & Smith Richard J.（eds.）*Entering China's Service：Robert Hart's Journals, 1854 – 1863*［C］. Cambridge：Harvard University Press, 1986.

（4）Smith Richard J.，Fairbank，John K. & Brunner，Katherine F.（eds.）*Robert Hart and China's Early Modernization*：*His Journals*，1863 – 1866 ［C］．Cambridge：Harvard University Press，1991.

（二）中国历史名人文献

1. 林则徐全集编辑委员会编：《林则徐全集》，海峡文艺出版社 2002 年版。

2. 魏源全集编辑委员会：《魏源全集》，岳麓书社 1998 年版。

3. （清）李瀚章编纂，李鸿章校勘：《足本曾文正公全集》，吉林人民出版社 1995 年版。

4. 李鸿章全集编辑工作委员会编：《李鸿章全集》，吉林人民出版社 1998 年版。

5. 苑书义、孙华锋、李秉新主编：《张之洞全集》，河北人民出版社 1998 年版。

6. 张品兴等主编：《梁启超全集》，北京出版社 1999 年版。

7. 张謇研究中心、南通市图书馆编：《张謇全集》，江苏古籍出版社 1994 年版。

8. 缪荃孙纂录，周骏富辑：《清代传记丛刊·综录类·续碑传集》，明文书局印行 1985 年版。

9. 郭嵩焘：《伦敦与巴黎日记》，岳麓书社出版社 1984 年版。

10. 王云五主编：《使德日记、英轺私记、澳太利亚洲新志（丛书集成本）》，商务印书馆 1936 年版。

11. 上海图书馆编：《汪康年师友书札》，上海古籍出版社 1986 年版。

12. 孔祥吉编著：《康有为变法奏章辑考》，北京图书馆出版社 2008 年版。

四　其他相关史料

1. （西汉）刘向集录：《战国策》，上海古籍出版社 1985 年版。

2. （西汉）司马迁撰，（宋）裴骃集解，（唐）司马贞索隐，（唐）张守节正义：《史记》，中华书局 1999 年版。

3. （东汉）班固撰，（唐）颜师古注：《汉书》，中华书局 1999 年版。

4. 赵尔巽等撰：《清史稿》，中华书局 1977 年版。

5. 《清实录》，中华书局 1985—1987 年版。

6. 王光越总编：《清代档案文献数据库·大清五部会典》，中国第一历史档案馆 2007 年版。

7. （清）王先谦撰，《续修四库全书》编纂委员会编：《续修四库全书·史部·编年类·东华录—东华续录》，上海古籍出版社 2008 年版。

8. （清）文庆、贾桢、宝鋆等纂辑，《续修四库全书》编纂委员会编：《续修四库全书·史部·纪事本末类·筹办夷务始末》，上海古籍出版社 2008 年版。

9. 蒋廷黻编：《筹办夷务始末补遗》（全九册），北京大学出版社 1988 年版。

10. 王彦威纂辑，王亮编，王敬立校：《清季外交史料》，书目文献出版社 1987 年版。

11. 中国第一历史档案馆编：《嘉庆道光两朝上谕档》，广西师范大学出版社 2000 年版。

12. 中国第一历史档案馆编：《咸丰同治两朝上谕档》，广西师范大学出版社 1998 年版。

13. 中国第一历史档案馆编：《光绪朝上谕档》，广西师范大学出版社 1996 年版。

14. 沈桐生辑：《光绪政要》，宣统元年（1909 年）上海崇义堂石印本。

15. 中国第一历史档案馆编：《鸦片战争档案史料》，天津古籍出版社 1992 年版。

16. 中国史学会主编：《中国近代史资料丛刊·鸦片战争》，神州国光社 1954 年版。

17. 中国史学会主编：《中国近代史资料丛刊·第二次鸦片战争》，上海人民出版社 1978 年版。

18. 中国史学会主编：《中国近代史资料丛刊·洋务运动》，上海人民出版社 1961 年版。

19. 中国史学会主编：《中国近代史资料丛刊·戊戌变法》，上海人民出版社 1957 年版。

20. 沈云龙主编，佚名辑：《近代中国史料丛刊·戊戌变法档案史料》，文海出版社有限公司印行。

21. 沈云龙主编，魏允恭编：《近代中国史料丛刊·江南制造局记》，文海出版社有限公司印行。

22. 故宫博物院明清档案部编：《清末筹备立宪档案史料》，中华书局

1979 年版。

23. 故宫博物院掌故部编：《掌故丛编》，中华书局 1990 年版。

24. 中国第一历史档案馆编：《英使马戛尔尼访华档案史料汇编》，国际文化出版公司 1996 年版。

25. 海关总署《中外旧约章大全》编纂委员会编：《中外旧约章大全》（第一分卷），中国海关出版社 2004 年版。

26. 张静庐辑注：《中国近代出版史料初编》，上海书店出版社 2003 年版。

27. 张静庐辑注：《中国近代出版史料二编》，上海书店出版社 2003 年版。

28. 《海防档·机器局》，中央研究院近代史研究所 1957 年版。

29. 《历代刑法志》，群众出版社 1988 年版。

30. （唐）长孙无忌等，刘俊文点校：《唐律疏议》，中华书局 1983 年版。

31. （清）吴坛著，马建石、杨育裳主编：《大清律例通考校注》，中国政法大学出版社 1992 年版。

32. 《江南制造局译书提要》，宣统元年（1909 年）七月印。

33. （明）沈德符撰，（清）钱枋编：《万历野获编》，中华书局 1959 年版。

34. 《经世报》第一册，光绪丁酉七月上（1897 年 8 月）。

35. *Records of the General Conference of the Protestant Missionaries of China Held at Shanghai, May* 10 – 24, 1877 ［C］. Shanghai：American Presbyterian Mission Press, 1878.

36. *Records of the General Conference of the Protestant Missionaries of China Held at Shanghai, May* 7 – 20, 1890 ［C］. Shanghai：American Presbyterian Mission Press, 1890.

37. *The Sessional Papers（Printed by Order of the House of Lords or Presented by Royal Command in the Session* 1840）, Vol. VIII.

38. *The Chinese Repository（from May* 1839, *to April* 1840）, Vol. VIII.

39. George III. *The King's Speech as It Might Have Been as It Is* ［M］. London：Piccadilly, 1798.

40. *A Letter by George III on the loss of America*（1780s）. From http：//www. royal. gov. uk/HistoryoftheMonarchy/KingsandQueensoftheUnitedKingdom/ TheHanoverians/ GeorgeIII. aspx.

41. *A Speech by Elizabeth I Addressing her Troops at Tilbury*（1588）. From ht-

tp：//www. royal. gov. uk/HistoryoftheMonarchy/KingsandQueensofEngland/TheTudors/ElizabethI. aspx.

42. *Extracts from Victoria's Diaries*. From http：//www. royal. gov. uk/HistoryoftheMonarchy/KingsandQueensoftheUnitedKingdom/TheHanoverians/Victoria. aspx.

五 典籍

（一）古代典籍

1. （汉）孔安国传，（唐）孔颖达疏，廖名春、陈明整理，吕绍纲审定：《十三经注疏·尚书正义》，北京大学出版社 1999 年版。

2. （汉）郑玄注，（唐）孔颖达疏，龚抗云整理，王文锦审定：《十三经注疏·礼记正义》，北京大学出版社 1999 年版。

3. （汉）公羊寿传，（汉）何休解诂，（唐）徐彦疏，浦卫忠整理，杨向奎审定：《十三经注疏·春秋公羊传注疏》，北京大学出版社 1999 年版。

4. （魏）何晏注，（宋）邢昺疏，朱汉民整理，张岂之审定：《十三经注疏·论语注疏》，北京大学出版社 1999 年版。

5. （汉）赵岐注，（宋）孙奭疏，廖名春、刘佑平整理，钱逊审定：《十三经注疏·孟子注疏》，北京大学出版社 1999 年版。

6. （清）王先谦撰，沈啸寰、王星贤点校：《荀子集解》，中华书局 1988 年版。

7. （清）王先谦撰：《庄子集解》，中华书局 1987 年版。

8. 蒋礼鸿撰：《商君书锥指》，中华书局 1986 年版。

9. （清）王先慎、钟哲点校：《韩非子集解》，中华书局 1998 年版。

10. 苏舆撰，钟哲点校：《春秋繁露义证》，中华书局 1992 年版。

11. 黄晖撰：《论衡校释（附刘盼遂集解）》，中华书局 1990 年版。

12. 徐元浩撰，王树民、沈长云点校：《国语集解》，中华书局 2002 年版。

13. （宋）黎靖德编，王星贤点校：《朱子语类》，中华书局 1985 年版。

14. （三国魏）张揖撰，（清）王念孙疏证，钟宇讯点校：《广雅疏证》，中华书局 1983 年版。

15. （东汉）许慎撰：《说文解字》，九州岛出版社 2001 年版。

16. 黄霖编著：《文心雕龙汇评》，上海古籍出版社 2005 年版。

（二）清季典籍

1. 《美理哥合省国志略》，裨治文著，刘路生点校。

2. 《海国四说》，梁廷枏著，中华书局 1993 年版。

3. 《瀛寰志略》，徐继畬著，上海书店出版社 2001 年版。

4. 《盛世危言》，郑观应著，华夏出版社 2002 年版。

5. 《西学书目表四卷附读西学书法一卷》，梁启超著，光绪丙申（1896年）冬十月质学会用时务报馆本重校付刊。

6. 《中西普通书目表》，黄庆澄著，光绪戊戌（1898 年）七月算学馆自刻本。

7. 《皇朝经世文新编续集》，晋安甘韩眠羊甫辑，析津杨凤藻兰坡校正。光绪壬寅（1902 年）五日商绛雪垒书局本。

8. 《观堂集林》，王国维著，中华书局 1961 年版。

9. 《化学鉴原》，韦而司撰，傅兰雅口译，徐寿笔述，同治十一年（1872年）江南制造总局版。

10. 《格致汇编》，傅兰雅辑。

11. 《续修四库全书总目提要》，中国科学院图书馆整理，齐鲁书社 1996年版。

六 本书研究的经典法律原著与译作列表

1. 原文：《钦定四库全书·大清律例》。

译文："Staunton, George Thomas."（tr.）1810. *Ta Tsing Leu Lee*；*Being the Fundamental Laws, and a Selection from the Supplementary Statutes, of the Penal Code of China*［C］. London：Strahan and Preston.

2. 原文："Vattel, Monsieur de. Chitty, Joseph".（tr.）1834. *The Law of Nations, or, Principles of the Law of Nature, Applied to the Conduct and Affairs of Nations and Sovereigns*［M］. London：Law Booksellers & Publishers.

译文：伯驾译《滑达尔各国律例》和袁德辉译《法律本性正理所载》。收录在魏源编《海国图志》第八十三卷。详见《魏源全集》，岳麓书社 1998 年版。

3. 原文：Wheaton, Henry. *Elements of International Law with a Sketch of the History of the Subject（Six Edition）*［M］. Boston：Little, Brown and

Company，1855.

译文：丁韪良译《万国公法》。同治三年岁在甲子孟冬月（1864 年 11 月）镌，京都崇实馆存板。

4. 原文：Woolsey，Theodore D. *Introduction to the Study of the International Law（Second Edition）*［M］. New York：Charles Scribner，1864.

译文：丁韪良译《公法便览》。光绪三年岁在丁丑（1877 年）同文馆聚珍版。

5. 原文：Phillimore，Robert. *Commentaries upon International Law*，*Vol.* 1&2（*Second Edition*）［M］. London：Butterworths，1871.

6. 原文：Phillimore，Robert. *Commentaries upon International Law*，*Vol.* 3［M］. Philadelphia：T. & J. W. Johnson & Co.，1857.

译文：傅兰雅口述《各国交涉公法论》。光绪二十二年（1896 年）小仓山房石印本。

7. 原文：Phillimore，Robert. *Commentaries on International Law*，*Private International Law on Comity*［M］. London：William Benning & Son，1861.

译文：傅兰雅口述《各国交涉便法论》。光绪二十七年（1901 年）小仓山房石印本。

8. 原文：Chambers，W. & R.（eds.）*Political Economy*［C］. Edinburgh：William and Robert Chambers，1852.

译文：傅兰雅口译. 佐治刍言［C］.
①光绪十一年（1885 年）江南制造总局刊本。
②叶斌点校本，上海书店出版社 2002 年版。

9. 原文：Skottowe，Britiffe Constable. *A Short History of Parliament*［M］. London：Swan Sonnenschein，Lowrey & Co.，1886.

译文：翰墨林编译印书局编译. 英国国会史［M］.
①光绪三十一年冬十一月（1905 年 12 月）初版。
②刘守刚点校本，中国政法大学出版社 2003 年版。

10. 原文：Darcy，A. V. *Introduction to the Study of the Law of the Constitution（8ᵗʰ Edition）*［M］. London：Macmillan，1915.

译文：雷沛鸿译. 英宪精义［M］.
①民国二十四年一月（1935 年 1 月）商务印书馆初版。
②戚渊序本，中国法制出版社 2001 年版。